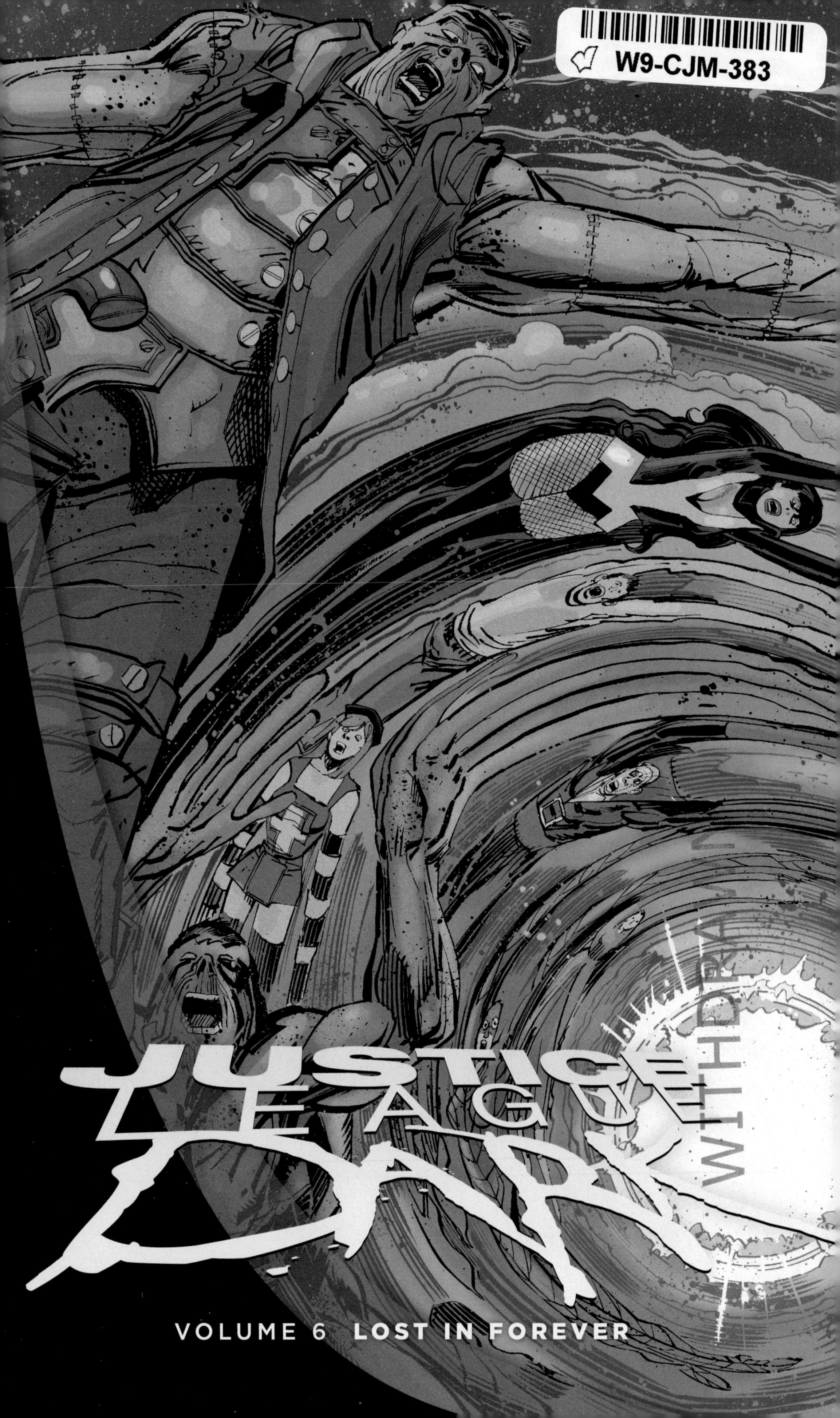
JUSTICE
LEAGUE
DARK
VOLUME 6 LOST IN FOREVER

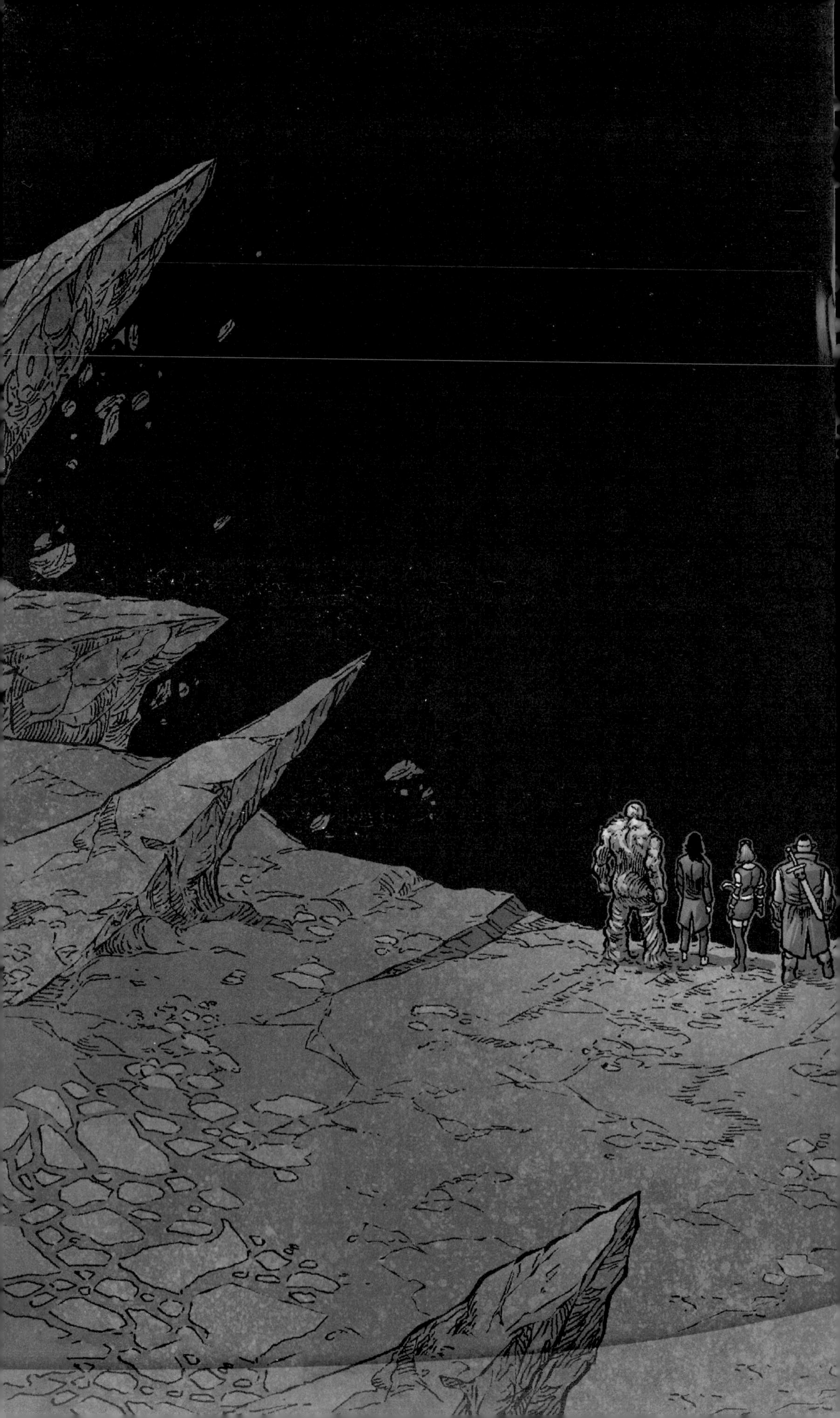

JUSTICE LEAGUE DARK

VOLUME 6
LOST IN FOREVER

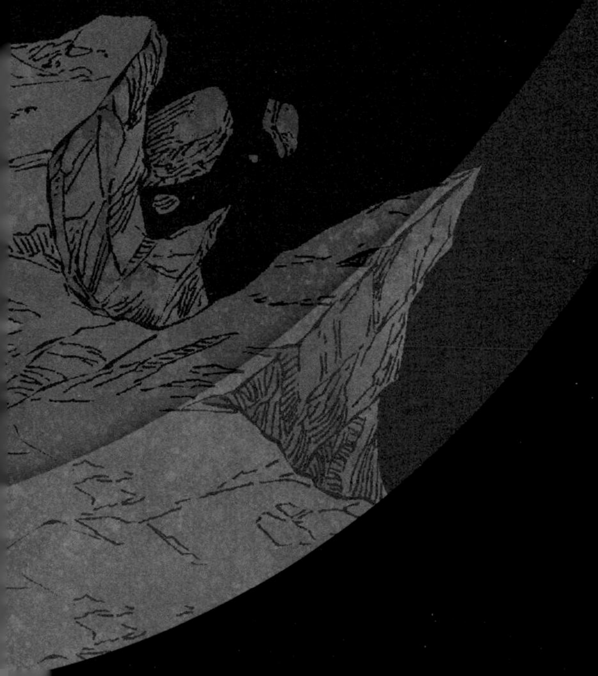

J.M. **DeMATTEIS** writer

ANDRES **GUINALDO** TOM **DERENICK**
KLAUS **JANSON** pencils

WALDEN **WONG** SCOTT **HANNA**
JOHN **STANISCI** inkers

CHRIS **SOTOMAYOR**
STEVE **BUCCELLATO** colorists

DEZI **SIENTY** TAYLOR **ESPOSITO**
TRAVIS **LANHAM** letterers

GUILLEM **MARCH** TOMEU **MOREY**
collection cover artists

FRANK·PITTARESE Editor – Original Series   HARVEY RICHARDS Associate Editor – Original Series
AMEDEO TURTURRO Assistant Editor – Original Series   JEB WOODARD Group Editor – Collected Editions
PAUL SANTOS Editor   DAMIAN RYLAND Publication Design

BOB HARRAS Senior VP – Editor-in-Chief, DC Comics

DIANE NELSON President   DAN DIDIO and JIM LEE Co-Publishers
GEOFF JOHNS Chief Creative Officer   AMIT DESAI Senior VP – Marketing & Global Franchise Management
NAIRI GARDINER Senior VP – Finance   SAM ADES VP – Digital Marketing
BOBBIE CHASE VP – Talent Development   MARK CHIARELLO Senior VP – Art, Design & Collected Editions
JOHN CUNNINGHAM VP – Content Strategy   ANNE DEPIES VP – Strategy Planning & Reporting
DON FALLETTI VP – Manufacturing Operations   LAWRENCE GANEM VP – Editorial Administration & Talent Relations
ALISON GILL Senior VP – Manufacturing & Operations   HANK KANALZ Senior VP – Editorial Strategy & Administration
JAY KOGAN VP – Legal Affairs   DEREK MADDALENA Senior VP – Sales & Business Development
DAN MIRON VP – Sales Planning & Trade Development   NICK NAPOLITANO VP – Manufacturing Administration
CAROL ROEDER VP – Marketing   EDDIE SCANNELL VP – Mass Account & Digital Sales
SUSAN SHEPPARD VP – Business Affairs   COURTNEY SIMMONS Senior VP – Publicity & Communications
JIM (SKI) SOKOLOWSKI VP – Comic Book Specialty & Newsstand Sales

JUSTICE LEAGUE DARK VOLUME 6: LOST IN FOREVER

DC Comics, 4000 Warner Blvd., Burbank, CA 91522
A Warner Bros. Entertainment Company
Printed by RR Donnelley, Owensville, MO, USA. 7/24/15.
ISBN: 978-1-4012-5481-0
First Printing.

Library of Congress Cataloging-in-Publication Data

DeMatteis, J. M.
Justice League Dark. Volume 6, / J.M. Dematteis, Andres Guinaldo.
pages cm
"Originally published in single magazine form in JUSTICE LEAGUE DARK 35-40, JUSTICE LEAGUE ANNUAL 2."
ISBN 978-1-4012-5481-0
1. Graphic novels. I. Guinaldo, Andres, illustrator. II. Title.
PN6728.J87D46 2015
741.5'973—dc23
2015011786

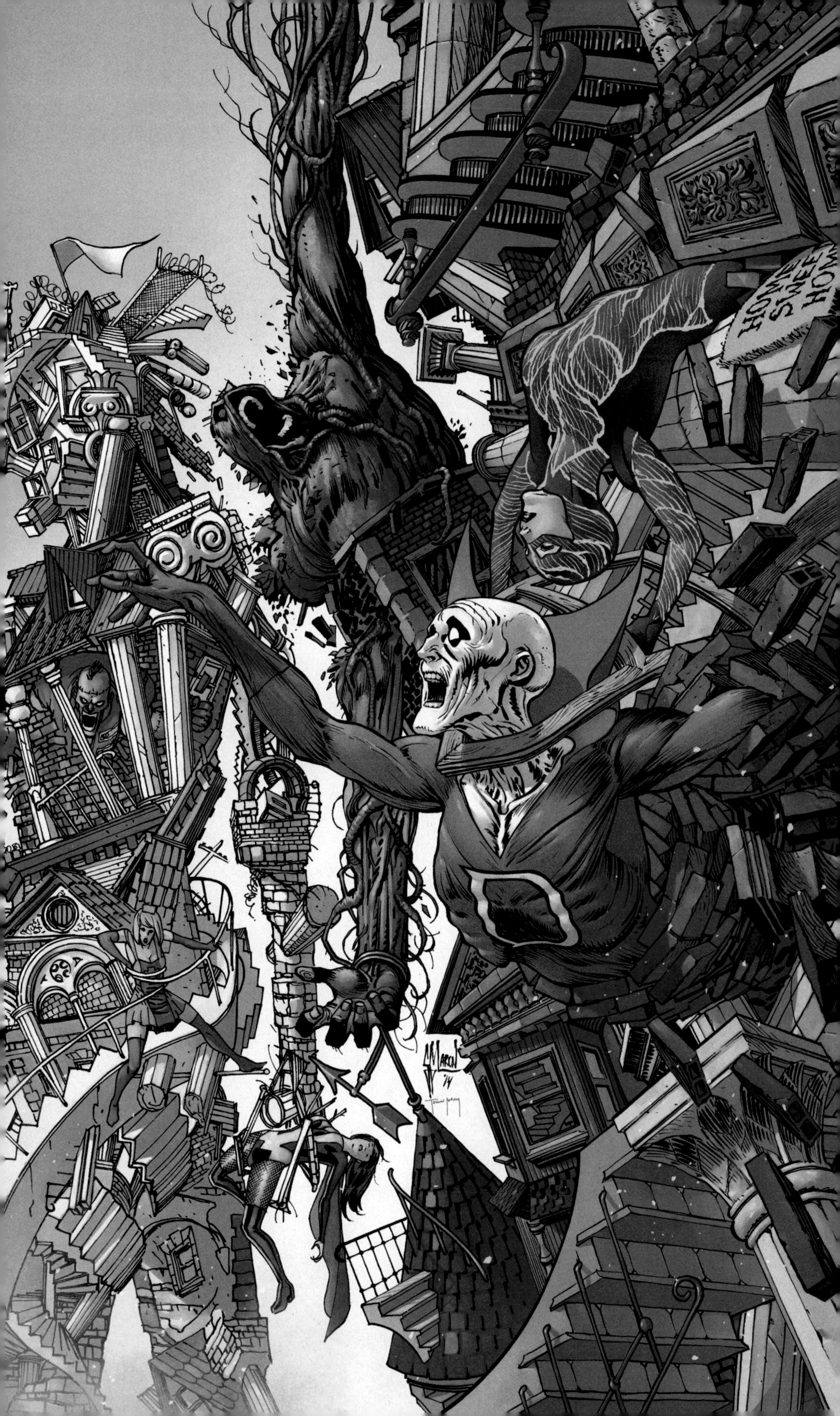
HOME
SWEET
HOME

WAR OF THE HOUSES

J.M. DEMATTEIS writer **KLAUS JANSON** penciller **JOHN STANISCI** inker **STEVE BUCCELLATO** colorist
DEZI SIENTY letterer cover by **GUILLEM MARCH & TOMEU MOREY**

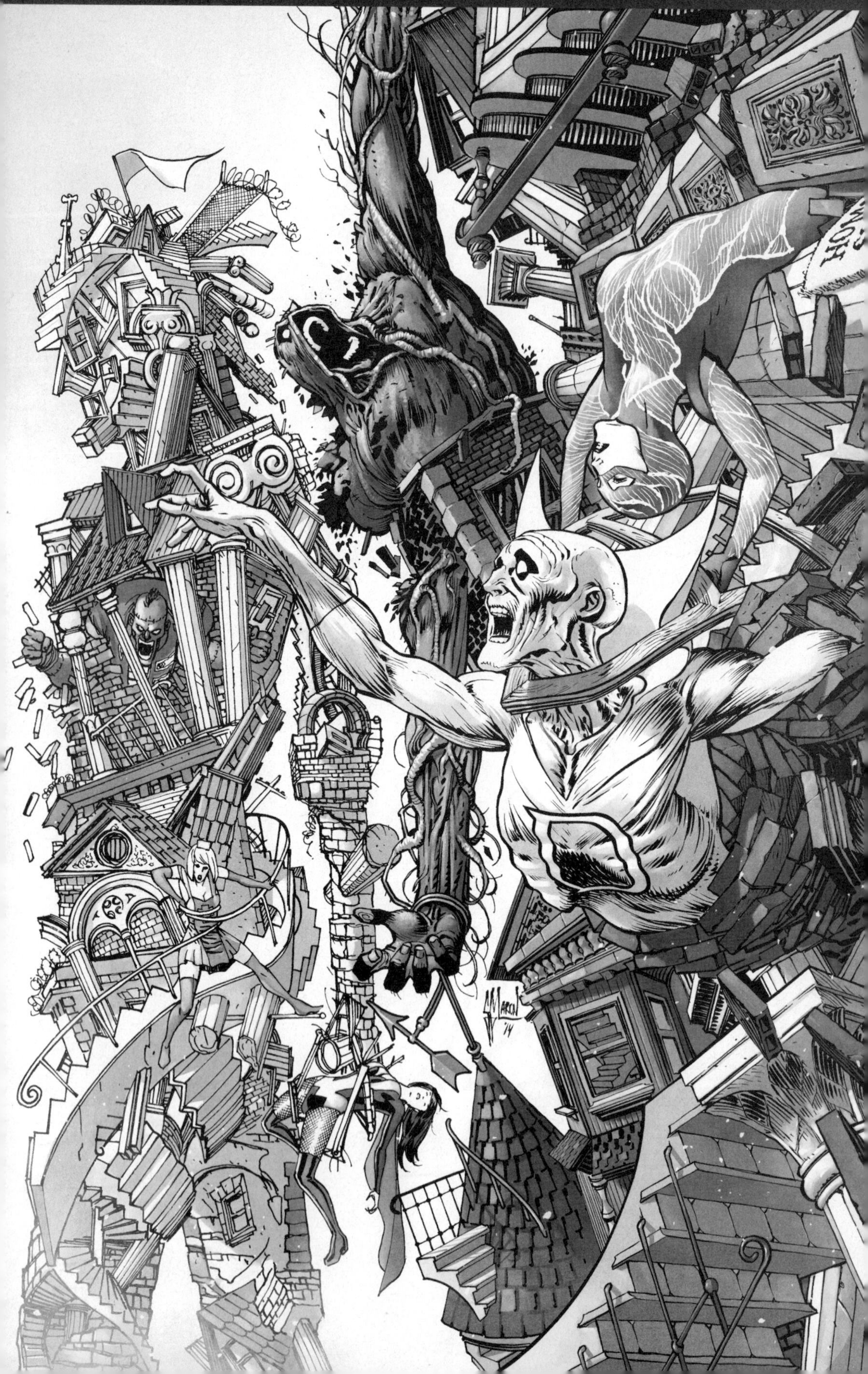

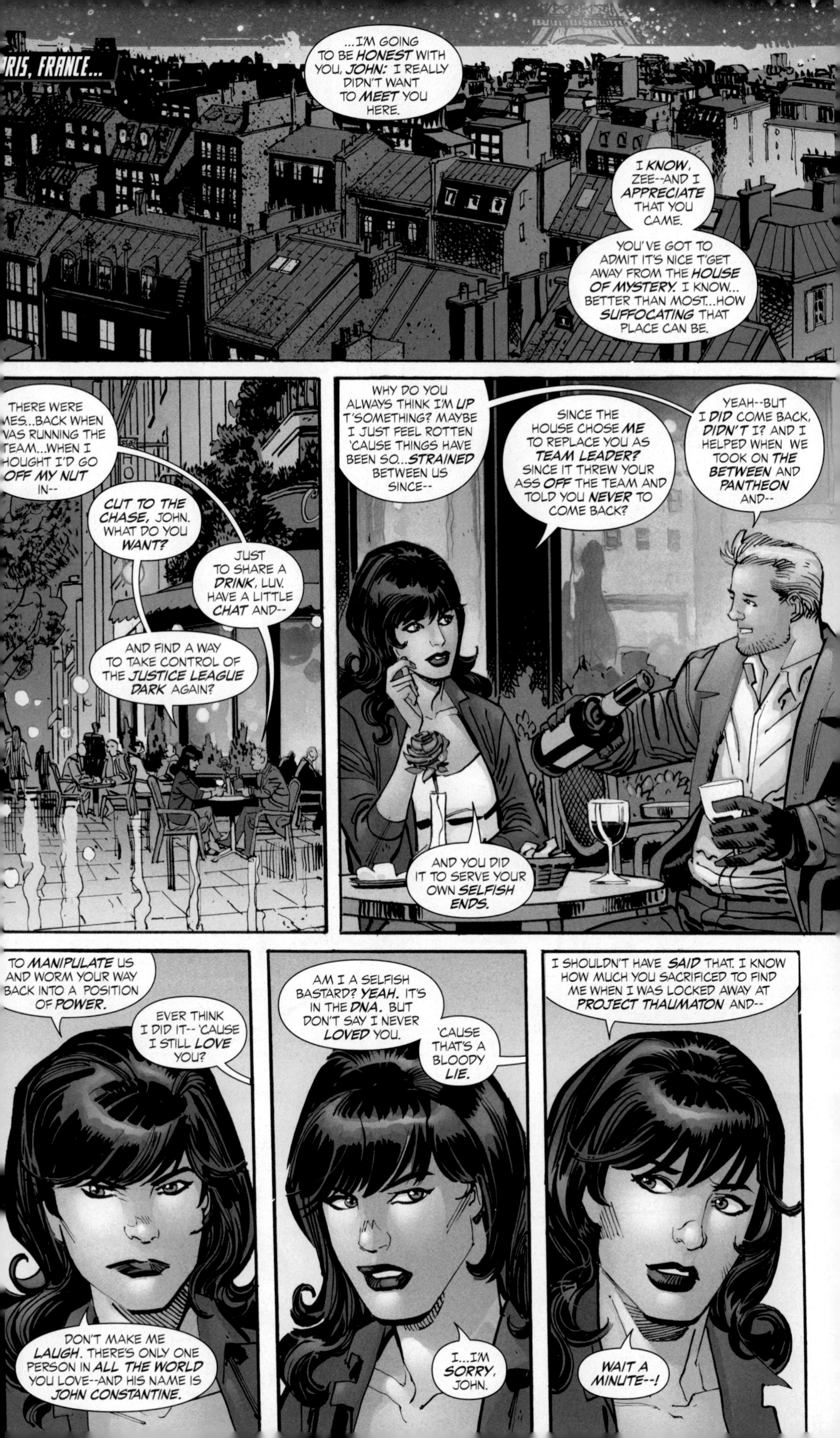
RIS, FRANCE...
...I'M GOING TO BE HONEST WITH YOU, JOHN: I REALLY DIDN'T WANT TO MEET YOU HERE.
I KNOW, ZEE--AND I APPRECIATE THAT YOU CAME.
YOU'VE GOT TO ADMIT IT'S NICE T'GET AWAY FROM THE HOUSE OF MYSTERY. I KNOW... BETTER THAN MOST...HOW SUFFOCATING THAT PLACE CAN BE.
THERE WERE MES...BACK WHEN VAS RUNNING THE TEAM...WHEN I HOUGHT I'D GO OFF MY NUT IN--
CUT TO THE CHASE, JOHN. WHAT DO YOU WANT?
JUST TO SHARE A DRINK, LUV. HAVE A LITTLE CHAT AND--
AND FIND A WAY TO TAKE CONTROL OF THE JUSTICE LEAGUE DARK AGAIN?
WHY DO YOU ALWAYS THINK I'M UP T'SOMETHING? MAYBE I JUST FEEL ROTTEN 'CAUSE THINGS HAVE BEEN SO...STRAINED BETWEEN US SINCE--
SINCE THE HOUSE CHOSE ME TO REPLACE YOU AS TEAM LEADER? SINCE IT THREW YOUR ASS OFF THE TEAM AND TOLD YOU NEVER TO COME BACK?
YEAH--BUT I DID COME BACK, DIDN'T I? AND I HELPED WHEN WE TOOK ON THE BETWEEN AND PANTHEON AND--
AND YOU DID IT TO SERVE YOUR OWN SELFISH ENDS.
TO MANIPULATE US AND WORM YOUR WAY BACK INTO A POSITION OF POWER.
EVER THINK I DID IT-- 'CAUSE I STILL LOVE YOU?
DON'T MAKE ME LAUGH. THERE'S ONLY ONE PERSON IN ALL THE WORLD YOU LOVE--AND HIS NAME IS JOHN CONSTANTINE.
AM I A SELFISH BASTARD? YEAH. IT'S IN THE DNA. BUT DON'T SAY I NEVER LOVED YOU.
'CAUSE THAT'S A BLOODY LIE.
I...I'M SORRY, JOHN.
I SHOULDN'T HAVE SAID THAT. I KNOW HOW MUCH YOU SACRIFICED TO FIND ME WHEN I WAS LOCKED AWAY AT PROJECT THAUMATON AND--
WAIT A MINUTE--!

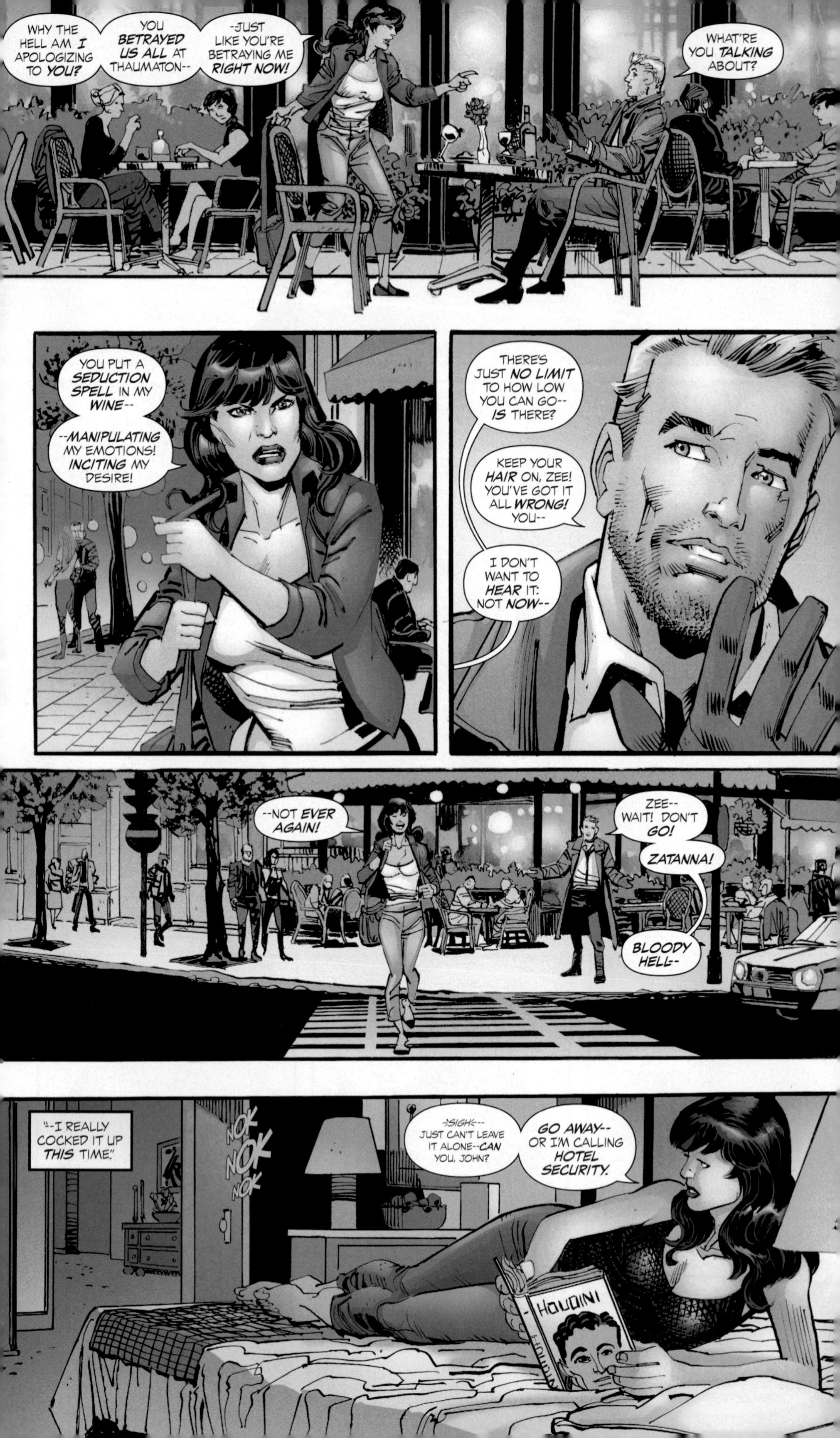
WHY THE HELL AM I APOLOGIZING TO YOU?
YOU BETRAYED US ALL AT THAUMATON--
--JUST LIKE YOU'RE BETRAYING ME RIGHT NOW!
WHAT'RE YOU TALKING ABOUT?
YOU PUT A SEDUCTION SPELL IN MY WINE--
--MANIPULATING MY EMOTIONS! INCITING MY DESIRE!
THERE'S JUST NO LIMIT TO HOW LOW YOU CAN GO--IS THERE?
KEEP YOUR HAIR ON, ZEE! YOU'VE GOT IT ALL WRONG! YOU--
I DON'T WANT TO HEAR IT: NOT NOW--
--NOT EVER AGAIN!
ZEE--WAIT! DON'T GO!
ZATANNA!
BLOODY HELL--
"--I REALLY COCKED IT UP THIS TIME."
NOK NOK NOK
SIGH--JUST CAN'T LEAVE IT ALONE--CAN YOU, JOHN?
GO AWAY--OR I'M CALLING HOTEL SECURITY.
HOUDINI

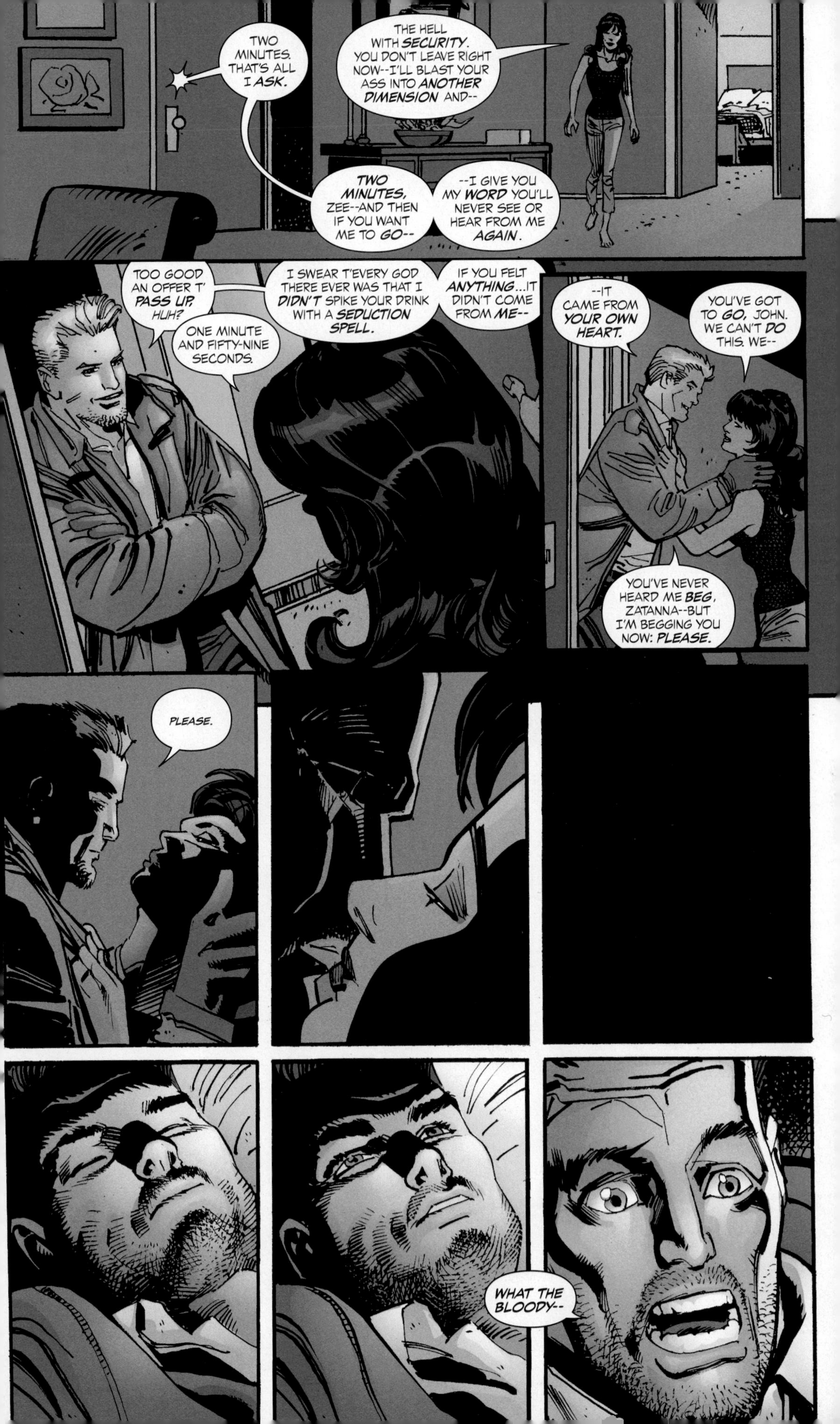

TWO MINUTES. THAT'S ALL I ASK.
THE HELL WITH SECURITY. YOU DON'T LEAVE RIGHT NOW--I'LL BLAST YOUR ASS INTO ANOTHER DIMENSION AND--
TWO MINUTES, ZEE--AND THEN IF YOU WANT ME TO GO--
--I GIVE YOU MY WORD YOU'LL NEVER SEE OR HEAR FROM ME AGAIN.
TOO GOOD AN OFFER T' PASS UP, HUH?
ONE MINUTE AND FIFTY-NINE SECONDS.
I SWEAR T'EVERY GOD THERE EVER WAS THAT I DIDN'T SPIKE YOUR DRINK WITH A SEDUCTION SPELL.
IF YOU FELT ANYTHING...IT DIDN'T COME FROM ME--
--IT CAME FROM YOUR OWN HEART.
YOU'VE GOT TO GO, JOHN. WE CAN'T DO THIS. WE--
YOU'VE NEVER HEARD ME BEG, ZATANNA--BUT I'M BEGGING YOU NOW: PLEASE.
PLEASE.
WHAT THE BLOODY--

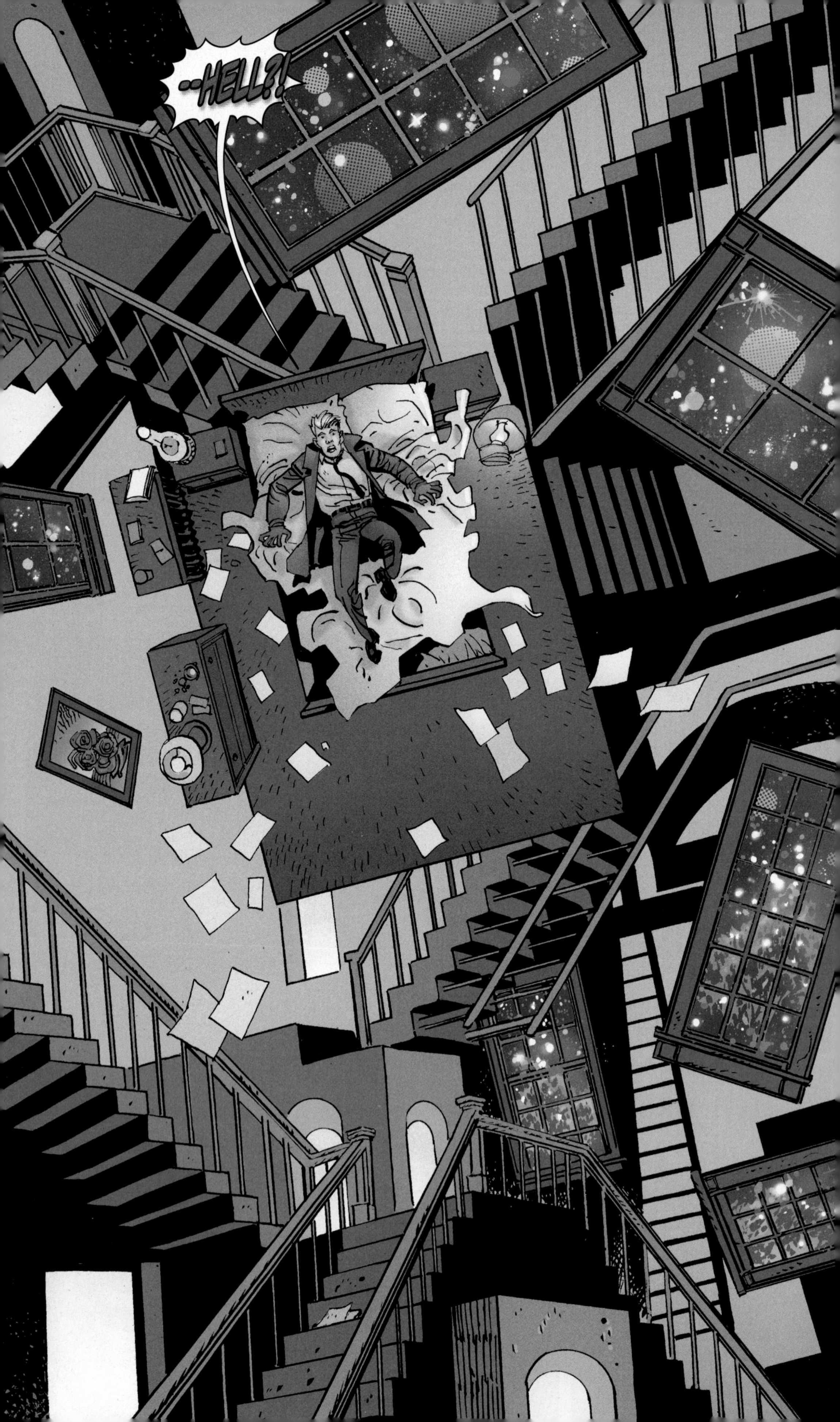
--HELL?!

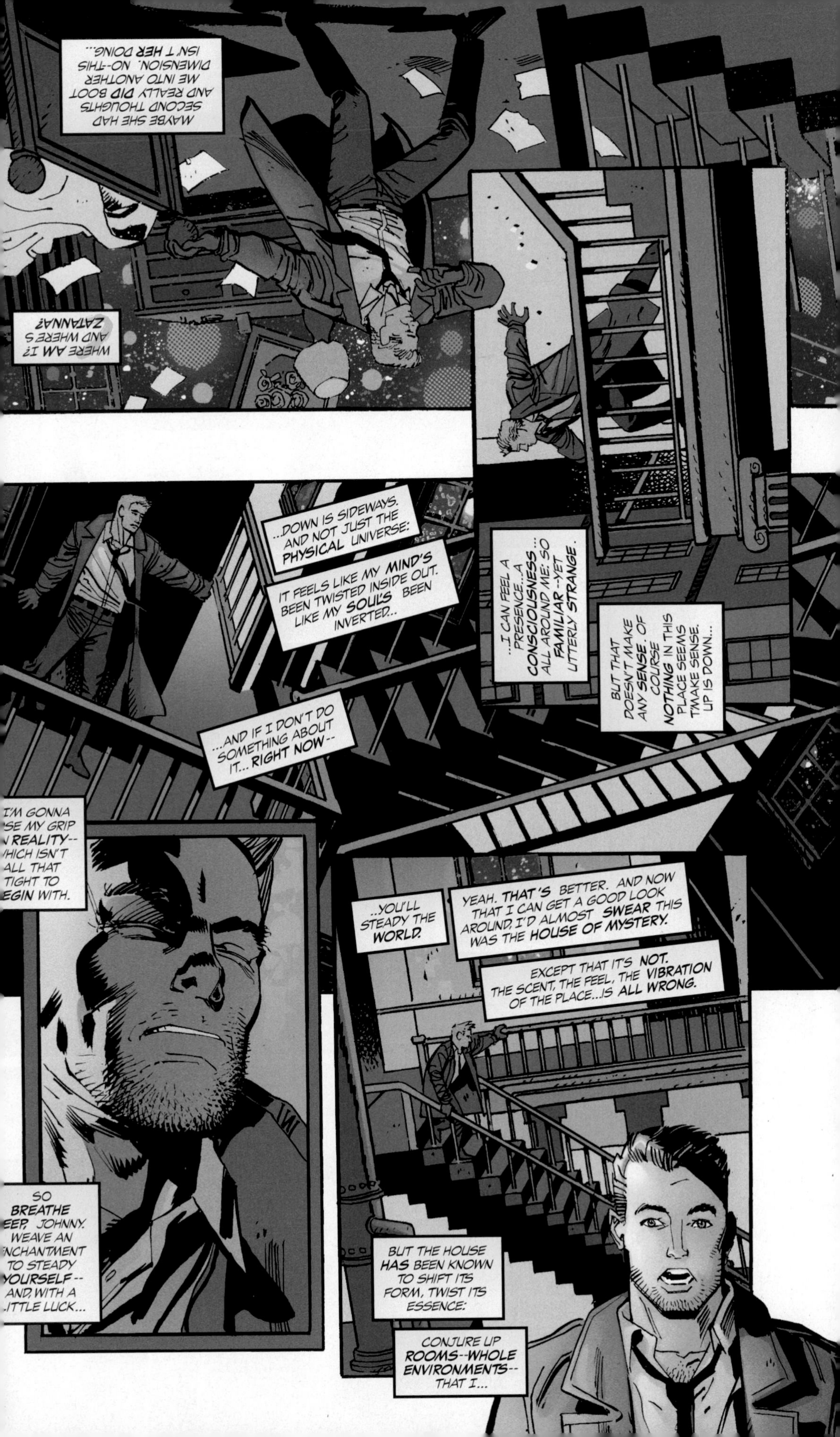

WHERE AM I? AND WHERE'S ZATANNA?
MAYBE SHE HAD SECOND THOUGHTS AND REALLY DID BOOT ME INTO ANOTHER DIMENSION. NO--THIS ISN'T HER DOING...
...I CAN FEEL A PRESENCE...A CONSCIOUSNESS... ALL AROUND ME: SO FAMILIAR--YET UTTERLY STRANGE.
BUT THAT DOESN'T MAKE ANY SENSE. OF COURSE NOTHING IN THIS PLACE SEEMS T'MAKE SENSE. UP IS DOWN...
...DOWN IS SIDEWAYS. AND NOT JUST THE PHYSICAL UNIVERSE:
IT FEELS LIKE MY MIND'S BEEN TWISTED INSIDE OUT. LIKE MY SOUL'S BEEN INVERTED...
...AND IF I DON'T DO SOMETHING ABOUT IT... RIGHT NOW--
I'M GONNA SE MY GRIP N REALITY-- HICH ISN'T ALL THAT TIGHT TO EGIN WITH.
SO BREATHE EEP, JOHNNY. WEAVE AN NCHANTMENT TO STEADY YOURSELF-- AND, WITH A ITTLE LUCK...
...YOU'LL STEADY THE WORLD.
YEAH. THAT'S BETTER. AND NOW THAT I CAN GET A GOOD LOOK AROUND, I'D ALMOST SWEAR THIS WAS THE HOUSE OF MYSTERY.
EXCEPT THAT IT'S NOT. THE SCENT, THE FEEL, THE VIBRATION OF THE PLACE...IS ALL WRONG.
BUT THE HOUSE HAS BEEN KNOWN TO SHIFT ITS FORM, TWIST ITS ESSENCE:
CONJURE UP ROOMS--WHOLE ENVIRONMENTS-- THAT I...

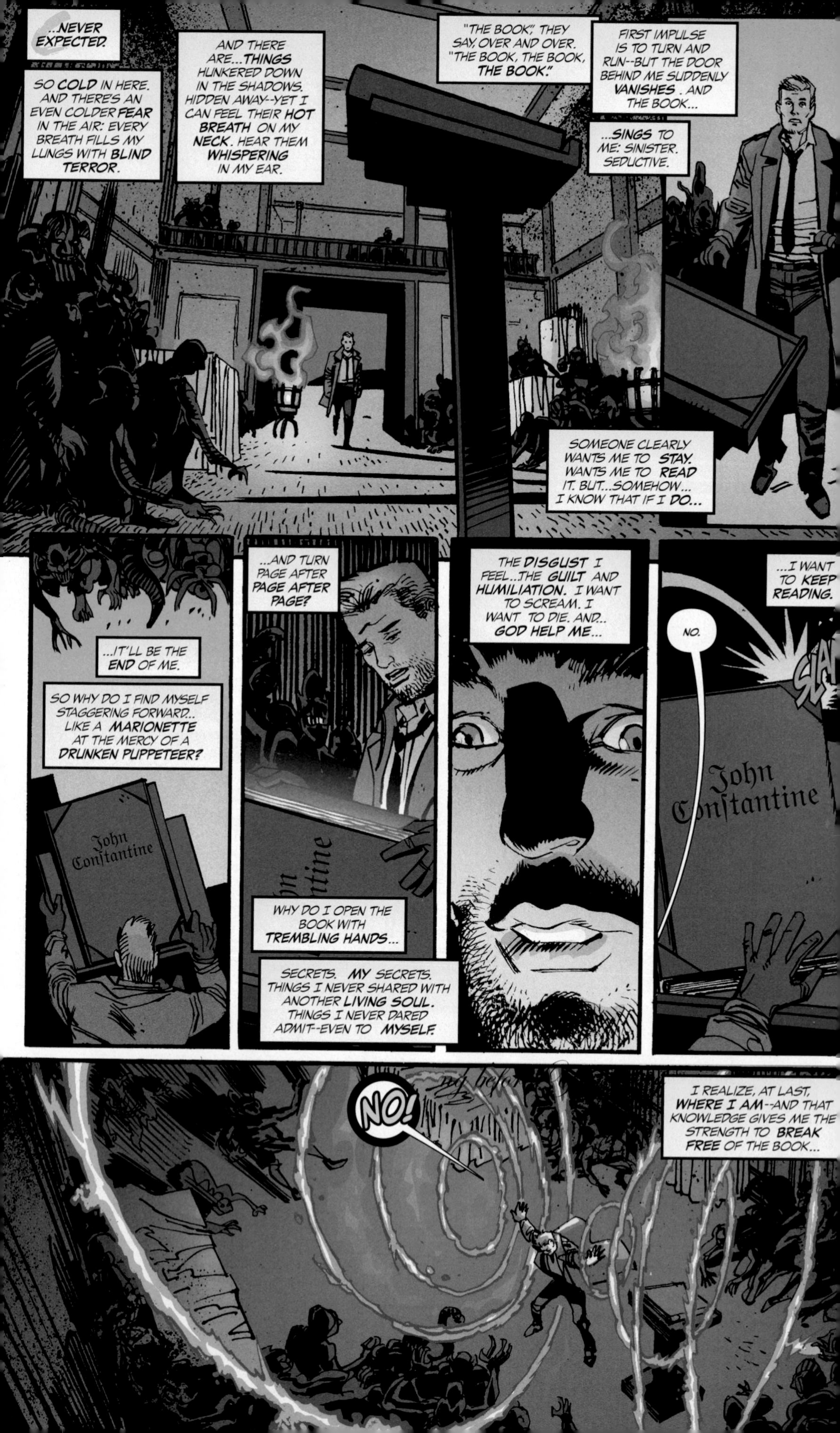
...NEVER EXPECTED.
SO COLD IN HERE. AND THERE'S AN EVEN COLDER FEAR IN THE AIR: EVERY BREATH FILLS MY LUNGS WITH BLIND TERROR.
AND THERE ARE...THINGS HUNKERED DOWN IN THE SHADOWS. HIDDEN AWAY--YET I CAN FEEL THEIR HOT BREATH ON MY NECK. HEAR THEM WHISPERING IN MY EAR.
"THE BOOK," THEY SAY, OVER AND OVER. "THE BOOK, THE BOOK, THE BOOK."
FIRST IMPULSE IS TO TURN AND RUN--BUT THE DOOR BEHIND ME SUDDENLY VANISHES. AND THE BOOK...
...SINGS TO ME: SINISTER. SEDUCTIVE.
SOMEONE CLEARLY WANTS ME TO STAY. WANTS ME TO READ IT. BUT...SOMEHOW... I KNOW THAT IF I DO...
...IT'LL BE THE END OF ME.
SO WHY DO I FIND MYSELF STAGGERING FORWARD... LIKE A MARIONETTE AT THE MERCY OF A DRUNKEN PUPPETEER?
John Constantine
...AND TURN PAGE AFTER PAGE AFTER PAGE?
WHY DO I OPEN THE BOOK WITH TREMBLING HANDS...
SECRETS. MY SECRETS. THINGS I NEVER SHARED WITH ANOTHER LIVING SOUL. THINGS I NEVER DARED ADMIT--EVEN TO MYSELF.
THE DISGUST I FEEL...THE GUILT AND HUMILIATION. I WANT TO SCREAM. I WANT TO DIE. AND... GOD HELP ME...
...I WANT TO KEEP READING.
NO.
John Constantine
NO!
I REALIZE, AT LAST, WHERE I AM--AND THAT KNOWLEDGE GIVES ME THE STRENGTH TO BREAK FREE OF THE BOOK...

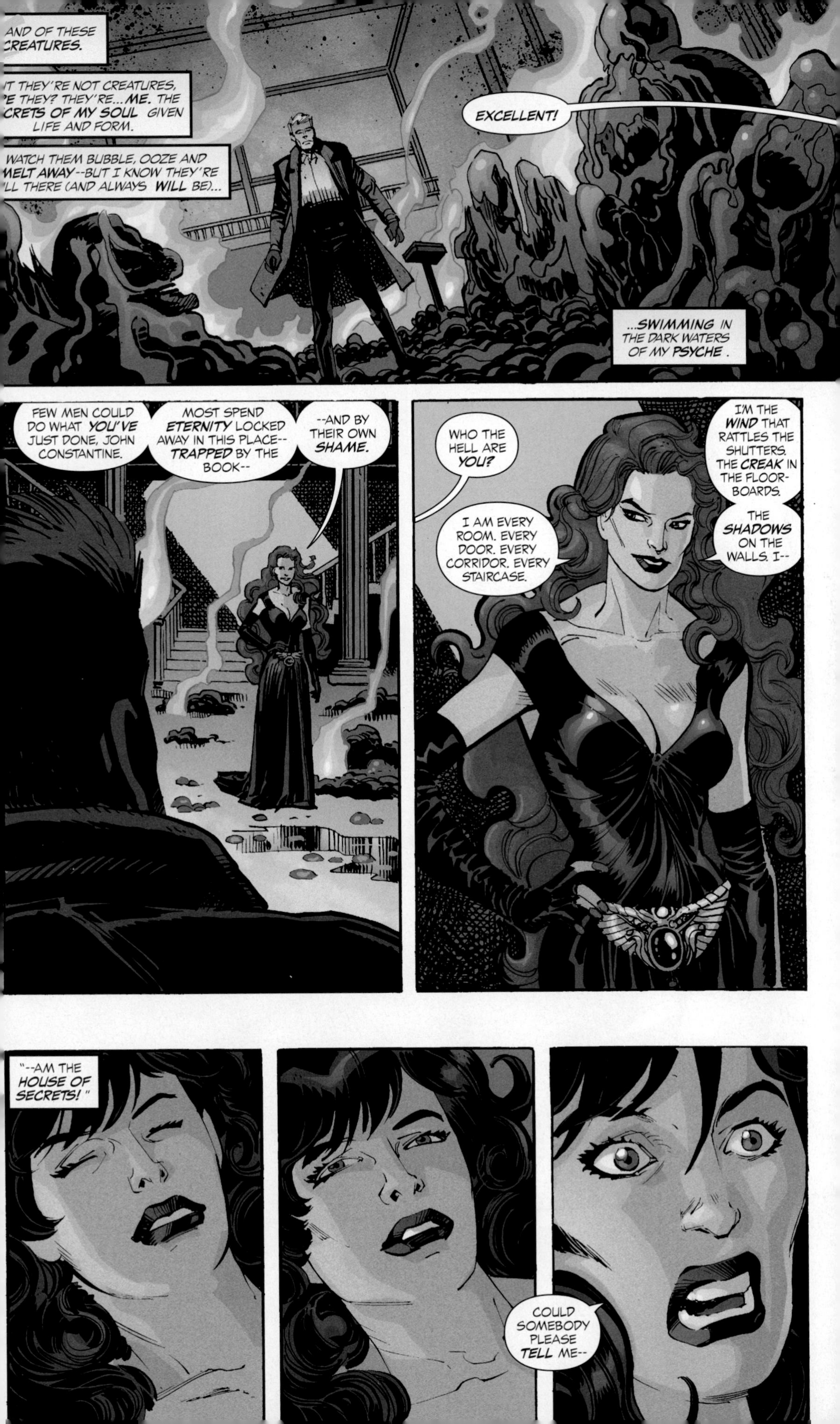

AND OF THESE CREATURES.
...T THEY'RE NOT CREATURES, ...E THEY? THEY'RE...ME. THE ...CRETS OF MY SOUL GIVEN LIFE AND FORM.
...WATCH THEM BUBBLE, OOZE AND MELT AWAY--BUT I KNOW THEY'RE ...LL THERE (AND ALWAYS WILL BE)...
EXCELLENT!
...SWIMMING IN THE DARK WATERS OF MY PSYCHE.
FEW MEN COULD DO WHAT YOU'VE JUST DONE, JOHN CONSTANTINE.
MOST SPEND ETERNITY LOCKED AWAY IN THIS PLACE-- TRAPPED BY THE BOOK--
--AND BY THEIR OWN SHAME.
WHO THE HELL ARE YOU?
I AM EVERY ROOM. EVERY DOOR. EVERY CORRIDOR. EVERY STAIRCASE.
I'M THE WIND THAT RATTLES THE SHUTTERS. THE CREAK IN THE FLOOR-BOARDS.
THE SHADOWS ON THE WALLS. I--
"--AM THE HOUSE OF SECRETS!"
COULD SOMEBODY PLEASE TELL ME--

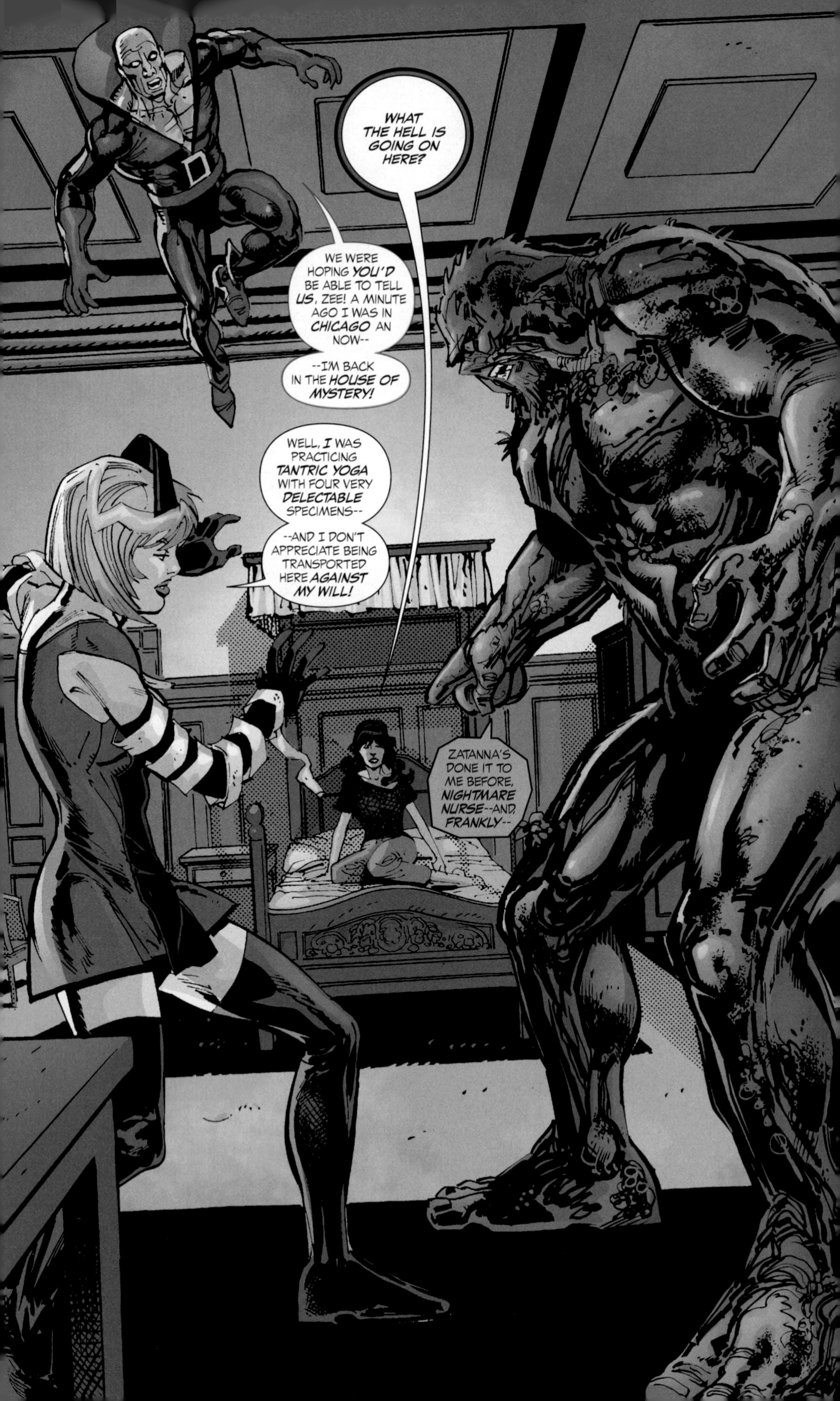
WHAT THE HELL IS GOING ON HERE?
WE WERE HOPING YOU'D BE ABLE TO TELL US, ZEE! A MINUTE AGO I WAS IN CHICAGO AN NOW--
--I'M BACK IN THE HOUSE OF MYSTERY!
WELL, I WAS PRACTICING TANTRIC YOGA WITH FOUR VERY DELECTABLE SPECIMENS--
--AND I DON'T APPRECIATE BEING TRANSPORTED HERE AGAINST MY WILL!
ZATANNA'S DONE IT TO ME BEFORE, NIGHTMARE NURSE--AND, FRANKLY--

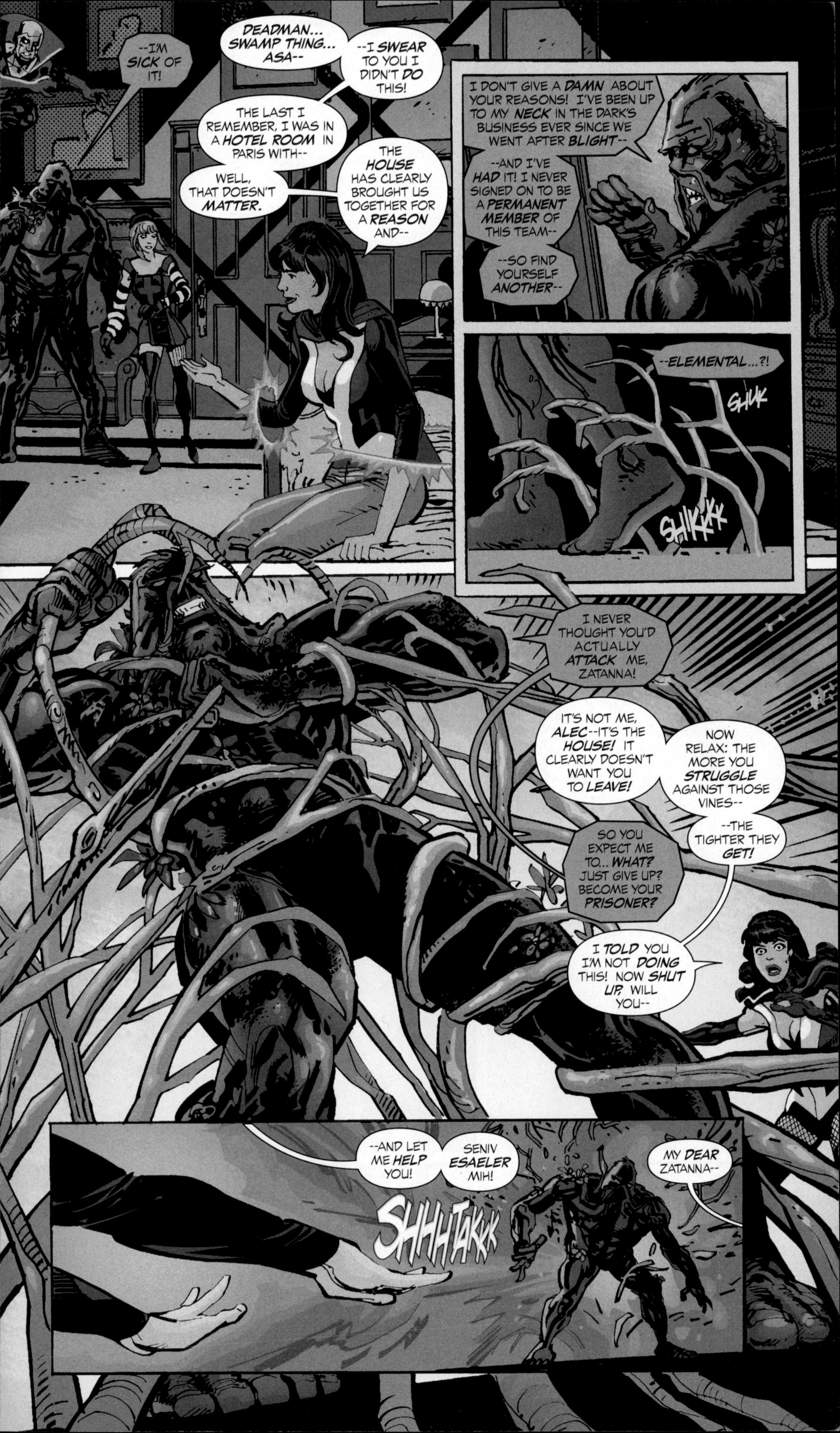
--I'M SICK OF IT!
DEADMAN... SWAMP THING... ASA--
--I SWEAR TO YOU I DIDN'T DO THIS!
THE LAST I REMEMBER, I WAS IN A HOTEL ROOM IN PARIS WITH--
WELL, THAT DOESN'T MATTER.
THE HOUSE HAS CLEARLY BROUGHT US TOGETHER FOR A REASON AND--
I DON'T GIVE A DAMN ABOUT YOUR REASONS! I'VE BEEN UP TO MY NECK IN THE DARK'S BUSINESS EVER SINCE WE WENT AFTER BLIGHT--
--AND I'VE HAD IT! I NEVER SIGNED ON TO BE A PERMANENT MEMBER OF THIS TEAM--
--SO FIND YOURSELF ANOTHER--
--ELEMENTAL...?!
SHUK
SHIKKKK
I NEVER THOUGHT YOU'D ACTUALLY ATTACK ME, ZATANNA!
IT'S NOT ME, ALEC--IT'S THE HOUSE! IT CLEARLY DOESN'T WANT YOU TO LEAVE!
NOW RELAX: THE MORE YOU STRUGGLE AGAINST THOSE VINES--
--THE TIGHTER THEY GET!
SO YOU EXPECT ME TO... WHAT? JUST GIVE UP? BECOME YOUR PRISONER?
I TOLD YOU I'M NOT DOING THIS! NOW SHUT UP, WILL YOU--
--AND LET ME HELP YOU!
SENIV ESAELER MIH!
SHHHTAKKK
MY DEAR ZATANNA--

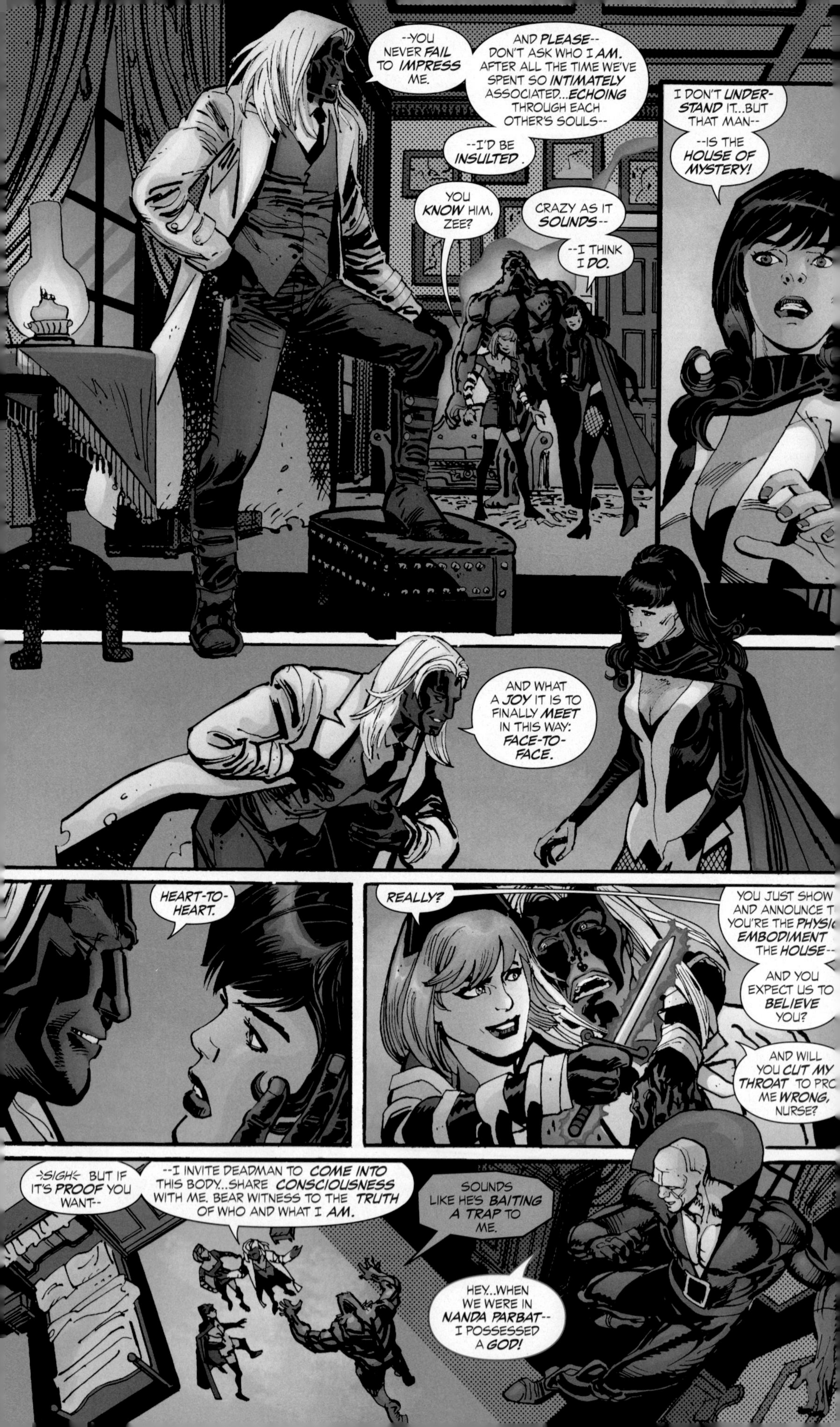
--YOU NEVER FAIL TO IMPRESS ME.
AND PLEASE-- DON'T ASK WHO I AM. AFTER ALL THE TIME WE'VE SPENT SO INTIMATELY ASSOCIATED...ECHOING THROUGH EACH OTHER'S SOULS--
--I'D BE INSULTED.
YOU KNOW HIM, ZEE?
CRAZY AS IT SOUNDS--
--I THINK I DO.
I DON'T UNDERSTAND IT...BUT THAT MAN--
--IS THE HOUSE OF MYSTERY!
AND WHAT A JOY IT IS TO FINALLY MEET IN THIS WAY: FACE-TO-FACE.
HEART-TO-HEART.
REALLY?
YOU JUST SHOW AND ANNOUNCE T YOU'RE THE PHYSIC EMBODIMENT THE HOUSE--
AND YOU EXPECT US TO BELIEVE YOU?
AND WILL YOU CUT MY THROAT TO PRO ME WRONG, NURSE?
SIGH BUT IF IT'S PROOF YOU WANT--
--I INVITE DEADMAN TO COME INTO THIS BODY...SHARE CONSCIOUSNESS WITH ME. BEAR WITNESS TO THE TRUTH OF WHO AND WHAT I AM.
SOUNDS LIKE HE'S BAITING A TRAP TO ME.
HEY...WHEN WE WERE IN NANDA PARBAT-- I POSSESSED A GOD!

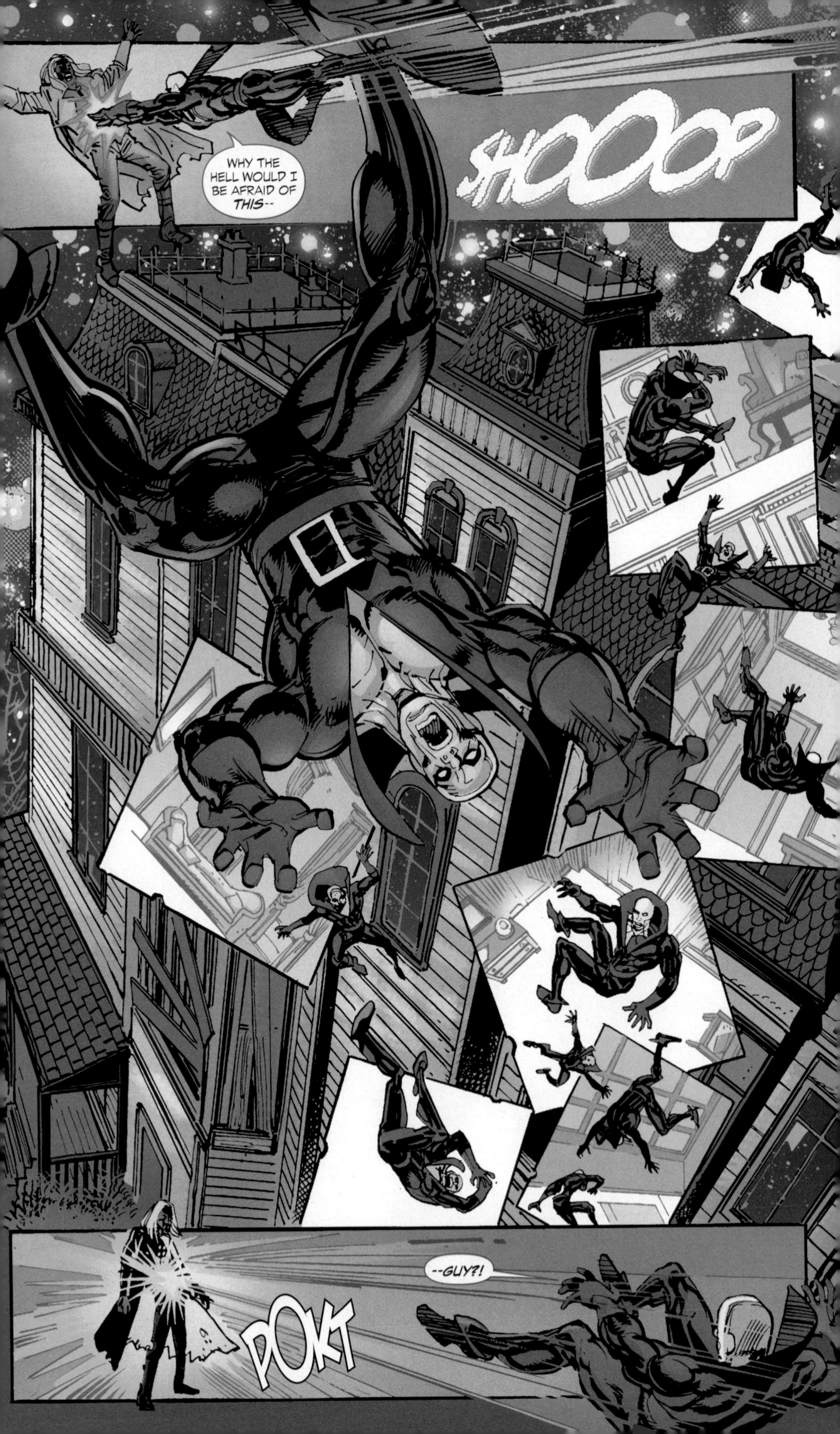
WHY THE HELL WOULD I BE AFRAID OF THIS--
SHOOOP
--GUY?!
POKT

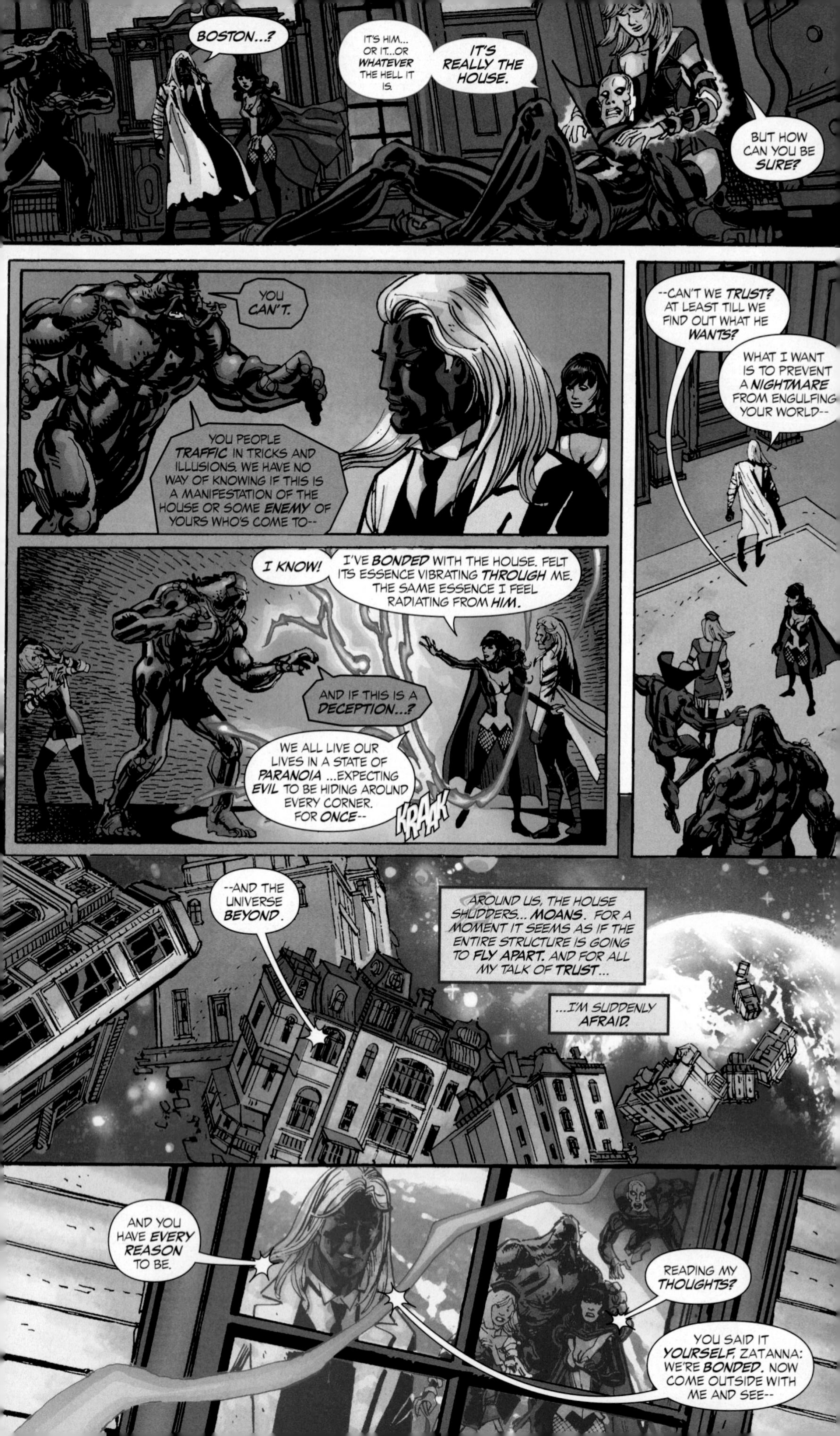
BOSTON...?
IT'S HIM... OR IT...OR WHATEVER THE HELL IT IS.
IT'S REALLY THE HOUSE.
BUT HOW CAN YOU BE SURE?
YOU CAN'T.
YOU PEOPLE TRAFFIC IN TRICKS AND ILLUSIONS. WE HAVE NO WAY OF KNOWING IF THIS IS A MANIFESTATION OF THE HOUSE OR SOME ENEMY OF YOURS WHO'S COME TO--
I KNOW!
I'VE BONDED WITH THE HOUSE. FELT ITS ESSENCE VIBRATING THROUGH ME. THE SAME ESSENCE I FEEL RADIATING FROM HIM.
AND IF THIS IS A DECEPTION...?
WE ALL LIVE OUR LIVES IN A STATE OF PARANOIA ...EXPECTING EVIL TO BE HIDING AROUND EVERY CORNER. FOR ONCE--
KRAAK
--CAN'T WE TRUST? AT LEAST TILL WE FIND OUT WHAT HE WANTS?
WHAT I WANT IS TO PREVENT A NIGHTMARE FROM ENGULFING YOUR WORLD--
--AND THE UNIVERSE BEYOND.
AROUND US, THE HOUSE SHUDDERS... MOANS. FOR A MOMENT IT SEEMS AS IF THE ENTIRE STRUCTURE IS GOING TO FLY APART. AND FOR ALL MY TALK OF TRUST...
...I'M SUDDENLY AFRAID.
AND YOU HAVE EVERY REASON TO BE.
READING MY THOUGHTS?
YOU SAID IT YOURSELF, ZATANNA: WE'RE BONDED. NOW COME OUTSIDE WITH ME AND SEE--

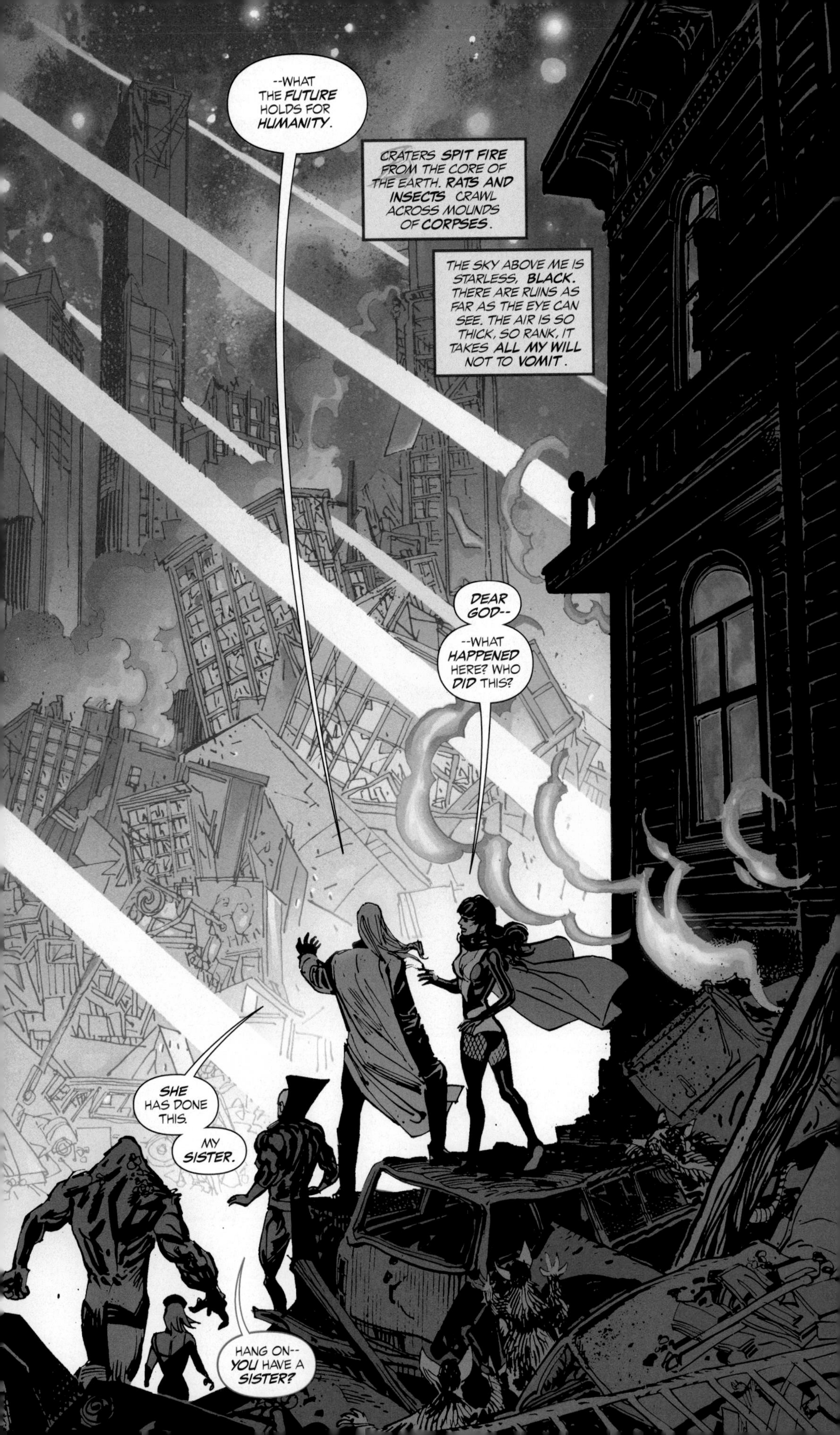
--WHAT THE FUTURE HOLDS FOR HUMANITY.
CRATERS SPIT FIRE FROM THE CORE OF THE EARTH. RATS AND INSECTS CRAWL ACROSS MOUNDS OF CORPSES.
THE SKY ABOVE ME IS STARLESS, BLACK. THERE ARE RUINS AS FAR AS THE EYE CAN SEE. THE AIR IS SO THICK, SO RANK, IT TAKES ALL MY WILL NOT TO VOMIT.
DEAR GOD--
--WHAT HAPPENED HERE? WHO DID THIS?
SHE HAS DONE THIS.
MY SISTER.
HANG ON-- YOU HAVE A SISTER?

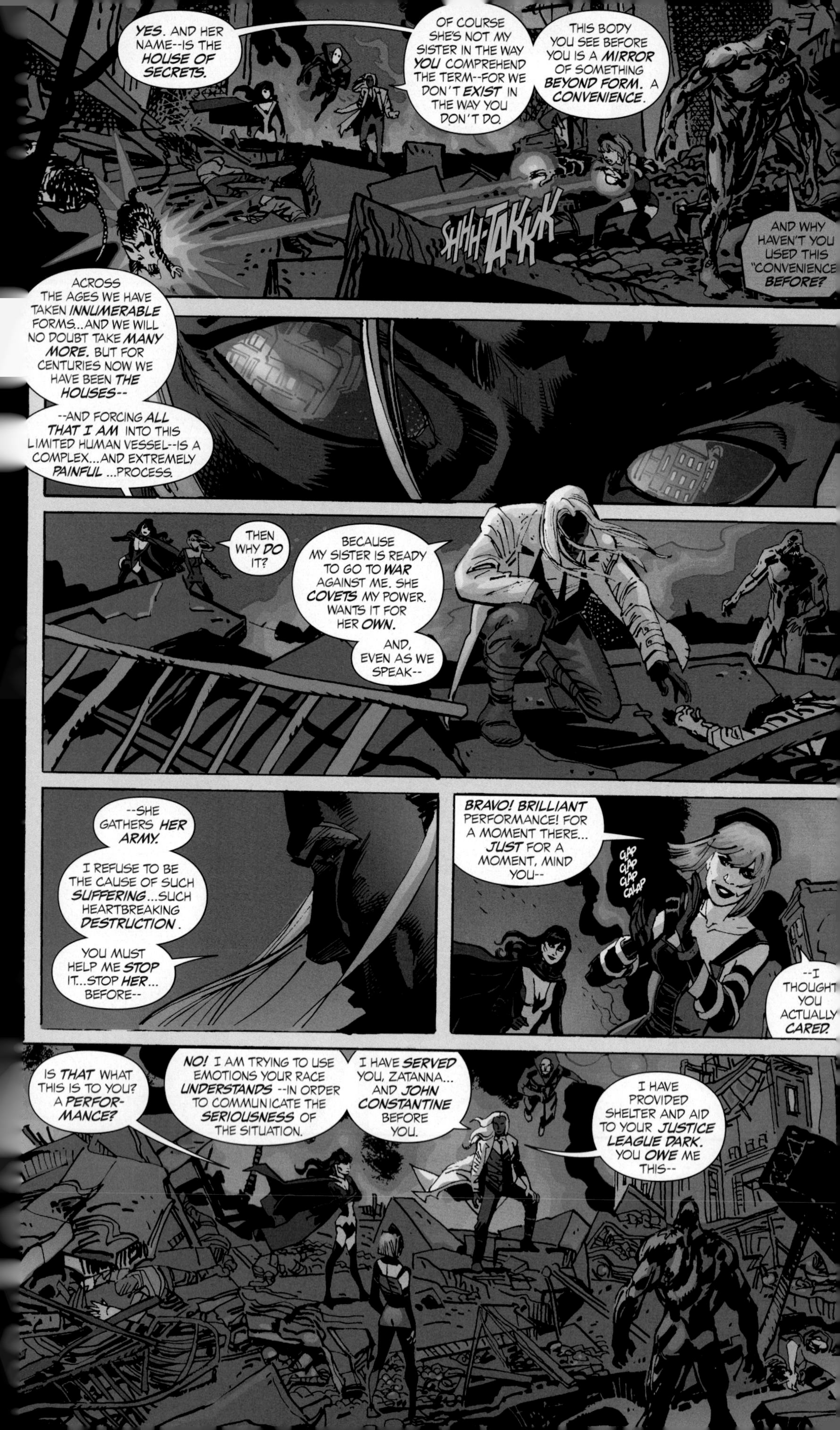
YES. AND HER NAME--IS THE HOUSE OF SECRETS.
OF COURSE SHE'S NOT MY SISTER IN THE WAY YOU COMPREHEND THE TERM--FOR WE DON'T EXIST IN THE WAY YOU DON'T DO.
THIS BODY YOU SEE BEFORE YOU IS A MIRROR OF SOMETHING BEYOND FORM. A CONVENIENCE.
SHHH-TAKKK
AND WHY HAVEN'T YOU USED THIS "CONVENIENCE" BEFORE?
ACROSS THE AGES WE HAVE TAKEN INNUMERABLE FORMS...AND WE WILL NO DOUBT TAKE MANY MORE. BUT FOR CENTURIES NOW WE HAVE BEEN THE HOUSES--
--AND FORCING ALL THAT I AM INTO THIS LIMITED HUMAN VESSEL--IS A COMPLEX...AND EXTREMELY PAINFUL ...PROCESS.
THEN WHY DO IT?
BECAUSE MY SISTER IS READY TO GO TO WAR AGAINST ME. SHE COVETS MY POWER. WANTS IT FOR HER OWN.
AND, EVEN AS WE SPEAK--
--SHE GATHERS HER ARMY.
I REFUSE TO BE THE CAUSE OF SUCH SUFFERING...SUCH HEARTBREAKING DESTRUCTION.
YOU MUST HELP ME STOP IT...STOP HER... BEFORE--
BRAVO! BRILLIANT PERFORMANCE! FOR A MOMENT THERE... JUST FOR A MOMENT, MIND YOU--
CLAP CLAP CLAP CLAP CALAP
--I THOUGHT YOU ACTUALLY CARED.
IS THAT WHAT THIS IS TO YOU? A PERFOR-MANCE?
NO! I AM TRYING TO USE EMOTIONS YOUR RACE UNDERSTANDS --IN ORDER TO COMMUNICATE THE SERIOUSNESS OF THE SITUATION.
I HAVE SERVED YOU, ZATANNA... AND JOHN CONSTANTINE BEFORE YOU.
I HAVE PROVIDED SHELTER AND AID TO YOUR JUSTICE LEAGUE DARK. YOU OWE ME THIS--

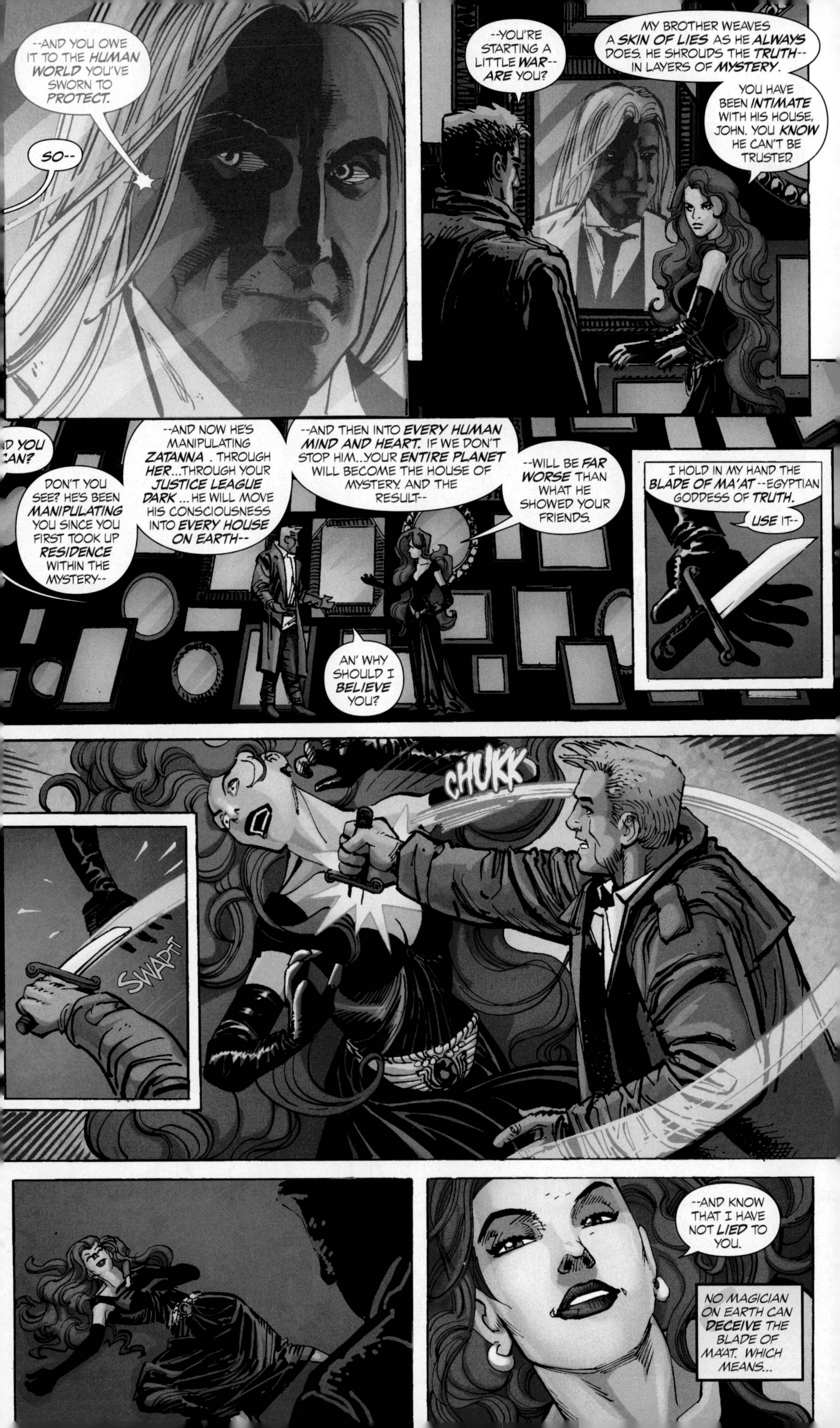

--AND YOU OWE IT TO THE HUMAN WORLD YOU'VE SWORN TO PROTECT.
SO--
--YOU'RE STARTING A LITTLE WAR-- ARE YOU?
MY BROTHER WEAVES A SKIN OF LIES AS HE ALWAYS DOES. HE SHROUDS THE TRUTH-- IN LAYERS OF MYSTERY.
YOU HAVE BEEN INTIMATE WITH HIS HOUSE, JOHN. YOU KNOW HE CAN'T BE TRUSTED.
DON'T YOU SEE? HE'S BEEN MANIPULATING YOU SINCE YOU FIRST TOOK UP RESIDENCE WITHIN THE MYSTERY--
--AND NOW HE'S MANIPULATING ZATANNA . THROUGH HER...THROUGH YOUR JUSTICE LEAGUE DARK ...HE WILL MOVE HIS CONSCIOUSNESS INTO EVERY HOUSE ON EARTH--
--AND THEN INTO EVERY HUMAN MIND AND HEART. IF WE DON'T STOP HIM...YOUR ENTIRE PLANET WILL BECOME THE HOUSE OF MYSTERY. AND THE RESULT--
--WILL BE FAR WORSE THAN WHAT HE SHOWED YOUR FRIENDS.
AN' WHY SHOULD I BELIEVE YOU?
I HOLD IN MY HAND THE BLADE OF MA'AT --EGYPTIAN GODDESS OF TRUTH.
USE IT--
CHUKK
SWAPT
--AND KNOW THAT I HAVE NOT LIED TO YOU.
NO MAGICIAN ON EARTH CAN DECEIVE THE BLADE OF MA'AT. WHICH MEANS...

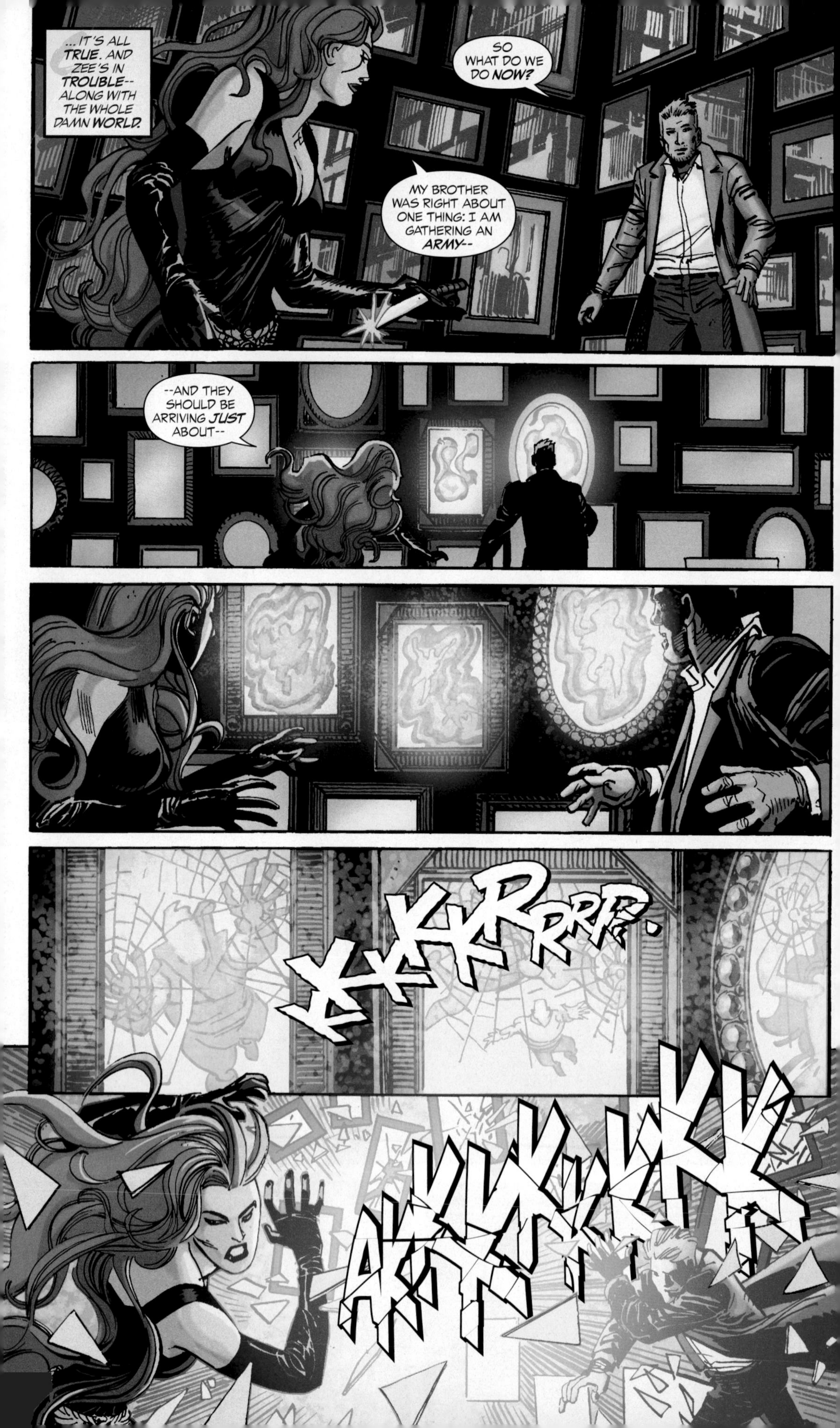
...IT'S ALL TRUE. AND ZEE'S IN TROUBLE-- ALONG WITH THE WHOLE DAMN WORLD.
SO WHAT DO WE DO NOW?
MY BROTHER WAS RIGHT ABOUT ONE THING: I AM GATHERING AN ARMY--
--AND THEY SHOULD BE ARRIVING JUST ABOUT--
KKKRRRR

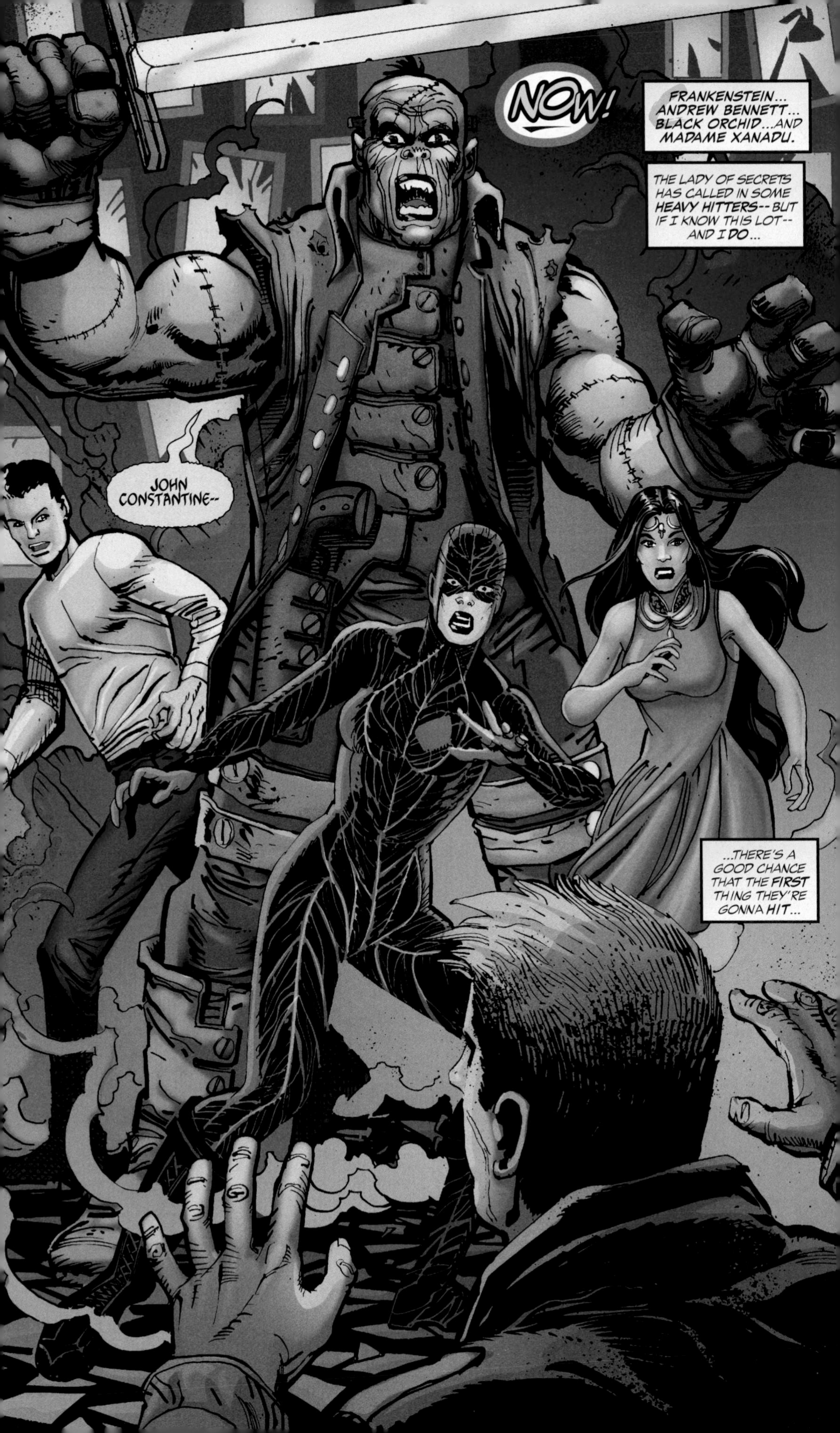
NOW!
FRANKENSTEIN... ANDREW BENNETT... BLACK ORCHID...AND MADAME XANADU.
THE LADY OF SECRETS HAS CALLED IN SOME HEAVY HITTERS-- BUT IF I KNOW THIS LOT-- AND I DO...
JOHN CONSTANTINE--
...THERE'S A GOOD CHANCE THAT THE FIRST THING THEY'RE GONNA HIT...

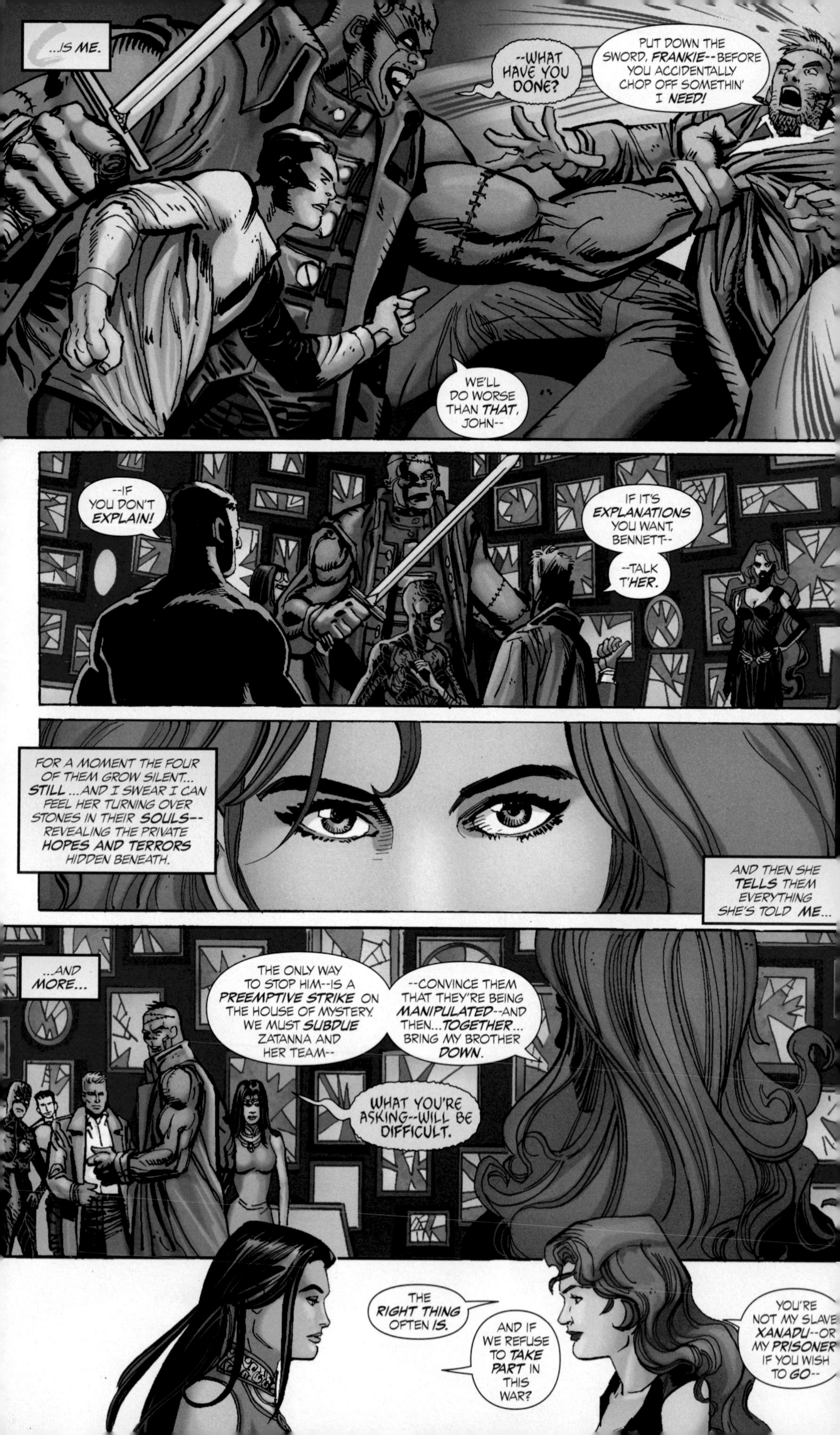
...IS ME.
--WHAT HAVE YOU DONE?
PUT DOWN THE SWORD, FRANKIE--BEFORE YOU ACCIDENTALLY CHOP OFF SOMETHIN' I NEED!
WE'LL DO WORSE THAN THAT, JOHN--
--IF YOU DON'T EXPLAIN!
IF IT'S EXPLANATIONS YOU WANT, BENNETT--
--TALK T'HER.
FOR A MOMENT THE FOUR OF THEM GROW SILENT... STILL ...AND I SWEAR I CAN FEEL HER TURNING OVER STONES IN THEIR SOULS--REVEALING THE PRIVATE HOPES AND TERRORS HIDDEN BENEATH.
AND THEN SHE TELLS THEM EVERYTHING SHE'S TOLD ME...
...AND MORE...
THE ONLY WAY TO STOP HIM--IS A PREEMPTIVE STRIKE ON THE HOUSE OF MYSTERY. WE MUST SUBDUE ZATANNA AND HER TEAM--
--CONVINCE THEM THAT THEY'RE BEING MANIPULATED--AND THEN...TOGETHER... BRING MY BROTHER DOWN.
WHAT YOU'RE ASKING--WILL BE DIFFICULT.
THE RIGHT THING OFTEN IS.
AND IF WE REFUSE TO TAKE PART IN THIS WAR?
YOU'RE NOT MY SLAVE XANADU--OR MY PRISONER IF YOU WISH TO GO--

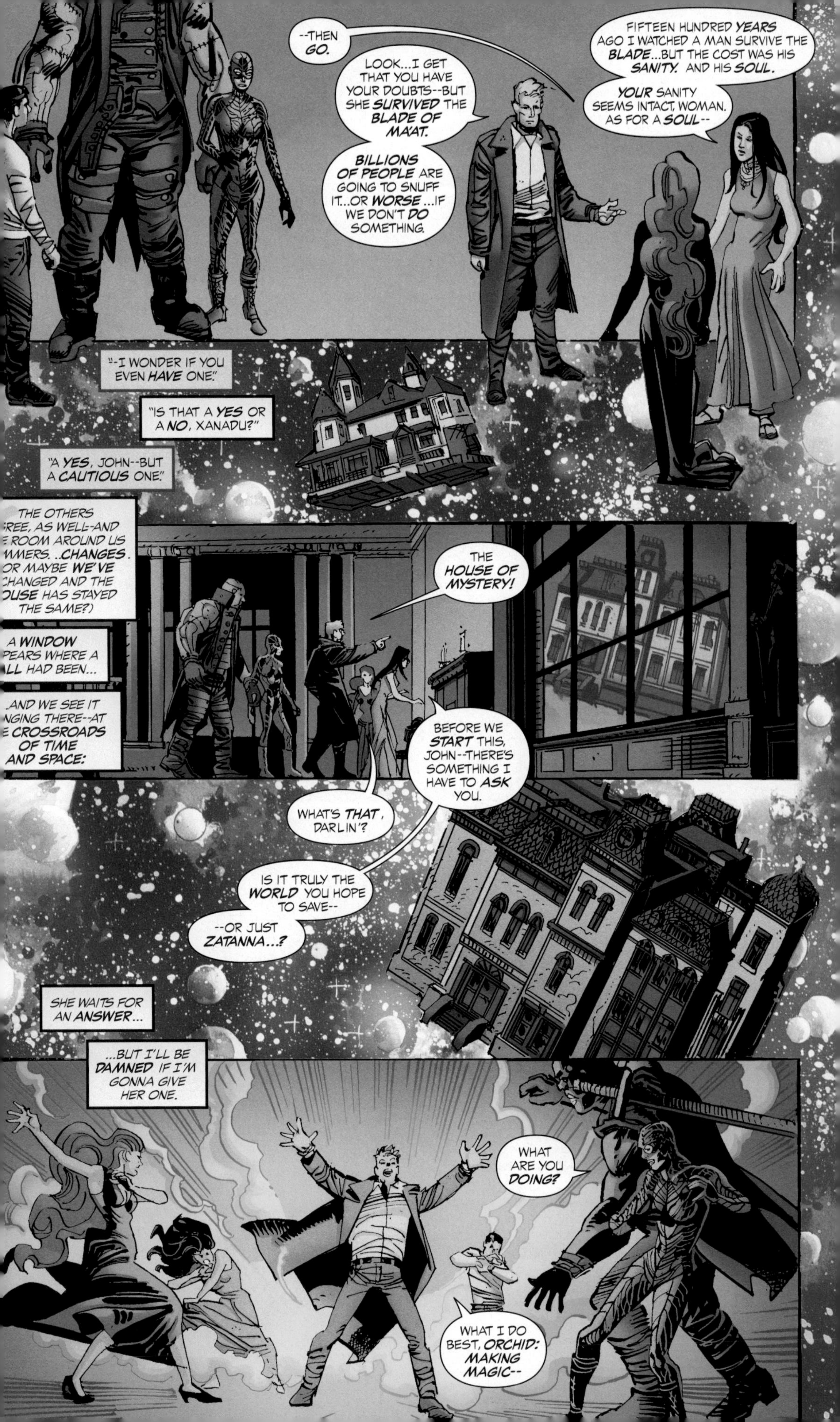
--THEN GO.
LOOK...I GET THAT YOU HAVE YOUR DOUBTS--BUT SHE SURVIVED THE BLADE OF MA'AT.
BILLIONS OF PEOPLE ARE GOING TO SNUFF IT...OR WORSE...IF WE DON'T DO SOMETHING.
FIFTEEN HUNDRED YEARS AGO I WATCHED A MAN SURVIVE THE BLADE...BUT THE COST WAS HIS SANITY. AND HIS SOUL.
YOUR SANITY SEEMS INTACT, WOMAN. AS FOR A SOUL--
"--I WONDER IF YOU EVEN HAVE ONE."
"IS THAT A YES OR A NO, XANADU?"
"A YES, JOHN--BUT A CAUTIOUS ONE."
THE OTHERS GREE, AS WELL--AND E ROOM AROUND US MMERS...CHANGES. OR MAYBE WE'VE CHANGED AND THE OUSE HAS STAYED THE SAME?)
A WINDOW PEARS WHERE A LL HAD BEEN...
...AND WE SEE IT NGING THERE--AT E CROSSROADS OF TIME AND SPACE:
THE HOUSE OF MYSTERY!
BEFORE WE START THIS, JOHN--THERE'S SOMETHING I HAVE TO ASK YOU.
WHAT'S THAT, DARLIN'?
IS IT TRULY THE WORLD YOU HOPE TO SAVE--
--OR JUST ZATANNA...?
SHE WAITS FOR AN ANSWER...
...BUT I'LL BE DAMNED IF I'M GONNA GIVE HER ONE.
WHAT ARE YOU DOING?
WHAT I DO BEST, ORCHID: MAKING MAGIC--

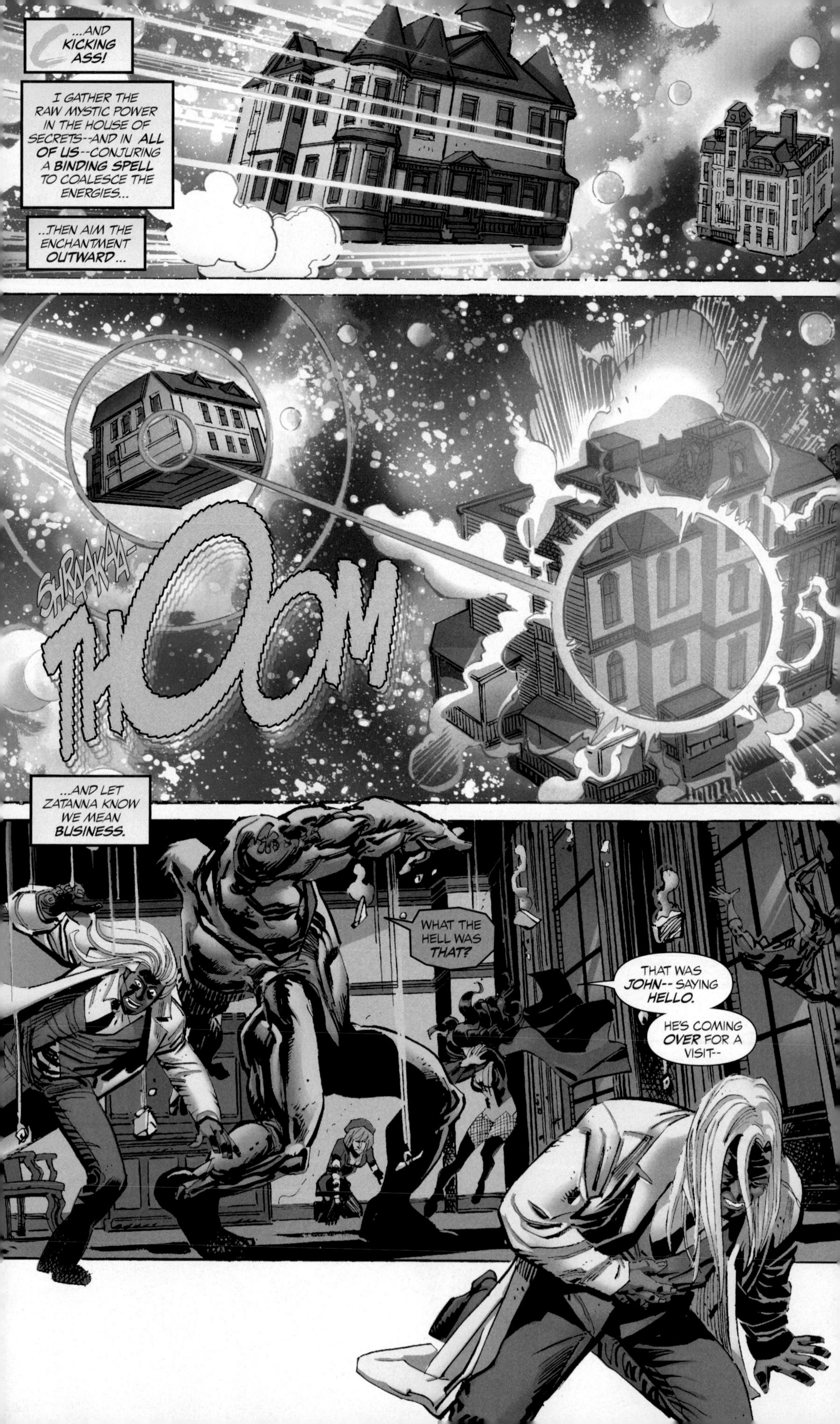
...AND KICKING ASS!
I GATHER THE RAW MYSTIC POWER IN THE HOUSE OF SECRETS--AND IN ALL OF US--CONJURING A BINDING SPELL TO COALESCE THE ENERGIES...
...THEN AIM THE ENCHANTMENT OUTWARD...
SHRAKAA-THOOM
...AND LET ZATANNA KNOW WE MEAN BUSINESS.
WHAT THE HELL WAS THAT?
THAT WAS JOHN-- SAYING HELLO.
HE'S COMING OVER FOR A VISIT--

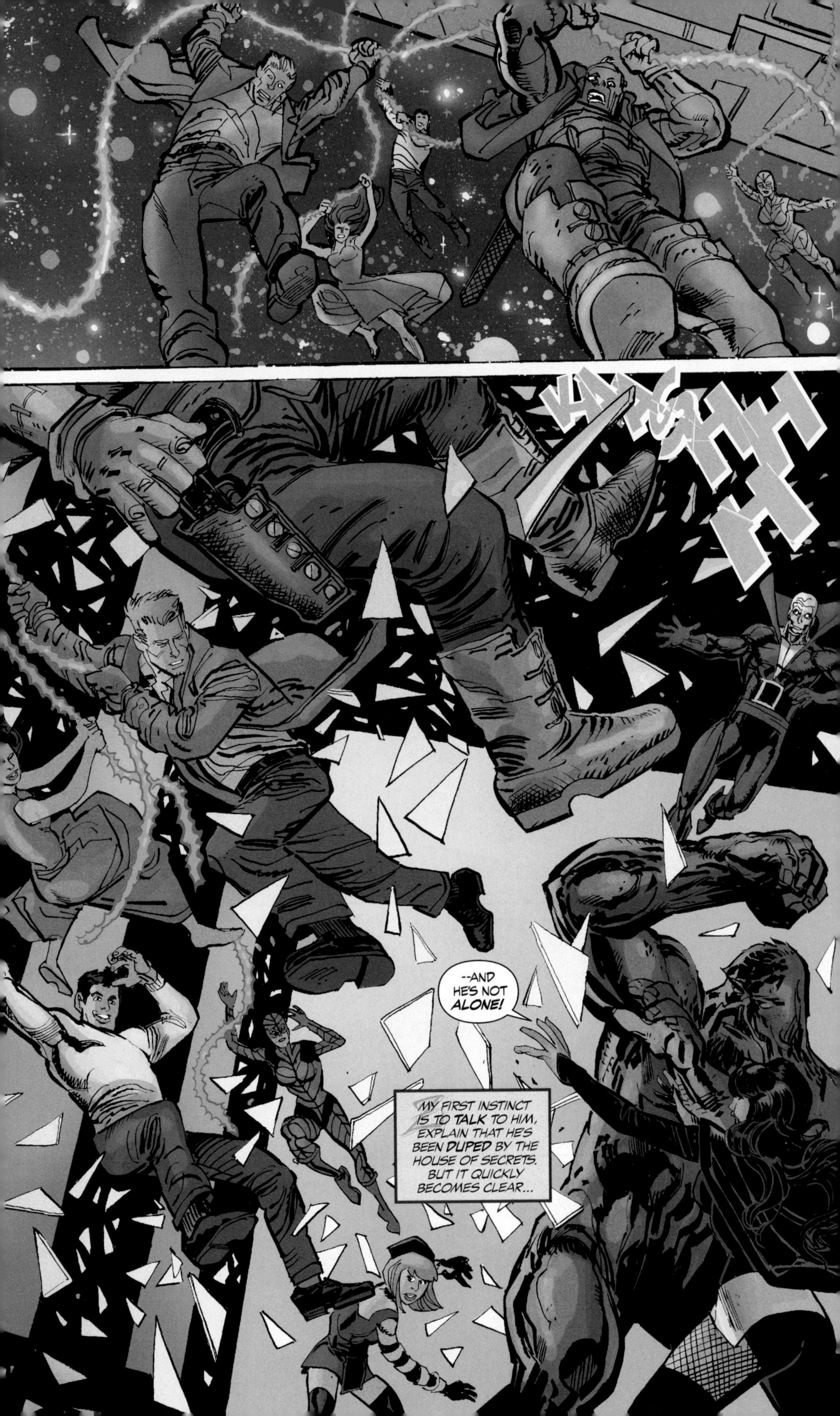
KRASHHH
--AND HE'S NOT ALONE!
MY FIRST INSTINCT IS TO TALK TO HIM, EXPLAIN THAT HE'S BEEN DUPED BY THE HOUSE OF SECRETS. BUT IT QUICKLY BECOMES CLEAR...

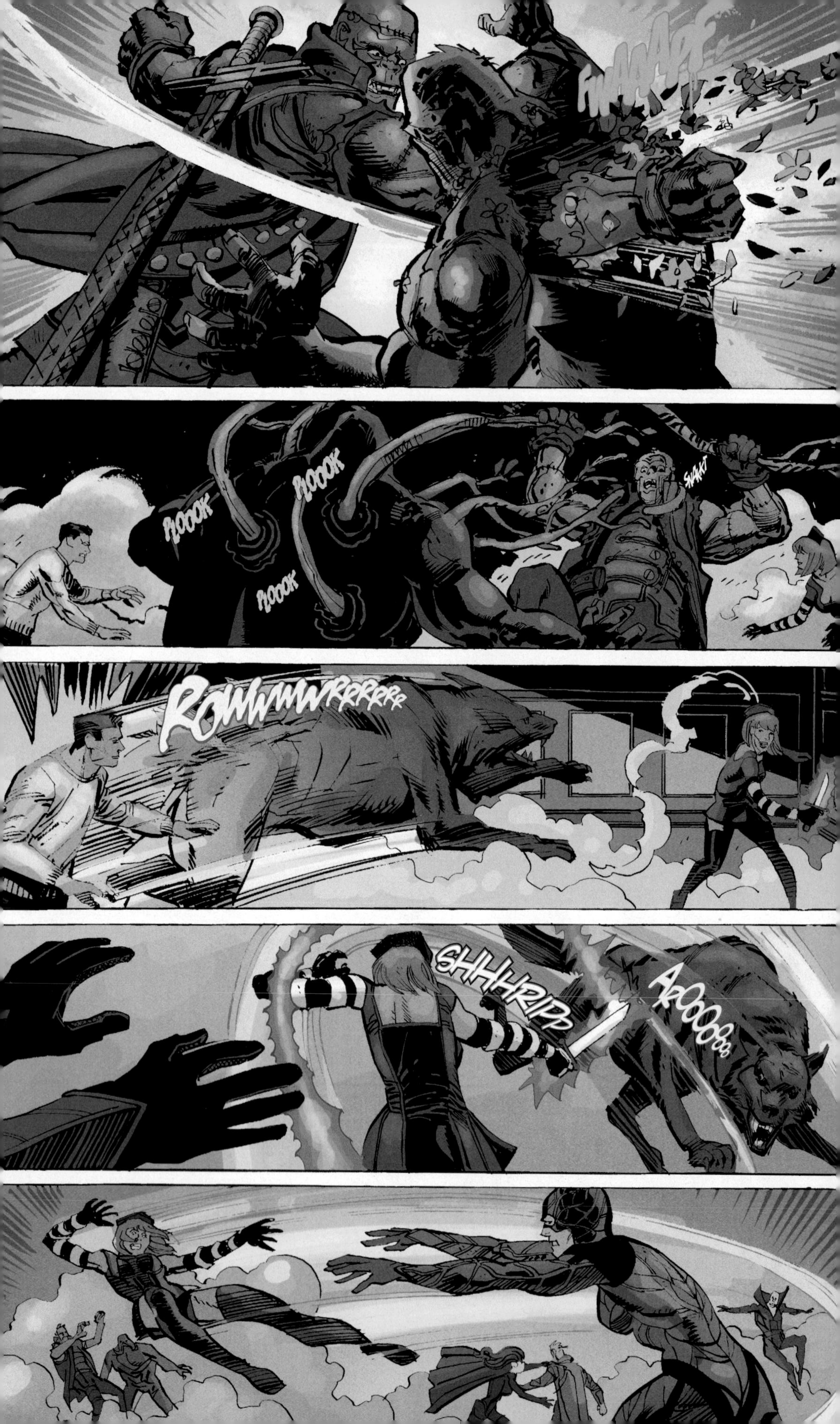
FWAAAPF
PLOOOK
PLOOOK
PLOOOK
SNAKT
ROWWWWRRRRRR
SHHHRIPP
AROOOOoo

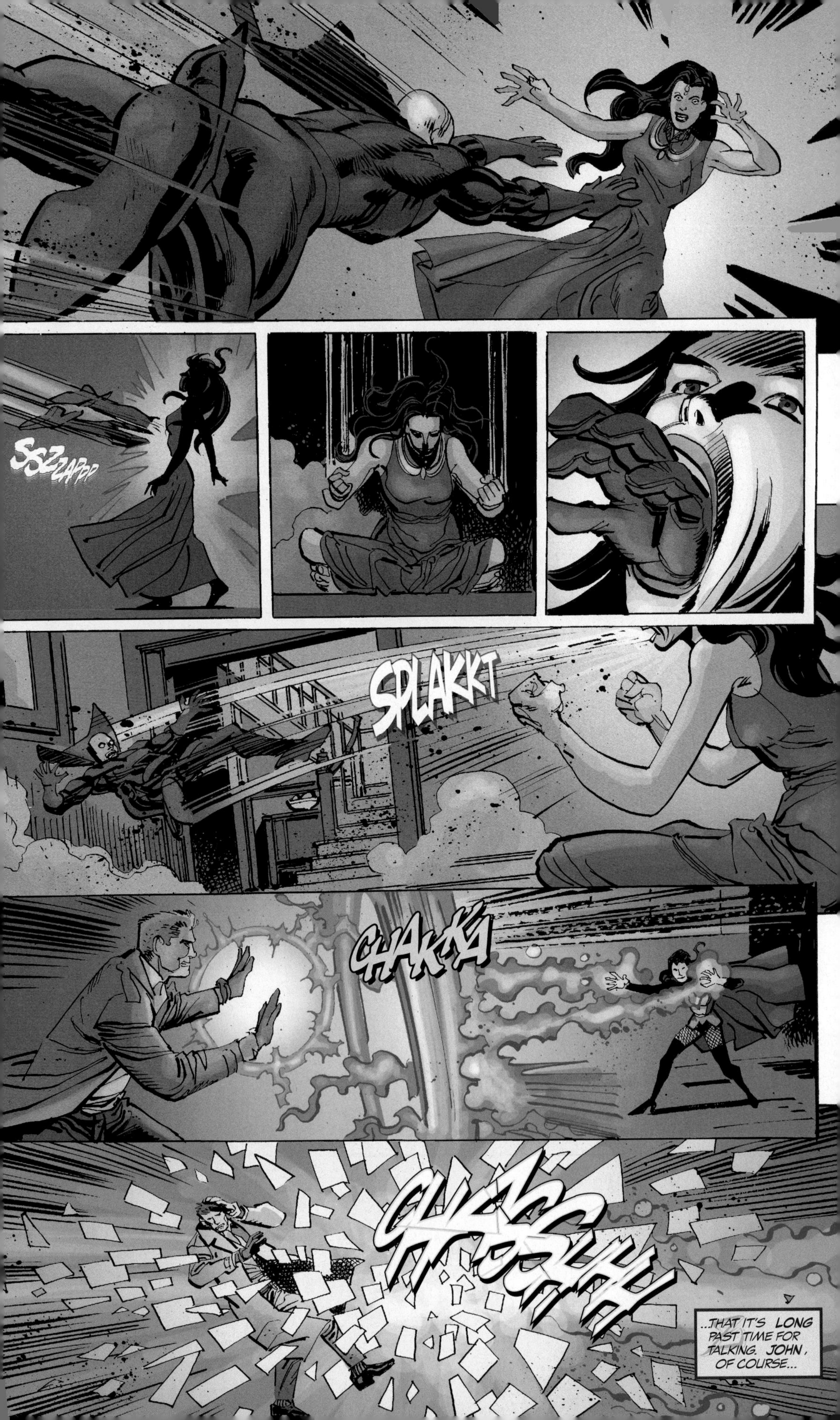
SSZZAPPP
SPLAKKT
CHAKKA
…THAT IT'S LONG PAST TIME FOR TALKING. JOHN, OF COURSE…

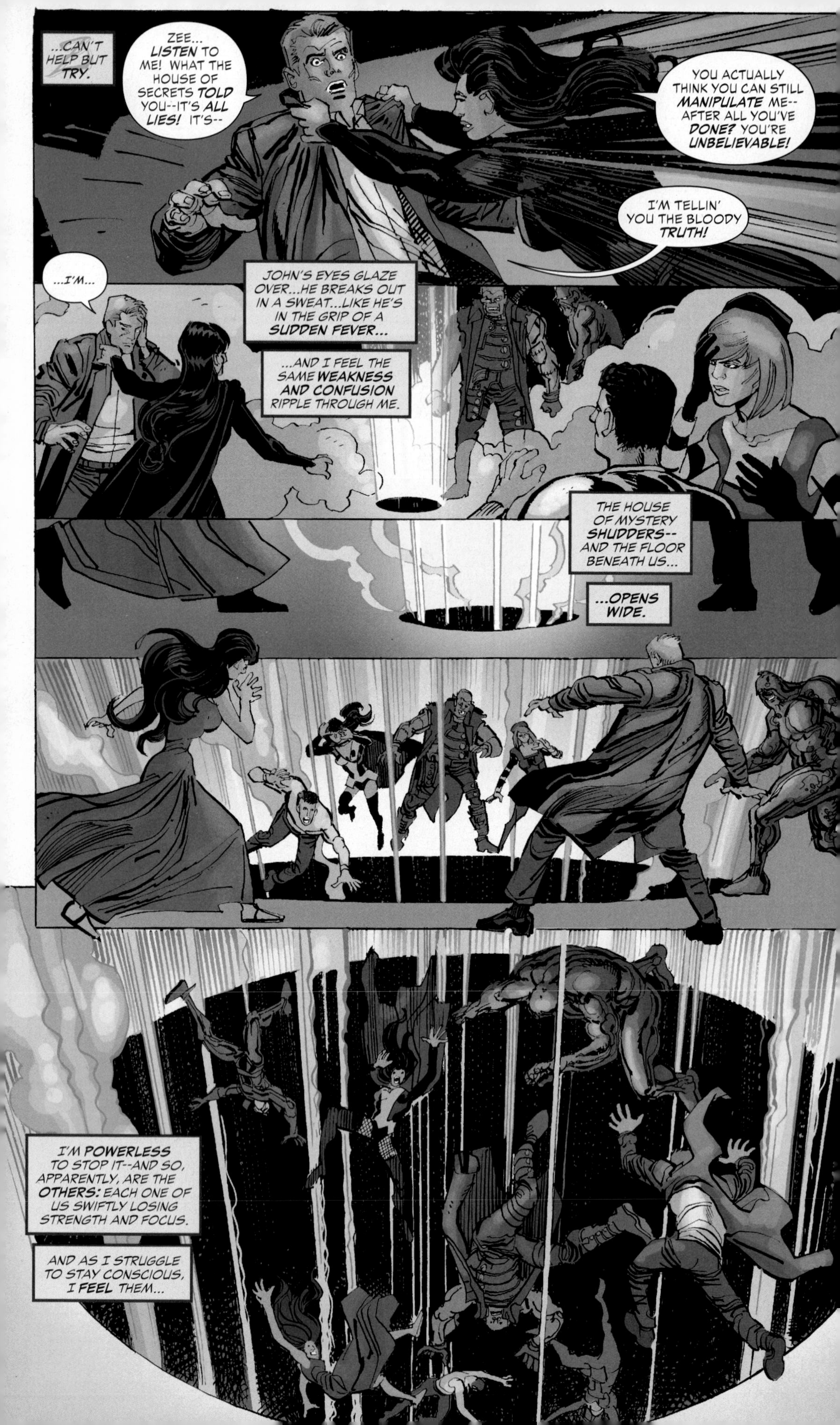
...CAN'T HELP BUT TRY.
ZEE... LISTEN TO ME! WHAT THE HOUSE OF SECRETS TOLD YOU--IT'S ALL LIES! IT'S--
YOU ACTUALLY THINK YOU CAN STILL MANIPULATE ME--AFTER ALL YOU'VE DONE? YOU'RE UNBELIEVABLE!
I'M TELLIN' YOU THE BLOODY TRUTH!
...I'M...
JOHN'S EYES GLAZE OVER...HE BREAKS OUT IN A SWEAT...LIKE HE'S IN THE GRIP OF A SUDDEN FEVER...
...AND I FEEL THE SAME WEAKNESS AND CONFUSION RIPPLE THROUGH ME.
THE HOUSE OF MYSTERY SHUDDERS--AND THE FLOOR BENEATH US...
...OPENS WIDE.
I'M POWERLESS TO STOP IT--AND SO, APPARENTLY, ARE THE OTHERS: EACH ONE OF US SWIFTLY LOSING STRENGTH AND FOCUS.
AND AS I STRUGGLE TO STAY CONSCIOUS, I FEEL THEM...

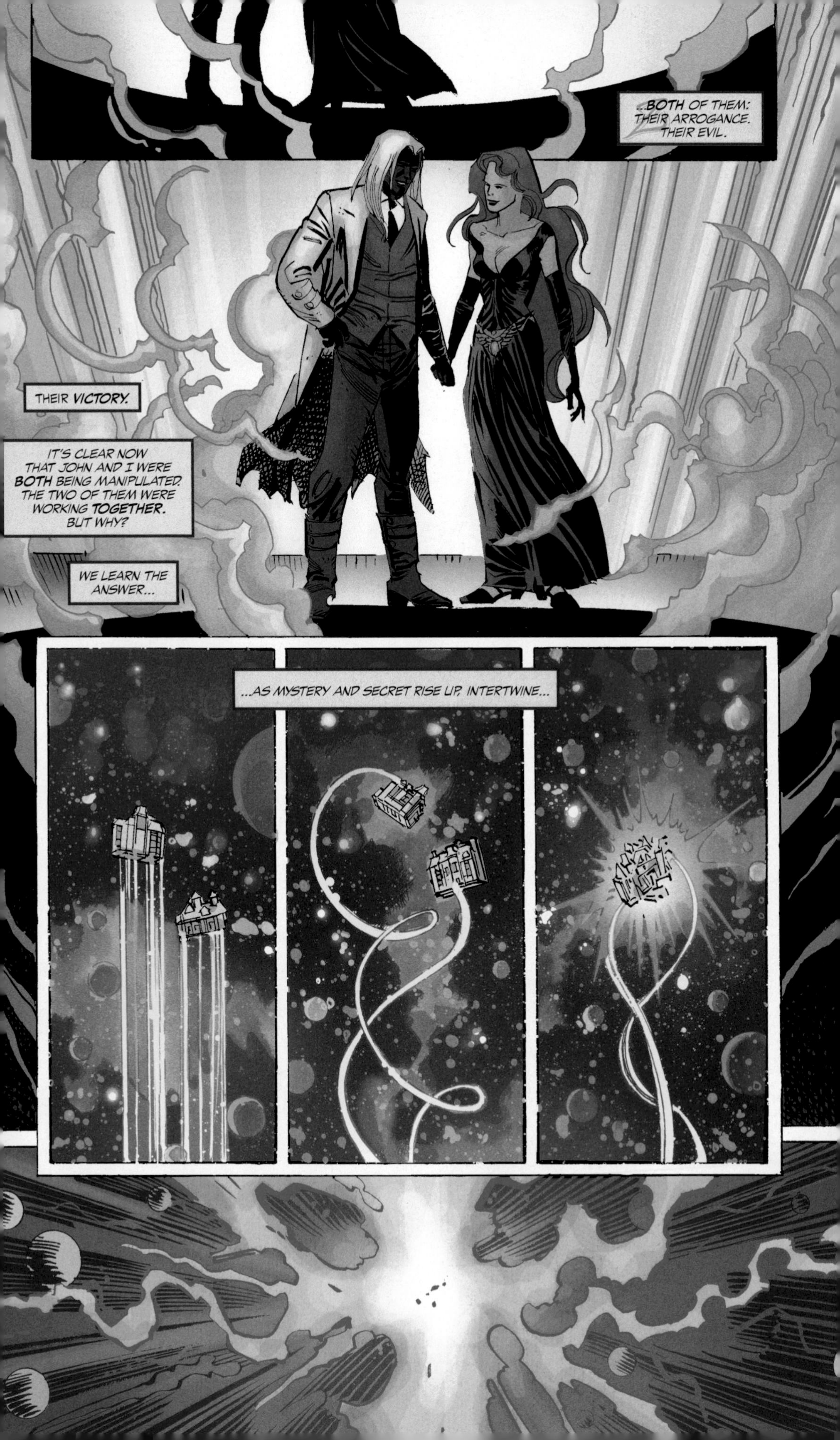
...BOTH OF THEM: THEIR ARROGANCE. THEIR EVIL.
THEIR VICTORY.
IT'S CLEAR NOW THAT JOHN AND I WERE BOTH BEING MANIPULATED. THE TWO OF THEM WERE WORKING TOGETHER. BUT WHY?
WE LEARN THE ANSWER...
...AS MYSTERY AND SECRET RISE UP, INTERTWINE...

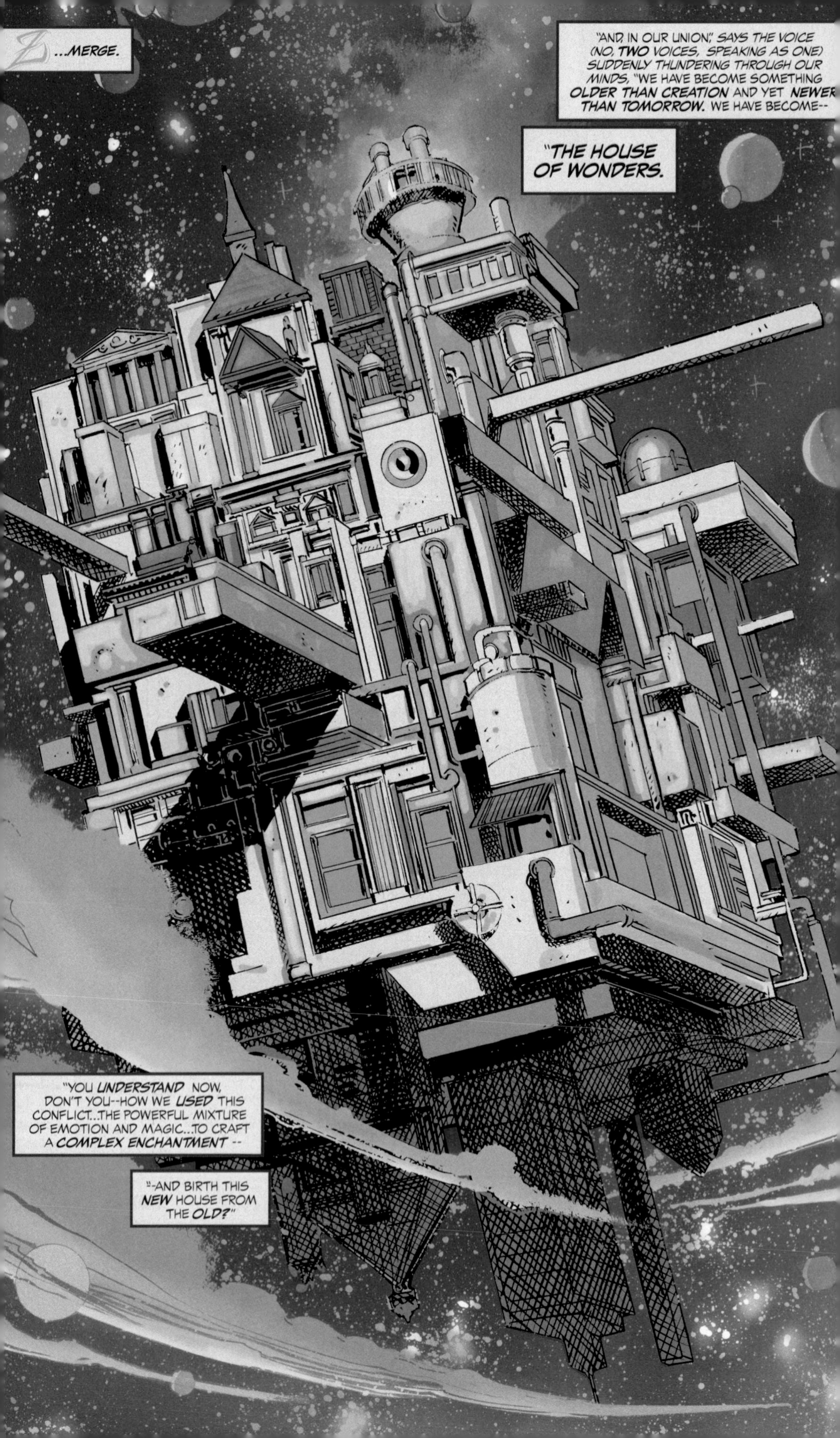
...MERGE.
"AND, IN OUR UNION," SAYS THE VOICE (NO, TWO VOICES, SPEAKING AS ONE) SUDDENLY THUNDERING THROUGH OUR MINDS, "WE HAVE BECOME SOMETHING OLDER THAN CREATION AND YET NEWER THAN TOMORROW. WE HAVE BECOME--
"THE HOUSE OF WONDERS.
"YOU UNDERSTAND NOW, DON'T YOU--HOW WE USED THIS CONFLICT...THE POWERFUL MIXTURE OF EMOTION AND MAGIC...TO CRAFT A COMPLEX ENCHANTMENT --
"-AND BIRTH THIS NEW HOUSE FROM THE OLD?"

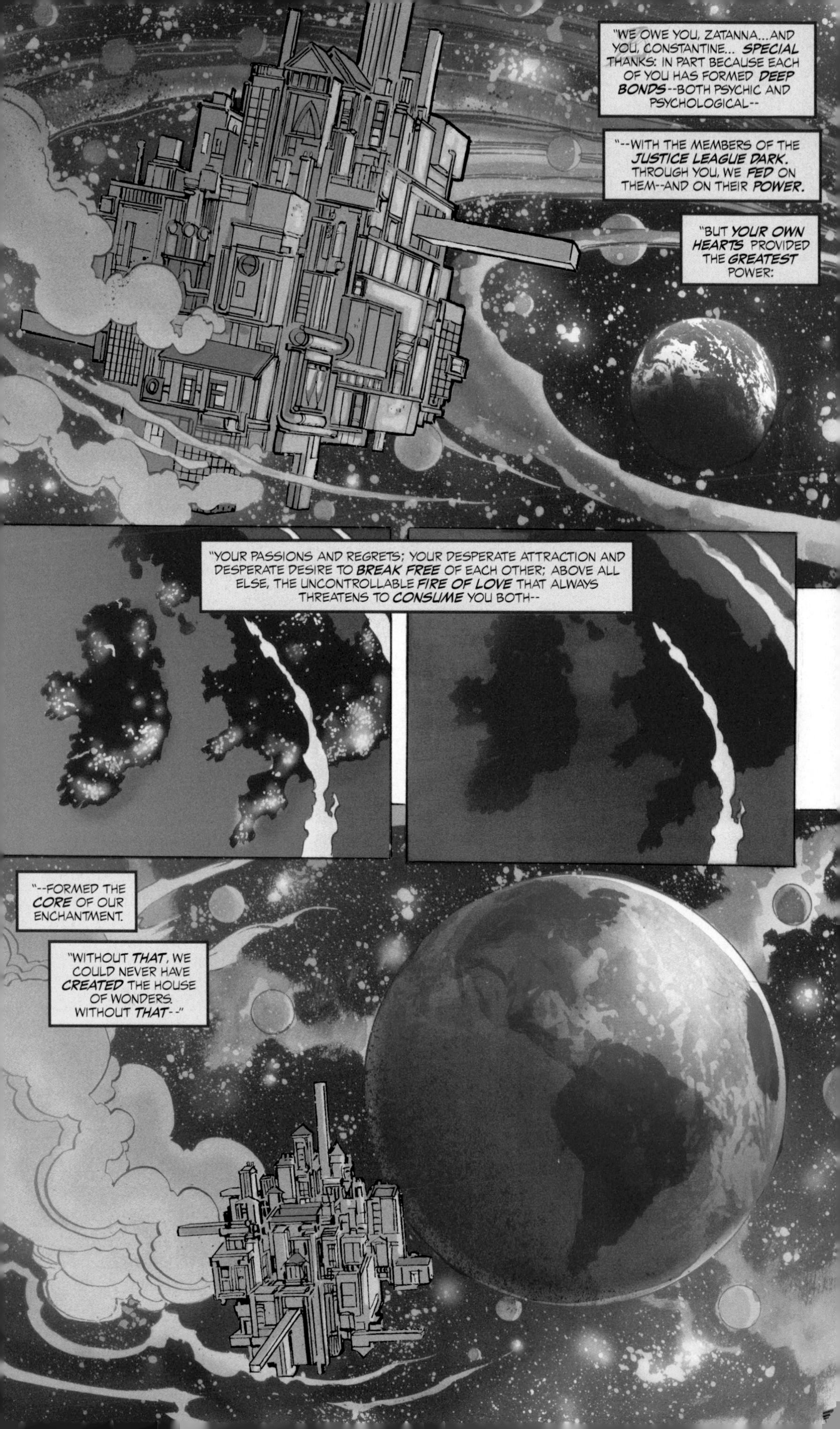
"WE OWE YOU, ZATANNA...AND YOU, CONSTANTINE... SPECIAL THANKS: IN PART BECAUSE EACH OF YOU HAS FORMED DEEP BONDS--BOTH PSYCHIC AND PSYCHOLOGICAL--
"--WITH THE MEMBERS OF THE JUSTICE LEAGUE DARK. THROUGH YOU, WE FED ON THEM--AND ON THEIR POWER.
"BUT YOUR OWN HEARTS PROVIDED THE GREATEST POWER:
"YOUR PASSIONS AND REGRETS; YOUR DESPERATE ATTRACTION AND DESPERATE DESIRE TO BREAK FREE OF EACH OTHER; ABOVE ALL ELSE, THE UNCONTROLLABLE FIRE OF LOVE THAT ALWAYS THREATENS TO CONSUME YOU BOTH--
"--FORMED THE CORE OF OUR ENCHANTMENT.
"WITHOUT THAT, WE COULD NEVER HAVE CREATED THE HOUSE OF WONDERS. WITHOUT THAT--"

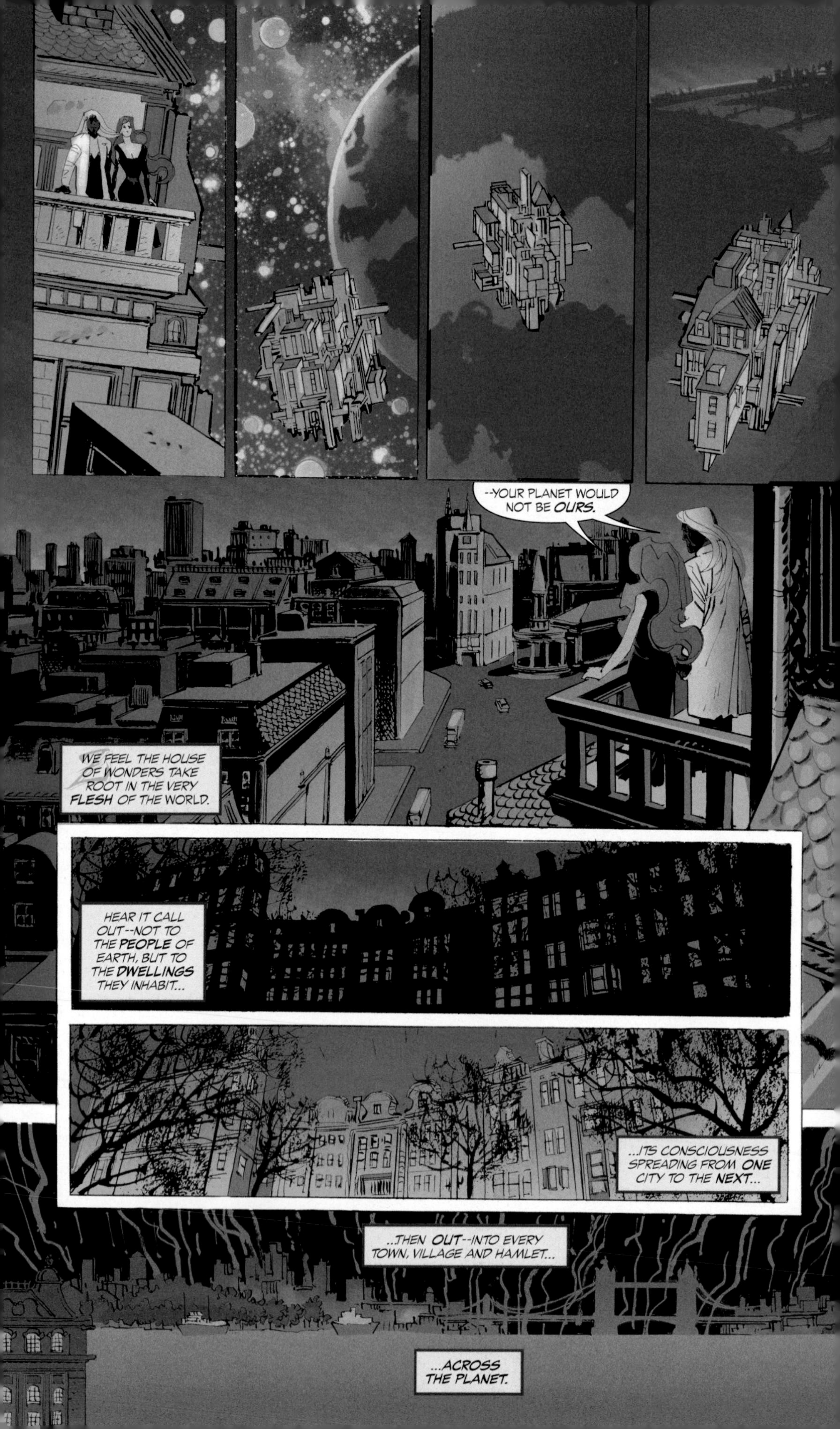

--YOUR PLANET WOULD NOT BE OURS.
WE FEEL THE HOUSE OF WONDERS TAKE ROOT IN THE VERY FLESH OF THE WORLD.
HEAR IT CALL OUT--NOT TO THE PEOPLE OF EARTH, BUT TO THE DWELLINGS THEY INHABIT...
...ITS CONSCIOUSNESS SPREADING FROM ONE CITY TO THE NEXT...
...THEN OUT--INTO EVERY TOWN, VILLAGE AND HAMLET...
...ACROSS THE PLANET.

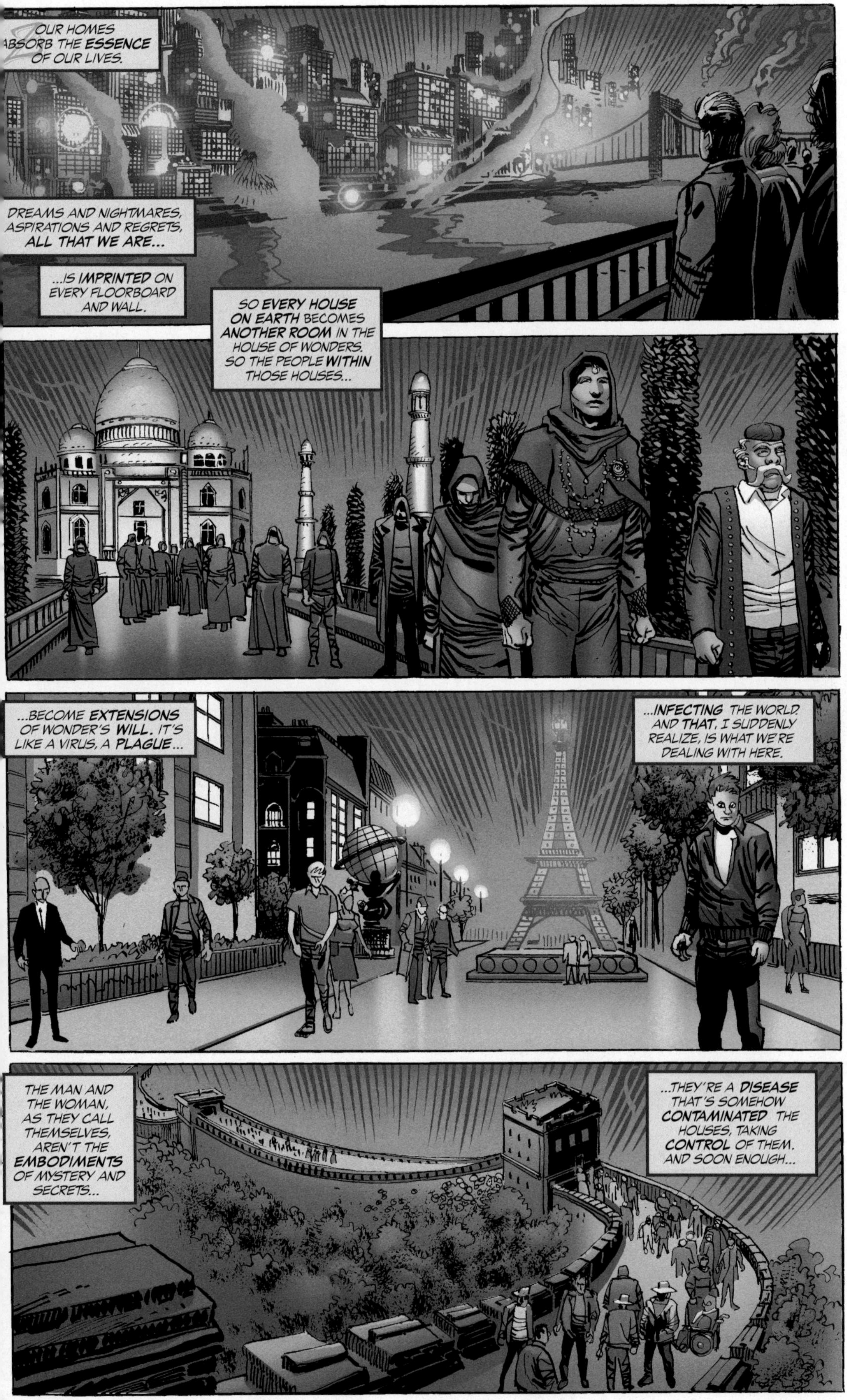
OUR HOMES ABSORB THE ESSENCE OF OUR LIVES.
DREAMS AND NIGHTMARES, ASPIRATIONS AND REGRETS, ALL THAT WE ARE...
...IS IMPRINTED ON EVERY FLOORBOARD AND WALL.
SO EVERY HOUSE ON EARTH BECOMES ANOTHER ROOM IN THE HOUSE OF WONDERS. SO THE PEOPLE WITHIN THOSE HOUSES...
...BECOME EXTENSIONS OF WONDER'S WILL. IT'S LIKE A VIRUS, A PLAGUE...
...INFECTING THE WORLD. AND THAT, I SUDDENLY REALIZE, IS WHAT WE'RE DEALING WITH HERE.
THE MAN AND THE WOMAN, AS THEY CALL THEMSELVES, AREN'T THE EMBODIMENTS OF MYSTERY AND SECRETS...
...THEY'RE A DISEASE THAT'S SOMEHOW CONTAMINATED THE HOUSES, TAKING CONTROL OF THEM. AND SOON ENOUGH...

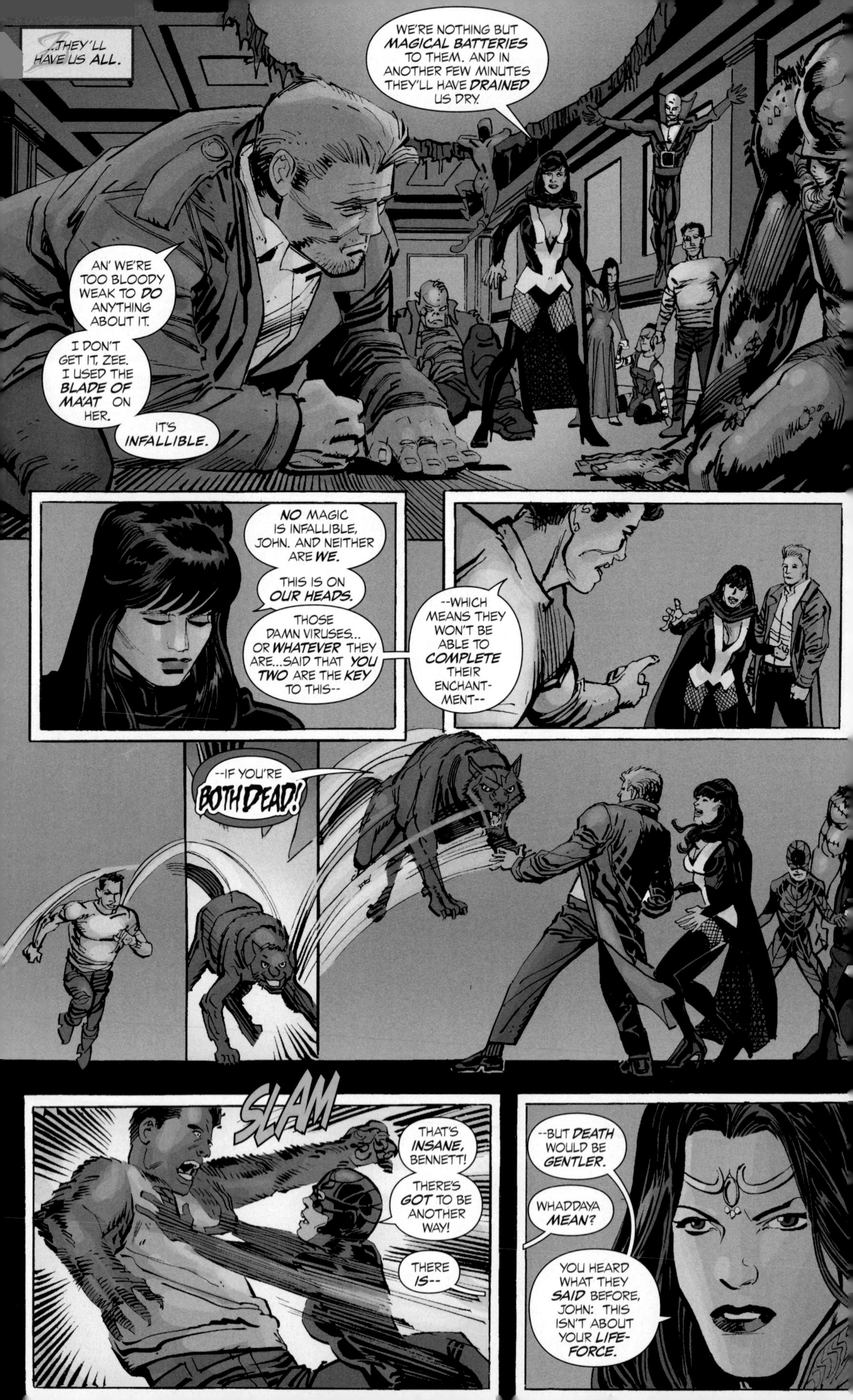
...THEY'LL HAVE US ALL.
WE'RE NOTHING BUT MAGICAL BATTERIES TO THEM. AND IN ANOTHER FEW MINUTES THEY'LL HAVE DRAINED US DRY.
AN' WE'RE TOO BLOODY WEAK TO DO ANYTHING ABOUT IT.
I DON'T GET IT, ZEE. I USED THE BLADE OF MA'AT ON HER.
IT'S INFALLIBLE.
NO MAGIC IS INFALLIBLE, JOHN. AND NEITHER ARE WE.
THIS IS ON OUR HEADS.
THOSE DAMN VIRUSES... OR WHATEVER THEY ARE...SAID THAT YOU TWO ARE THE KEY TO THIS--
--WHICH MEANS THEY WON'T BE ABLE TO COMPLETE THEIR ENCHANT-MENT--
--IF YOU'RE BOTH DEAD!
SLAM
THAT'S INSANE, BENNETT!
THERE'S GOT TO BE ANOTHER WAY!
THERE IS--
--BUT DEATH WOULD BE GENTLER.
WHADDAYA MEAN?
YOU HEARD WHAT THEY SAID BEFORE, JOHN: THIS ISN'T ABOUT YOUR LIFE-FORCE.

THIS IS ABOUT *YOUR* LOVE. CUT THAT LOVE *OUT*--AND THEIR SPELL *COLLAPSES.*

CUT IT *OUT?* WHAT THE HELL ARE YOU *TALKIN'* ABOUT?

IF I KNOW MY MAGIC--AND I *DO*--SHE'S TALKING ABOUT *THE K'AM'DEVA CURSE.* IT *EXTRACTS* THE LOVE FROM A PERSON'S HEART--

--ERASING *ALL TRACES* OF IT IN *EVERY DIRECTION OF TIME*--

--SO THAT IT *NEVER EXISTED.*

CAN YOU...CAN *YOU* DO IT, XANADU? I DON'T THINK EITHER ONE OF *US* HAS THE--

YOU CAN'T BE *SERIOUS!*

YOU GOT A *BETTER* PLAN, DARLIN'?

BE *CERTAIN*, JOHN: THE WAY THE K'AM'DEVA WORKS, ONLY *ONE* OF YOU WILL HAVE THE MEMORY OF YOUR LOVE DISSOLVED THE *OTHER*--

--WILL *REMEMBER FOREVER.* AND THAT *IS* THE *TRUE* CURSE.

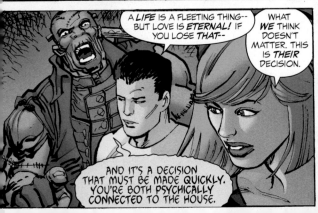

A *LIFE* IS A FLEETING THING--BUT LOVE IS *ETERNAL!* IF YOU LOSE *THAT*--

WHAT *WE* THINK DOESN'T MATTER. THIS IS *THEIR* DECISION.

AND IT'S A DECISION THAT MUST BE MADE QUICKLY. YOU'RE BOTH PSYCHICALLY CONNECTED TO THE HOUSE.

IT...THEY...WILL SURELY KNOW WHAT WE'RE PLANNING.

THEN WE'RE GONNA NEED A *DISTRAC-TION.*

HOLLAND'S BARELY GOT THE STRENGTH TO STAND...

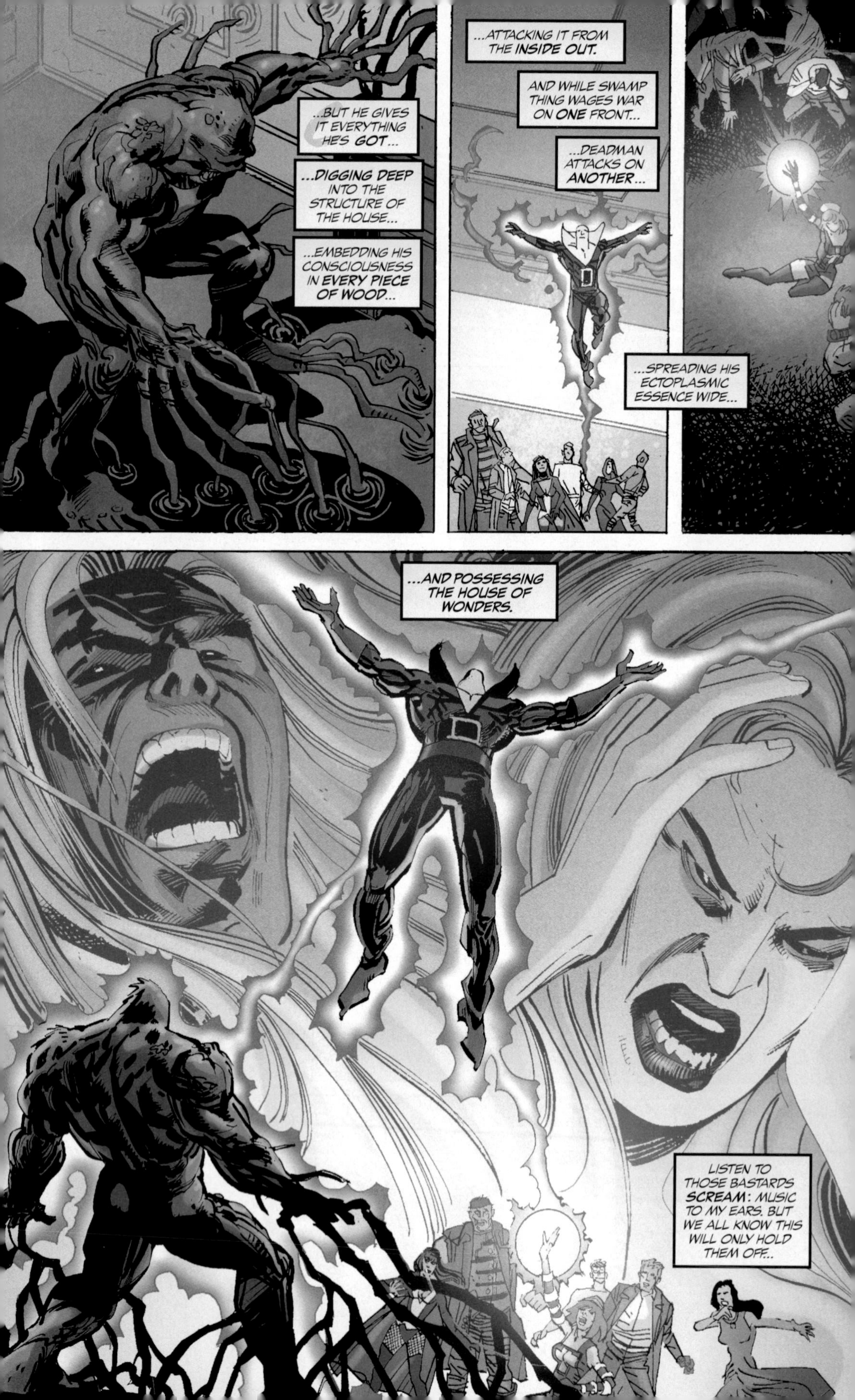
...BUT HE GIVES IT EVERYTHING HE'S GOT...
...DIGGING DEEP INTO THE STRUCTURE OF THE HOUSE...
...EMBEDDING HIS CONSCIOUSNESS IN EVERY PIECE OF WOOD...
...ATTACKING IT FROM THE INSIDE OUT.
AND WHILE SWAMP THING WAGES WAR ON ONE FRONT...
...DEADMAN ATTACKS ON ANOTHER...
...SPREADING HIS ECTOPLASMIC ESSENCE WIDE...
...AND POSSESSING THE HOUSE OF WONDERS.
LISTEN TO THOSE BASTARDS SCREAM: MUSIC TO MY EARS. BUT WE ALL KNOW THIS WILL ONLY HOLD THEM OFF...

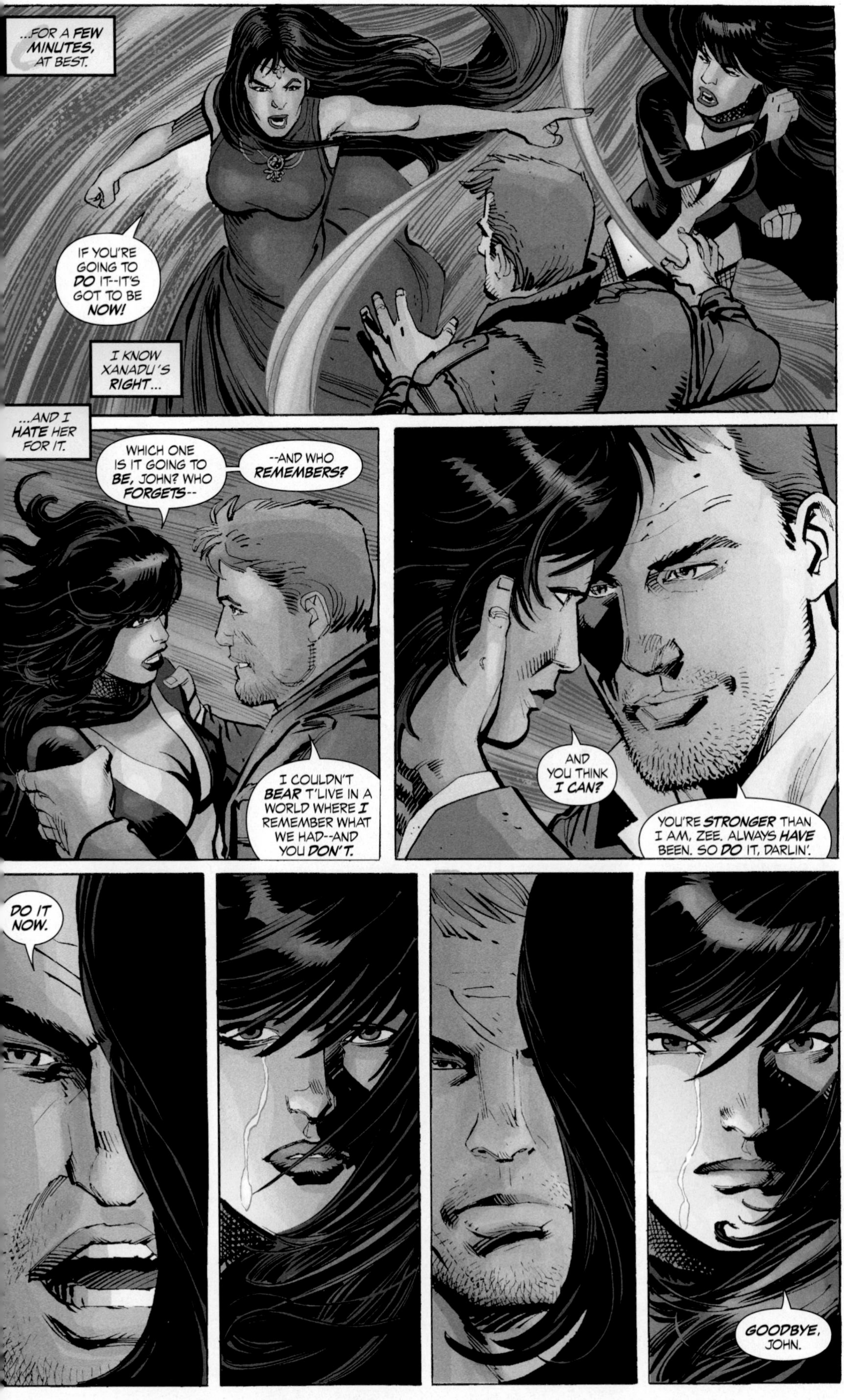
...FOR A FEW MINUTES, AT BEST.
IF YOU'RE GOING TO DO IT--IT'S GOT TO BE NOW!
I KNOW XANADU'S RIGHT...
...AND I HATE HER FOR IT.
WHICH ONE IS IT GOING TO BE, JOHN? WHO FORGETS--
--AND WHO REMEMBERS?
I COULDN'T BEAR T'LIVE IN A WORLD WHERE I REMEMBER WHAT WE HAD--AND YOU DON'T.
AND YOU THINK I CAN?
YOU'RE STRONGER THAN I AM, ZEE. ALWAYS HAVE BEEN. SO DO IT, DARLIN'.
DO IT NOW.
GOODBYE, JOHN.

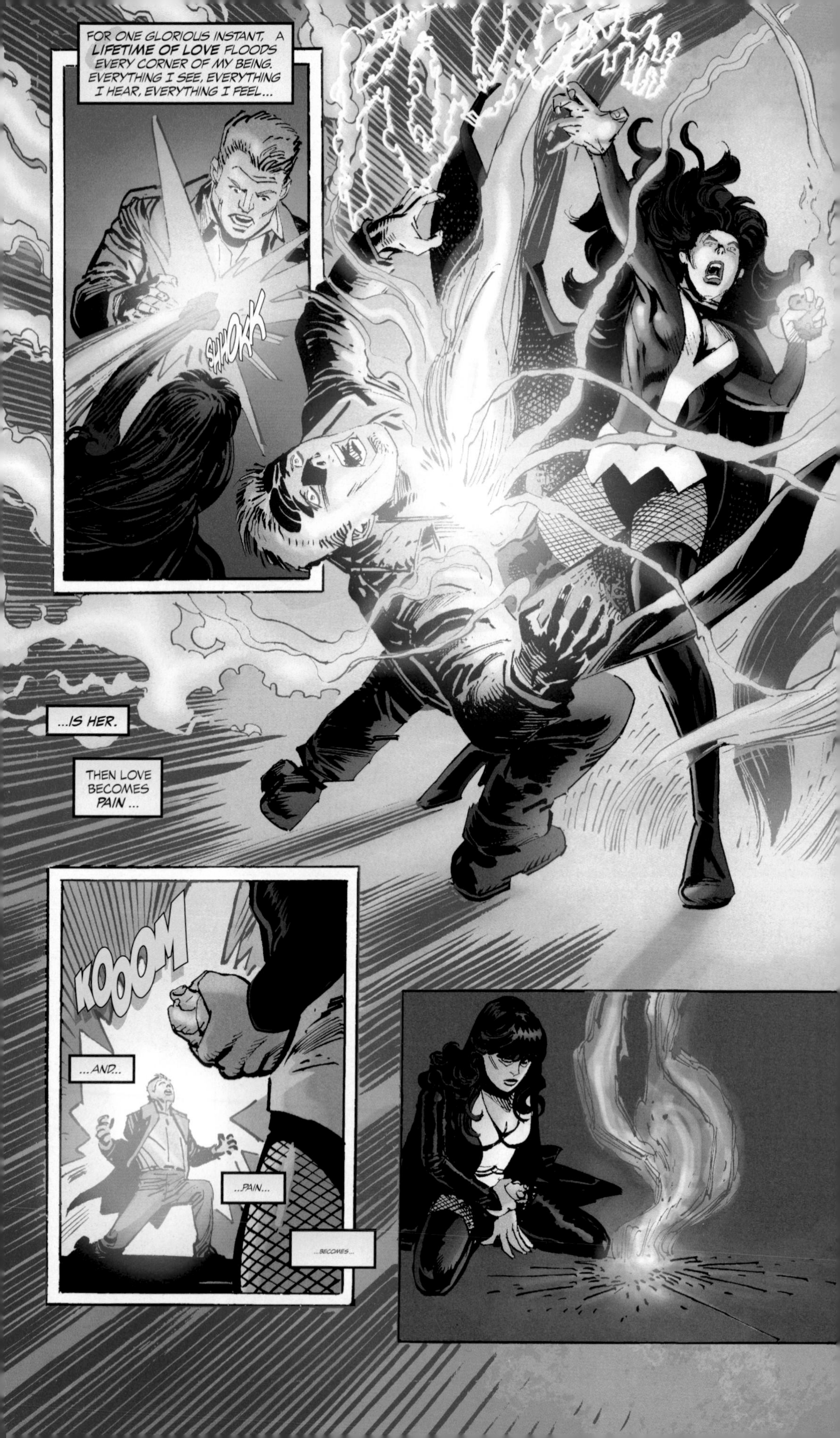

FOR ONE GLORIOUS INSTANT, A **LIFETIME OF LOVE** FLOODS EVERY CORNER OF MY BEING. EVERYTHING I SEE, EVERYTHING I HEAR, EVERYTHING I FEEL...
SHHOKK
...IS HER.
THEN LOVE BECOMES PAIN...
KOOOM
...AND...
...PAIN...
...BECOMES...

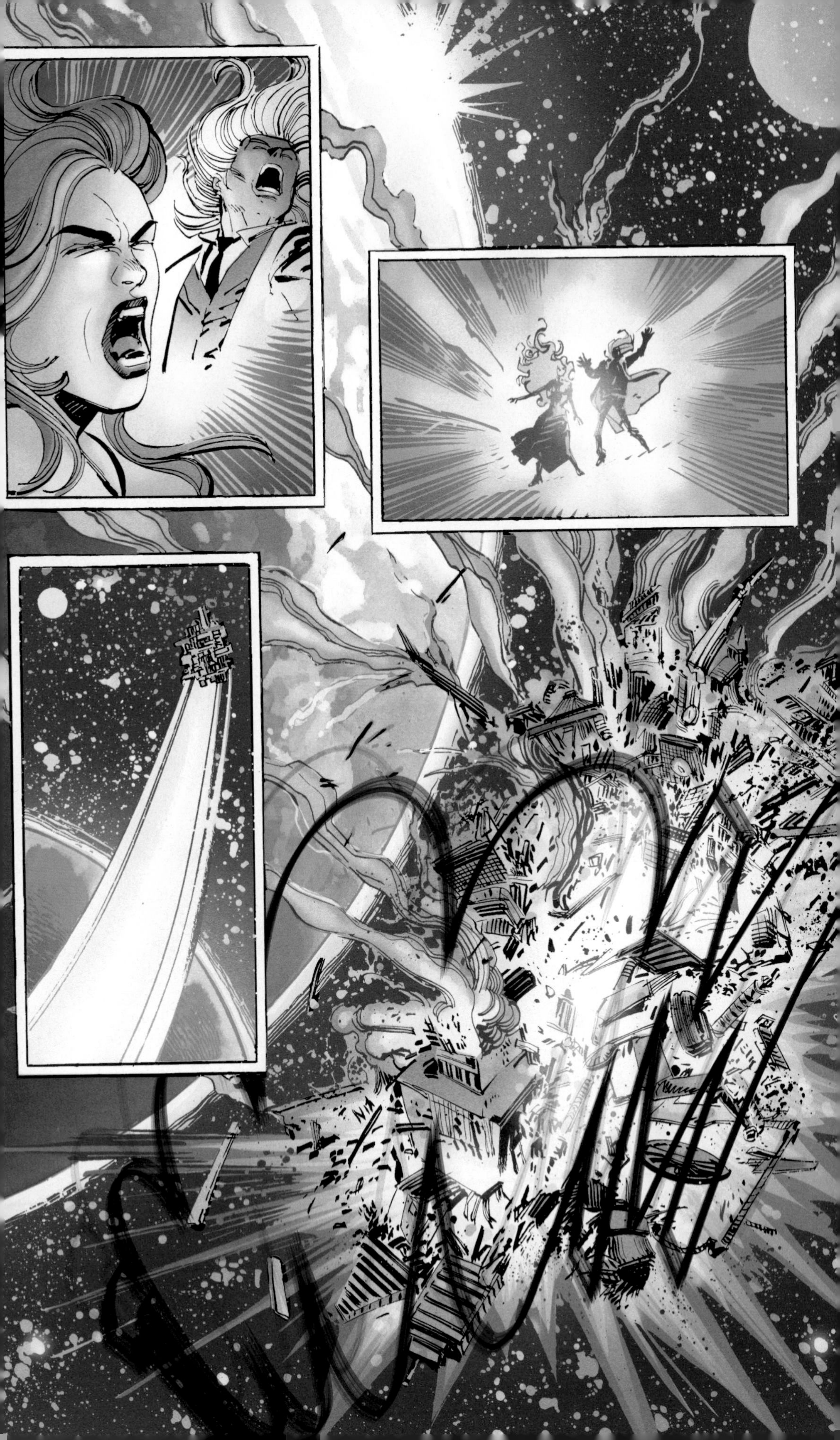

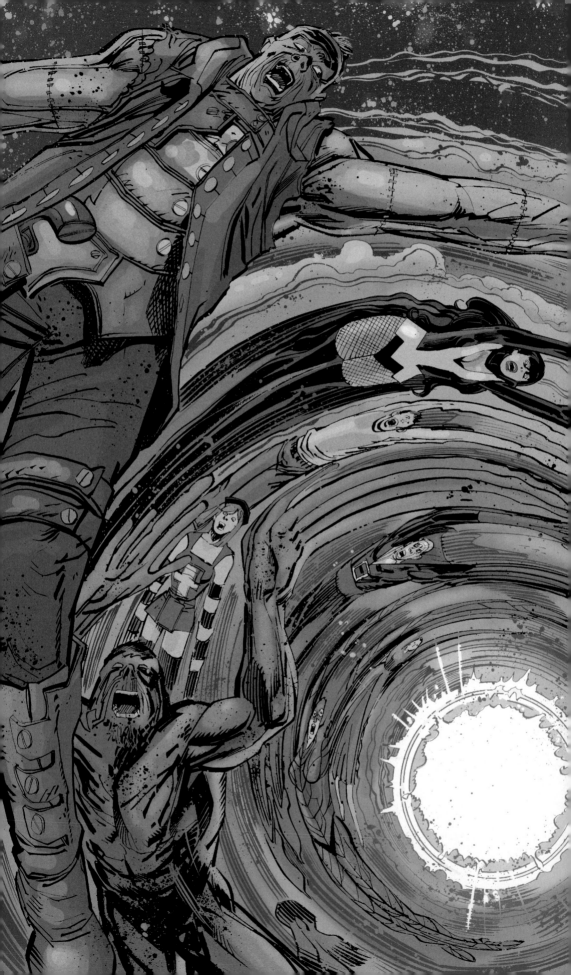

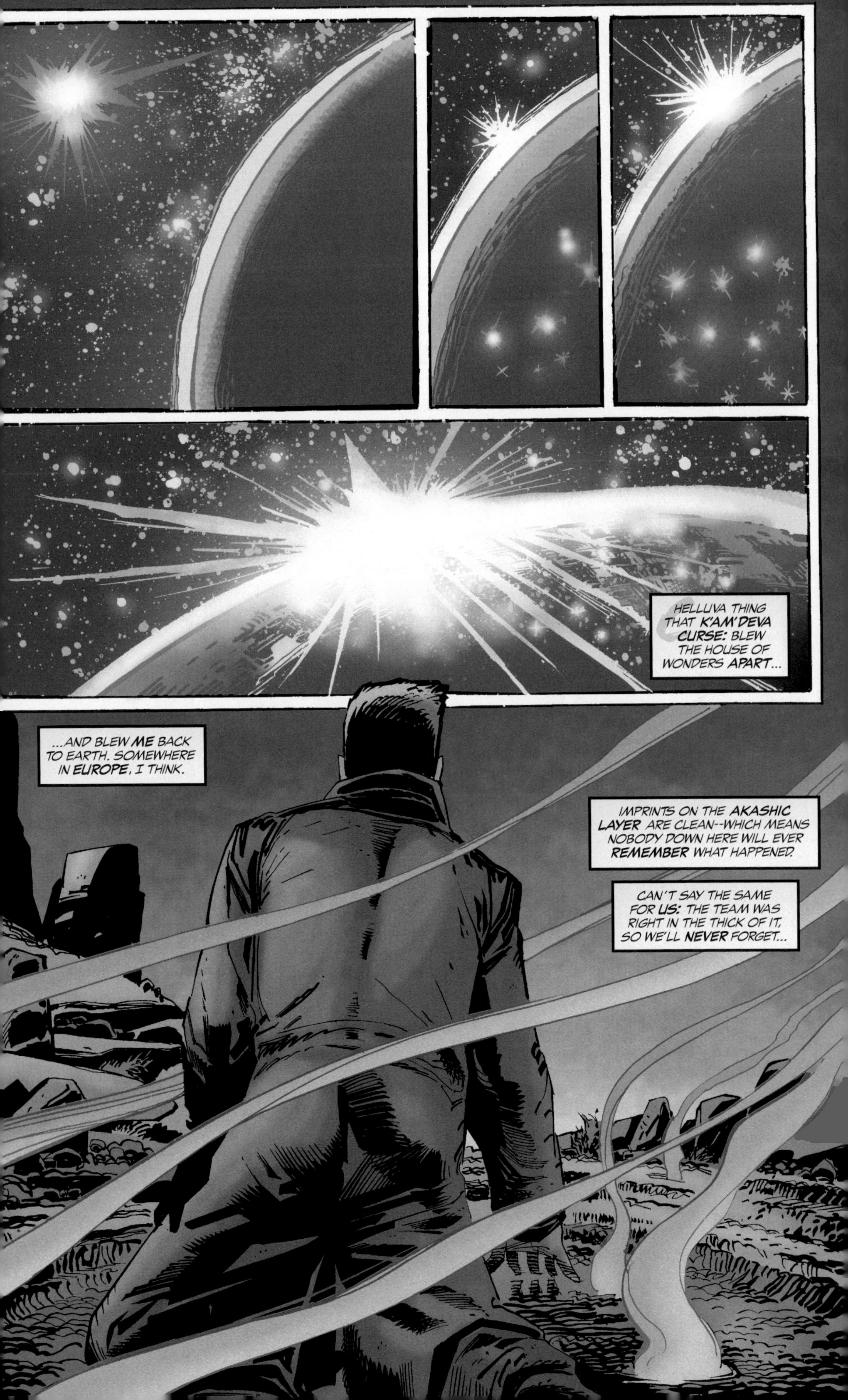
HELLUVA THING THAT K'AM'DEVA CURSE: BLEW THE HOUSE OF WONDERS APART...
...AND BLEW ME BACK TO EARTH. SOMEWHERE IN EUROPE, I THINK.
IMPRINTS ON THE AKASHIC LAYER ARE CLEAN--WHICH MEANS NOBODY DOWN HERE WILL EVER REMEMBER WHAT HAPPENED.
CAN'T SAY THE SAME FOR US: THE TEAM WAS RIGHT IN THE THICK OF IT, SO WE'LL NEVER FORGET...

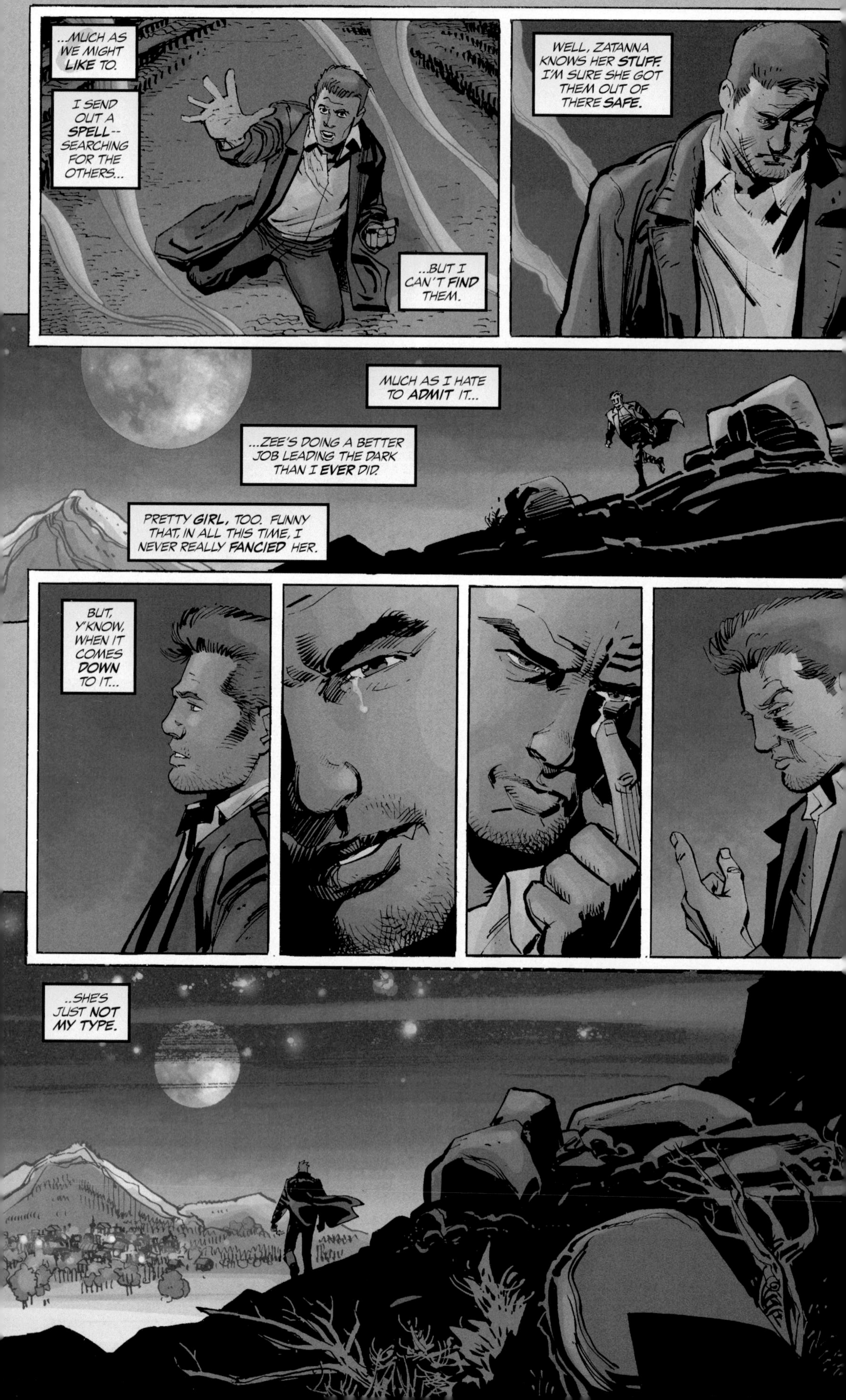

...MUCH AS WE MIGHT LIKE TO.
I SEND OUT A SPELL-- SEARCHING FOR THE OTHERS...
...BUT I CAN'T FIND THEM.
WELL, ZATANNA KNOWS HER STUFF. I'M SURE SHE GOT THEM OUT OF THERE SAFE.
MUCH AS I HATE TO ADMIT IT...
...ZEE'S DOING A BETTER JOB LEADING THE DARK THAN I EVER DID.
PRETTY GIRL, TOO. FUNNY THAT, IN ALL THIS TIME, I NEVER REALLY FANCIED HER.
BUT, Y'KNOW, WHEN IT COMES DOWN TO IT...
..SHE'S JUST NOT MY TYPE.

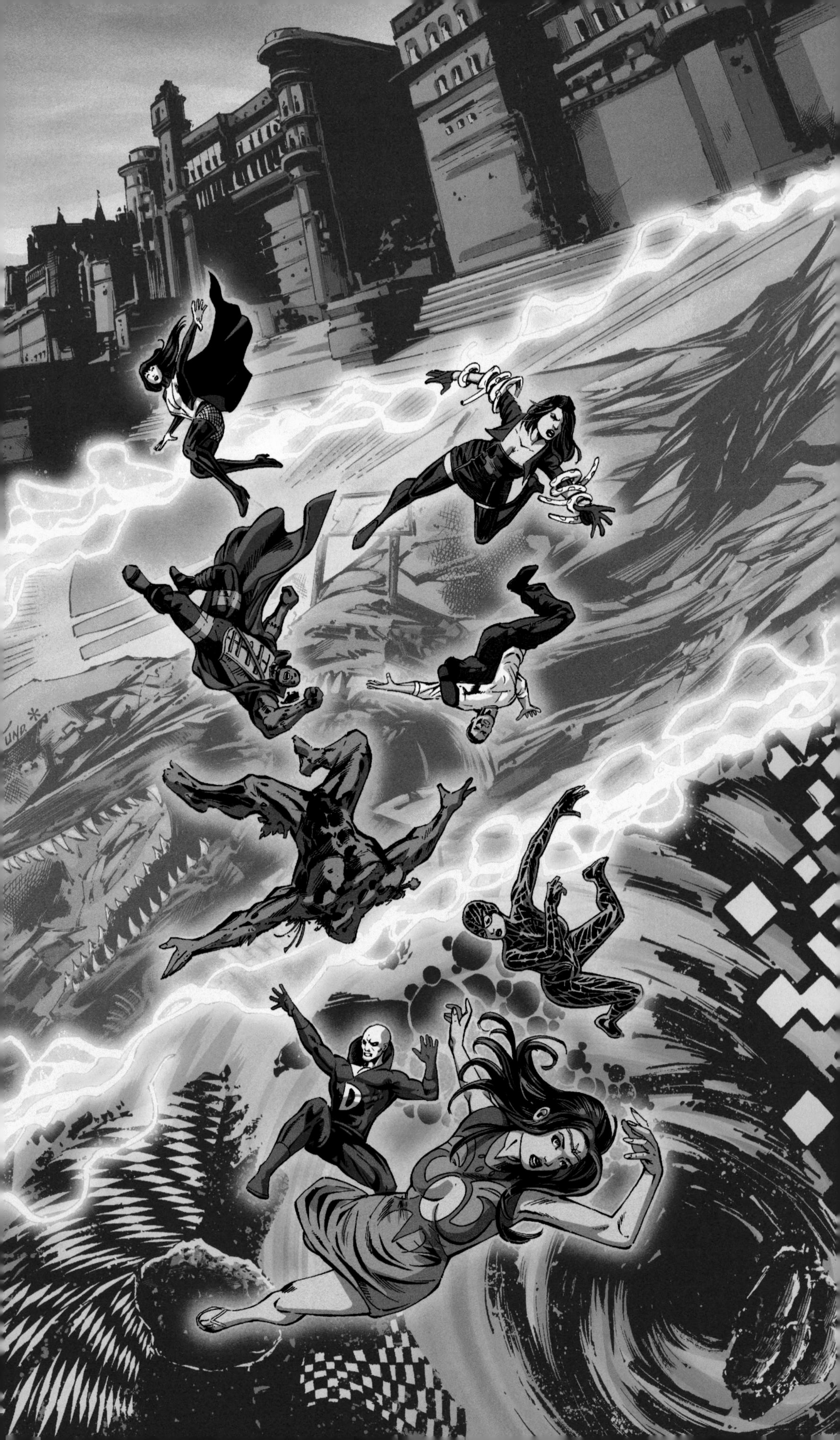

THE AMBER OF THE MOMENT PART 1: LONG BEFORE YESTERDAY

J.M. DEMATTEIS writer **TOM DERENICK** penciller **SCOTT HANNA** inker **CHRIS SOTOMAYOR** colorist
TAYLOR ESPOSITO DEZI SIENTY letterers cover by **GUILLEM MARCH & TOMEU MOREY**

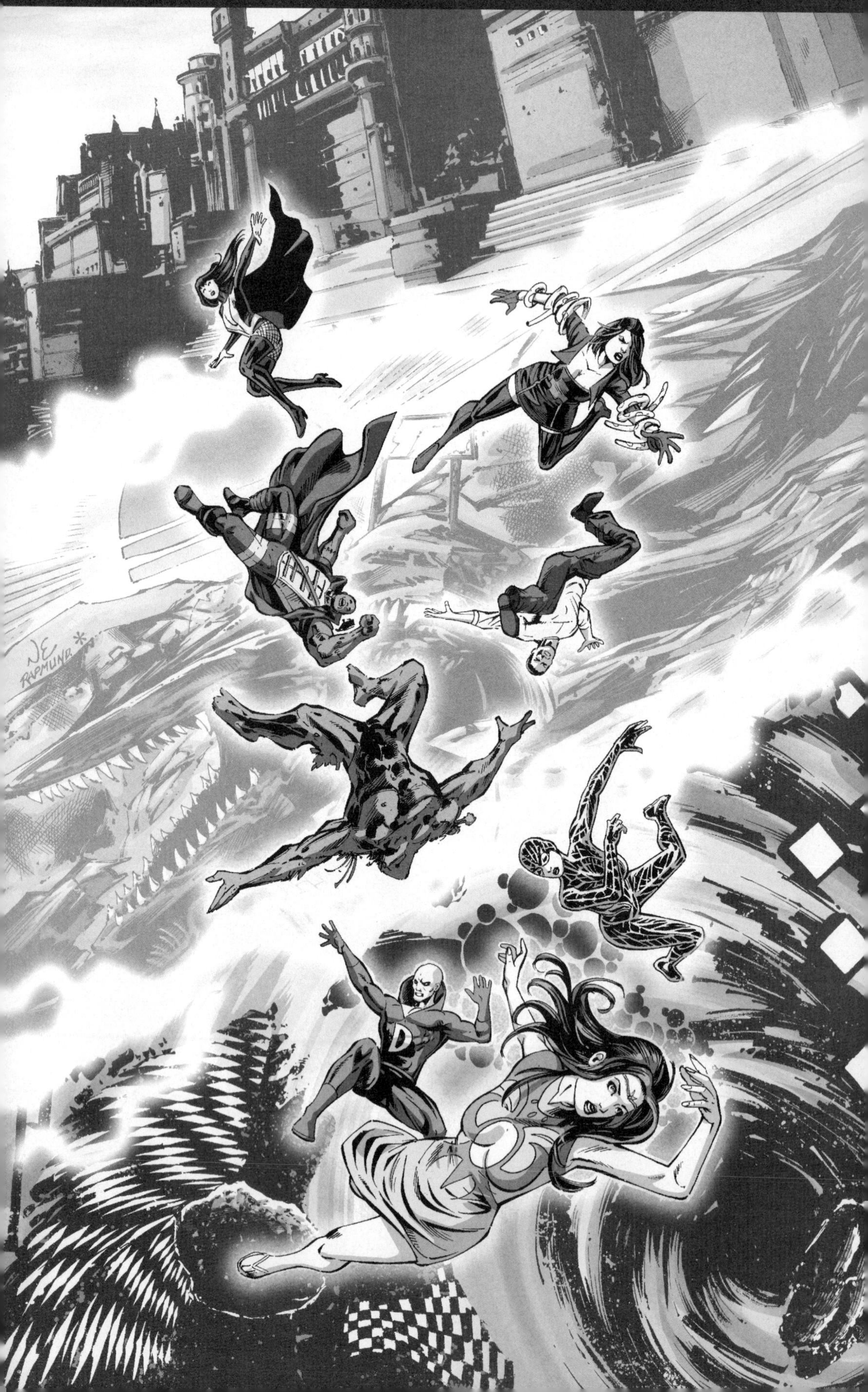

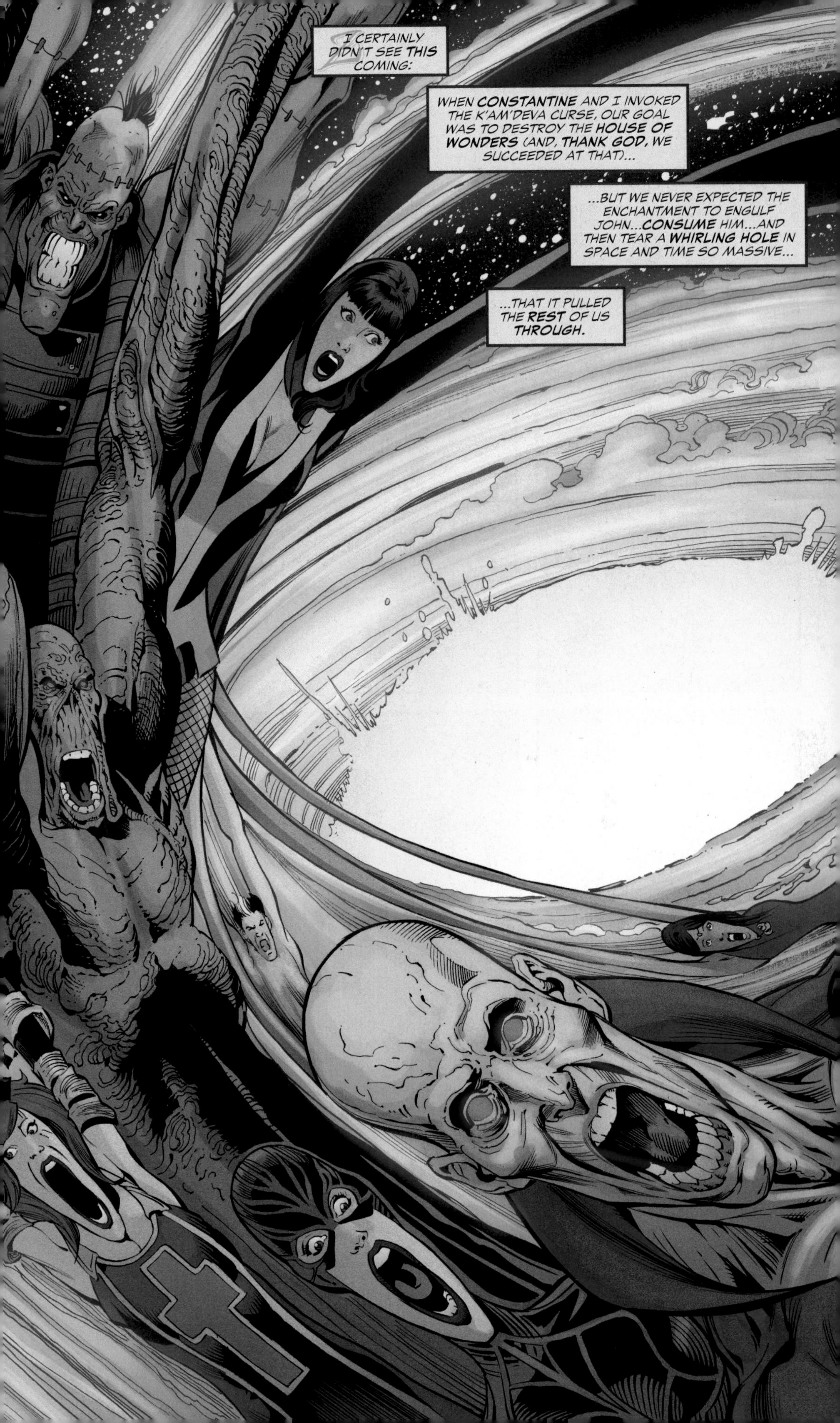
I CERTAINLY DIDN'T SEE THIS COMING:
WHEN CONSTANTINE AND I INVOKED THE K'AM'DEVA CURSE, OUR GOAL WAS TO DESTROY THE HOUSE OF WONDERS (AND, THANK GOD, WE SUCCEEDED AT THAT)...
...BUT WE NEVER EXPECTED THE ENCHANTMENT TO ENGULF JOHN...CONSUME HIM...AND THEN TEAR A WHIRLING HOLE IN SPACE AND TIME SO MASSIVE...
...THAT IT PULLED THE REST OF US THROUGH.

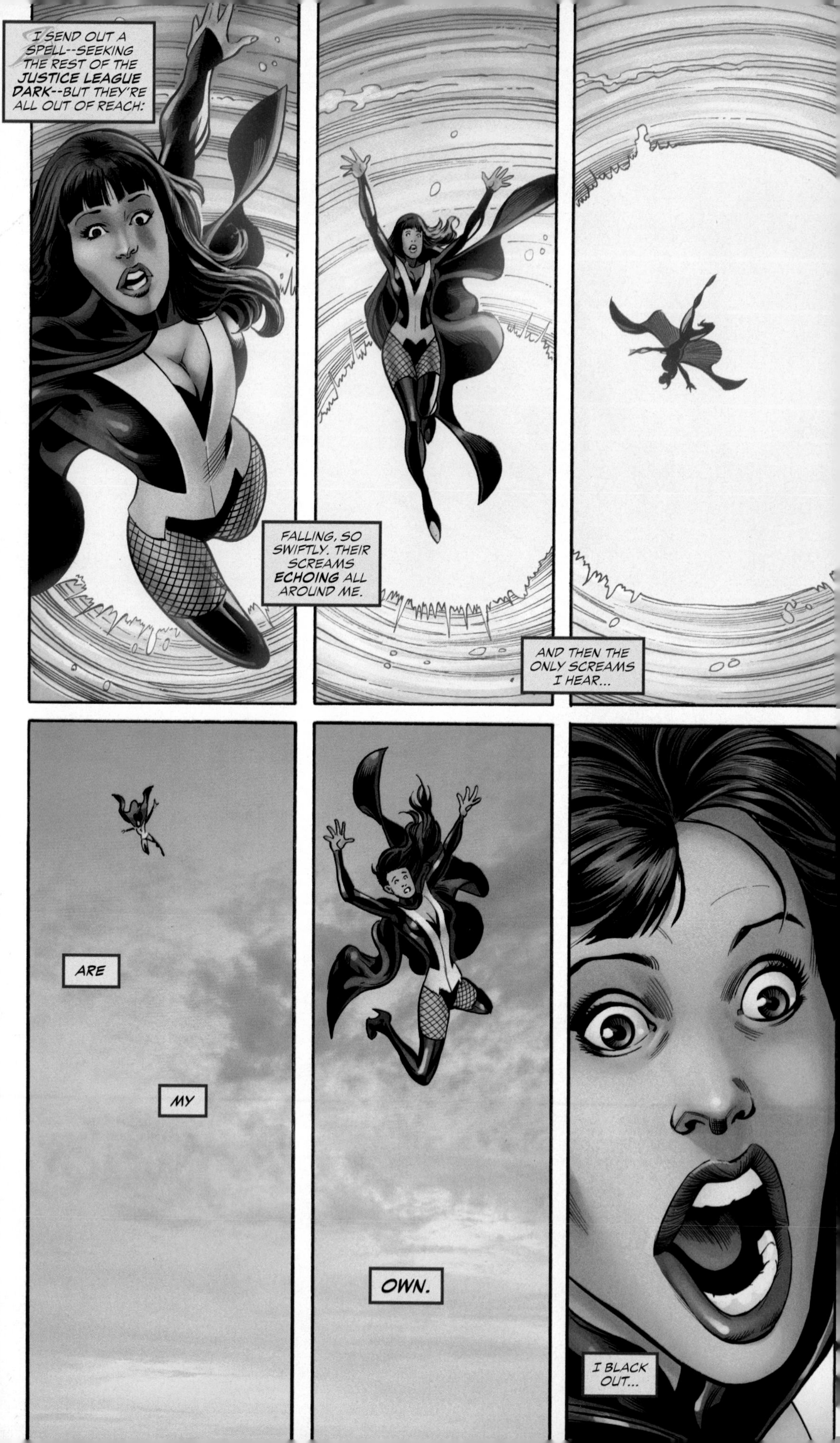
I SEND OUT A SPELL--SEEKING THE REST OF THE JUSTICE LEAGUE DARK--BUT THEY'RE ALL OUT OF REACH:
FALLING, SO SWIFTLY. THEIR SCREAMS ECHOING ALL AROUND ME.
AND THEN THE ONLY SCREAMS I HEAR...
ARE
MY
OWN.
I BLACK OUT...

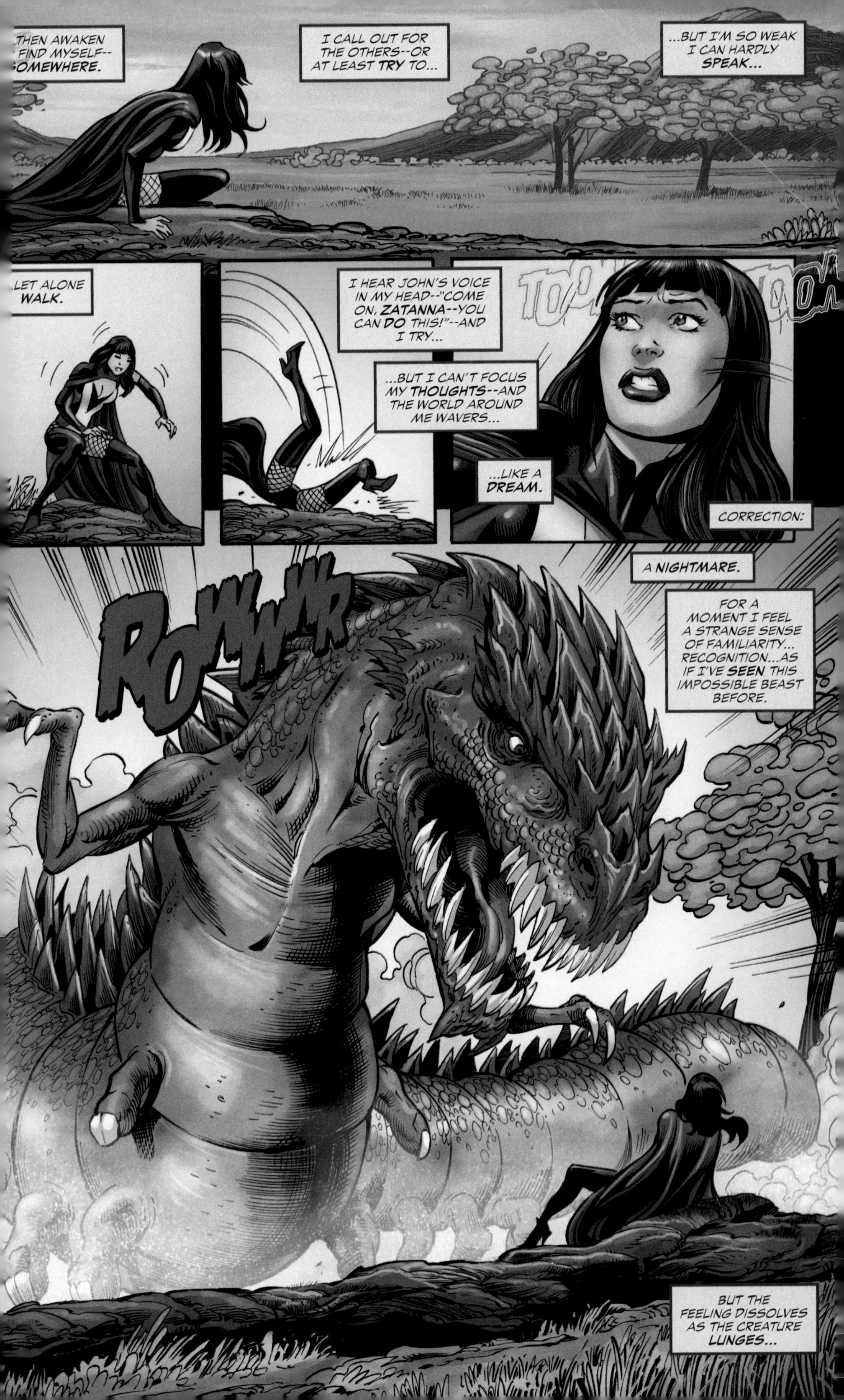

...THEN AWAKEN
...FIND MYSELF--
SOMEWHERE.
I CALL OUT FOR THE OTHERS--OR AT LEAST TRY TO...
...BUT I'M SO WEAK I CAN HARDLY SPEAK...
...LET ALONE WALK.
I HEAR JOHN'S VOICE IN MY HEAD--"COME ON, ZATANNA--YOU CAN DO THIS!"--AND I TRY...
...BUT I CAN'T FOCUS MY THOUGHTS--AND THE WORLD AROUND ME WAVERS...
...LIKE A DREAM.
CORRECTION:
A NIGHTMARE.
ROWWR
FOR A MOMENT I FEEL A STRANGE SENSE OF FAMILIARITY... RECOGNITION...AS IF I'VE SEEN THIS IMPOSSIBLE BEAST BEFORE.
BUT THE FEELING DISSOLVES AS THE CREATURE LUNGES...

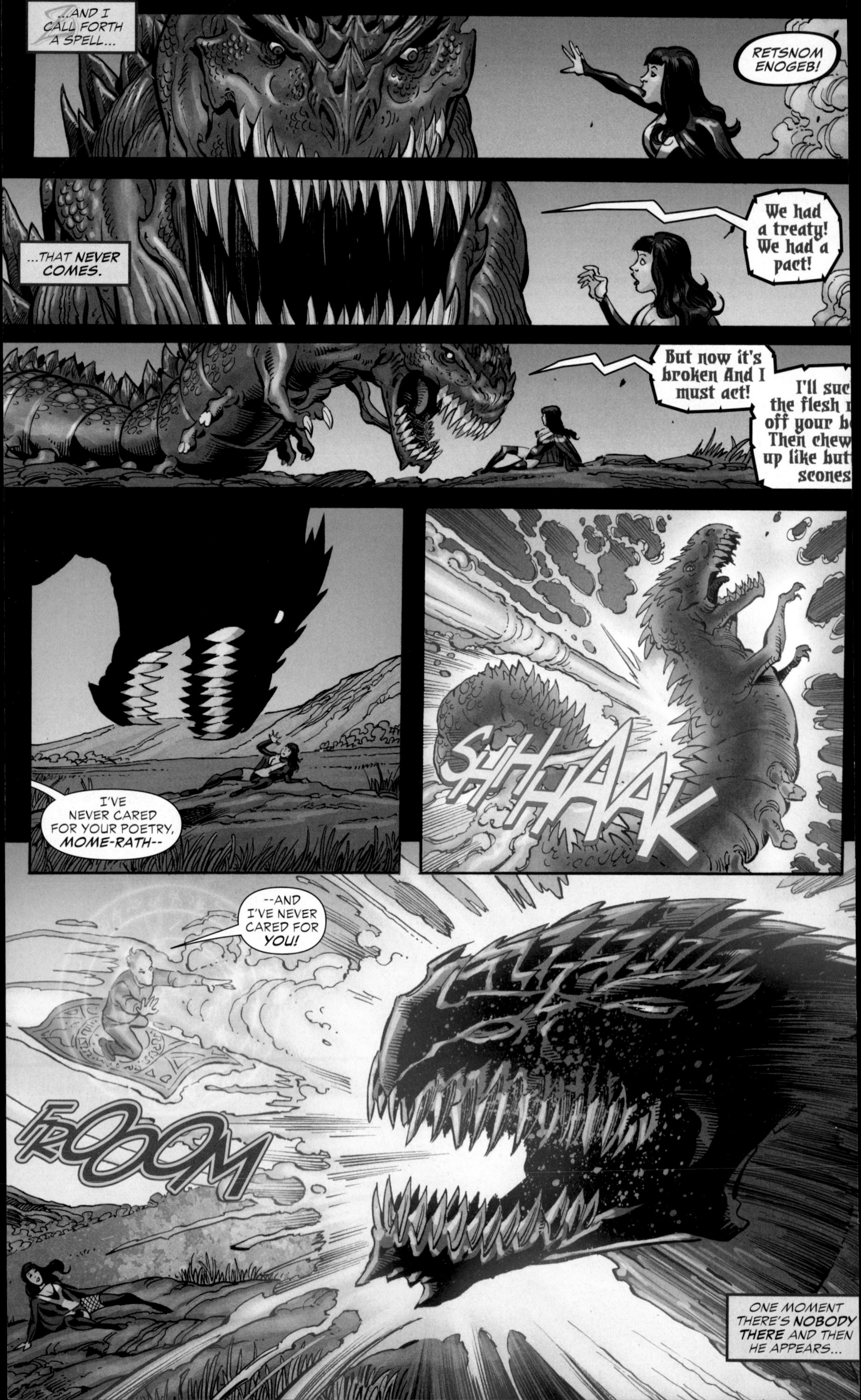
...AND I CALL FORTH A SPELL...
RETSNOM ENOGEB!
...THAT NEVER COMES.
We had a treaty! We had a pact!
But now it's broken And I must act!
I'll suc the flesh r off your b Then chew up like but scones
I'VE NEVER CARED FOR YOUR POETRY, MOME-RATH--
SHHAAAK
--AND I'VE NEVER CARED FOR YOU!
FROOOM
ONE MOMENT THERE'S NOBODY THERE AND THEN HE APPEARS...

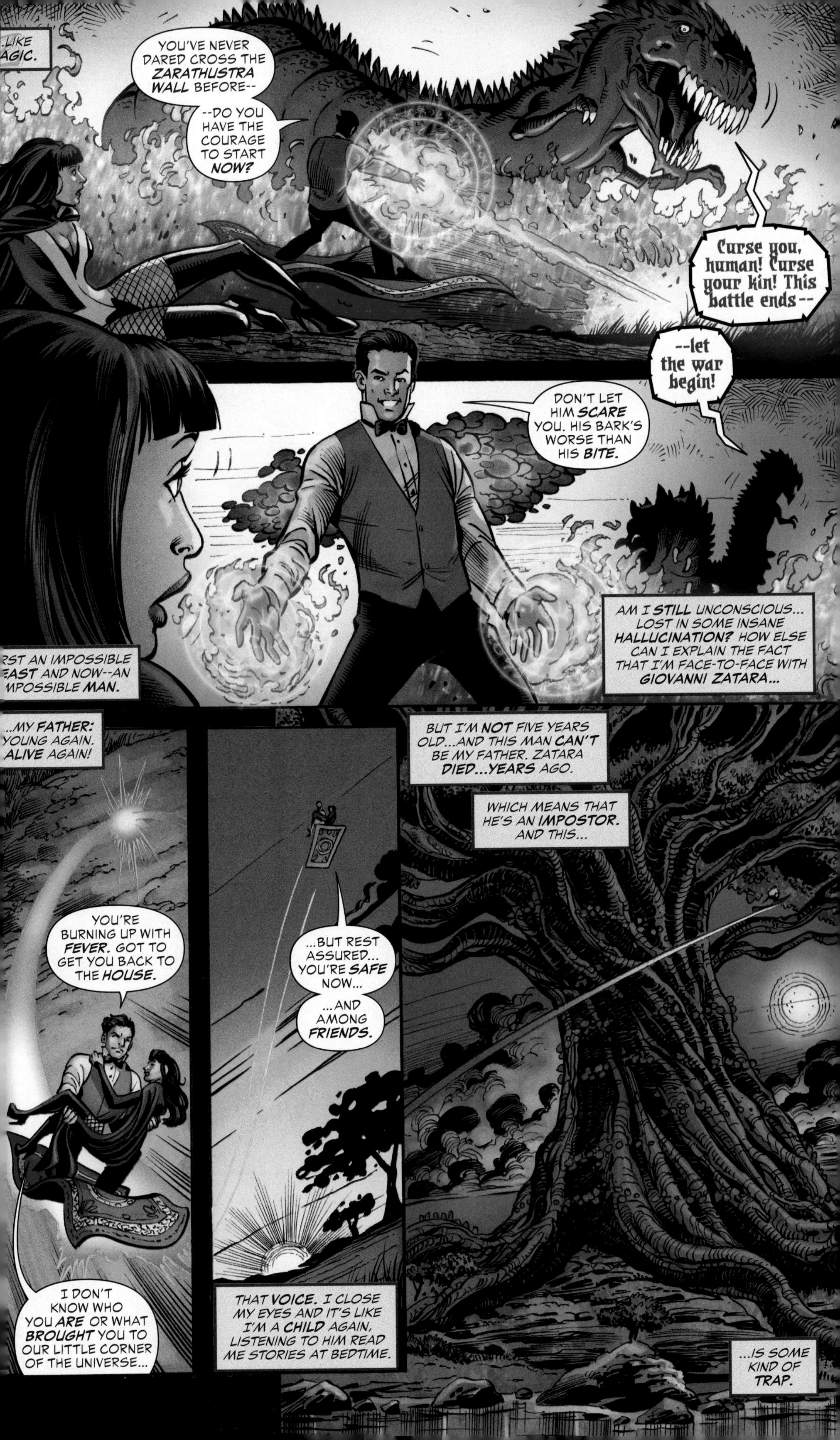

...LIKE MAGIC.
YOU'VE NEVER DARED CROSS THE ZARATHUSTRA WALL BEFORE--
--DO YOU HAVE THE COURAGE TO START NOW?
Curse you, human! Curse your kin! This battle ends--
--let the war begin!
DON'T LET HIM SCARE YOU. HIS BARK'S WORSE THAN HIS BITE.
...RST AN IMPOSSIBLE ...EAST AND NOW--AN ...MPOSSIBLE MAN.
AM I STILL UNCONSCIOUS... LOST IN SOME INSANE HALLUCINATION? HOW ELSE CAN I EXPLAIN THE FACT THAT I'M FACE-TO-FACE WITH GIOVANNI ZATARA...
...MY FATHER: YOUNG AGAIN. ALIVE AGAIN!
YOU'RE BURNING UP WITH FEVER. GOT TO GET YOU BACK TO THE HOUSE.
I DON'T KNOW WHO YOU ARE OR WHAT BROUGHT YOU TO OUR LITTLE CORNER OF THE UNIVERSE...
...BUT REST ASSURED... YOU'RE SAFE NOW...
...AND AMONG FRIENDS.
THAT VOICE. I CLOSE MY EYES AND IT'S LIKE I'M A CHILD AGAIN, LISTENING TO HIM READ ME STORIES AT BEDTIME.
BUT I'M NOT FIVE YEARS OLD...AND THIS MAN CAN'T BE MY FATHER. ZATARA DIED...YEARS AGO.
WHICH MEANS THAT HE'S AN IMPOSTOR. AND THIS...
...IS SOME KIND OF TRAP.

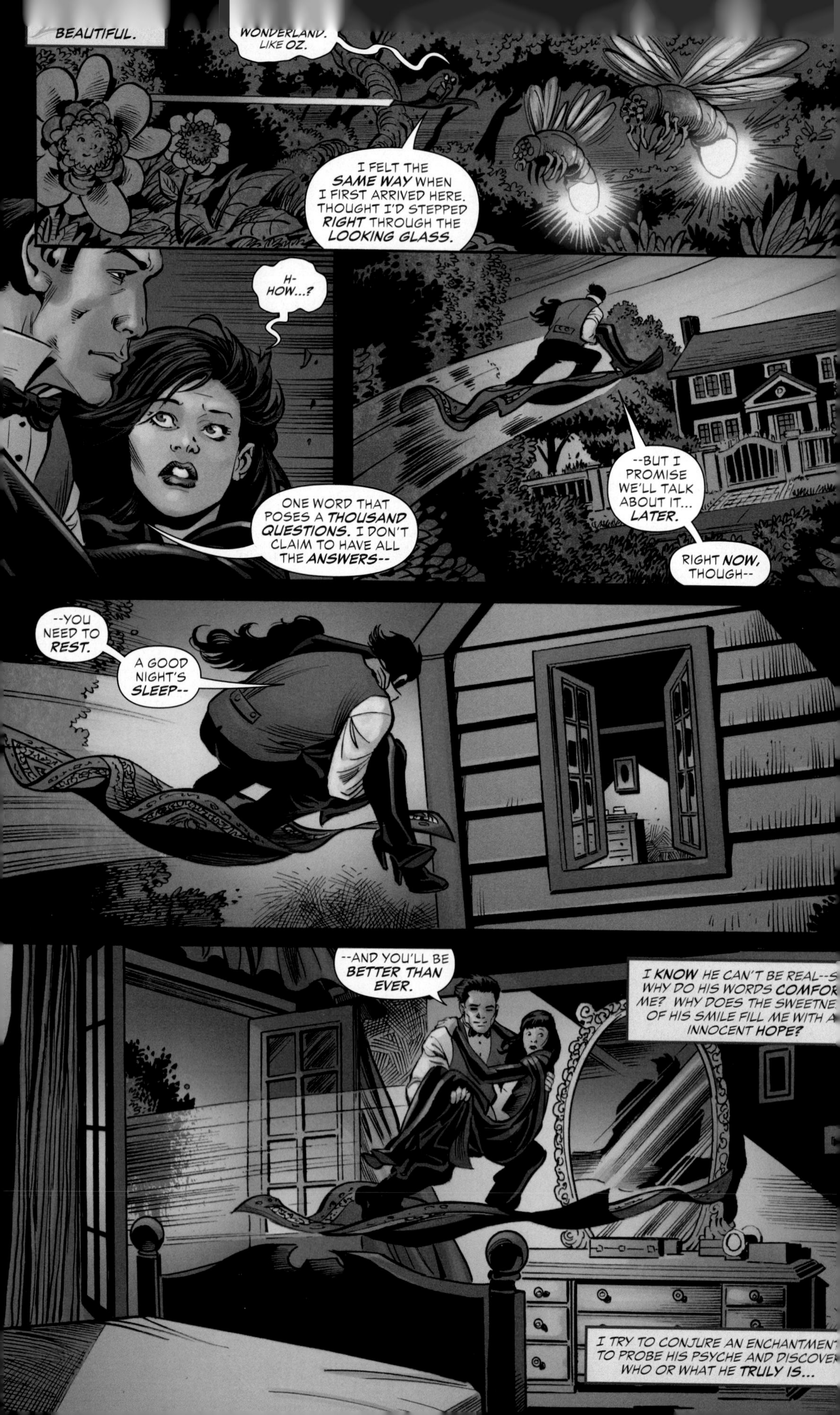

BEAUTIFUL.
WONDERLAND. LIKE OZ.
I FELT THE SAME WAY WHEN I FIRST ARRIVED HERE. THOUGHT I'D STEPPED RIGHT THROUGH THE LOOKING GLASS.
H- HOW...?
ONE WORD THAT POSES A THOUSAND QUESTIONS. I DON'T CLAIM TO HAVE ALL THE ANSWERS--
--BUT I PROMISE WE'LL TALK ABOUT IT... LATER.
RIGHT NOW, THOUGH--
--YOU NEED TO REST.
A GOOD NIGHT'S SLEEP--
--AND YOU'LL BE BETTER THAN EVER.
I KNOW HE CAN'T BE REAL--S WHY DO HIS WORDS COMFOR ME? WHY DOES THE SWEETNE OF HIS SMILE FILL ME WITH A INNOCENT HOPE?
I TRY TO CONJURE AN ENCHANTMEN TO PROBE HIS PSYCHE AND DISCOVE WHO OR WHAT HE TRULY IS...

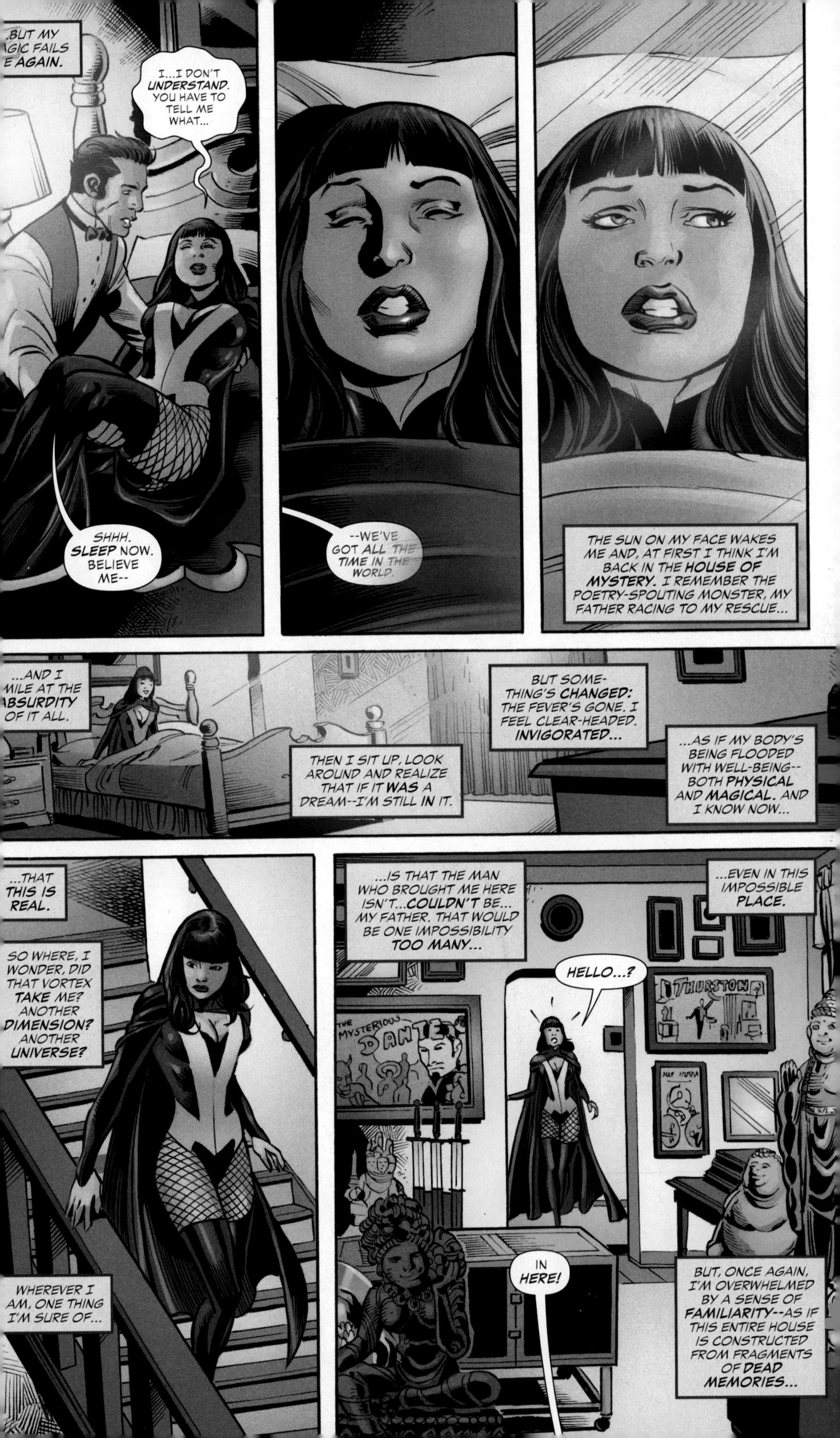

...BUT MY MAGIC FAILS ME AGAIN.
I...I DON'T UNDERSTAND. YOU HAVE TO TELL ME WHAT...
SHHH. SLEEP NOW. BELIEVE ME--
--WE'VE GOT ALL THE TIME IN THE WORLD.
THE SUN ON MY FACE WAKES ME AND, AT FIRST I THINK I'M BACK IN THE HOUSE OF MYSTERY. I REMEMBER THE POETRY-SPOUTING MONSTER, MY FATHER RACING TO MY RESCUE...
...AND I SMILE AT THE ABSURDITY OF IT ALL.
THEN I SIT UP, LOOK AROUND AND REALIZE THAT IF IT WAS A DREAM--I'M STILL IN IT.
BUT SOMETHING'S CHANGED: THE FEVER'S GONE. I FEEL CLEAR-HEADED. INVIGORATED...
...AS IF MY BODY'S BEING FLOODED WITH WELL-BEING--BOTH PHYSICAL AND MAGICAL. AND I KNOW NOW...
...THAT THIS IS REAL.
SO WHERE, I WONDER, DID THAT VORTEX TAKE ME? ANOTHER DIMENSION? ANOTHER UNIVERSE?
WHEREVER I AM, ONE THING I'M SURE OF...
...IS THAT THE MAN WHO BROUGHT ME HERE ISN'T...COULDN'T BE... MY FATHER. THAT WOULD BE ONE IMPOSSIBILITY TOO MANY...
...EVEN IN THIS IMPOSSIBLE PLACE.
HELLO...?
THE MYSTERIOUS DANTE
THURSTON
IN HERE!
BUT, ONCE AGAIN, I'M OVERWHELMED BY A SENSE OF FAMILIARITY--AS IF THIS ENTIRE HOUSE IS CONSTRUCTED FROM FRAGMENTS OF DEAD MEMORIES...

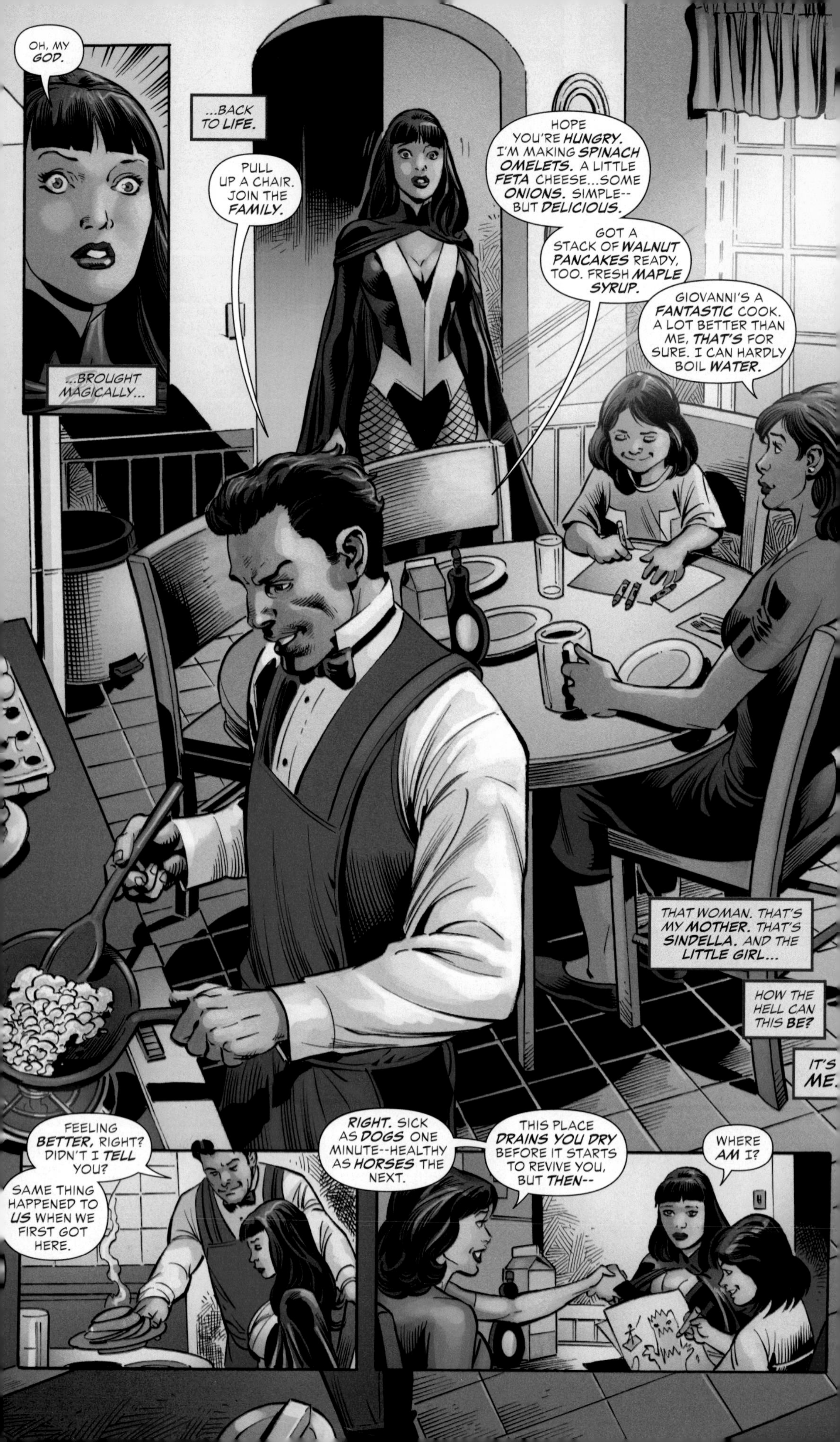
OH, MY GOD.
...BROUGHT MAGICALLY...
...BACK TO LIFE.
PULL UP A CHAIR. JOIN THE FAMILY.
HOPE YOU'RE HUNGRY. I'M MAKING SPINACH OMELETS. A LITTLE FETA CHEESE...SOME ONIONS. SIMPLE-- BUT DELICIOUS.
GOT A STACK OF WALNUT PANCAKES READY, TOO. FRESH MAPLE SYRUP.
GIOVANNI'S A FANTASTIC COOK. A LOT BETTER THAN ME, THAT'S FOR SURE. I CAN HARDLY BOIL WATER.
THAT WOMAN. THAT'S MY MOTHER. THAT'S SINDELLA. AND THE LITTLE GIRL...
HOW THE HELL CAN THIS BE?
IT'S ME.
FEELING BETTER, RIGHT? DIDN'T I TELL YOU?
SAME THING HAPPENED TO US WHEN WE FIRST GOT HERE.
RIGHT. SICK AS DOGS ONE MINUTE--HEALTHY AS HORSES THE NEXT.
THIS PLACE DRAINS YOU DRY BEFORE IT STARTS TO REVIVE YOU, BUT THEN--
WHERE AM I?

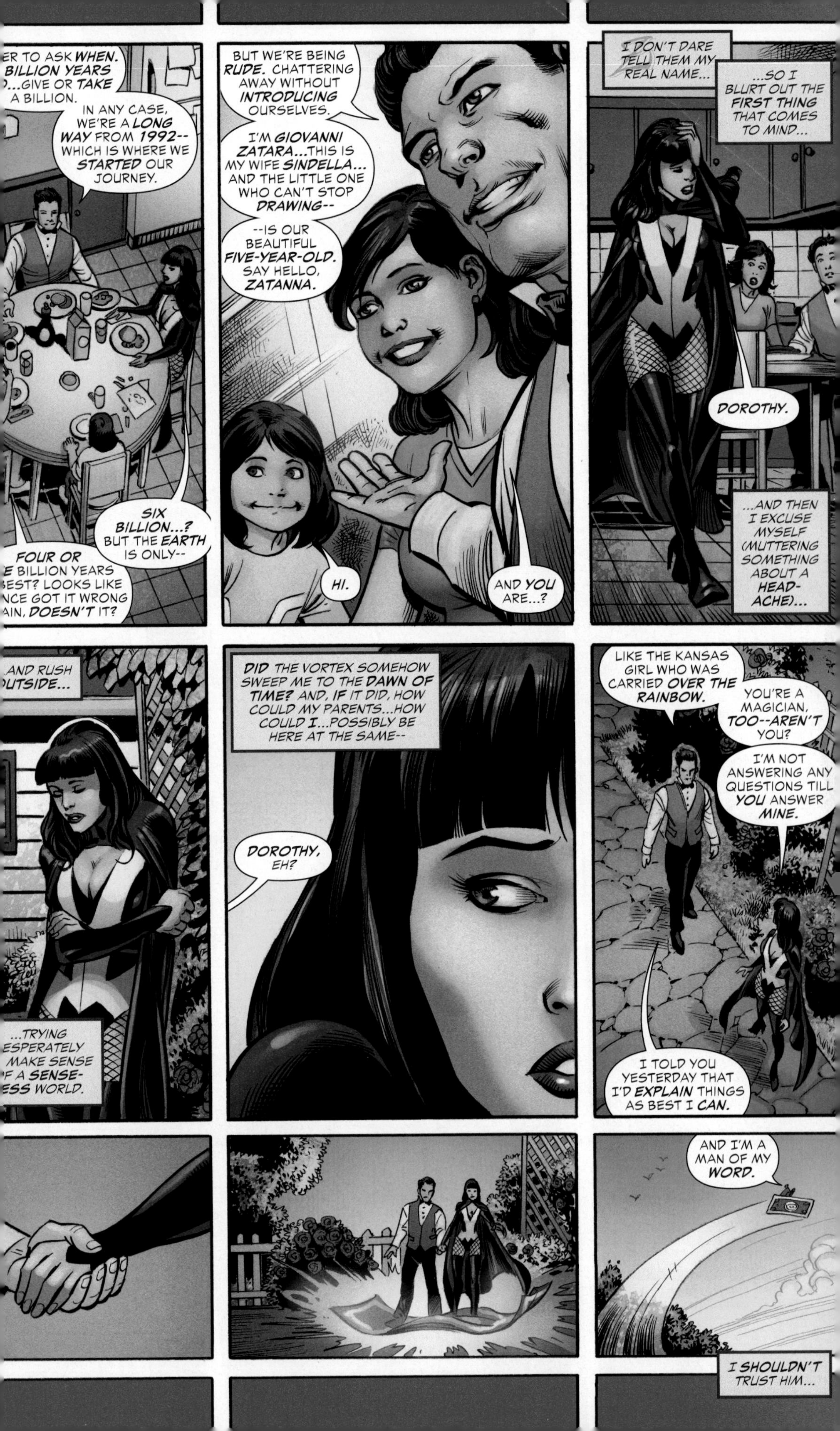

ER TO ASK WHEN. BILLION YEARS ...GIVE OR TAKE A BILLION.
IN ANY CASE, WE'RE A LONG WAY FROM 1992--WHICH IS WHERE WE STARTED OUR JOURNEY.
SIX BILLION...? BUT THE EARTH IS ONLY--
FOUR OR E BILLION YEARS BEST? LOOKS LIKE NCE GOT IT WRONG AIN, DOESN'T IT?
BUT WE'RE BEING RUDE. CHATTERING AWAY WITHOUT INTRODUCING OURSELVES.
I'M GIOVANNI ZATARA...THIS IS MY WIFE SINDELLA...AND THE LITTLE ONE WHO CAN'T STOP DRAWING--
--IS OUR BEAUTIFUL FIVE-YEAR-OLD. SAY HELLO, ZATANNA.
HI.
AND YOU ARE...?
I DON'T DARE TELL THEM MY REAL NAME...
...SO I BLURT OUT THE FIRST THING THAT COMES TO MIND...
DOROTHY.
...AND THEN I EXCUSE MYSELF (MUTTERING SOMETHING ABOUT A HEAD-ACHE)...
..AND RUSH UTSIDE...
...TRYING ESPERATELY MAKE SENSE F A SENSE-ESS WORLD.
DID THE VORTEX SOMEHOW SWEEP ME TO THE DAWN OF TIME? AND, IF IT DID, HOW COULD MY PARENTS...HOW COULD I...POSSIBLY BE HERE AT THE SAME--
DOROTHY, EH?
LIKE THE KANSAS GIRL WHO WAS CARRIED OVER THE RAINBOW.
YOU'RE A MAGICIAN, TOO--AREN'T YOU?
I'M NOT ANSWERING ANY QUESTIONS TILL YOU ANSWER MINE.
I TOLD YOU YESTERDAY THAT I'D EXPLAIN THINGS AS BEST I CAN.
AND I'M A MAN OF MY WORD.
I SHOULDN'T TRUST HIM...

...BUT I **DO**. AT LEAST ENOUGH TO LET HIM TELL ME HIS **STORY**:

"*I'D SPENT YEARS*," HE SAYS, "RESEARCHING A TIME **BEFORE** TIME--WHEN THE EARTH WAS **PERMEATED** BY A MAGIC SO PURE THAT JUST BREATHING THE AIR WOULD INFUSE YOU WITH **INCALCULABLE POWER**.

"--I FOUND THE **DOORWAY THROUGH TIME**. BUT I DIDN'T WANT TO LEAVE MY FAMILY BEHIND--SO I TOOK SINDELLA AND ZATANNA **WITH ME**...NEVER DREAMING THAT, ONCE HERE, WE'D NEVER BE ABLE TO FIND A **WAY BACK**.

"NO SPELLS, THE LEGENDS SAID, WERE NECESSARY: **THOUGHT** ITSELF WOULD INSTANTLY BECOME **MANIFEST REALITY**.

"**PREPOSTEROUS** LEGENDS? MOST MAGICAL SCHOLARS THOUGHT SO...BUT, FROM THE TIME I WAS A BOY, I BELIEVED; AND, EVENTUALLY--

"AT FIRST, THE ENCHANTMENT OF THIS PLACE WAS **OVERWHELMING**... CHANGING REALITY WITH A THOUGHT WAS **INTOXICATING**.

"WE LIVED IN A HUNDRED, A **THOUSAND**, DIFFERENT WORLDS-- FROM THE ORDINARY TO THE INCONCEIVABLE--BUT EVENTUALLY--

"--WE SETTLED ON OUR SIMPLE HOUSE. OUR SIMPLE LIFE. WE TRAVELLED BILLION**S** OF YEARS IN SEARC**H** OF MAGIC...AND, IN THE END--

"--FOUND IT IN **EACH OTHER'S** EYES."

"HOW LONG HAVE YO**U** BEEN HERE?" I ASK**ED** "NO IDEA," HE REPLIE**S**

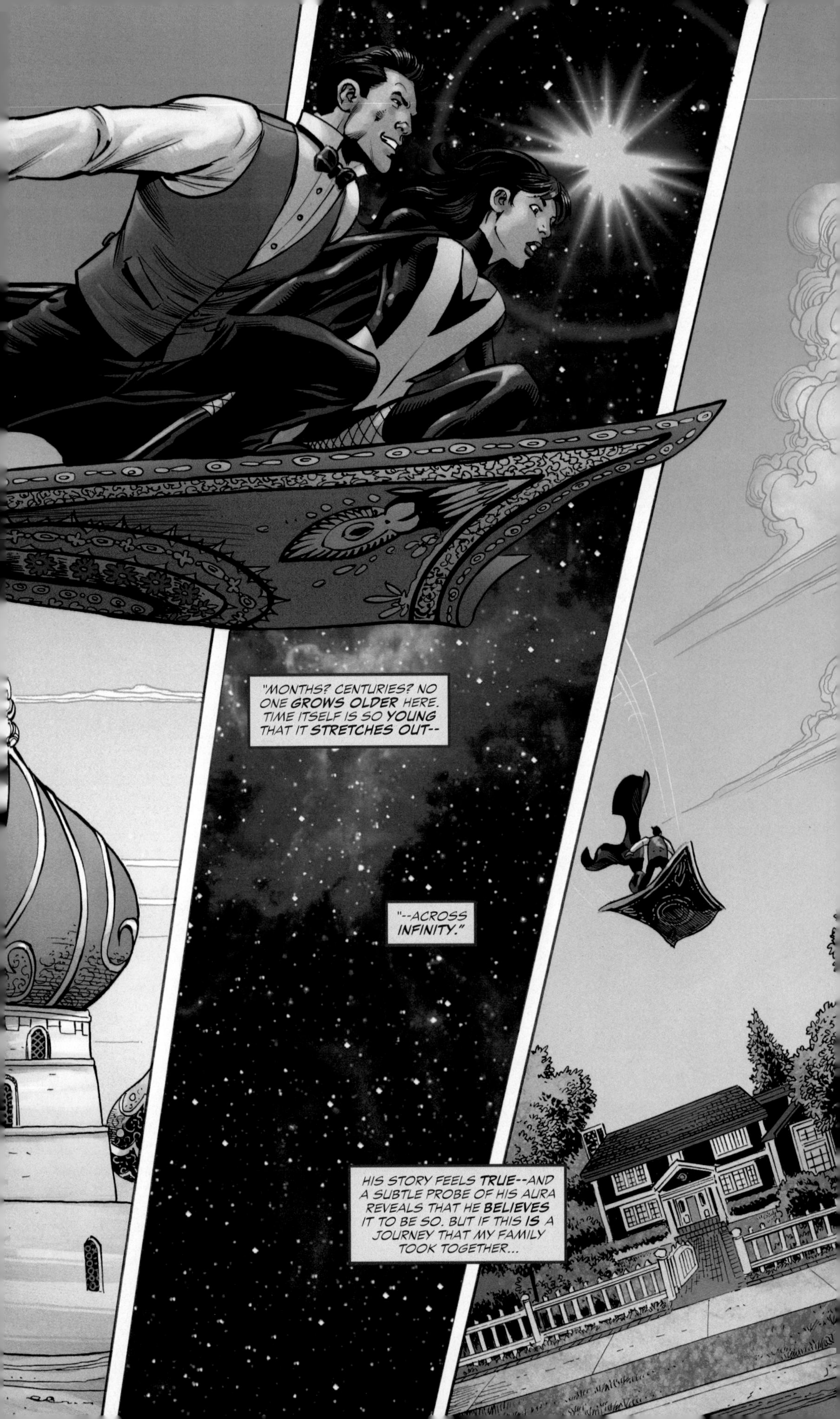
"MONTHS? CENTURIES? NO ONE GROWS OLDER HERE. TIME ITSELF IS SO YOUNG THAT IT STRETCHES OUT--
"--ACROSS INFINITY."
HIS STORY FEELS TRUE--AND A SUBTLE PROBE OF HIS AURA REVEALS THAT HE BELIEVES IT TO BE SO. BUT IF THIS IS A JOURNEY THAT MY FAMILY TOOK TOGETHER...

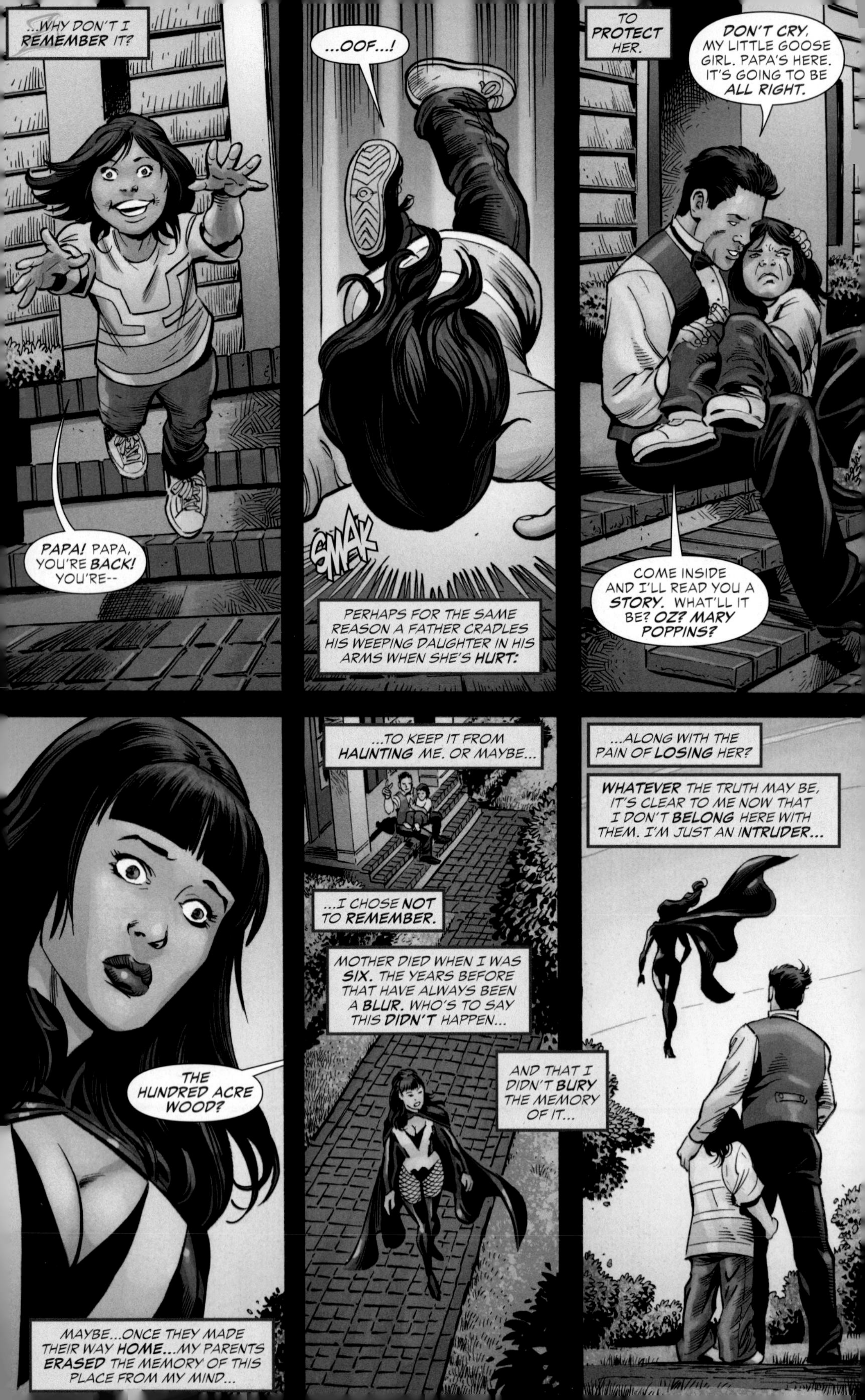
...WHY DON'T I REMEMBER IT?
PAPA! PAPA, YOU'RE BACK! YOU'RE--
...OOF...!
SMAK
PERHAPS FOR THE SAME REASON A FATHER CRADLES HIS WEEPING DAUGHTER IN HIS ARMS WHEN SHE'S HURT:
TO PROTECT HER.
DON'T CRY, MY LITTLE GOOSE GIRL. PAPA'S HERE. IT'S GOING TO BE ALL RIGHT.
COME INSIDE AND I'LL READ YOU A STORY. WHAT'LL IT BE? OZ? MARY POPPINS?
THE HUNDRED ACRE WOOD?
MAYBE...ONCE THEY MADE THEIR WAY HOME...MY PARENTS ERASED THE MEMORY OF THIS PLACE FROM MY MIND...
...TO KEEP IT FROM HAUNTING ME. OR MAYBE...
...I CHOSE NOT TO REMEMBER.
MOTHER DIED WHEN I WAS SIX. THE YEARS BEFORE THAT HAVE ALWAYS BEEN A BLUR. WHO'S TO SAY THIS DIDN'T HAPPEN...
AND THAT I DIDN'T BURY THE MEMORY OF IT...
...ALONG WITH THE PAIN OF LOSING HER?
WHATEVER THE TRUTH MAY BE, IT'S CLEAR TO ME NOW THAT I DON'T BELONG HERE WITH THEM. I'M JUST AN INTRUDER...

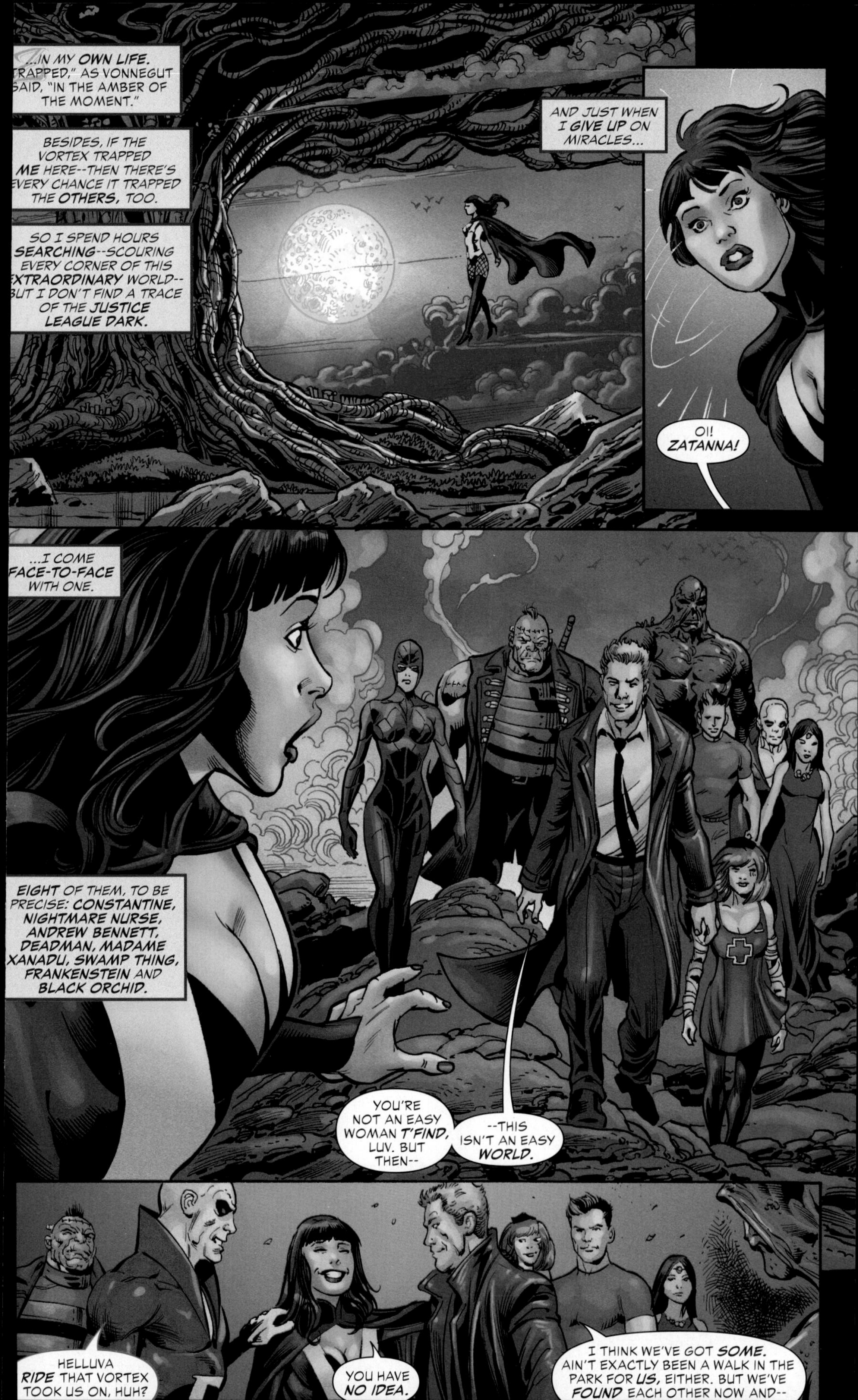
...IN MY OWN LIFE. TRAPPED," AS VONNEGUT SAID, "IN THE AMBER OF THE MOMENT."
BESIDES, IF THE VORTEX TRAPPED ME HERE--THEN THERE'S EVERY CHANCE IT TRAPPED THE OTHERS, TOO.
SO I SPEND HOURS SEARCHING--SCOURING EVERY CORNER OF THIS EXTRAORDINARY WORLD--BUT I DON'T FIND A TRACE OF THE JUSTICE LEAGUE DARK.
AND JUST WHEN I GIVE UP ON MIRACLES...
OI! ZATANNA!
...I COME FACE-TO-FACE WITH ONE.
EIGHT OF THEM, TO BE PRECISE: CONSTANTINE, NIGHTMARE NURSE, ANDREW BENNETT, DEADMAN, MADAME XANADU, SWAMP THING, FRANKENSTEIN AND BLACK ORCHID.
YOU'RE NOT AN EASY WOMAN T'FIND, LUV. BUT THEN--
--THIS ISN'T AN EASY WORLD.
HELLUVA RIDE THAT VORTEX TOOK US ON, HUH?
YOU HAVE NO IDEA.
I THINK WE'VE GOT SOME. AIN'T EXACTLY BEEN A WALK IN THE PARK FOR US, EITHER. BUT WE'VE FOUND EACH OTHER NOW AND--

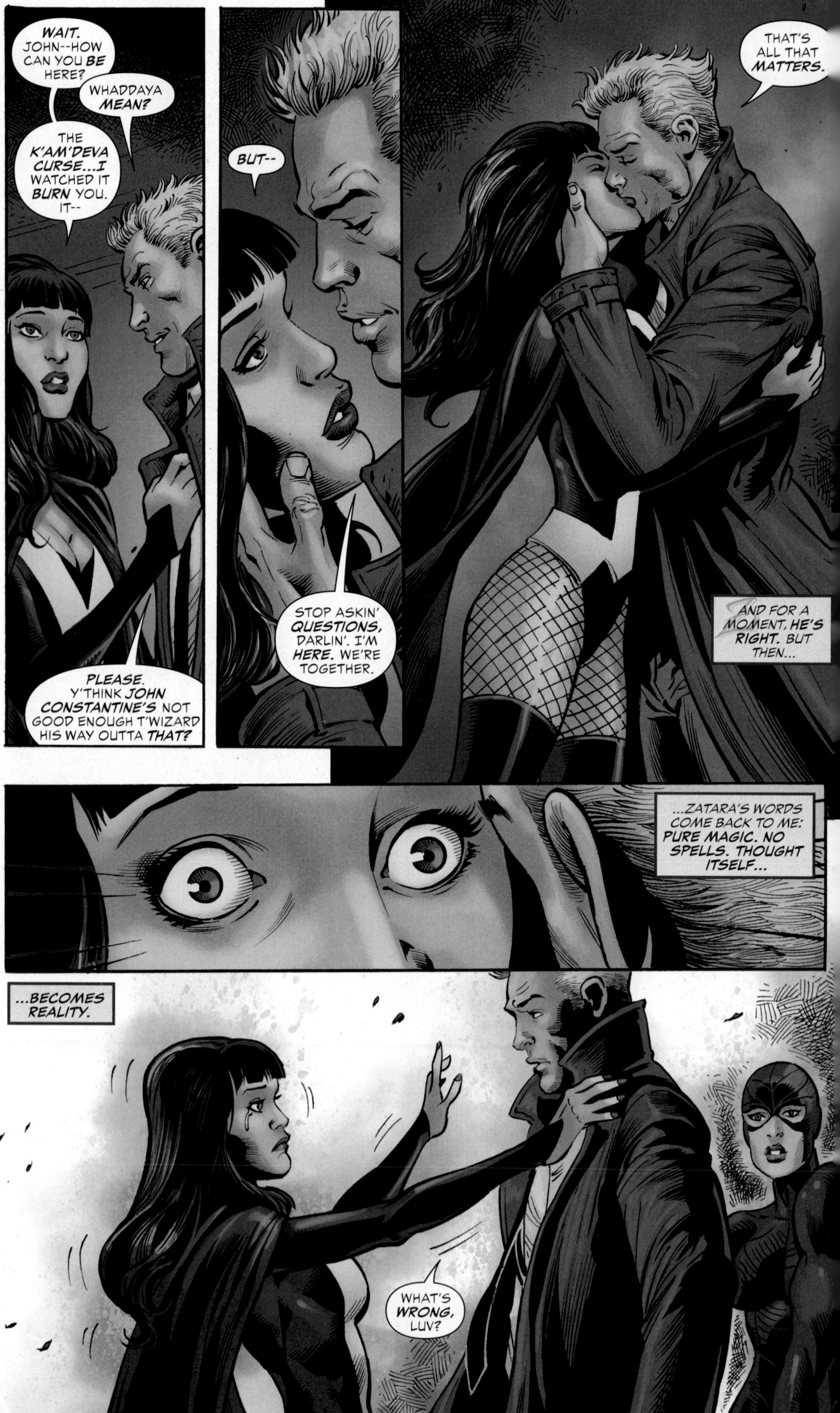
WAIT. JOHN--HOW CAN YOU BE HERE?
WHADDAYA MEAN?
THE K'AM'DEVA CURSE...I WATCHED IT BURN YOU. IT--
PLEASE. Y'THINK JOHN CONSTANTINE'S NOT GOOD ENOUGH T'WIZARD HIS WAY OUTTA THAT?
BUT--
STOP ASKIN' QUESTIONS, DARLIN'. I'M HERE. WE'RE TOGETHER.
THAT'S ALL THAT MATTERS.
AND FOR A MOMENT, HE'S RIGHT. BUT THEN...
...ZATARA'S WORDS COME BACK TO ME: PURE MAGIC. NO SPELLS. THOUGHT ITSELF...
...BECOMES REALITY.
WHAT'S WRONG, LUV?

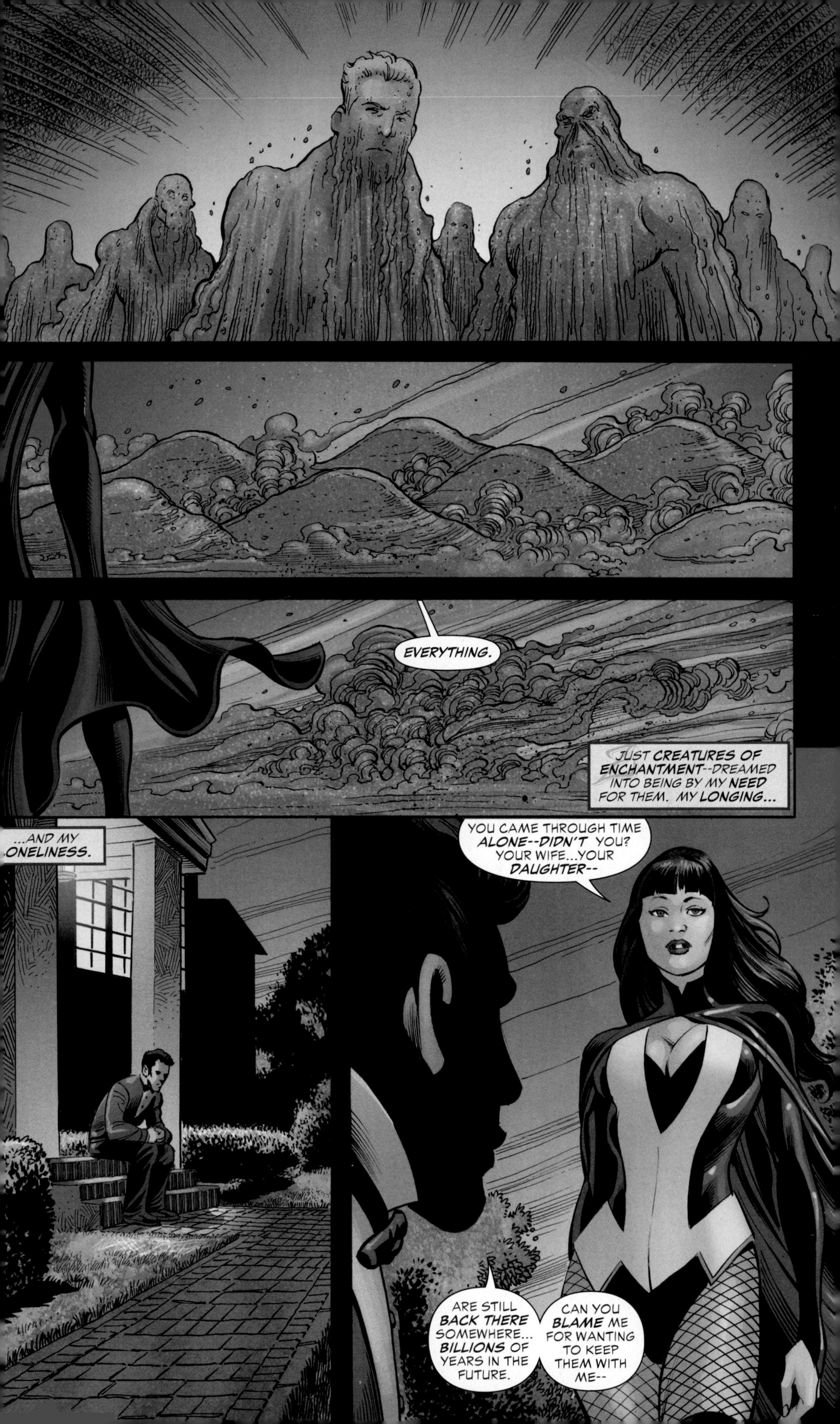
EVERYTHING.
JUST CREATURES OF ENCHANTMENT--DREAMED INTO BEING BY MY NEED FOR THEM. MY LONGING...
...AND MY ONELINESS.
YOU CAME THROUGH TIME ALONE--DIDN'T YOU? YOUR WIFE...YOUR DAUGHTER--
ARE STILL BACK THERE SOMEWHERE... BILLIONS OF YEARS IN THE FUTURE.
CAN YOU BLAME ME FOR WANTING TO KEEP THEM WITH ME--

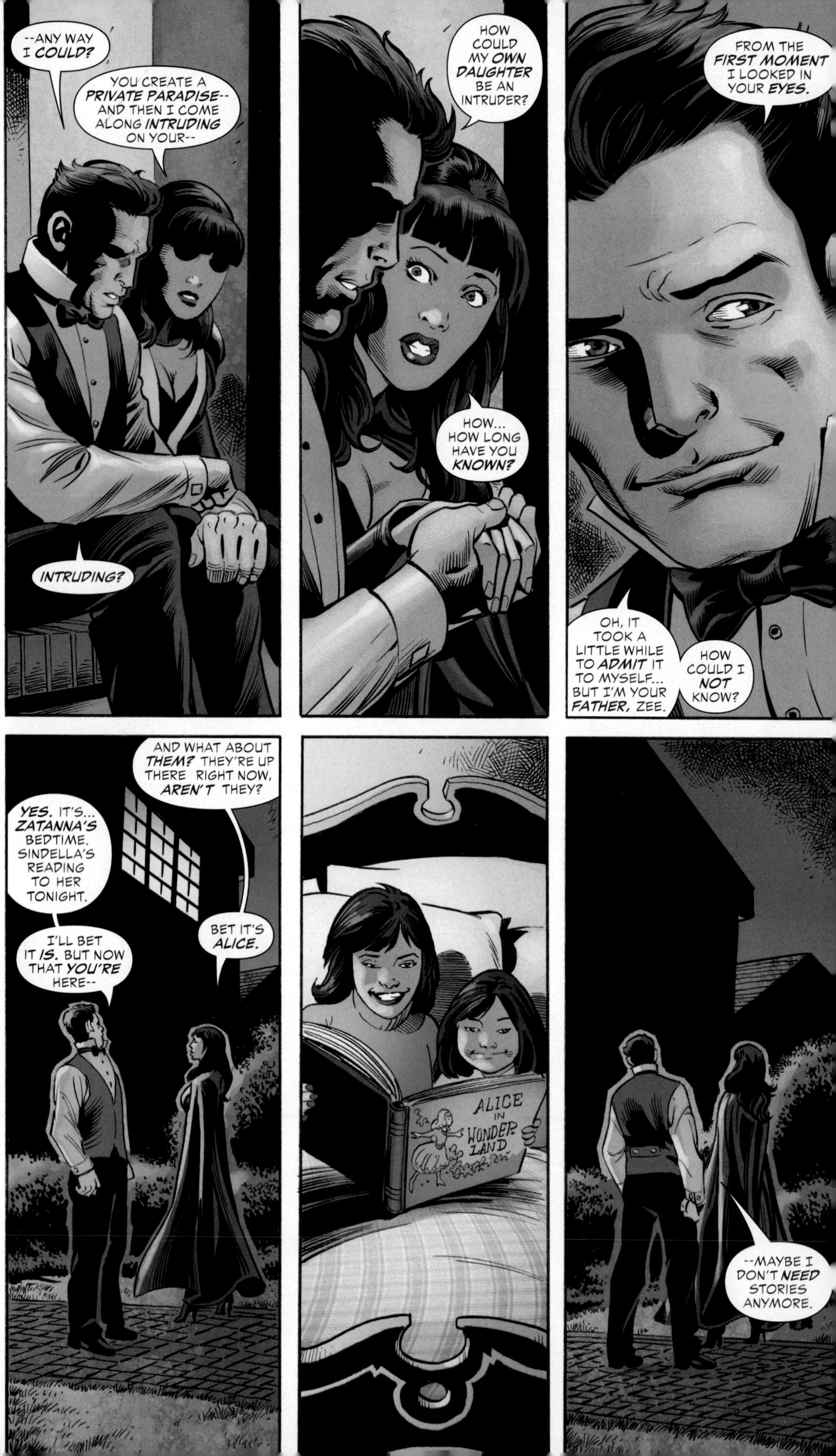
--ANY WAY I *COULD?*
YOU CREATE A *PRIVATE PARADISE*-- AND THEN I COME ALONG *INTRUDING* ON YOUR--
INTRUDING?
HOW COULD MY *OWN DAUGHTER* BE AN INTRUDER?
HOW... HOW LONG HAVE YOU *KNOWN?*
FROM THE *FIRST MOMENT* I LOOKED IN YOUR *EYES.*
OH, IT TOOK A LITTLE WHILE TO *ADMIT* IT TO MYSELF... BUT I'M YOUR *FATHER,* ZEE.
HOW COULD I *NOT* KNOW?
AND WHAT ABOUT *THEM?* THEY'RE UP THERE RIGHT NOW, *AREN'T* THEY?
YES. IT'S... *ZATANNA'S* BEDTIME. SINDELLA'S READING TO HER TONIGHT.
BET IT'S *ALICE.*
I'LL BET IT *IS.* BUT NOW THAT *YOU'RE* HERE--
ALICE IN WONDER LAND
--MAYBE I DON'T *NEED* STORIES ANYMORE.

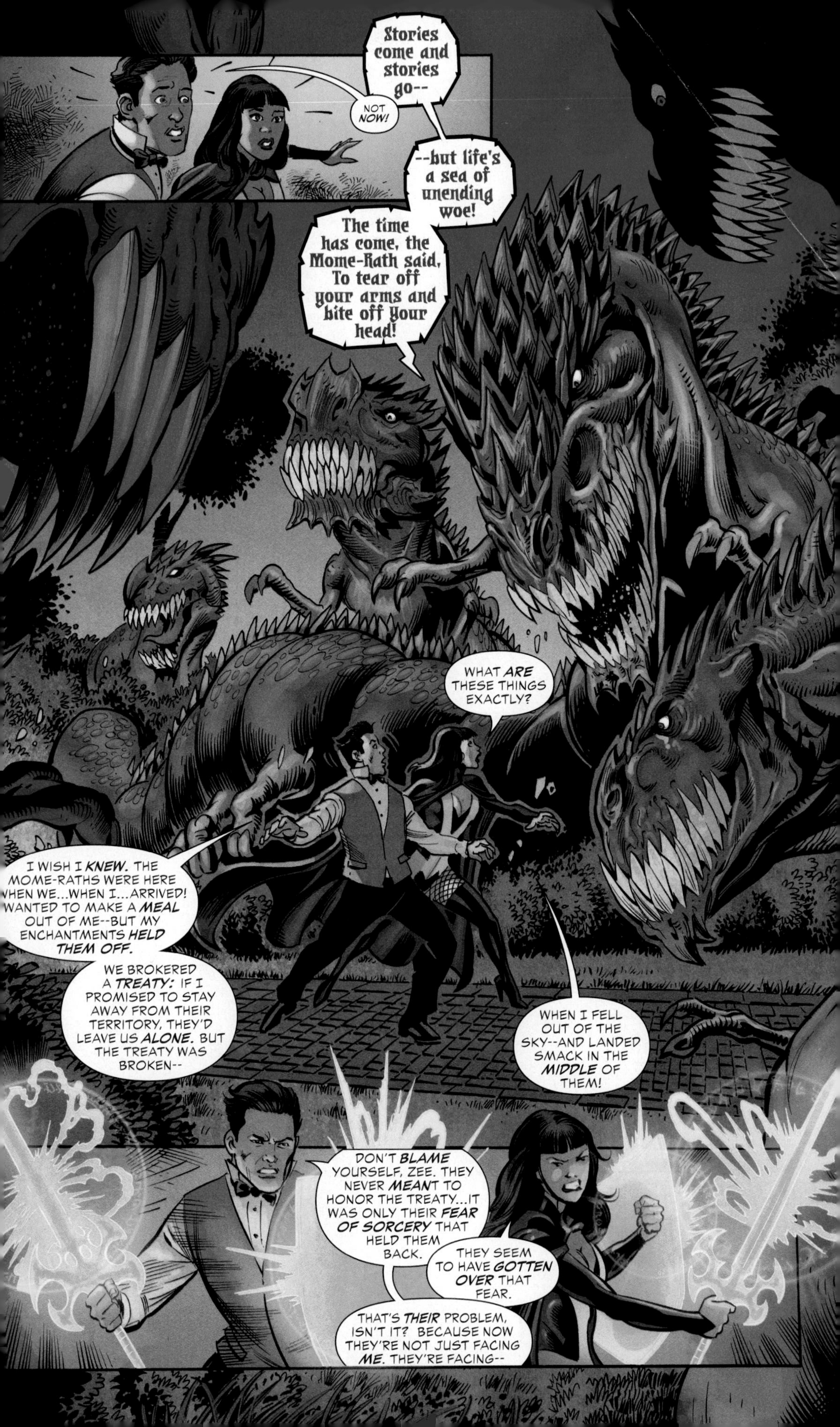
Stories come and stories go--
NOT NOW!
--but life's a sea of unending woe!
The time has come, the Mome-Rath said, To tear off your arms and bite off Your head!
WHAT ARE THESE THINGS EXACTLY?
I WISH I KNEW. THE MOME-RATHS WERE HERE WHEN WE...WHEN I...ARRIVED! WANTED TO MAKE A MEAL OUT OF ME--BUT MY ENCHANTMENTS HELD THEM OFF.
WE BROKERED A TREATY: IF I PROMISED TO STAY AWAY FROM THEIR TERRITORY, THEY'D LEAVE US ALONE. BUT THE TREATY WAS BROKEN--
WHEN I FELL OUT OF THE SKY--AND LANDED SMACK IN THE MIDDLE OF THEM!
DON'T BLAME YOURSELF, ZEE. THEY NEVER MEANT TO HONOR THE TREATY...IT WAS ONLY THEIR FEAR OF SORCERY THAT HELD THEM BACK.
THEY SEEM TO HAVE GOTTEN OVER THAT FEAR.
THAT'S THEIR PROBLEM, ISN'T IT? BECAUSE NOW THEY'RE NOT JUST FACING ME. THEY'RE FACING--

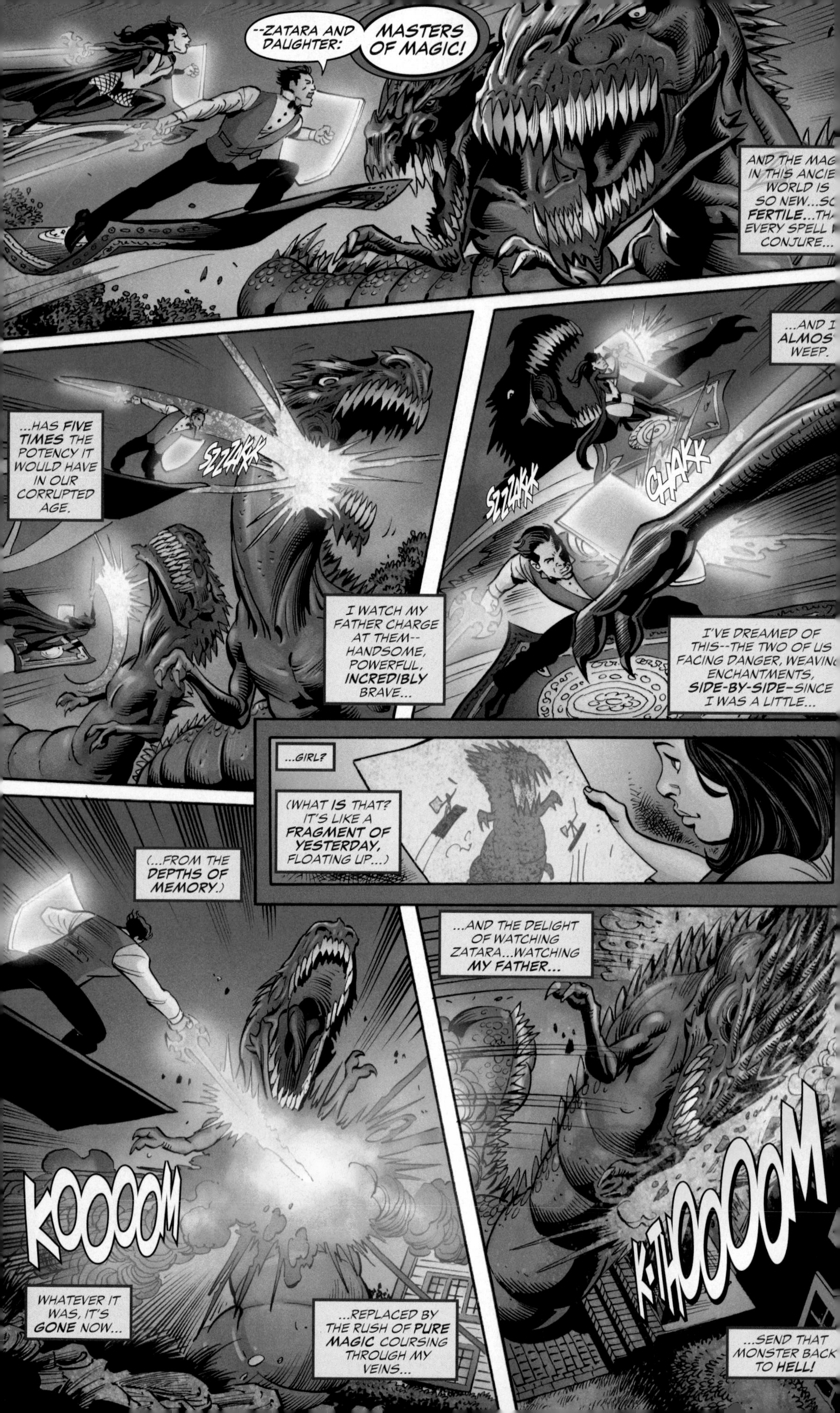

--ZATARA AND DAUGHTER:
MASTERS OF MAGIC!
AND THE MAG IN THIS ANCIE WORLD IS SO NEW...SC FERTILE...THA EVERY SPELL I CONJURE...
...HAS FIVE TIMES THE POTENCY IT WOULD HAVE IN OUR CORRUPTED AGE.
SZZZAKKK
...AND I ALMOS WEEP.
SZZZAKKK
CHAKK
I WATCH MY FATHER CHARGE AT THEM--HANDSOME, POWERFUL, INCREDIBLY BRAVE...
I'VE DREAMED OF THIS--THE TWO OF US FACING DANGER, WEAVING ENCHANTMENTS, SIDE-BY-SIDE--SINCE I WAS A LITTLE...
...GIRL?
(WHAT IS THAT? IT'S LIKE A FRAGMENT OF YESTERDAY, FLOATING UP...)
(...FROM THE DEPTHS OF MEMORY.)
KOOOOM
WHATEVER IT WAS, IT'S GONE NOW...
...REPLACED BY THE RUSH OF PURE MAGIC COURSING THROUGH MY VEINS...
...AND THE DELIGHT OF WATCHING ZATARA...WATCHING MY FATHER...
K-THOOOOM
...SEND THAT MONSTER BACK TO HELL!

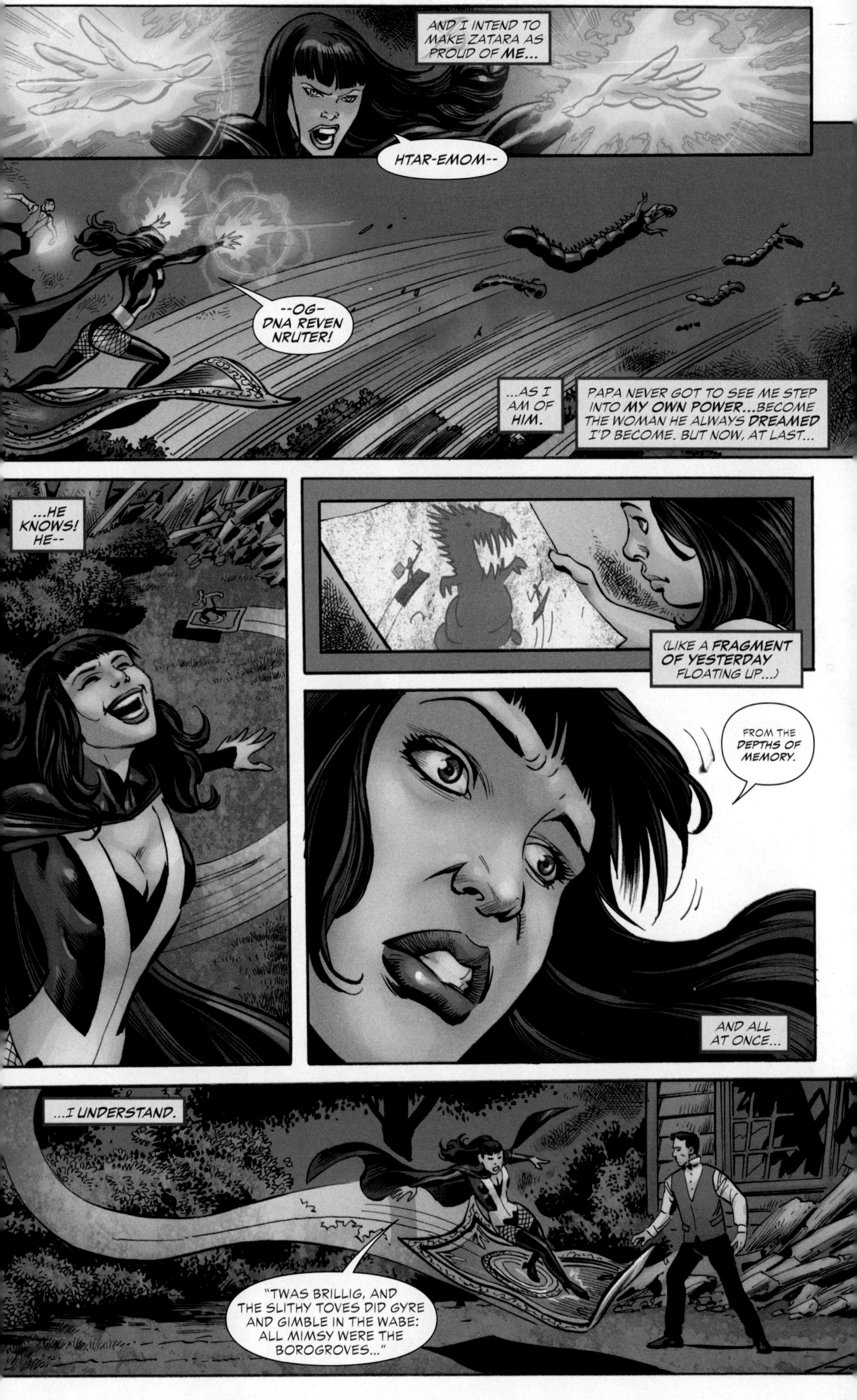
AND I INTEND TO MAKE ZATARA AS PROUD OF ME...
HTAR-EMOM--
--OG-DNA REVEN NRUTER!
...AS I AM OF HIM.
PAPA NEVER GOT TO SEE ME STEP INTO MY OWN POWER...BECOME THE WOMAN HE ALWAYS DREAMED I'D BECOME. BUT NOW, AT LAST...
...HE KNOWS! HE--
(LIKE A FRAGMENT OF YESTERDAY FLOATING UP...)
FROM THE DEPTHS OF MEMORY.
AND ALL AT ONCE...
...I UNDERSTAND.
"TWAS BRILLIG, AND THE SLITHY TOVES DID GYRE AND GIMBLE IN THE WABE: ALL MIMSY WERE THE BOROGROVES..."

"...AND THE MOME RATHS OUTGRABE."

LEWIS CARROLL AGAIN. "JABBERWOCKY." GOD, HOW YOU LOVED THAT POEM. YOU'D READ IT OVER AND OVER--

AND I'D SPEND HOURS DRAWING MY OWN VERSION OF THE MOME RATH. IMAGINING THE TWO OF US BATTLING IT... TOGETHER.

STRANGE, ISN'T IT--THAT A LITTLE GIRL'S FANTASY--

--HAS SOMEHOW COME TO LIFE?

IT'S THE MAGIC HER ZATANNA. S STRONG...TH EVEN AN UNCONSCIO WHISPER C MANIFEST T HEART'S DESIRE.

SO I DREAMED YOU... DREAMING THEM.

AND NOW THAT I KNOW WHAT I REALLY AM--

--I HAVE TO GO.

NO! NO, YOU DON'T!

YOU CAN'T LET A DREAM KEEP YOU HERE, ZEE. YOU HAVE TO FIND YOUR WAY HOME.

PLEASE DON'T LEAVE.

DON'T CRY, MY LITTLE GOOSE GIRL. PAPA'S--

--HERE

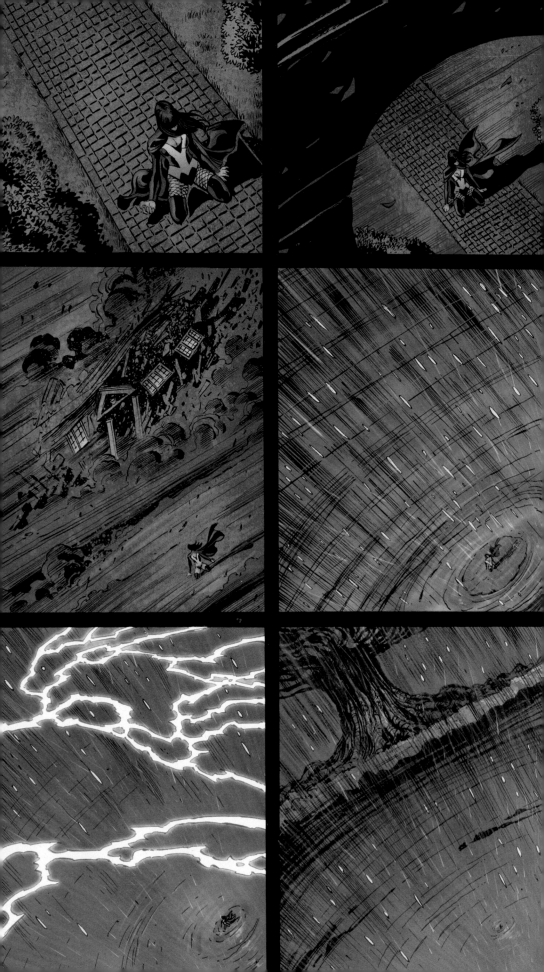

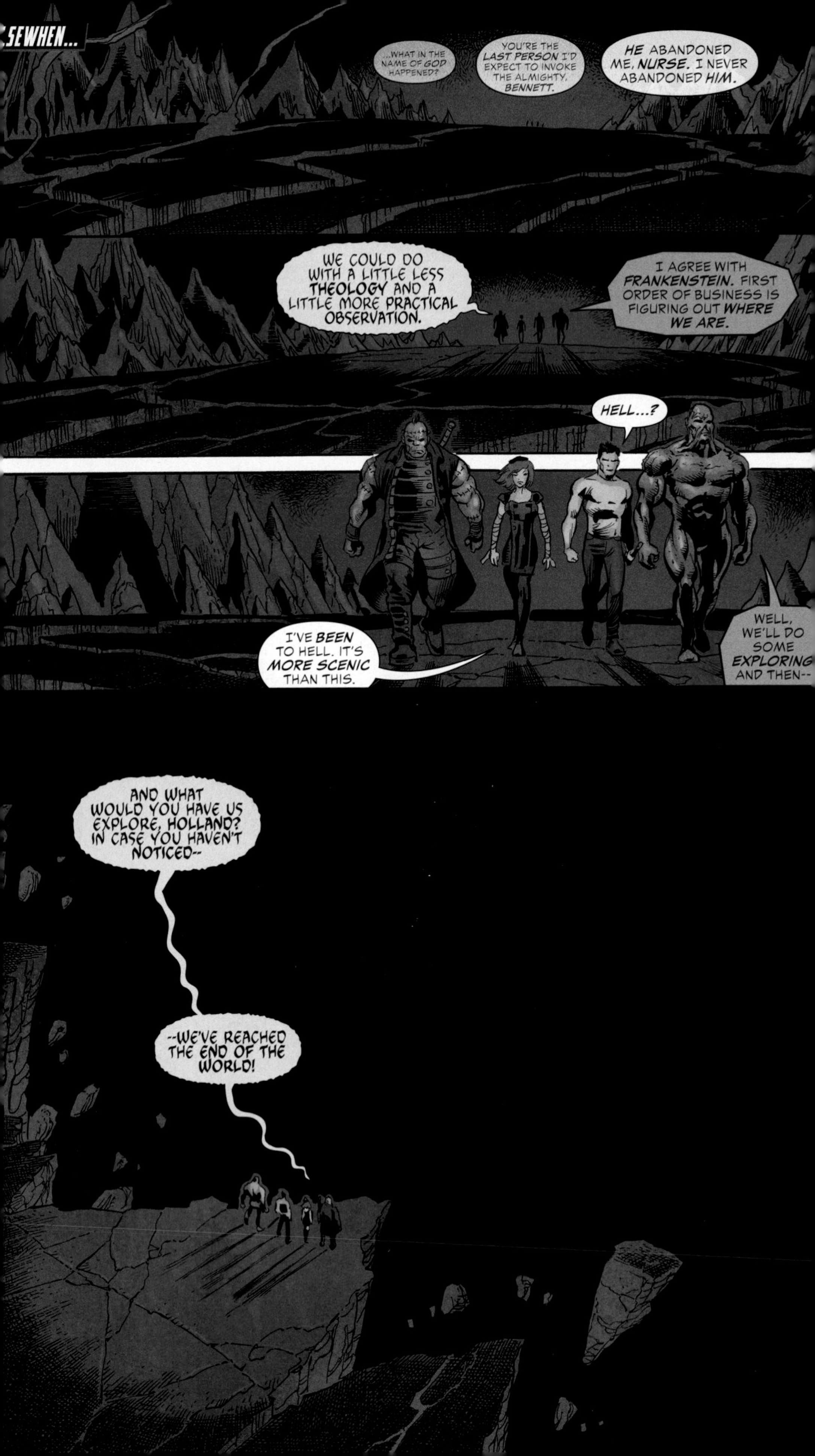
SEWHEN...
...WHAT IN THE NAME OF GOD HAPPENED?
YOU'RE THE LAST PERSON I'D EXPECT TO INVOKE THE ALMIGHTY, BENNETT.
HE ABANDONED ME, NURSE. I NEVER ABANDONED HIM.
WE COULD DO WITH A LITTLE LESS THEOLOGY AND A LITTLE MORE PRACTICAL OBSERVATION.
I AGREE WITH FRANKENSTEIN. FIRST ORDER OF BUSINESS IS FIGURING OUT WHERE WE ARE.
HELL...?
I'VE BEEN TO HELL. IT'S MORE SCENIC THAN THIS.
WELL, WE'LL DO SOME EXPLORING AND THEN--
AND WHAT WOULD YOU HAVE US EXPLORE, HOLLAND? IN CASE YOU HAVEN'T NOTICED--
--WE'VE REACHED THE END OF THE WORLD!

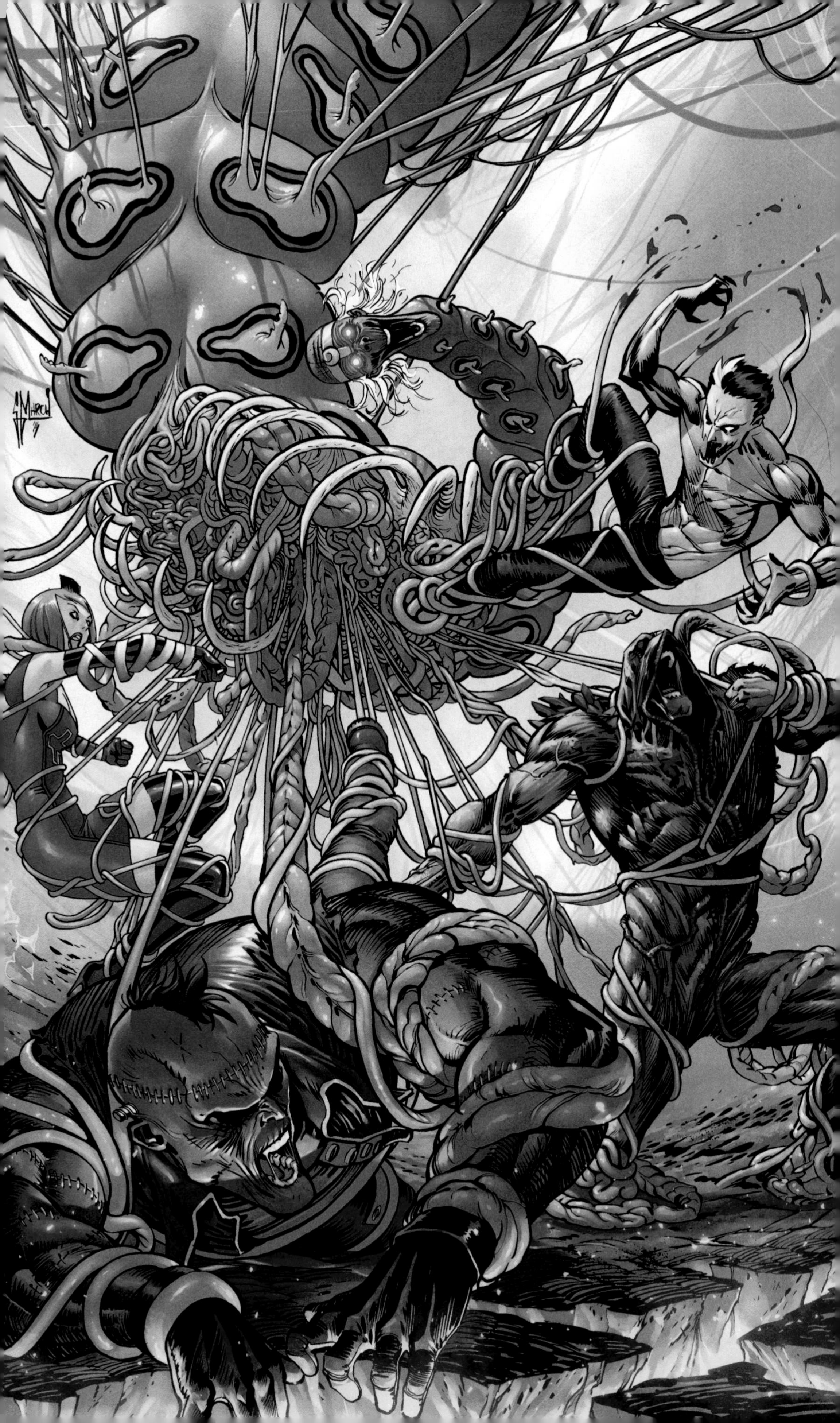

THE AMBER OF THE MOMENT PART 2: LONG AFTER TOMORROW

J.M. DEMATTEIS writer **ANDRES GUINALDO** penciller **WALDEN WONG** inker **CHRIS SOTOMAYOR** colorist
DEZI SIENTY letterer cover by **GUILLEM MARCH & TOMEU MOREY**

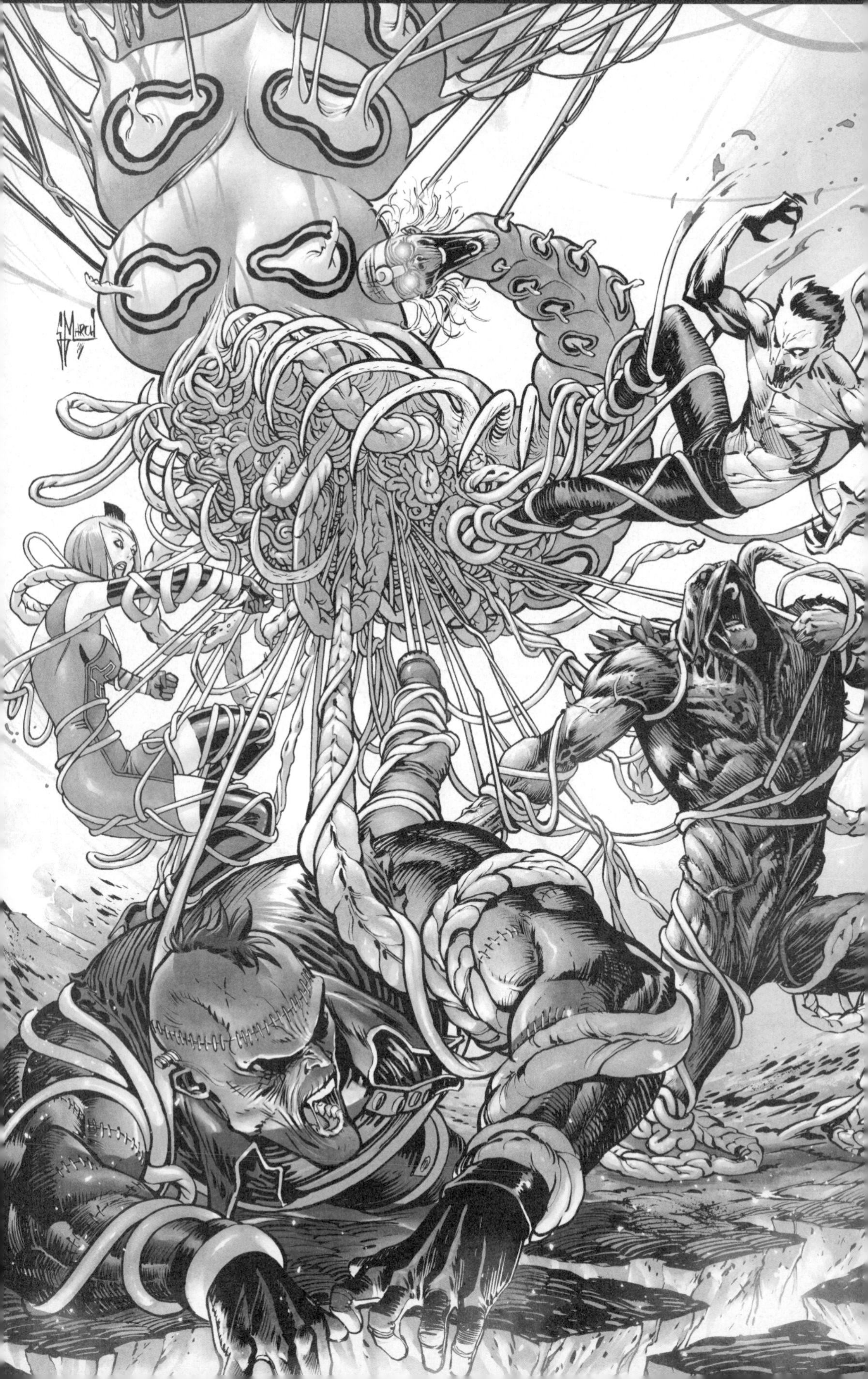

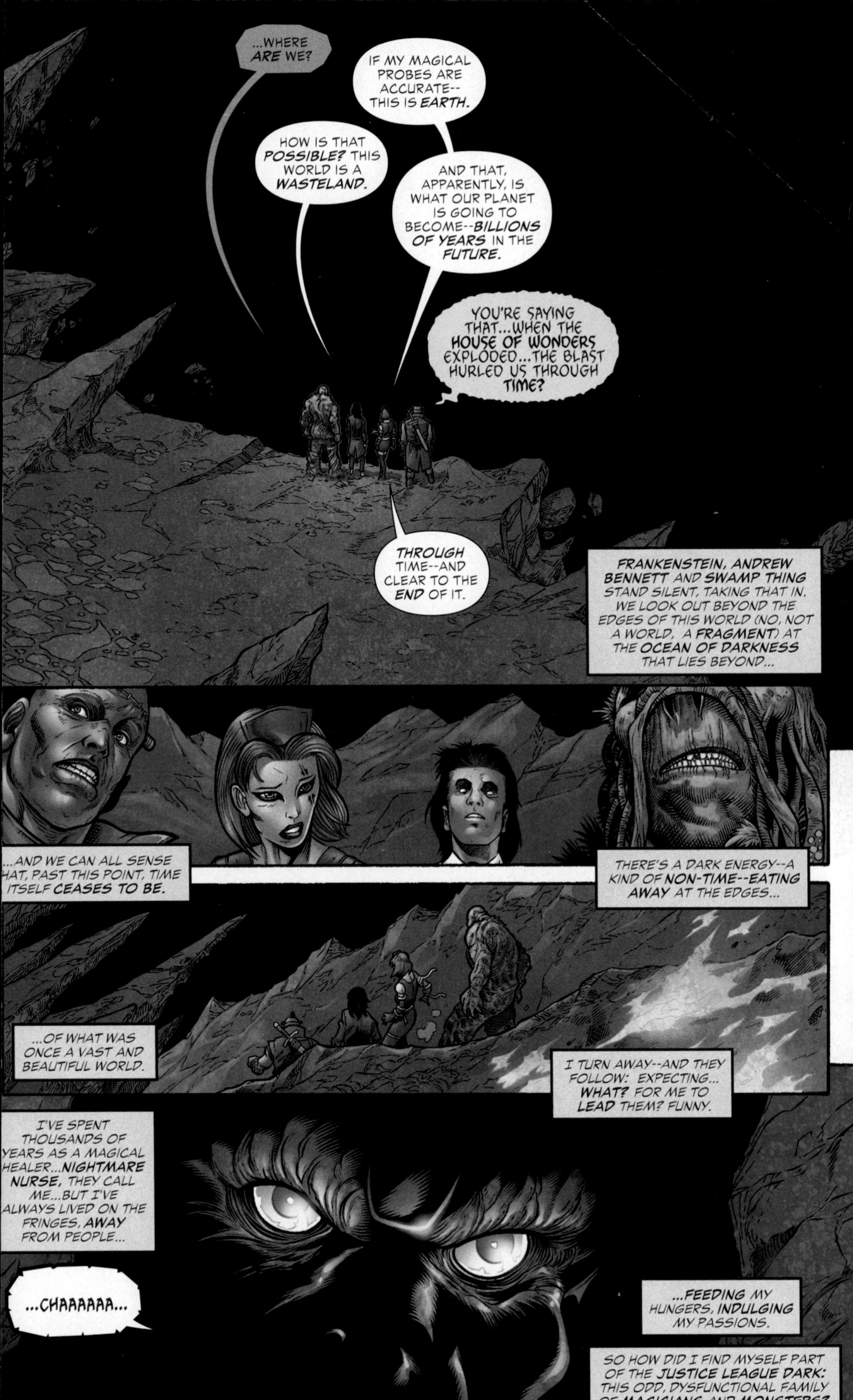
...WHERE ARE WE?
IF MY MAGICAL PROBES ARE ACCURATE-- THIS IS EARTH.
HOW IS THAT POSSIBLE? THIS WORLD IS A WASTELAND.
AND THAT, APPARENTLY, IS WHAT OUR PLANET IS GOING TO BECOME--BILLIONS OF YEARS IN THE FUTURE.
YOU'RE SAYING THAT...WHEN THE HOUSE OF WONDERS EXPLODED...THE BLAST HURLED US THROUGH TIME?
THROUGH TIME--AND CLEAR TO THE END OF IT.
FRANKENSTEIN, ANDREW BENNETT AND SWAMP THING STAND SILENT, TAKING THAT IN. WE LOOK OUT BEYOND THE EDGES OF THIS WORLD (NO, NOT A WORLD, A FRAGMENT) AT THE OCEAN OF DARKNESS THAT LIES BEYOND...
...AND WE CAN ALL SENSE HAT, PAST THIS POINT, TIME ITSELF CEASES TO BE.
THERE'S A DARK ENERGY--A KIND OF NON-TIME--EATING AWAY AT THE EDGES...
...OF WHAT WAS ONCE A VAST AND BEAUTIFUL WORLD.
I TURN AWAY--AND THEY FOLLOW: EXPECTING... WHAT? FOR ME TO LEAD THEM? FUNNY.
I'VE SPENT THOUSANDS OF YEARS AS A MAGICAL HEALER...NIGHTMARE NURSE, THEY CALL ME...BUT I'VE ALWAYS LIVED ON THE FRINGES, AWAY FROM PEOPLE...
...CHAAAAAAA...
...FEEDING MY HUNGERS, INDULGING MY PASSIONS.
SO HOW DID I FIND MYSELF PART OF THE JUSTICE LEAGUE DARK: THIS ODD, DYSFUNCTIONAL FAMILY

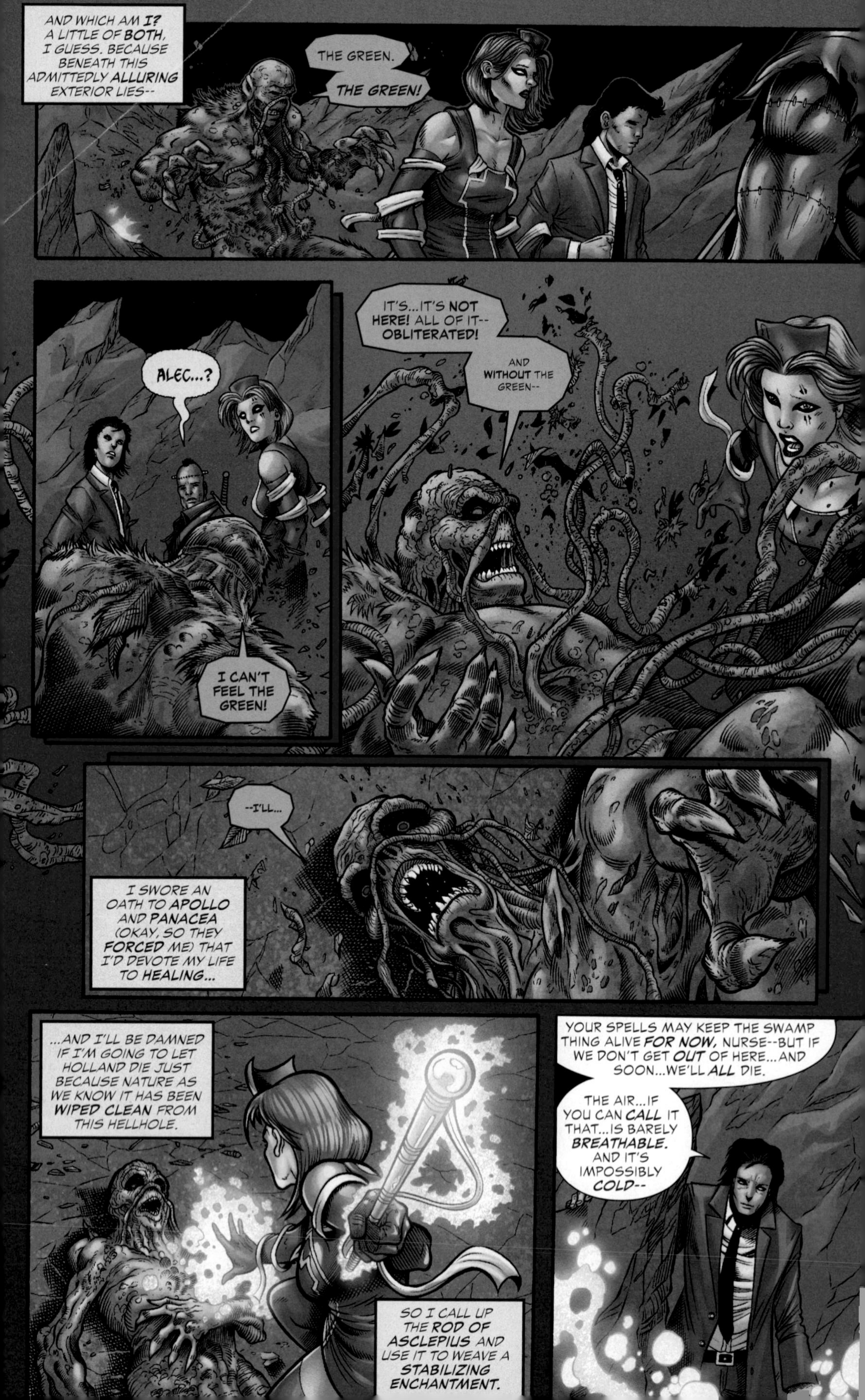
AND WHICH AM **I?** A LITTLE OF **BOTH**, I GUESS. BECAUSE BENEATH THIS ADMITTEDLY **ALLURING** EXTERIOR LIES--
THE GREEN.
THE GREEN!
ALEC...?
I CAN'T FEEL THE GREEN!
IT'S...IT'S **NOT HERE!** ALL OF IT-- **OBLITERATED!**
AND **WITHOUT** THE GREEN--
--I'LL...
I SWORE AN OATH TO **APOLLO** AND **PANACEA** (OKAY, SO THEY **FORCED** ME) THAT I'D DEVOTE MY LIFE TO **HEALING**...
...AND I'LL BE DAMNED IF I'M GOING TO LET HOLLAND DIE JUST BECAUSE NATURE AS WE KNOW IT HAS BEEN **WIPED CLEAN** FROM THIS HELLHOLE.
SO I CALL UP THE **ROD OF ASCLEPIUS** AND USE IT TO WEAVE A **STABILIZING ENCHANTMENT.**
YOUR SPELLS MAY KEEP THE SWAMP THING ALIVE **FOR NOW,** NURSE--BUT IF WE DON'T GET **OUT** OF HERE...AND SOON...WE'LL **ALL** DIE.
THE AIR...IF YOU CAN **CALL** THAT...IS BARELY **BREATHABLE.** AND IT'S IMPOSSIBLY **COLD--**

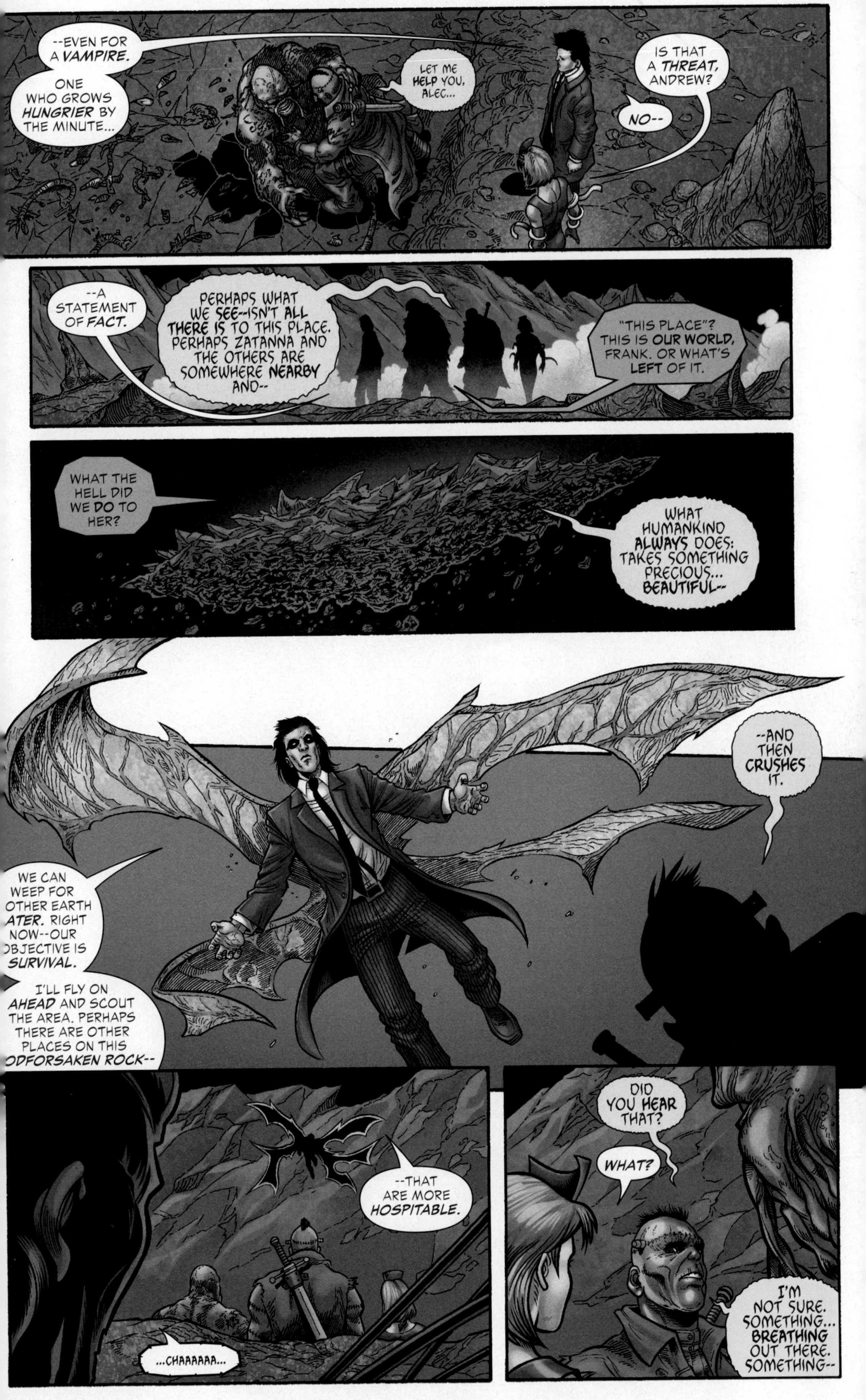

--EVEN FOR A VAMPIRE.
ONE WHO GROWS HUNGRIER BY THE MINUTE...
LET ME HELP YOU, ALEC...
IS THAT A THREAT, ANDREW?
NO--
--A STATEMENT OF FACT.
PERHAPS WHAT WE SEE--ISN'T ALL THERE IS TO THIS PLACE. PERHAPS ZATANNA AND THE OTHERS ARE SOMEWHERE NEARBY AND--
"THIS PLACE"? THIS IS OUR WORLD, FRANK. OR WHAT'S LEFT OF IT.
WHAT THE HELL DID WE DO TO HER?
WHAT HUMANKIND ALWAYS DOES: TAKES SOMETHING PRECIOUS... BEAUTIFUL--
--AND THEN CRUSHES IT.
WE CAN WEEP FOR OTHER EARTH ATER. RIGHT NOW--OUR OBJECTIVE IS SURVIVAL.
I'LL FLY ON AHEAD AND SCOUT THE AREA. PERHAPS THERE ARE OTHER PLACES ON THIS ODFORSAKEN ROCK--
--THAT ARE MORE HOSPITABLE.
...CHAAAAAA...
DID YOU HEAR THAT?
WHAT?
I'M NOT SURE. SOMETHING... BREATHING OUT THERE. SOMETHING--

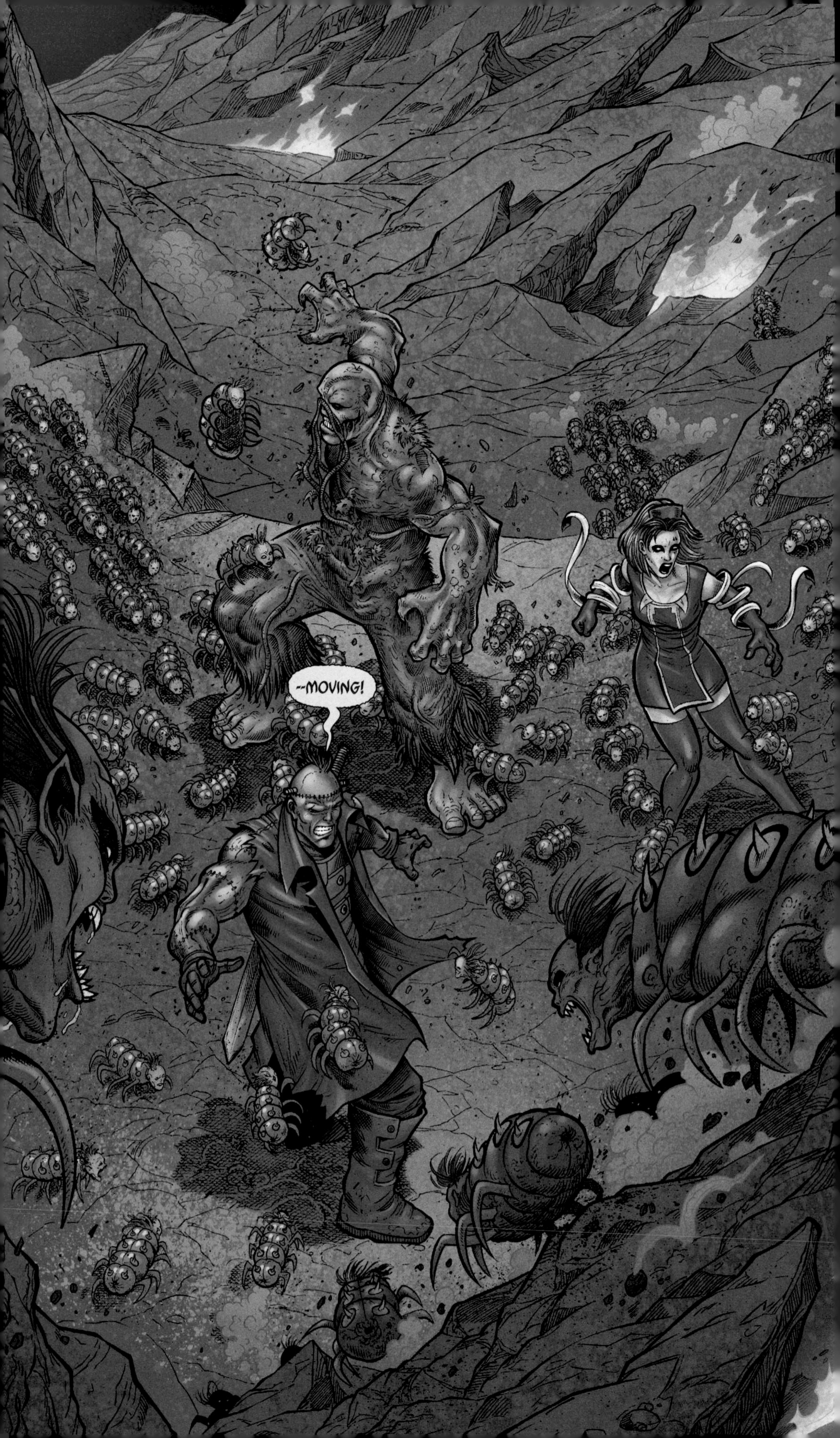
--MOVING!

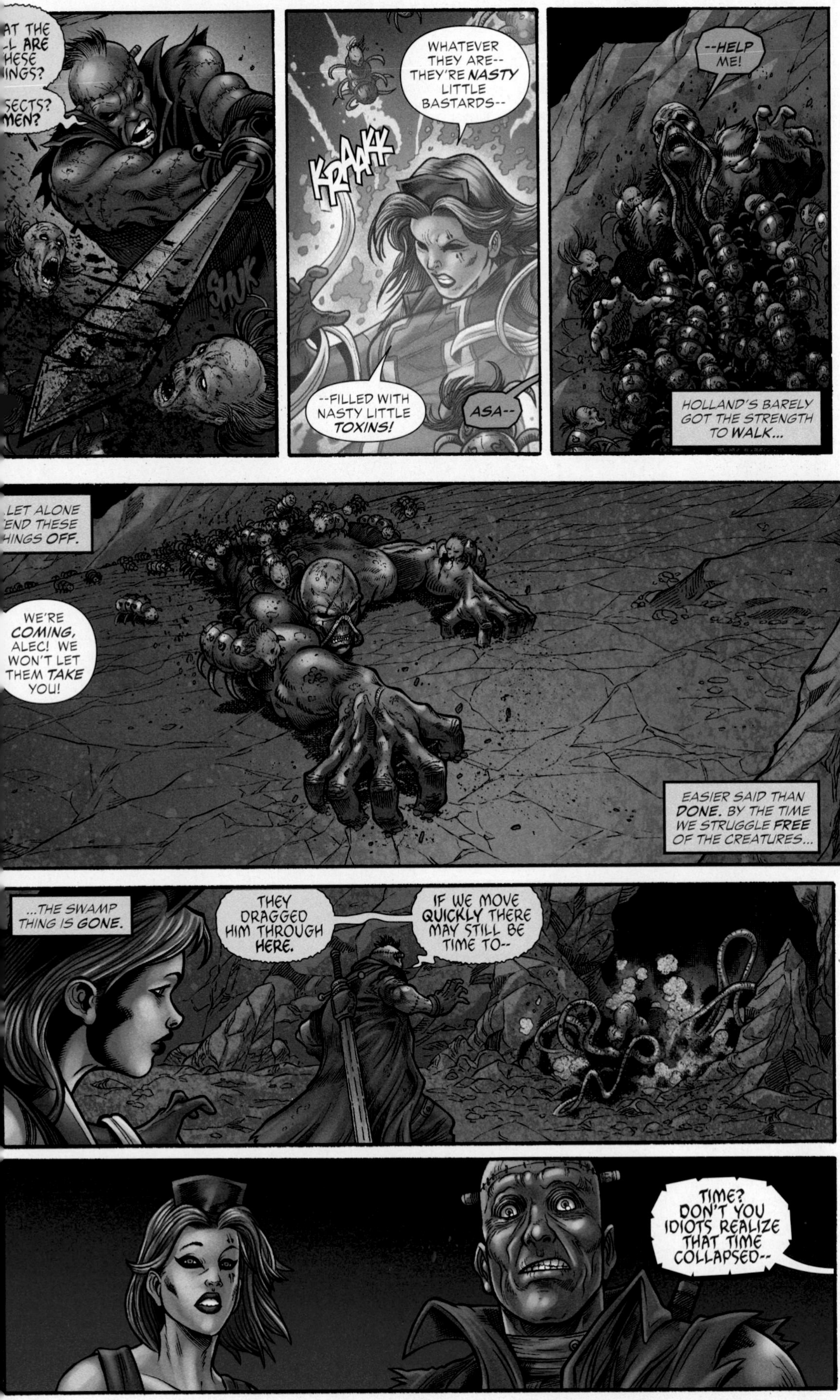
AT THE -L ARE HESE INGS? SECTS? MEN?
SHUK
WHATEVER THEY ARE-- THEY'RE NASTY LITTLE BASTARDS--
KRAAKK
--FILLED WITH NASTY LITTLE TOXINS!
ASA--
--HELP ME!
HOLLAND'S BARELY GOT THE STRENGTH TO WALK...
LET ALONE END THESE HINGS OFF.
WE'RE COMING, ALEC! WE WON'T LET THEM TAKE YOU!
EASIER SAID THAN DONE. BY THE TIME WE STRUGGLE FREE OF THE CREATURES...
...THE SWAMP THING IS GONE.
THEY DRAGGED HIM THROUGH HERE.
IF WE MOVE QUICKLY THERE MAY STILL BE TIME TO--
TIME? DON'T YOU IDIOTS REALIZE THAT TIME COLLAPSED--

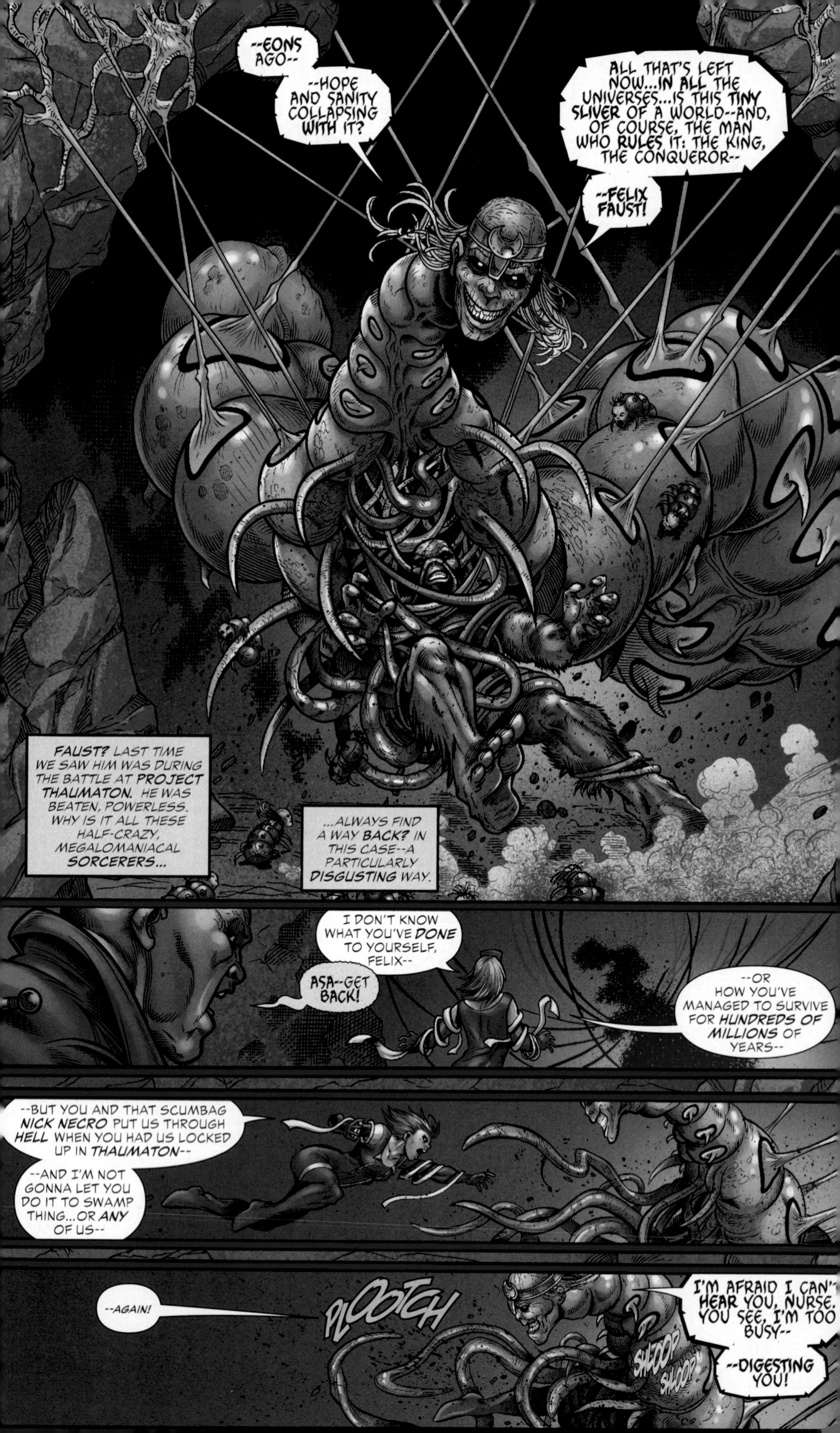
--EONS AGO--
--HOPE AND SANITY COLLAPSING WITH IT?
ALL THAT'S LEFT NOW...IN ALL THE UNIVERSES...IS THIS TINY SLIVER OF A WORLD--AND, OF COURSE, THE MAN WHO RULES IT: THE KING, THE CONQUEROR--
--FELIX FAUST!
FAUST? LAST TIME WE SAW HIM WAS DURING THE BATTLE AT PROJECT THAUMATON. HE WAS BEATEN, POWERLESS. WHY IS IT ALL THESE HALF-CRAZY, MEGALOMANIACAL SORCERERS...
...ALWAYS FIND A WAY BACK? IN THIS CASE--A PARTICULARLY DISGUSTING WAY.
I DON'T KNOW WHAT YOU'VE DONE TO YOURSELF, FELIX--
ASA--GET BACK!
--OR HOW YOU'VE MANAGED TO SURVIVE FOR HUNDREDS OF MILLIONS OF YEARS--
--BUT YOU AND THAT SCUMBAG NICK NECRO PUT US THROUGH HELL WHEN YOU HAD US LOCKED UP IN THAUMATON--
--AND I'M NOT GONNA LET YOU DO IT TO SWAMP THING...OR ANY OF US--
--AGAIN!
PLOOTCH
I'M AFRAID I CAN'T HEAR YOU, NURSE. YOU SEE, I'M TOO BUSY--
SHLOOP
SHLOOP
--DIGESTING YOU!

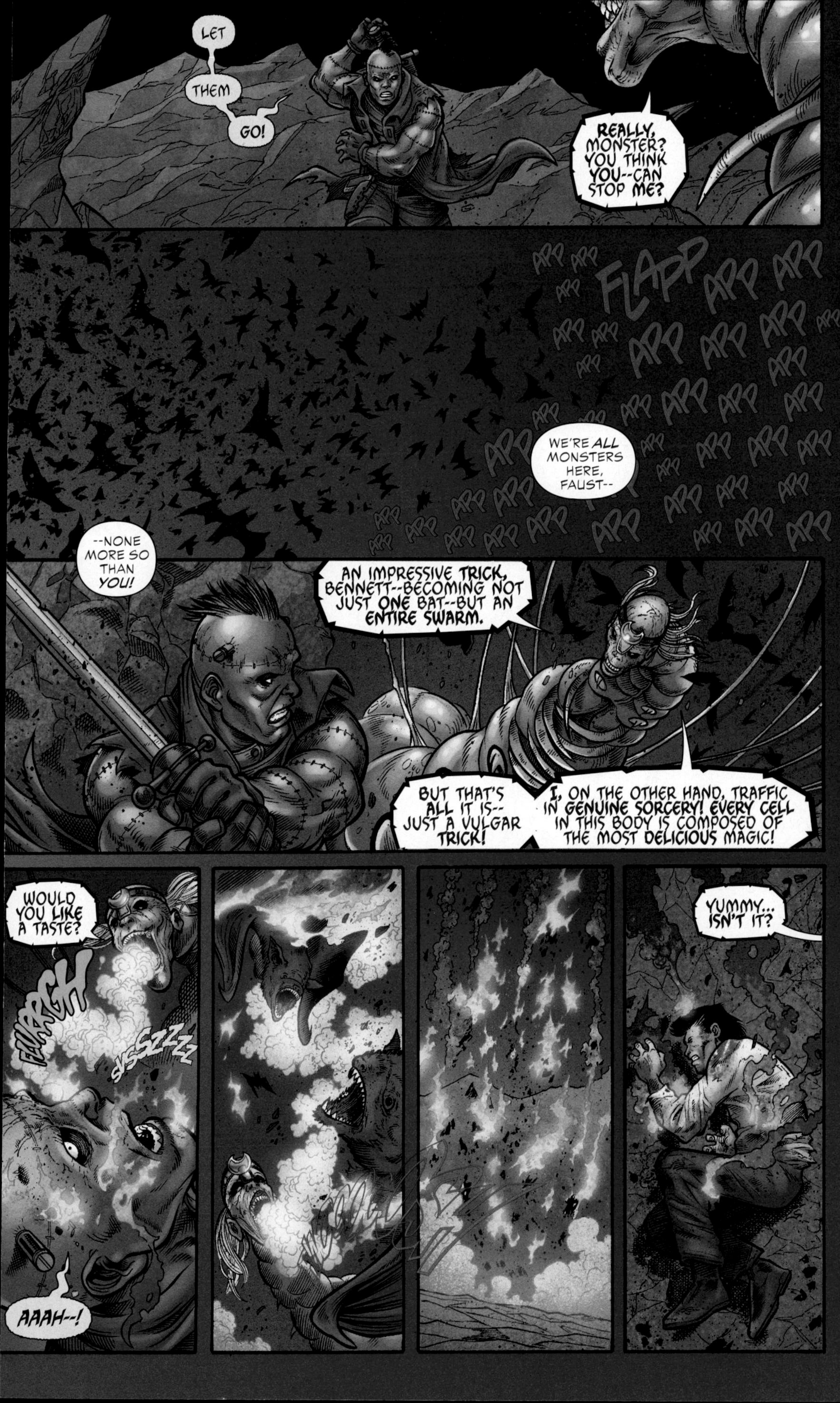
LET THEM GO!
REALLY, MONSTER? YOU THINK YOU--CAN STOP ME?
FLAPP APP APP APP
WE'RE ALL MONSTERS HERE, FAUST--
--NONE MORE SO THAN YOU!
AN IMPRESSIVE TRICK, BENNETT--BECOMING NOT JUST ONE BAT--BUT AN ENTIRE SWARM.
BUT THAT'S ALL IT IS--JUST A VULGAR TRICK!
I, ON THE OTHER HAND, TRAFFIC IN GENUINE SORCERY! EVERY CELL IN THIS BODY IS COMPOSED OF THE MOST DELICIOUS MAGIC!
WOULD YOU LIKE A TASTE?
FWARGH
SSSSZZZZ
AAAH--!
YUMMY... ISN'T IT?

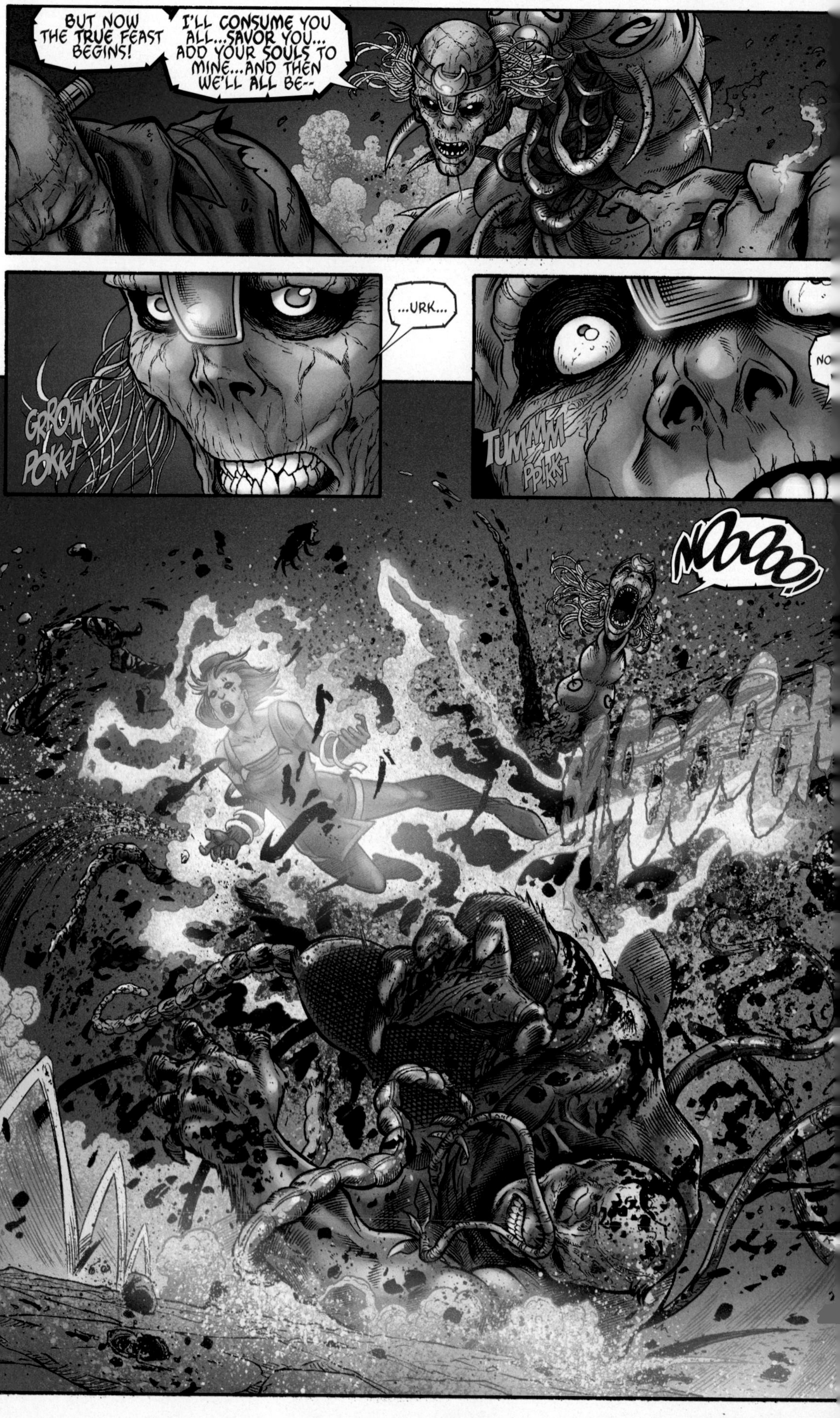
BUT NOW THE TRUE FEAST BEGINS!
I'LL CONSUME YOU ALL...SAVOR YOU... ADD YOUR SOULS TO MINE...AND THEN WE'LL ALL BE--
GRROWKK POKK-T
...URK...
TUMMM PPKKT
NO
NOOOOO!

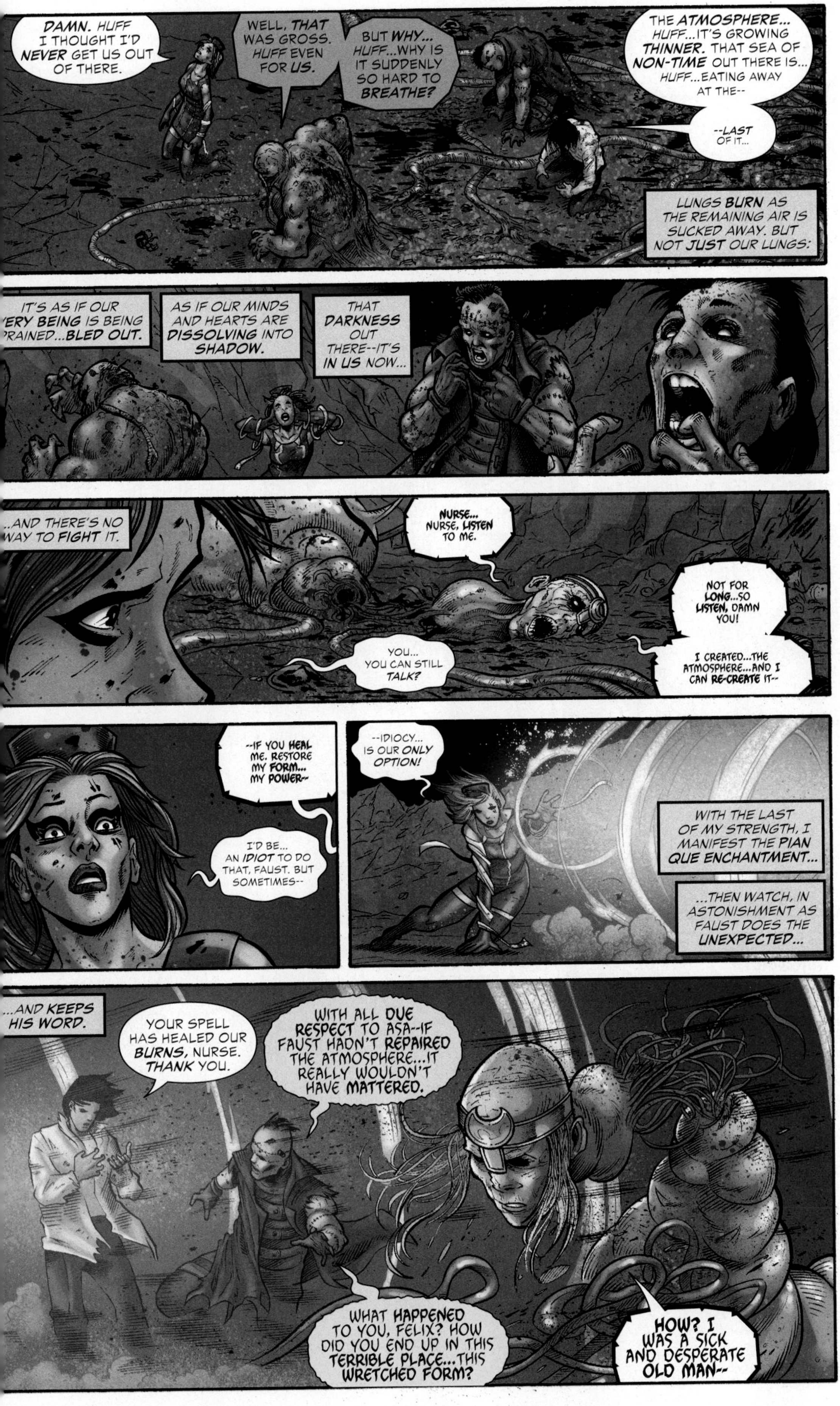
DAMN. HUFF I THOUGHT I'D NEVER GET US OUT OF THERE.
WELL, THAT WAS GROSS. HUFF EVEN FOR US.
BUT WHY... HUFF...WHY IS IT SUDDENLY SO HARD TO BREATHE?
THE ATMOSPHERE... HUFF...IT'S GROWING THINNER. THAT SEA OF NON-TIME OUT THERE IS... HUFF...EATING AWAY AT THE--
--LAST OF IT...
LUNGS BURN AS THE REMAINING AIR IS SUCKED AWAY. BUT NOT JUST OUR LUNGS:
IT'S AS IF OUR VERY BEING IS BEING DRAINED...BLED OUT.
AS IF OUR MINDS AND HEARTS ARE DISSOLVING INTO SHADOW.
THAT DARKNESS OUT THERE--IT'S IN US NOW...
...AND THERE'S NO WAY TO FIGHT IT.
NURSE... NURSE, LISTEN TO ME.
YOU... YOU CAN STILL TALK?
NOT FOR LONG...SO LISTEN, DAMN YOU!
I CREATED...THE ATMOSPHERE...AND I CAN RE-CREATE IT--
--IF YOU HEAL ME. RESTORE MY FORM... MY POWER--
I'D BE... AN IDIOT TO DO THAT, FAUST. BUT SOMETIMES--
--IDIOCY... IS OUR ONLY OPTION!
WITH THE LAST OF MY STRENGTH, I MANIFEST THE PIAN QUE ENCHANTMENT...
...THEN WATCH, IN ASTONISHMENT AS FAUST DOES THE UNEXPECTED...
...AND KEEPS HIS WORD.
YOUR SPELL HAS HEALED OUR BURNS, NURSE. THANK YOU.
WITH ALL DUE RESPECT TO ASA--IF FAUST HADN'T REPAIRED THE ATMOSPHERE...IT REALLY WOULDN'T HAVE MATTERED.
WHAT HAPPENED TO YOU, FELIX? HOW DID YOU END UP IN THIS TERRIBLE PLACE...THIS WRETCHED FORM?
HOW? I WAS A SICK AND DESPERATE OLD MAN--

--AND...AFTER DECADES OF SEARCHING...I FOUND IT: THE LOST BOOK OF TITHONUS. AND WITHIN THAT BOOK:

THE KEY TO IMMORTALITY.

EVERY MAN DREAMS OF ETERNAL LIFE--

--BUT FAUST ALONE ACHIEVED IT: LIVING ON AGE--

--AF AG

--AF AG

BUT IN ORDER TO SURVIVE THE INEVITABLE CHANGES TO THE EARTH'S ENVIRONMENT--

--I HAD TO EVOLVE. MUTATE. BECOME--

--THIS.

HUMANKIND ABANDONED THE WORLD LONG AGO...BUT I REMAINED:

THE KING. THE CONQUEROR. LORD AND MASTER.

FOOL.

SUCH TERRIBLE LONELINESS.

MORE THAN ANY OF YOU COULD EVER IMAGINE.

SO...TO ASSUAGE MY COSMIC LONELINESS... I BIRTHED MY OTHER-SELVES--

--OUT OF MY OWN FLESH AND CONSCIOUSNESS.

BUT STILL THE EONS CRAWLED ON. ALL LIFEFORMS ON ALL WORLDS PASSED AWAY.

TIME ITSEL PERISHED BUT FAUS

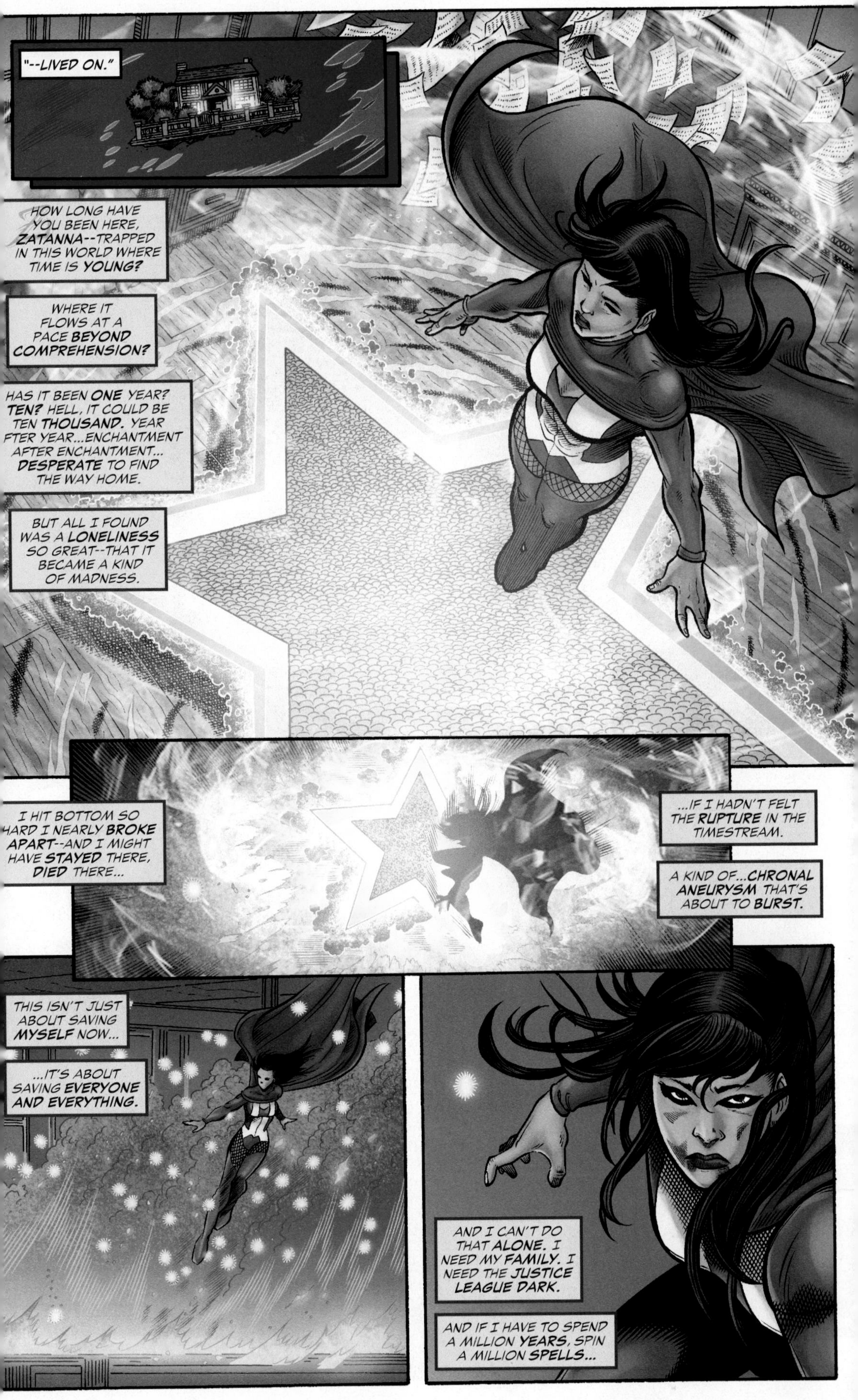

"--LIVED ON."
HOW LONG HAVE YOU BEEN HERE, ZATANNA--TRAPPED IN THIS WORLD WHERE TIME IS YOUNG?
WHERE IT FLOWS AT A PACE BEYOND COMPREHENSION?
HAS IT BEEN ONE YEAR? TEN? HELL, IT COULD BE TEN THOUSAND. YEAR FTER YEAR...ENCHANTMENT AFTER ENCHANTMENT... DESPERATE TO FIND THE WAY HOME.
BUT ALL I FOUND WAS A LONELINESS SO GREAT--THAT IT BECAME A KIND OF MADNESS.
I HIT BOTTOM SO HARD I NEARLY BROKE APART--AND I MIGHT HAVE STAYED THERE, DIED THERE...
...IF I HADN'T FELT THE RUPTURE IN THE TIMESTREAM.
A KIND OF...CHRONAL ANEURYSM THAT'S ABOUT TO BURST.
THIS ISN'T JUST ABOUT SAVING MYSELF NOW...
...IT'S ABOUT SAVING EVERYONE AND EVERYTHING.
AND I CAN'T DO THAT ALONE. I NEED MY FAMILY. I NEED THE JUSTICE LEAGUE DARK.
AND IF I HAVE TO SPEND A MILLION YEARS, SPIN A MILLION SPELLS...

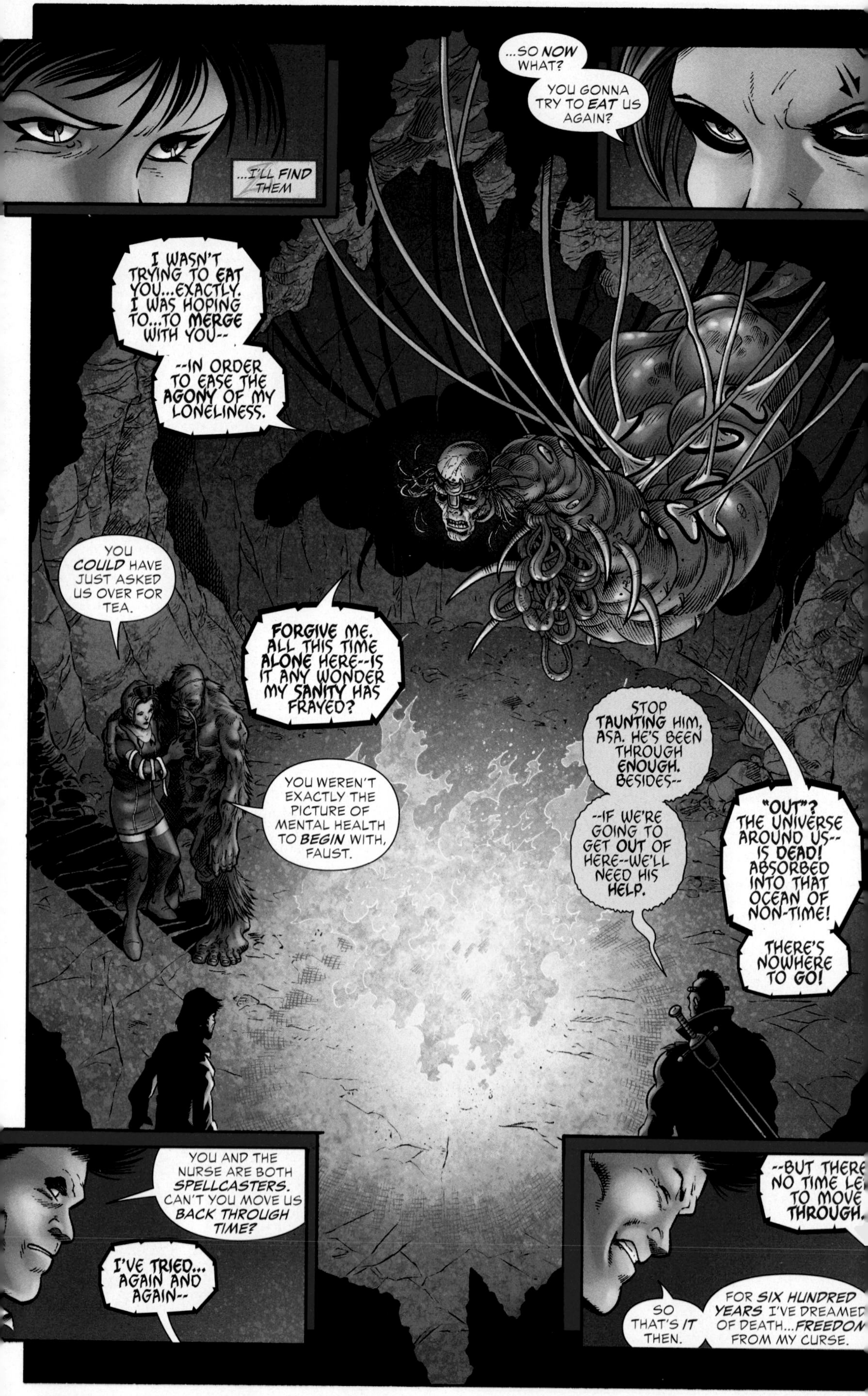

...I'LL FIND THEM
...SO NOW WHAT?
YOU GONNA TRY TO EAT US AGAIN?
I WASN'T TRYING TO EAT YOU...EXACTLY. I WAS HOPING TO...TO MERGE WITH YOU--
--IN ORDER TO EASE THE AGONY OF MY LONELINESS.
YOU COULD HAVE JUST ASKED US OVER FOR TEA.
FORGIVE ME. ALL THIS TIME ALONE HERE--IS IT ANY WONDER MY SANITY HAS FRAYED?
YOU WEREN'T EXACTLY THE PICTURE OF MENTAL HEALTH TO BEGIN WITH, FAUST.
STOP TAUNTING HIM, ASA. HE'S BEEN THROUGH ENOUGH. BESIDES--
--IF WE'RE GOING TO GET OUT OF HERE--WE'LL NEED HIS HELP.
"OUT"? THE UNIVERSE AROUND US--IS DEAD! ABSORBED INTO THAT OCEAN OF NON-TIME!
THERE'S NOWHERE TO GO!
YOU AND THE NURSE ARE BOTH SPELLCASTERS. CAN'T YOU MOVE US BACK THROUGH TIME?
I'VE TRIED... AGAIN AND AGAIN--
--BUT THERE NO TIME LE TO MOVE THROUGH.
SO THAT'S IT THEN.
FOR SIX HUNDRED YEARS I'VE DREAMED OF DEATH...FREEDOM FROM MY CURSE.

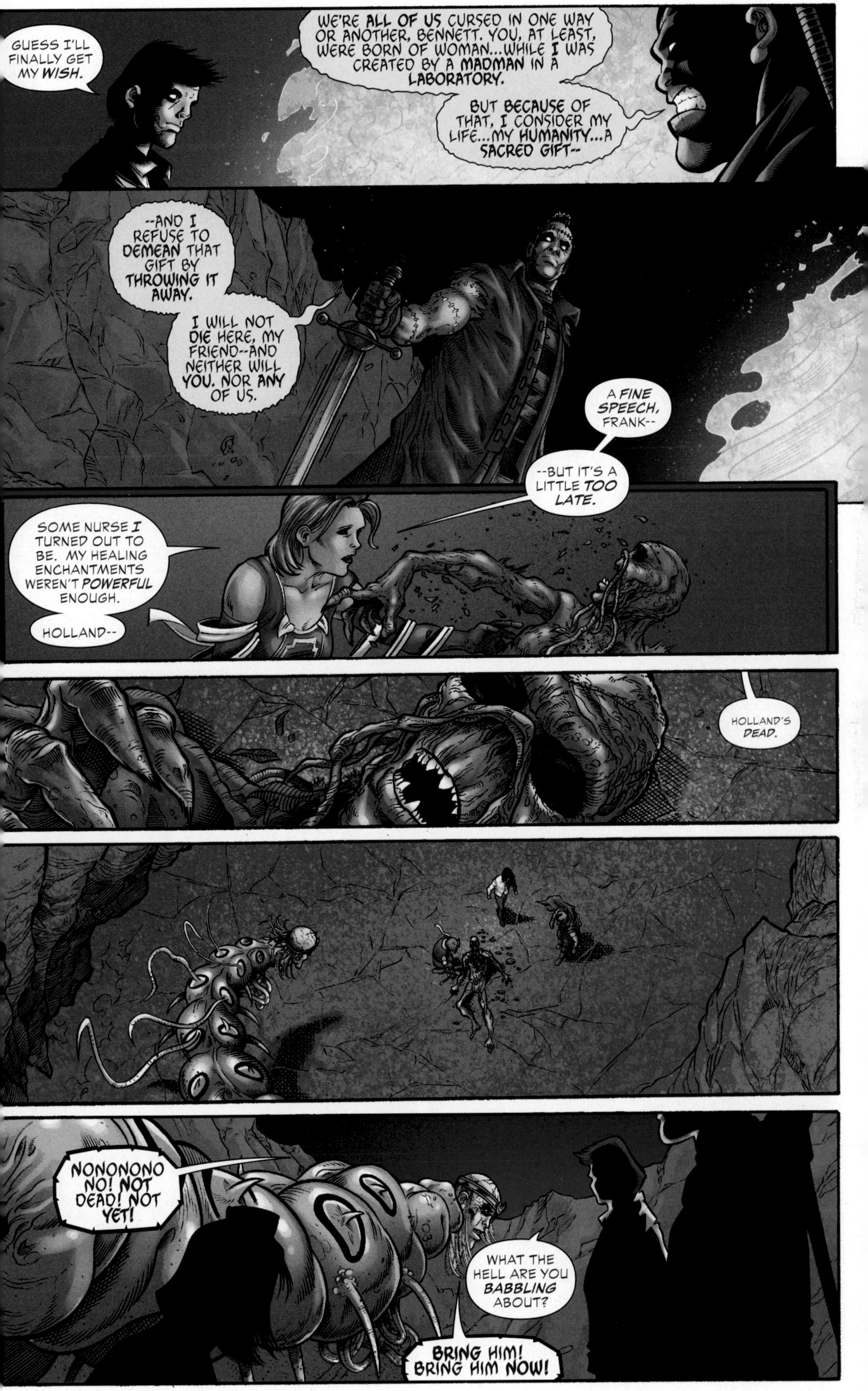
GUESS I'LL FINALLY GET MY WISH.
WE'RE ALL OF US CURSED IN ONE WAY OR ANOTHER, BENNETT. YOU, AT LEAST, WERE BORN OF WOMAN...WHILE I WAS CREATED BY A MADMAN IN A LABORATORY.
BUT BECAUSE OF THAT, I CONSIDER MY LIFE...MY HUMANITY...A SACRED GIFT--
--AND I REFUSE TO DEMEAN THAT GIFT BY THROWING IT AWAY.
I WILL NOT DIE HERE, MY FRIEND--AND NEITHER WILL YOU. NOR ANY OF US.
A FINE SPEECH, FRANK--
--BUT IT'S A LITTLE TOO LATE.
SOME NURSE I TURNED OUT TO BE. MY HEALING ENCHANTMENTS WEREN'T POWERFUL ENOUGH.
HOLLAND--
HOLLAND'S DEAD.
NONONONO NO! NOT DEAD! NOT YET!
WHAT THE HELL ARE YOU BABBLING ABOUT?
BRING HIM! BRING HIM NOW!

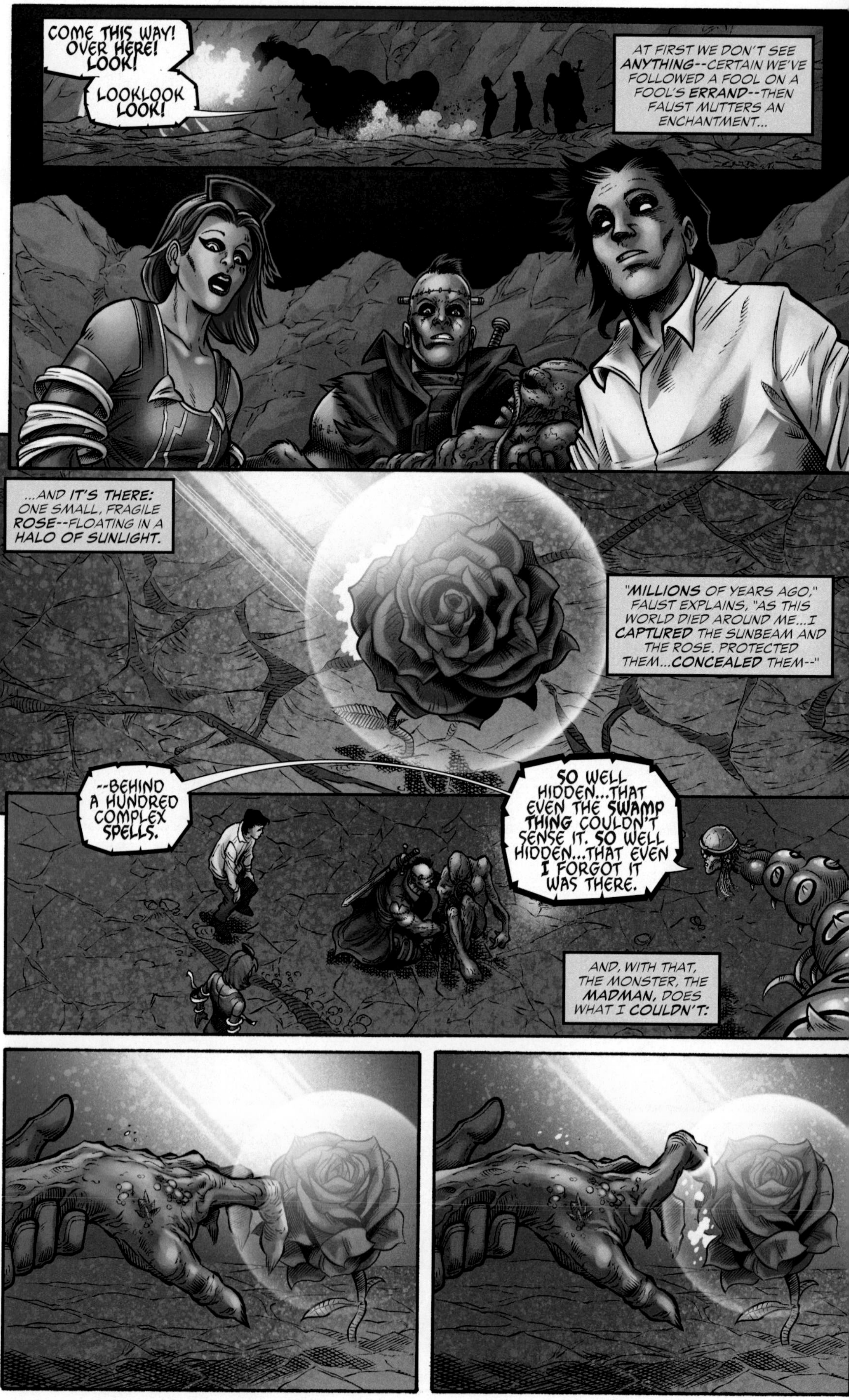

COME THIS WAY! OVER HERE! LOOK!
LOOKLOOK LOOK!
AT FIRST WE DON'T SEE ANYTHING--CERTAIN WE'VE FOLLOWED A FOOL ON A FOOL'S ERRAND--THEN FAUST MUTTERS AN ENCHANTMENT...
...AND IT'S THERE: ONE SMALL, FRAGILE ROSE--FLOATING IN A HALO OF SUNLIGHT.
"MILLIONS OF YEARS AGO," FAUST EXPLAINS, "AS THIS WORLD DIED AROUND ME...I CAPTURED THE SUNBEAM AND THE ROSE. PROTECTED THEM...CONCEALED THEM--"
--BEHIND A HUNDRED COMPLEX SPELLS.
SO WELL HIDDEN...THAT EVEN THE SWAMP THING COULDN'T SENSE IT. SO WELL HIDDEN...THAT EVEN I FORGOT IT WAS THERE.
AND, WITH THAT, THE MONSTER, THE MADMAN, DOES WHAT I COULDN'T:

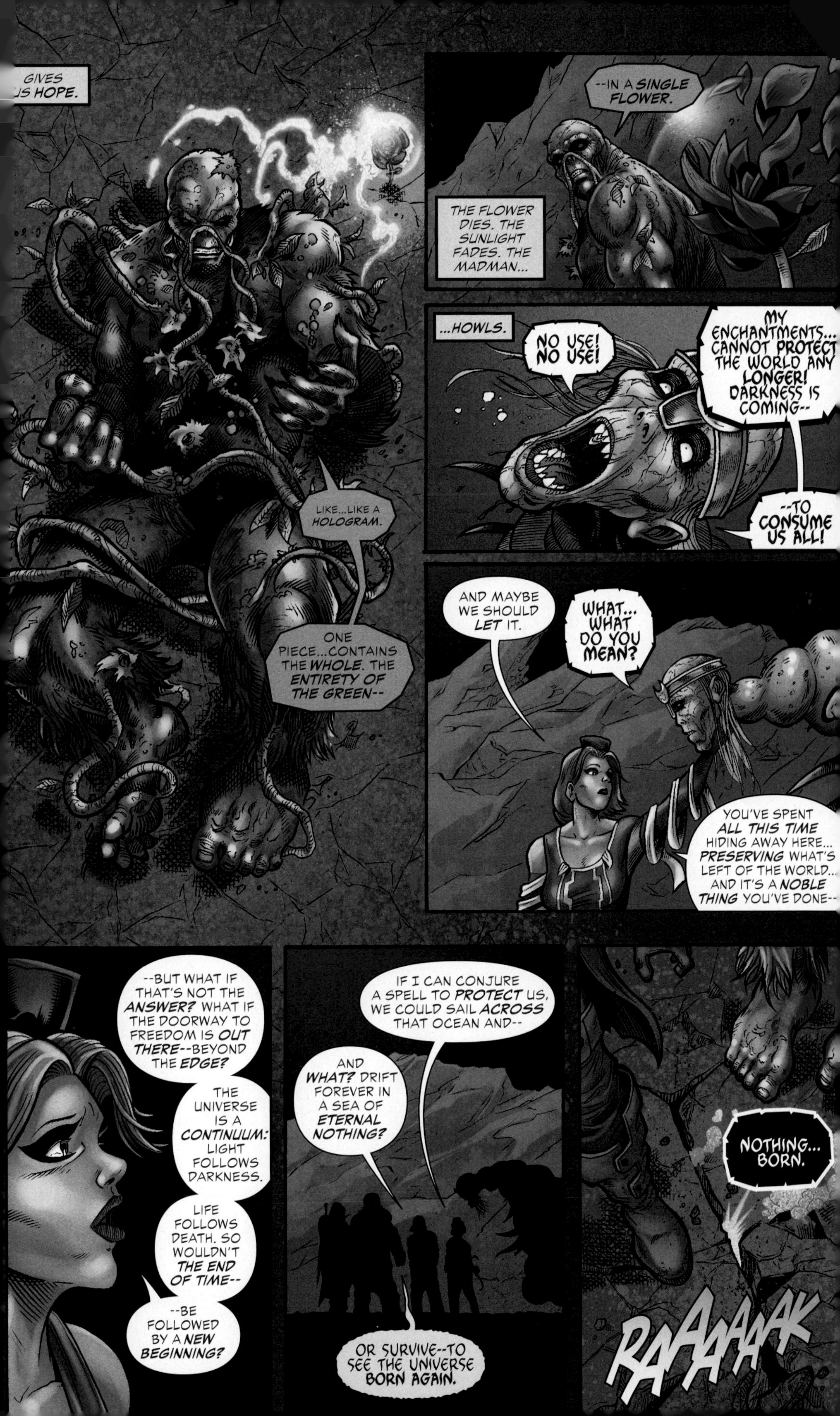
GIVES US HOPE.
--IN A SINGLE FLOWER.
THE FLOWER DIES. THE SUNLIGHT FADES. THE MADMAN...
...HOWLS.
NO USE! NO USE!
MY ENCHANTMENTS... CANNOT PROTECT THE WORLD ANY LONGER! DARKNESS IS COMING--
--TO CONSUME US ALL!
LIKE...LIKE A HOLOGRAM.
ONE PIECE...CONTAINS THE WHOLE. THE ENTIRETY OF THE GREEN--
AND MAYBE WE SHOULD LET IT.
WHAT... WHAT DO YOU MEAN?
YOU'VE SPENT ALL THIS TIME HIDING AWAY HERE... PRESERVING WHAT'S LEFT OF THE WORLD... AND IT'S A NOBLE THING YOU'VE DONE--
--BUT WHAT IF THAT'S NOT THE ANSWER? WHAT IF THE DOORWAY TO FREEDOM IS OUT THERE--BEYOND THE EDGE?
THE UNIVERSE IS A CONTINUUM: LIGHT FOLLOWS DARKNESS.
LIFE FOLLOWS DEATH. SO WOULDN'T THE END OF TIME--
--BE FOLLOWED BY A NEW BEGINNING?
IF I CAN CONJURE A SPELL TO PROTECT US, WE COULD SAIL ACROSS THAT OCEAN AND--
AND WHAT? DRIFT FOREVER IN A SEA OF ETERNAL NOTHING?
OR SURVIVE--TO SEE THE UNIVERSE BORN AGAIN.
NOTHING... BORN.
RAAAAAAK

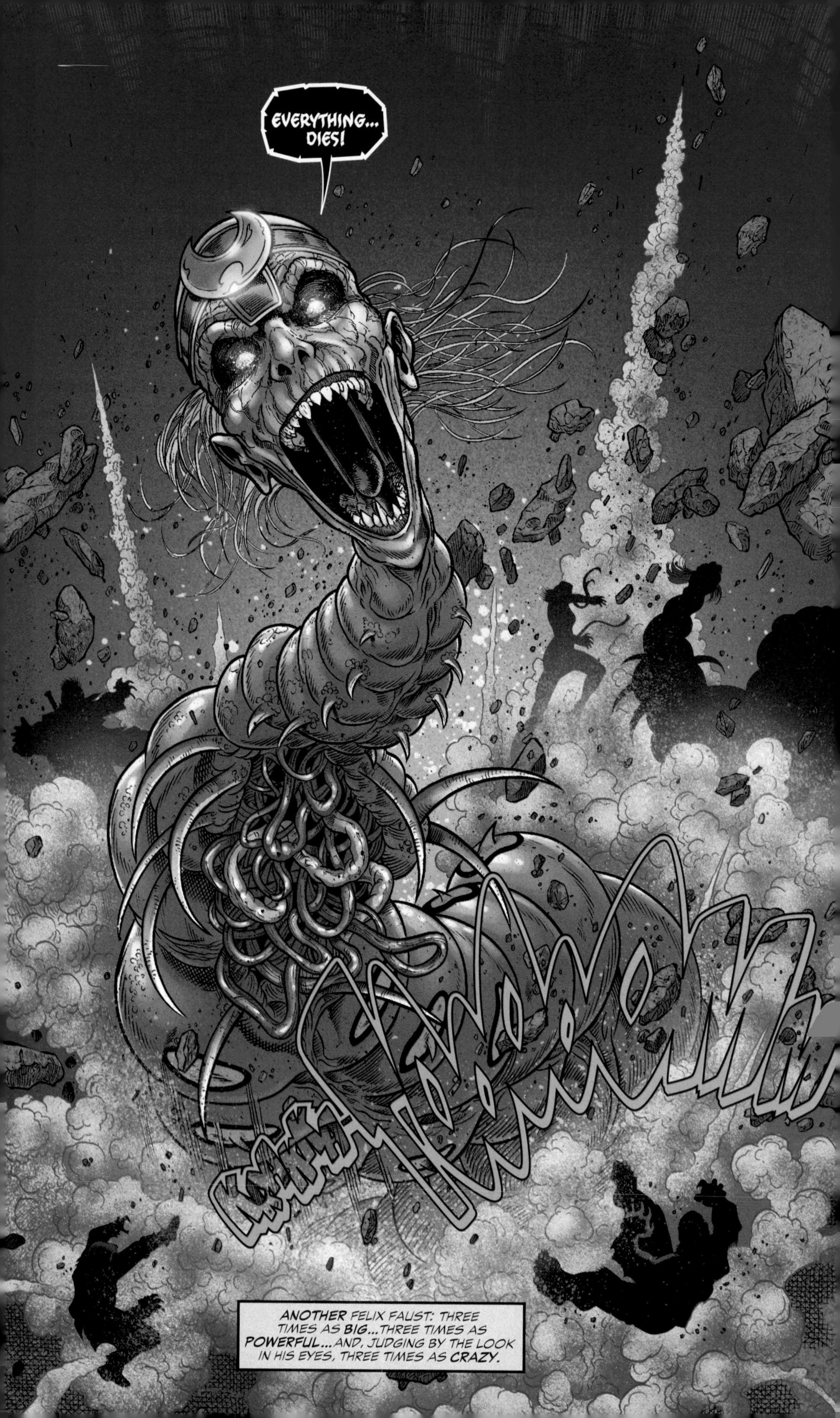
EVERYTHING... DIES!
ANOTHER FELIX FAUST: THREE TIMES AS BIG...THREE TIMES AS POWERFUL...AND, JUDGING BY THE LOOK IN HIS EYES, THREE TIMES AS CRAZY.

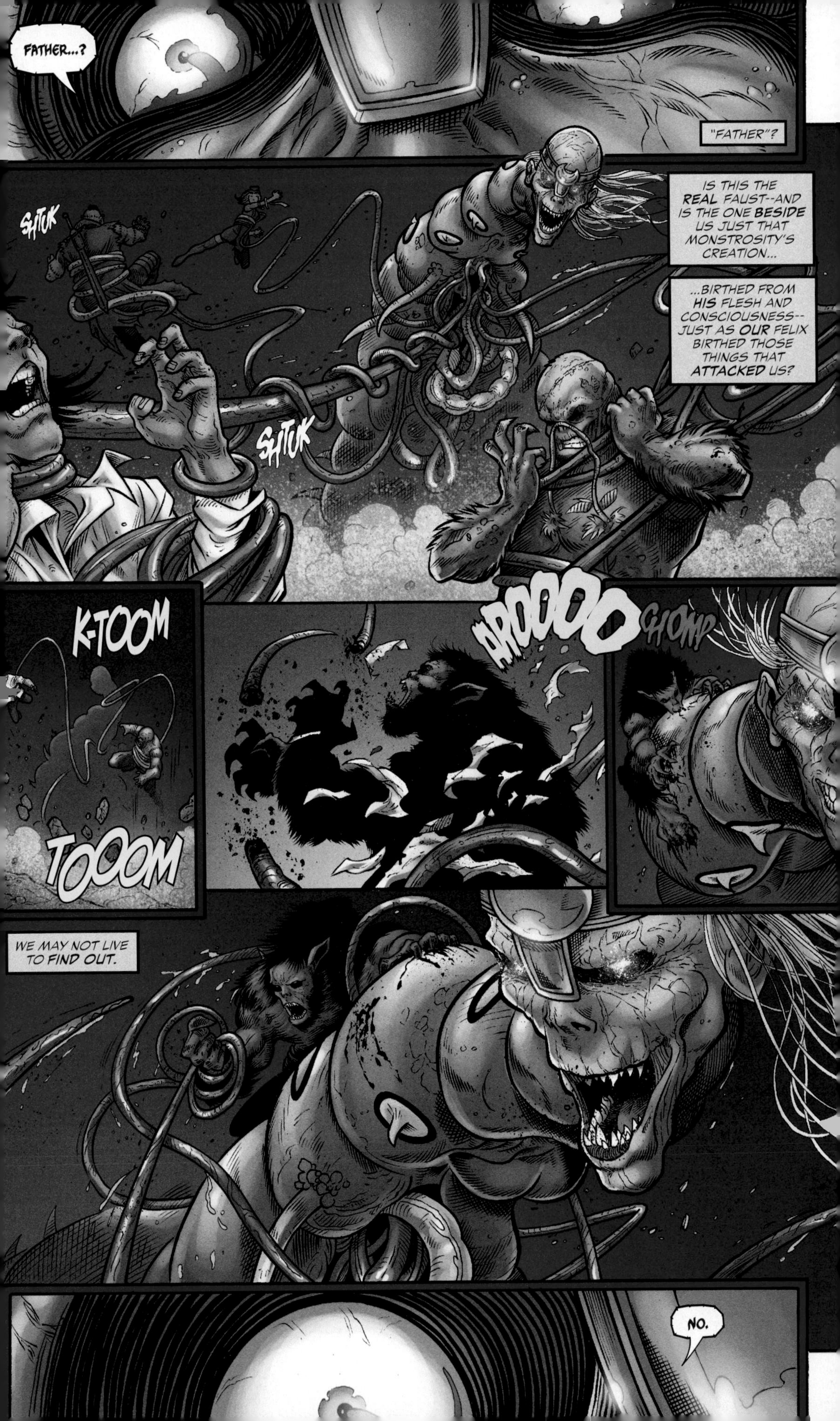
FATHER...?
"FATHER"?
SHTUK
IS THIS THE REAL FAUST--AND IS THE ONE BESIDE US JUST THAT MONSTROSITY'S CREATION...
...BIRTHED FROM HIS FLESH AND CONSCIOUSNESS-- JUST AS OUR FELIX BIRTHED THOSE THINGS THAT ATTACKED US?
SHTUK
K-TOOM
TOOOM
AROOOOO
CHOMP
WE MAY NOT LIVE TO FIND OUT.
NO.

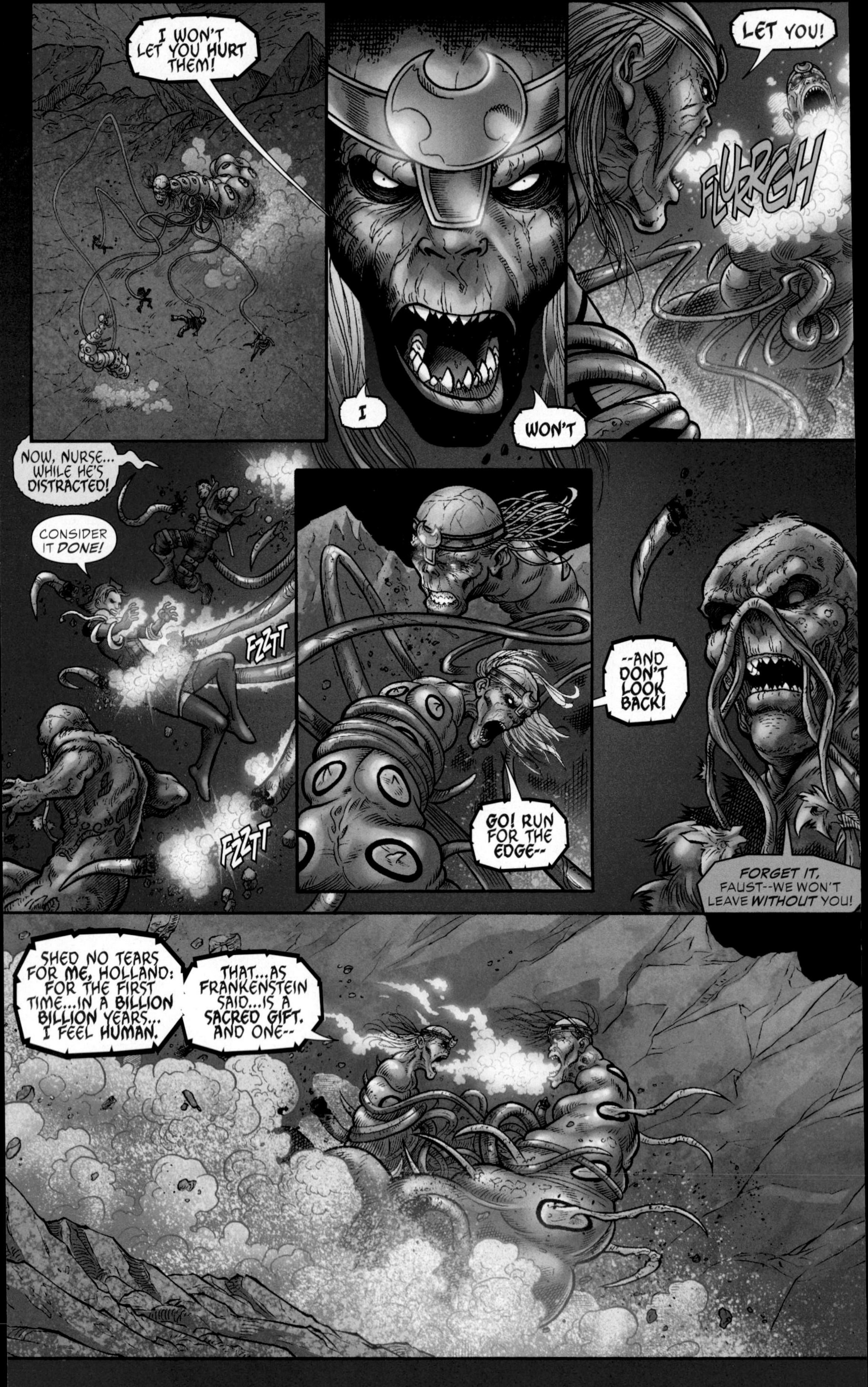

I WON'T LET YOU HURT THEM!
I
WON'T
LET YOU!
FLURGH
NOW, NURSE... WHILE HE'S DISTRACTED!
CONSIDER IT DONE!
FZZTT
FZZTT
GO! RUN FOR THE EDGE--
--AND DON'T LOOK BACK!
FORGET IT, FAUST--WE WON'T LEAVE WITHOUT YOU!
SHED NO TEARS FOR ME, HOLLAND: FOR THE FIRST TIME...IN A BILLION BILLION YEARS... I FEEL HUMAN.
THAT...AS FRANKENSTEIN SAID...IS A SACRED GIFT. AND ONE--

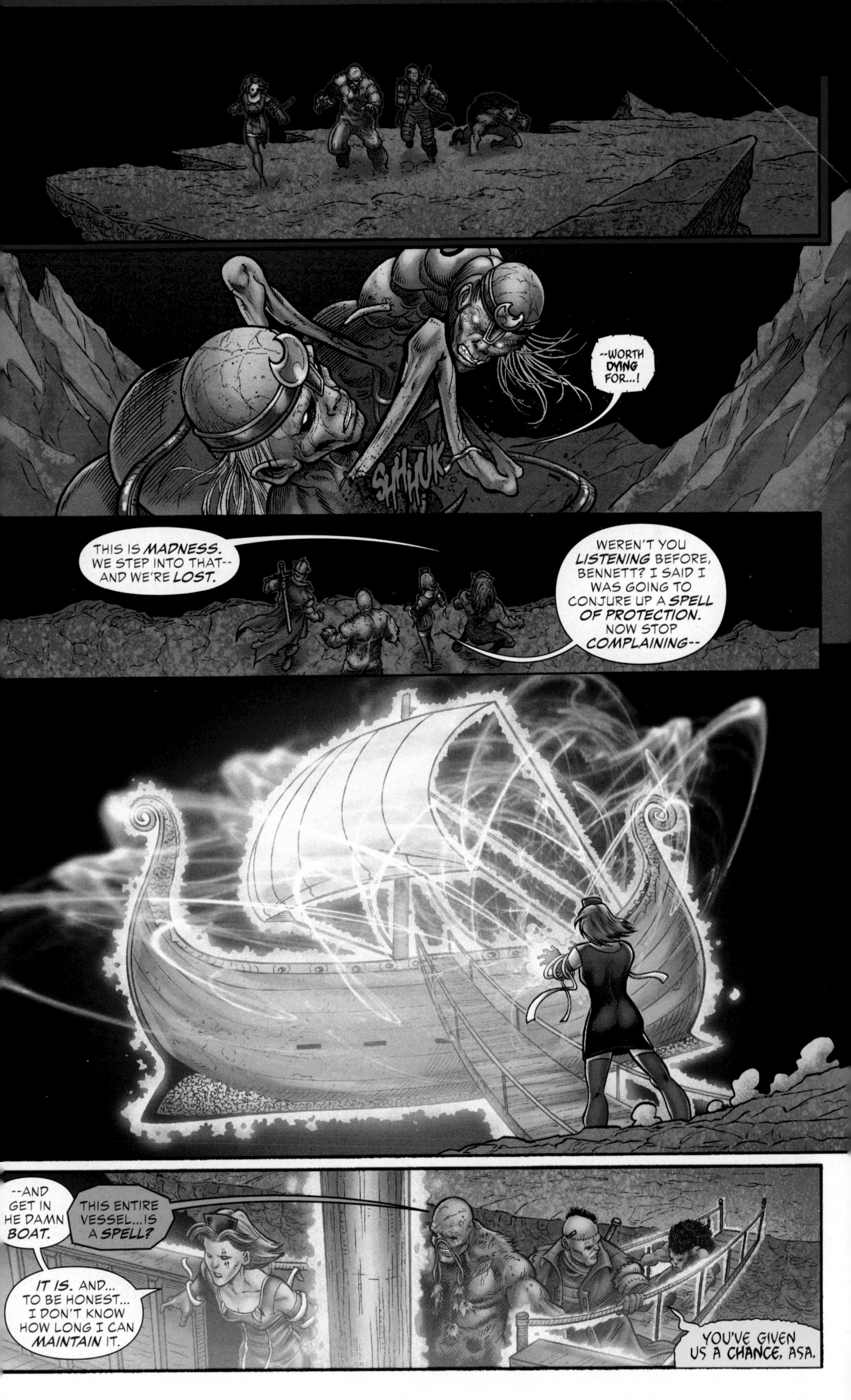
--WORTH DYING FOR...!
SHHUK
THIS IS MADNESS. WE STEP INTO THAT-- AND WE'RE LOST.
WEREN'T YOU LISTENING BEFORE, BENNETT? I SAID I WAS GOING TO CONJURE UP A SPELL OF PROTECTION. NOW STOP COMPLAINING--
--AND GET IN HE DAMN BOAT.
THIS ENTIRE VESSEL...IS A SPELL?
IT IS. AND... TO BE HONEST... I DON'T KNOW HOW LONG I CAN MAINTAIN IT.
YOU'VE GIVEN US A CHANCE, ASA.

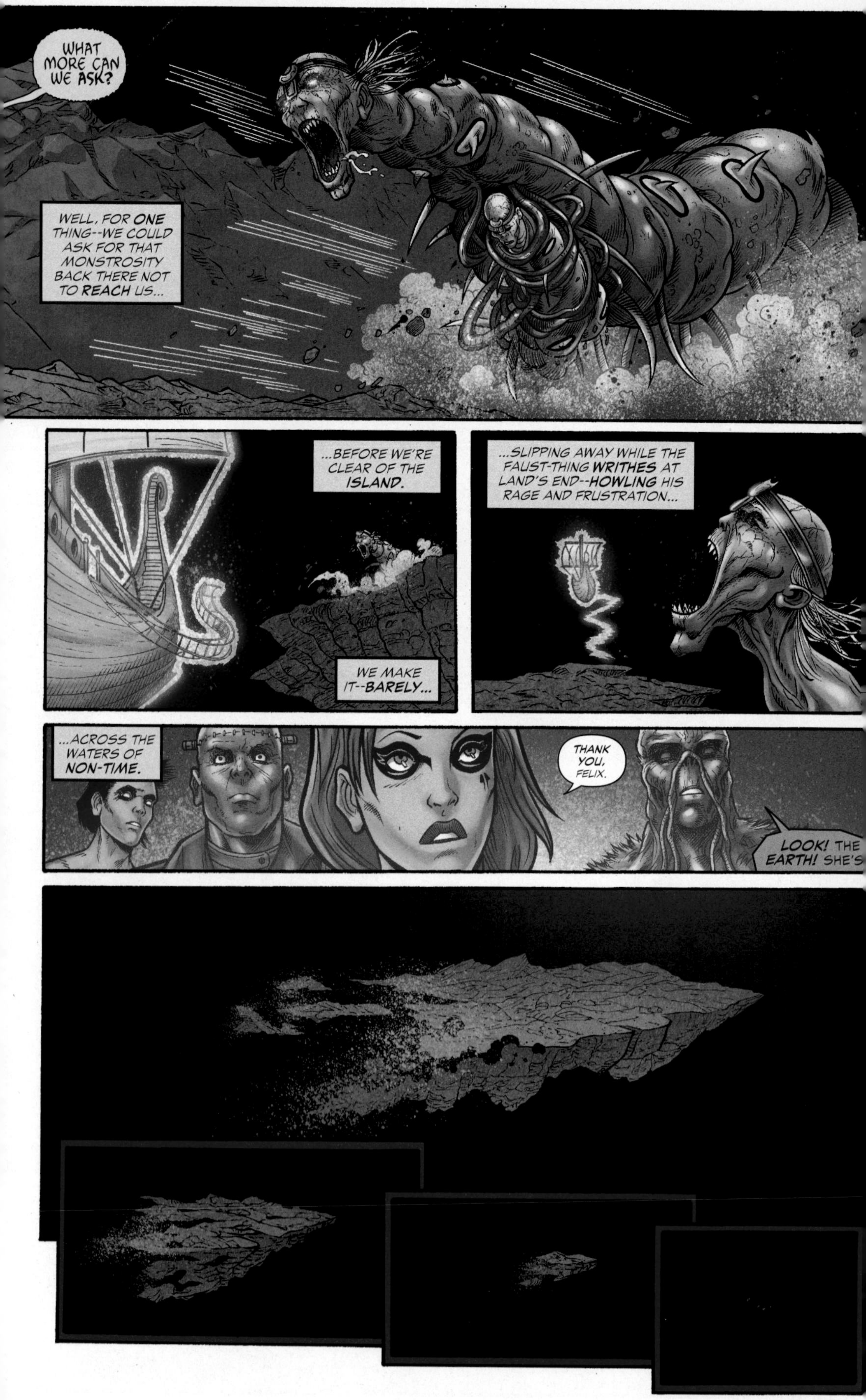
WHAT MORE CAN WE ASK?
WELL, FOR ONE THING--WE COULD ASK FOR THAT MONSTROSITY BACK THERE NOT TO REACH US...
...BEFORE WE'RE CLEAR OF THE ISLAND.
WE MAKE IT--BARELY...
...SLIPPING AWAY WHILE THE FAUST-THING WRITHES AT LAND'S END--HOWLING HIS RAGE AND FRUSTRATION...
...ACROSS THE WATERS OF NON-TIME.
THANK YOU, FELIX.
LOOK! THE EARTH! SHE'S

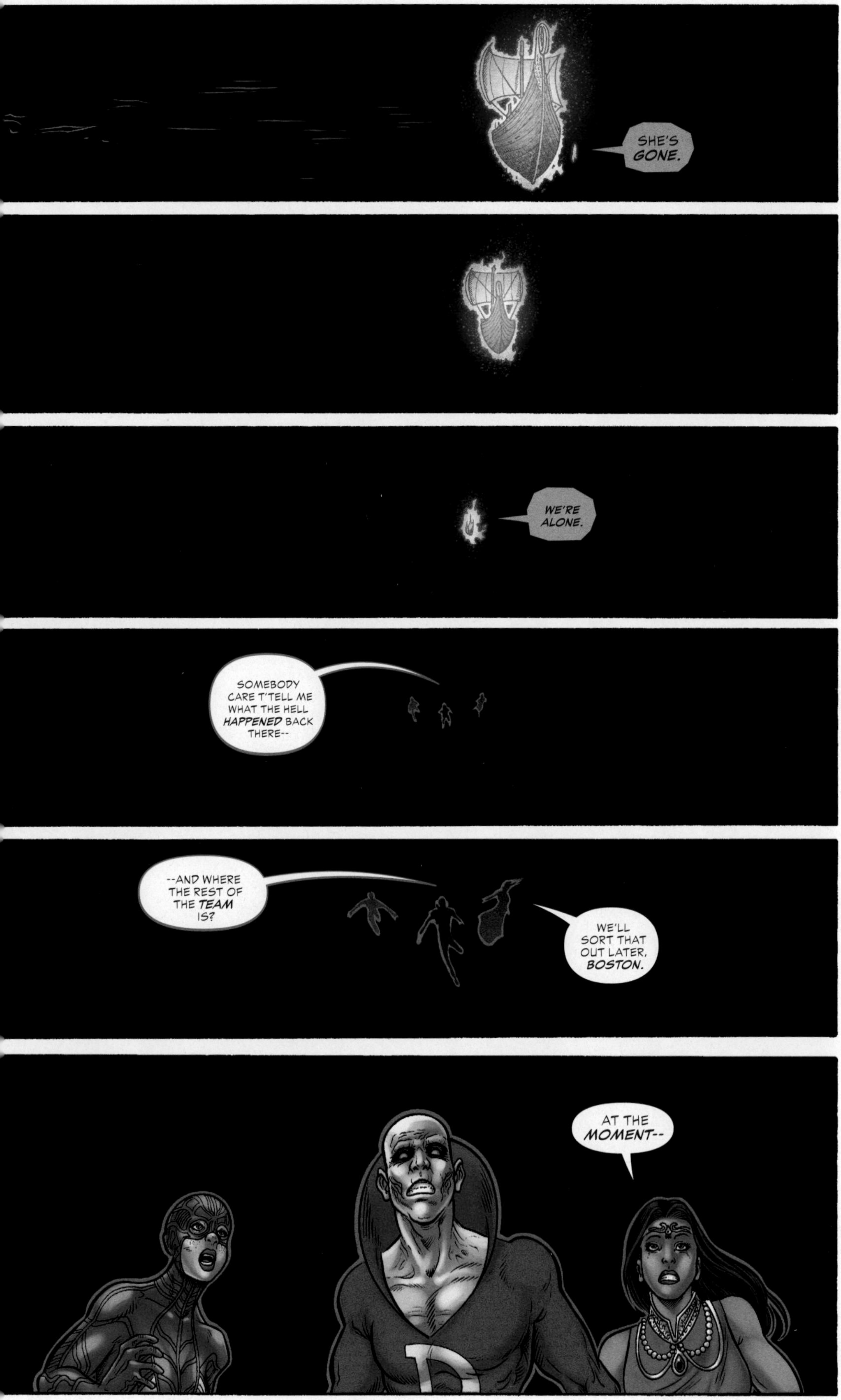
SHE'S GONE.
WE'RE ALONE.
SOMEBODY CARE T'TELL ME WHAT THE HELL HAPPENED BACK THERE--
--AND WHERE THE REST OF THE TEAM IS?
WE'LL SORT THAT OUT LATER, BOSTON.
AT THE MOMENT--

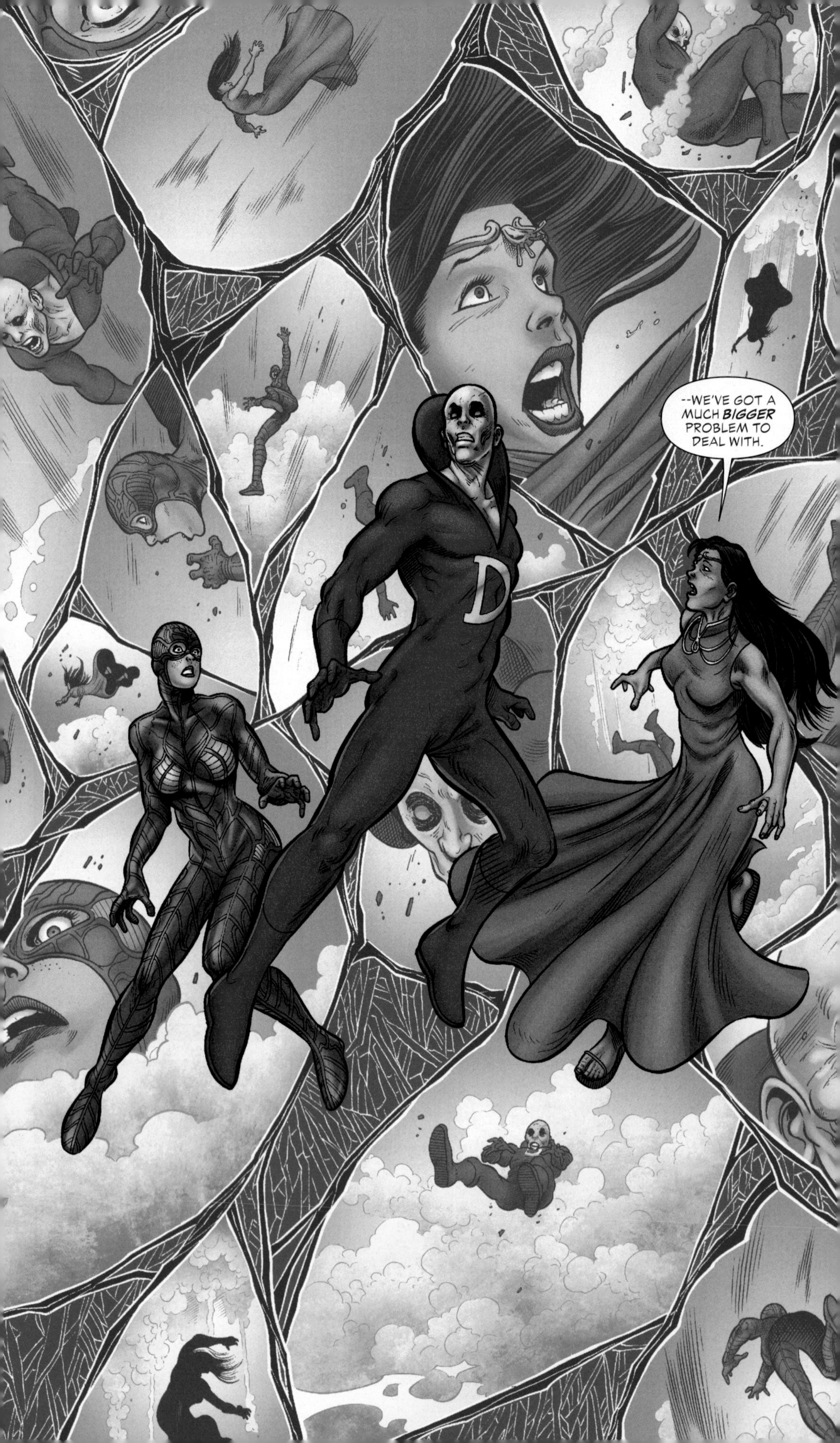
--WE'VE GOT A MUCH BIGGER PROBLEM TO DEAL WITH.

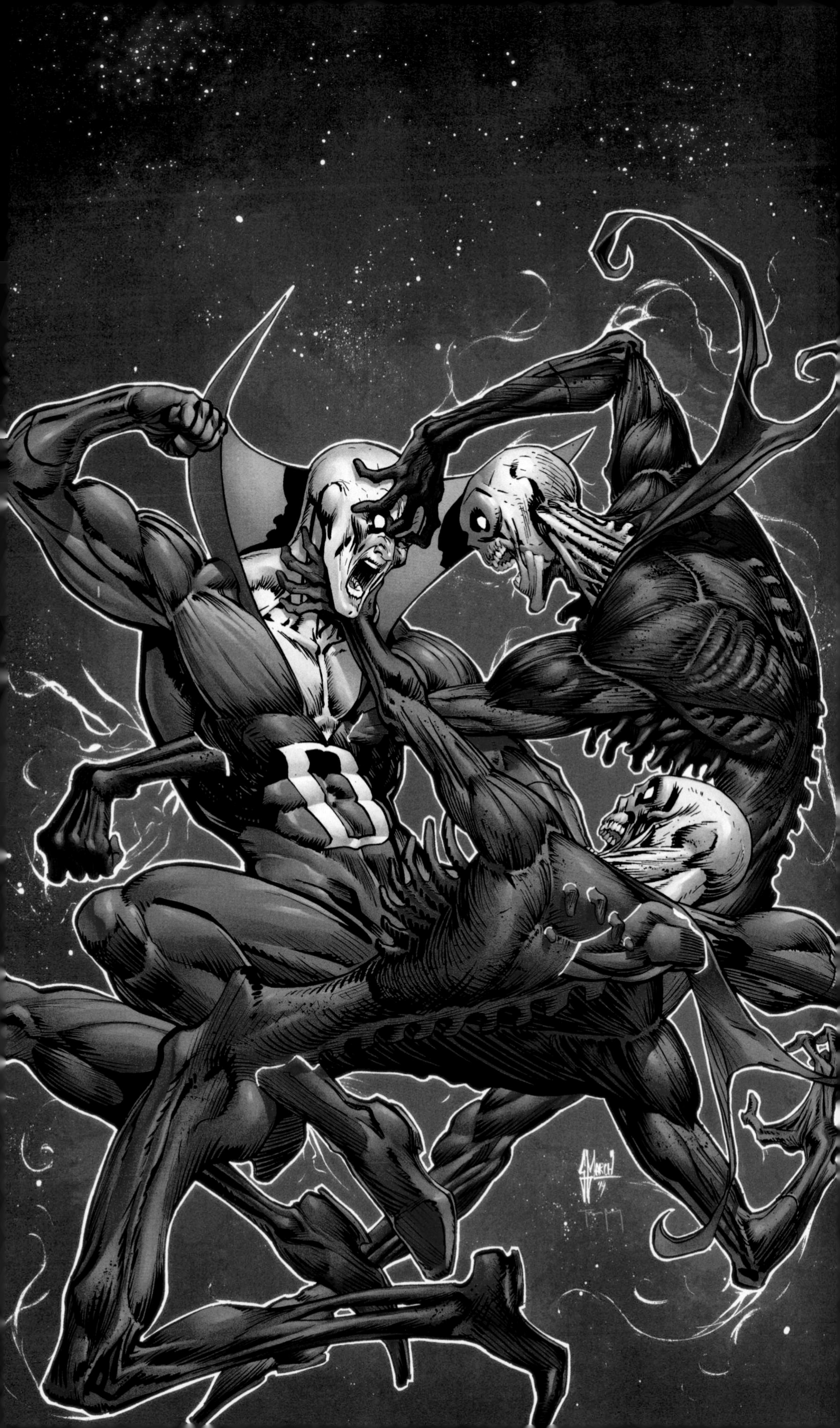

THE AMBER OF THE MOMENT PART 3: THE SHATTERED NOW

J.M. DEMATTEIS writer **ANDRES GUINALDO** penciller **WALDEN WONG** inker **CHRIS SOTOMAYOR** colorist
TAYLOR ESPOSITO letterer cover by **GUILLEM MARCH & TOMEU MOREY**

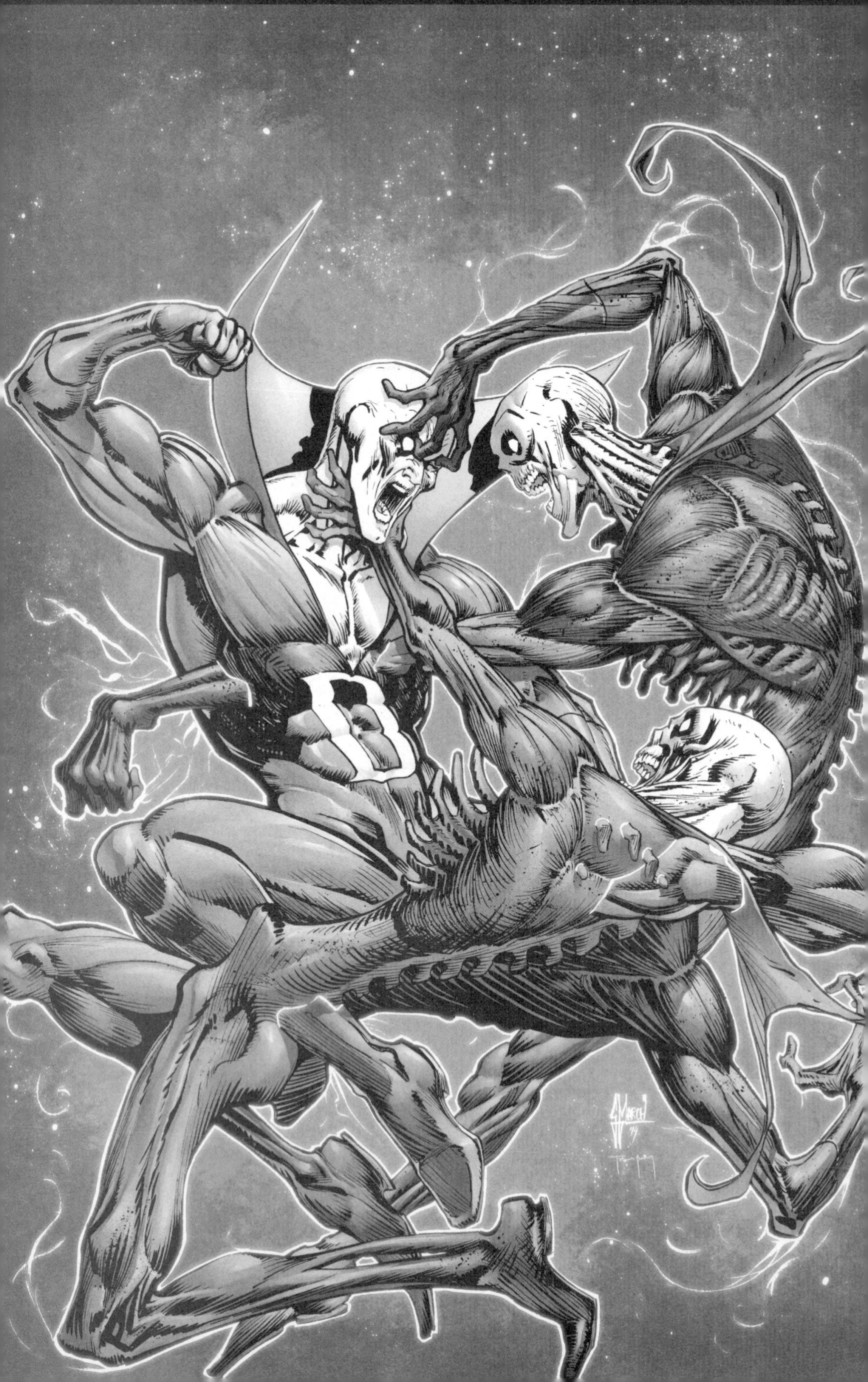

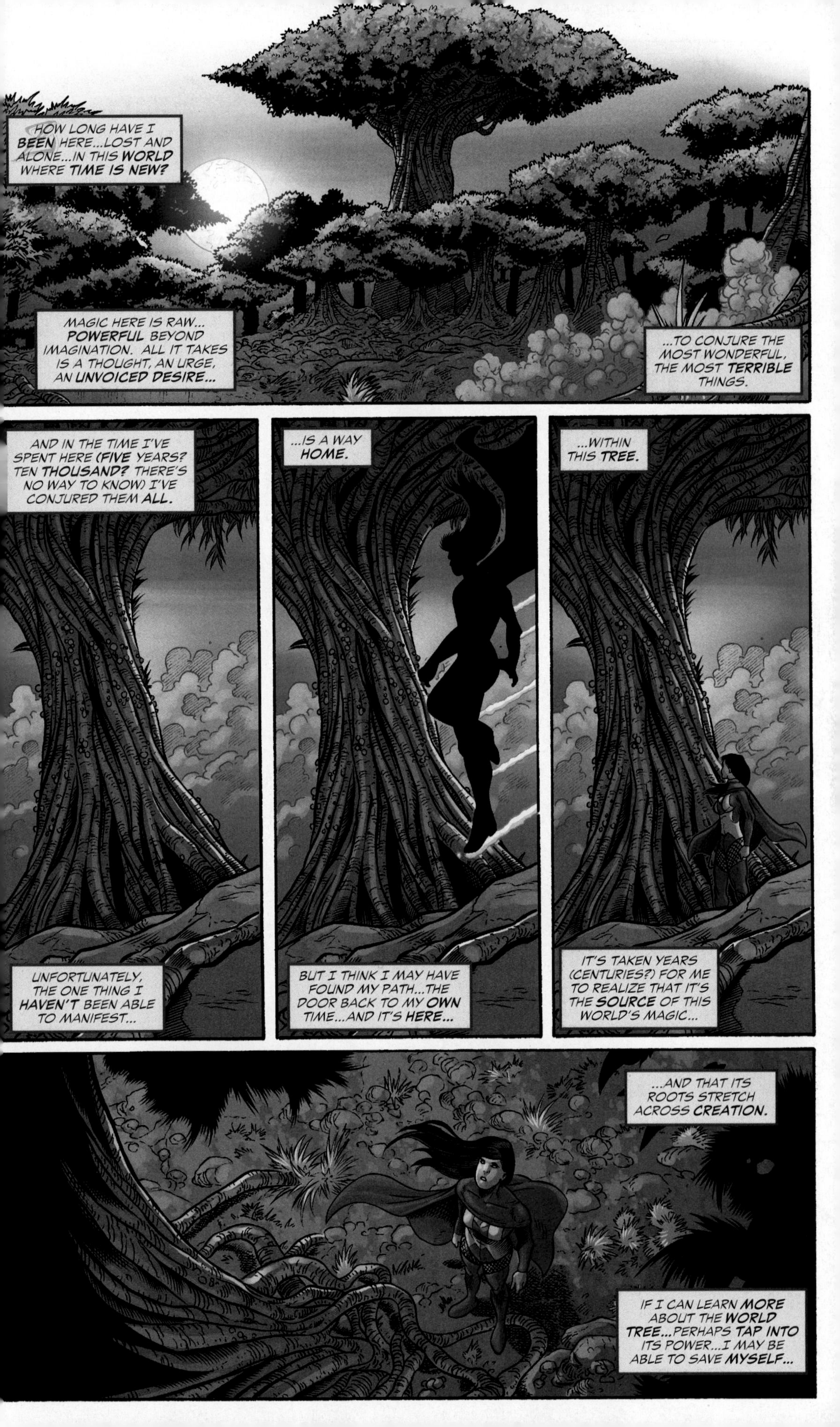

HOW LONG HAVE I BEEN HERE...LOST AND ALONE...IN THIS WORLD WHERE TIME IS NEW?
MAGIC HERE IS RAW... POWERFUL BEYOND IMAGINATION. ALL IT TAKES IS A THOUGHT, AN URGE, AN UNVOICED DESIRE...
...TO CONJURE THE MOST WONDERFUL, THE MOST TERRIBLE THINGS.
AND IN THE TIME I'VE SPENT HERE (FIVE YEARS? TEN THOUSAND? THERE'S NO WAY TO KNOW) I'VE CONJURED THEM ALL.
UNFORTUNATELY, THE ONE THING I HAVEN'T BEEN ABLE TO MANIFEST...
...IS A WAY HOME.
BUT I THINK I MAY HAVE FOUND MY PATH...THE DOOR BACK TO MY OWN TIME...AND IT'S HERE...
...WITHIN THIS TREE.
IT'S TAKEN YEARS (CENTURIES?) FOR ME TO REALIZE THAT IT'S THE SOURCE OF THIS WORLD'S MAGIC...
...AND THAT ITS ROOTS STRETCH ACROSS CREATION.
IF I CAN LEARN MORE ABOUT THE WORLD TREE...PERHAPS TAP INTO ITS POWER...I MAY BE ABLE TO SAVE MYSELF...

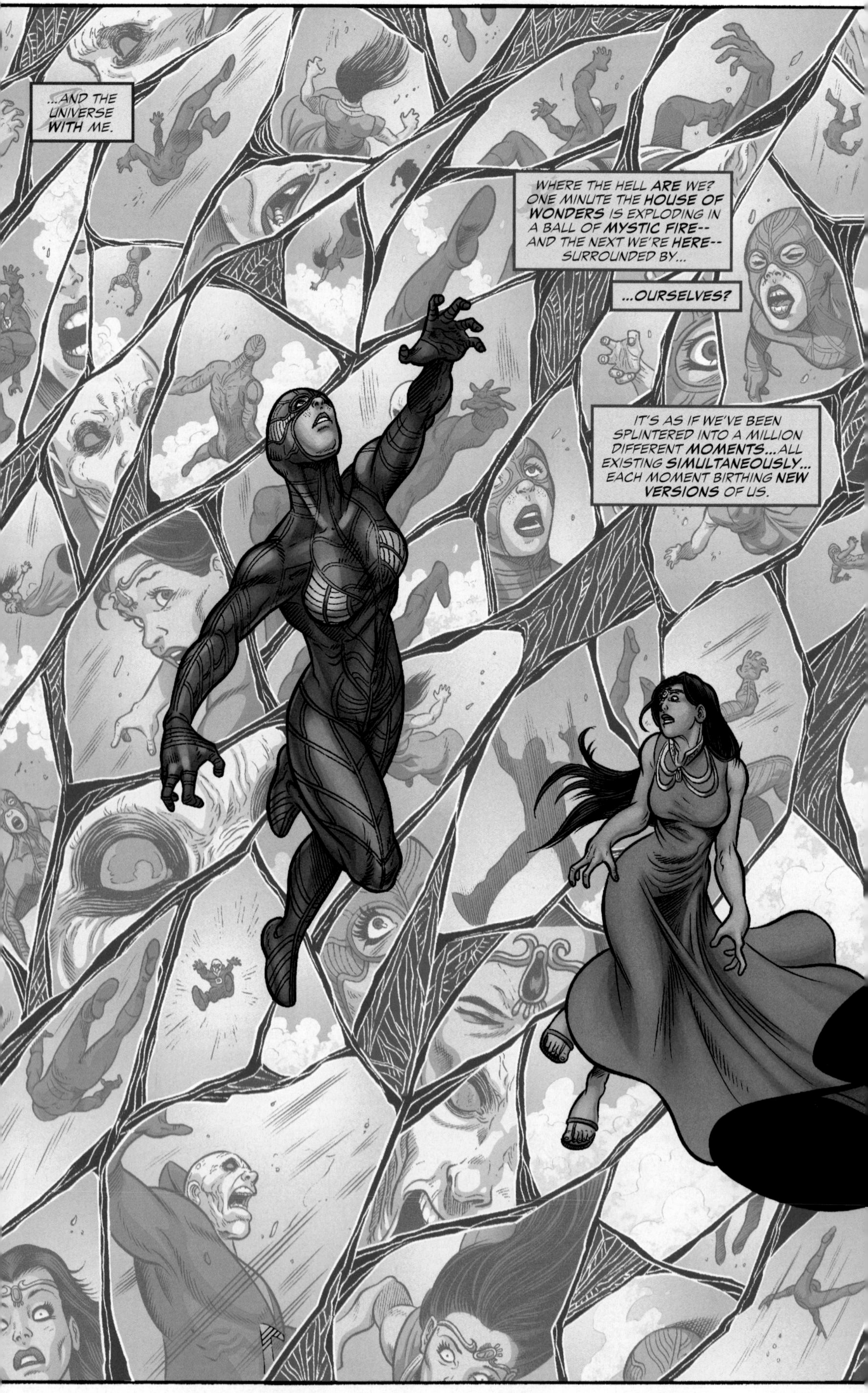
...AND THE UNIVERSE WITH ME.
WHERE THE HELL ARE WE? ONE MINUTE THE HOUSE OF WONDERS IS EXPLODING IN A BALL OF MYSTIC FIRE-- AND THE NEXT WE'RE HERE-- SURROUNDED BY...
...OURSELVES?
IT'S AS IF WE'VE BEEN SPLINTERED INTO A MILLION DIFFERENT MOMENTS...ALL EXISTING SIMULTANEOUSLY... EACH MOMENT BIRTHING NEW VERSIONS OF US.

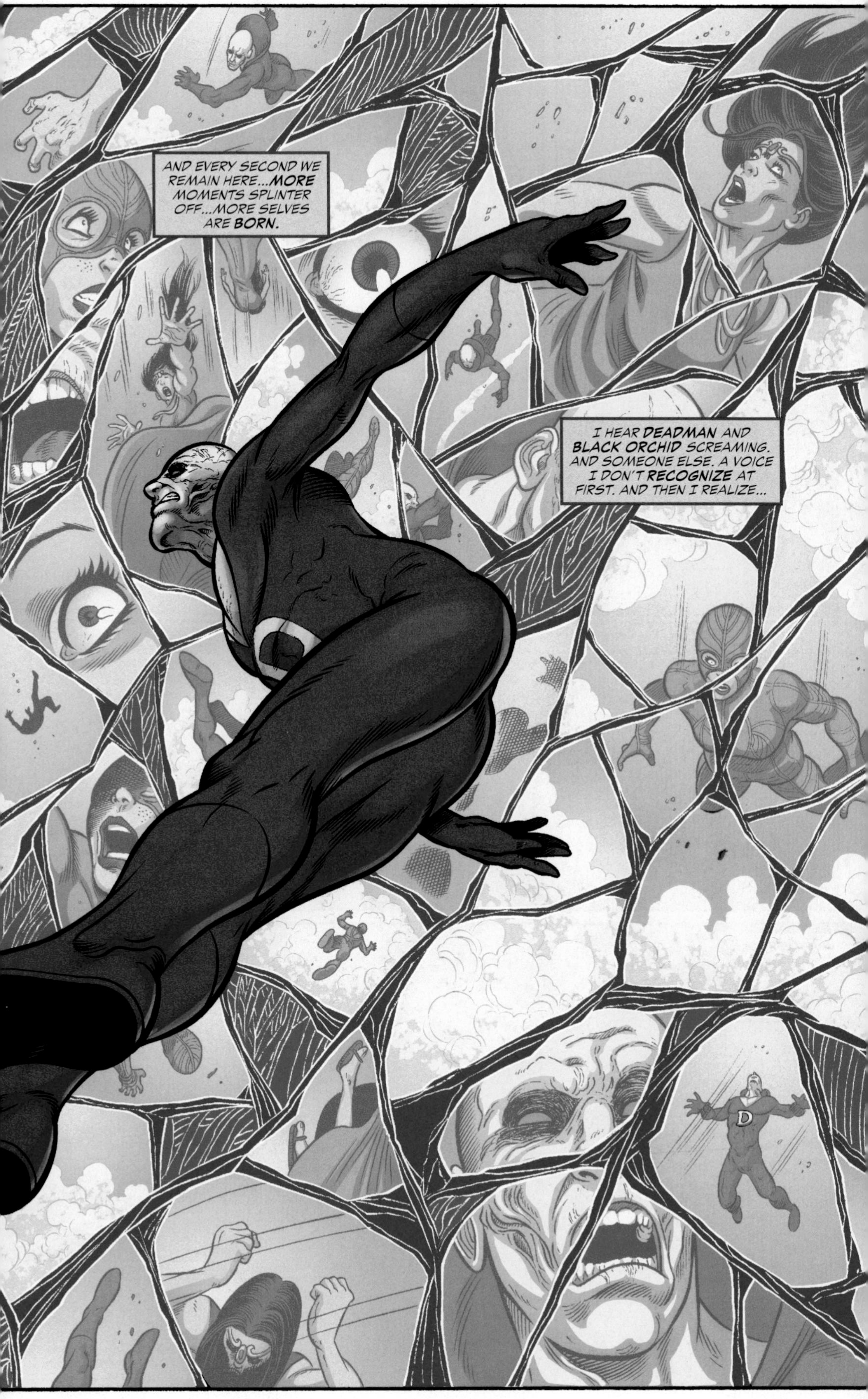
AND EVERY SECOND WE REMAIN HERE...MORE MOMENTS SPLINTER OFF...MORE SELVES ARE BORN.
I HEAR DEADMAN AND BLACK ORCHID SCREAMING. AND SOMEONE ELSE. A VOICE I DON'T RECOGNIZE AT FIRST. AND THEN I REALIZE...

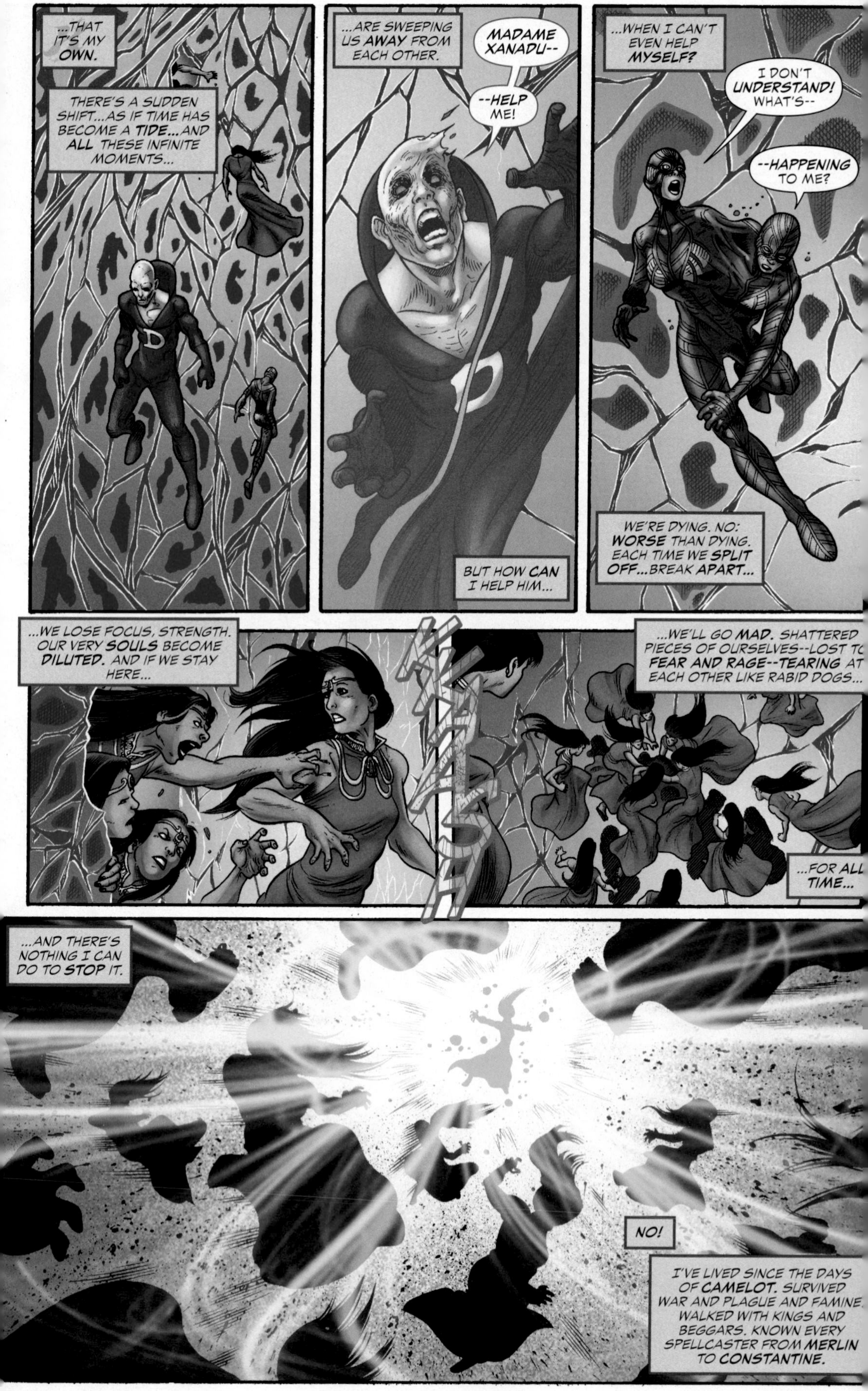
...THAT IT'S MY OWN.
THERE'S A SUDDEN SHIFT...AS IF TIME HAS BECOME A TIDE...AND ALL THESE INFINITE MOMENTS...
...ARE SWEEPING US AWAY FROM EACH OTHER.
MADAME XANADU--
--HELP ME!
BUT HOW CAN I HELP HIM...
...WHEN I CAN'T EVEN HELP MYSELF?
I DON'T UNDERSTAND! WHAT'S--
--HAPPENING TO ME?
WE'RE DYING. NO: WORSE THAN DYING. EACH TIME WE SPLIT OFF...BREAK APART...
...WE LOSE FOCUS, STRENGTH. OUR VERY SOULS BECOME DILUTED. AND IF WE STAY HERE...
...WE'LL GO MAD. SHATTERED PIECES OF OURSELVES--LOST TO FEAR AND RAGE--TEARING AT EACH OTHER LIKE RABID DOGS...
...FOR ALL TIME...
...AND THERE'S NOTHING I CAN DO TO STOP IT.
NO!
I'VE LIVED SINCE THE DAYS OF CAMELOT. SURVIVED WAR AND PLAGUE AND FAMINE. WALKED WITH KINGS AND BEGGARS. KNOWN EVERY SPELLCASTER FROM MERLIN TO CONSTANTINE.

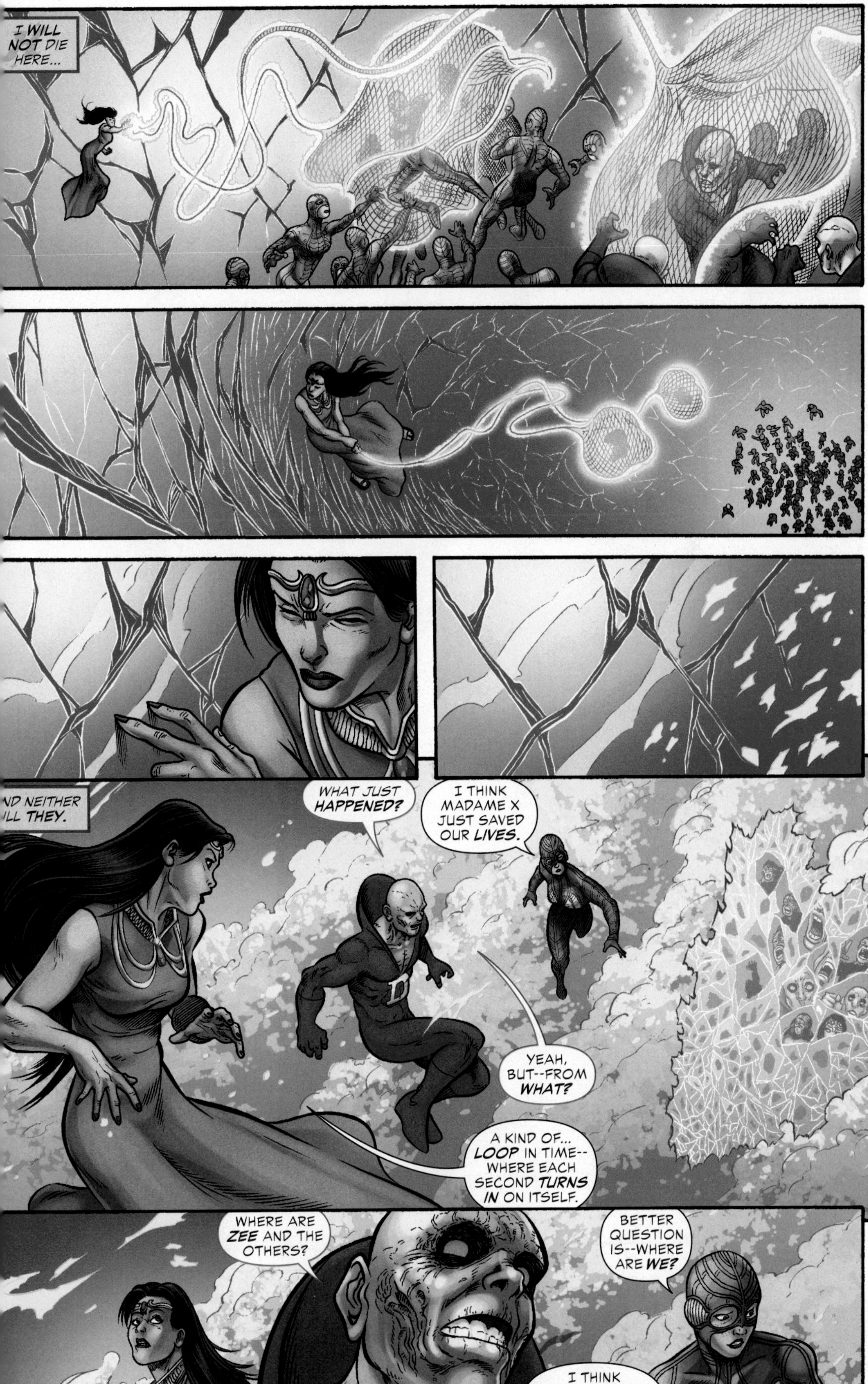
I WILL NOT DIE HERE...
ND NEITHER ILL THEY.
WHAT JUST HAPPENED?
I THINK MADAME X JUST SAVED OUR LIVES.
YEAH, BUT--FROM WHAT?
A KIND OF... LOOP IN TIME-- WHERE EACH SECOND TURNS IN ON ITSELF.
WHERE ARE ZEE AND THE OTHERS?
BETTER QUESTION IS--WHERE ARE WE?
I THINK WE'VE MOVED FROM A PLACE OF INVERTED TIME--

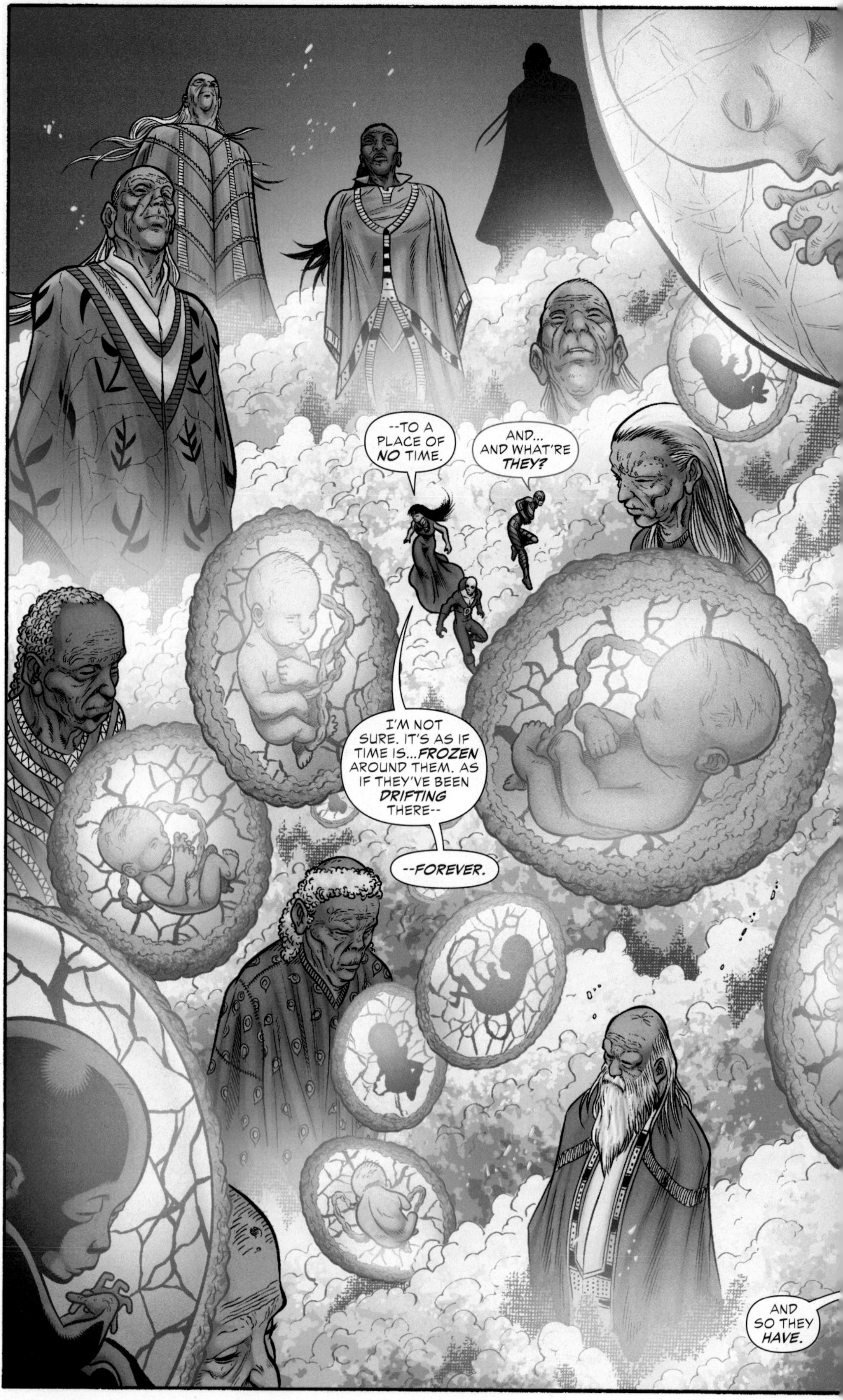
--TO A PLACE OF NO TIME.
AND... AND WHAT'RE THEY?
I'M NOT SURE. IT'S AS IF TIME IS...FROZEN AROUND THEM. AS IF THEY'VE BEEN DRIFTING THERE--
--FOREVER.
AND SO THEY HAVE.

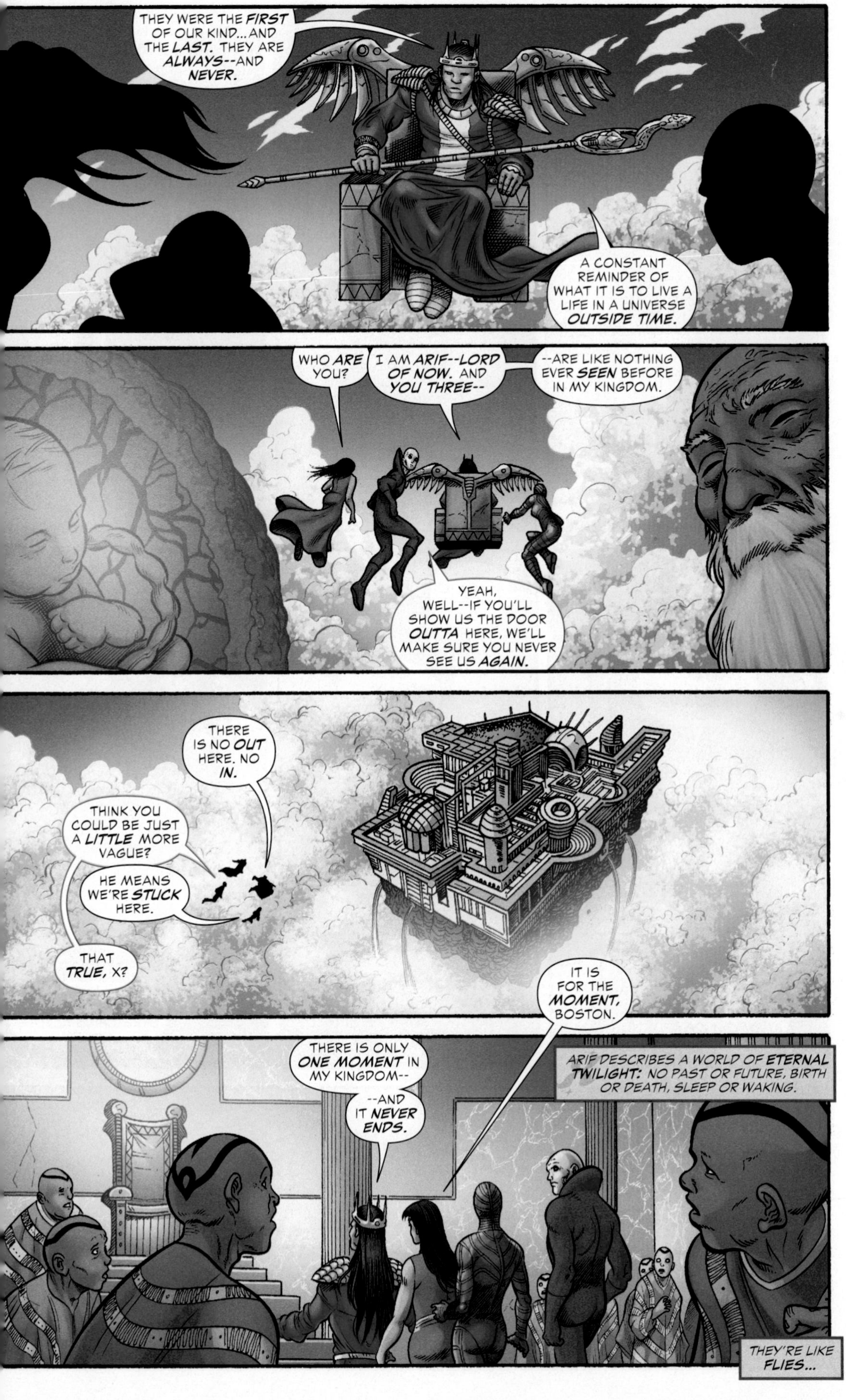
THEY WERE THE FIRST OF OUR KIND...AND THE LAST. THEY ARE ALWAYS--AND NEVER.
A CONSTANT REMINDER OF WHAT IT IS TO LIVE A LIFE IN A UNIVERSE OUTSIDE TIME.
WHO ARE YOU?
I AM ARIF--LORD OF NOW. AND YOU THREE--
--ARE LIKE NOTHING EVER SEEN BEFORE IN MY KINGDOM.
YEAH, WELL--IF YOU'LL SHOW US THE DOOR OUTTA HERE, WE'LL MAKE SURE YOU NEVER SEE US AGAIN.
THERE IS NO OUT HERE. NO IN.
THINK YOU COULD BE JUST A LITTLE MORE VAGUE?
HE MEANS WE'RE STUCK HERE.
THAT TRUE, X?
IT IS FOR THE MOMENT, BOSTON.
THERE IS ONLY ONE MOMENT IN MY KINGDOM--
--AND IT NEVER ENDS.
ARIF DESCRIBES A WORLD OF ETERNAL TWILIGHT: NO PAST OR FUTURE, BIRTH OR DEATH, SLEEP OR WAKING.
THEY'RE LIKE FLIES...

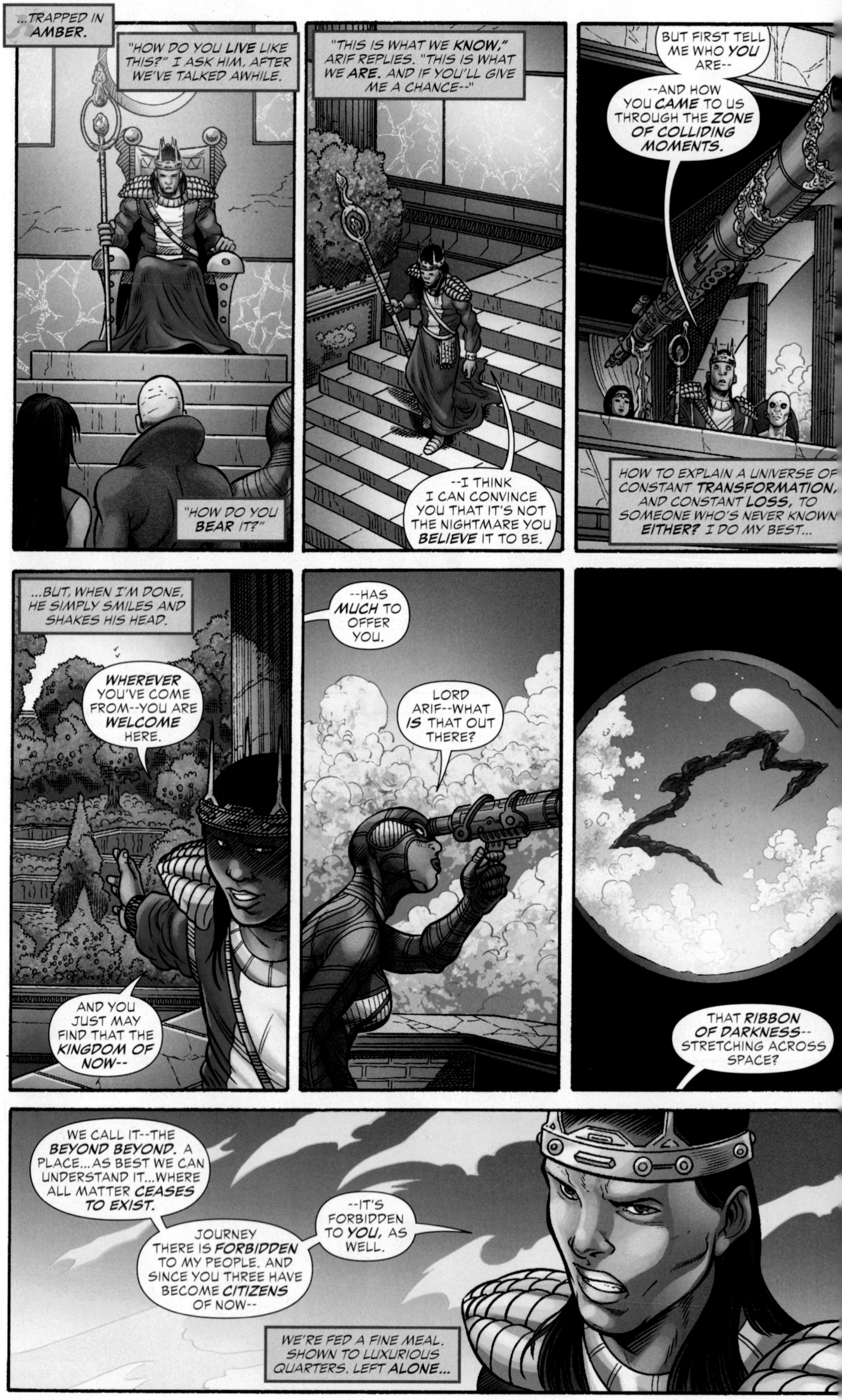
...TRAPPED IN AMBER.
"HOW DO YOU LIVE LIKE THIS?" I ASK HIM, AFTER WE'VE TALKED AWHILE.
"HOW DO YOU BEAR IT?"
"THIS IS WHAT WE KNOW," ARIF REPLIES. "THIS IS WHAT WE ARE. AND IF YOU'LL GIVE ME A CHANCE--"
--I THINK I CAN CONVINCE YOU THAT IT'S NOT THE NIGHTMARE YOU BELIEVE IT TO BE.
BUT FIRST TELL ME WHO YOU ARE--
--AND HOW YOU CAME TO US THROUGH THE ZONE OF COLLIDING MOMENTS.
HOW TO EXPLAIN A UNIVERSE OF CONSTANT TRANSFORMATION, AND CONSTANT LOSS, TO SOMEONE WHO'S NEVER KNOWN EITHER? I DO MY BEST...
...BUT, WHEN I'M DONE, HE SIMPLY SMILES AND SHAKES HIS HEAD.
WHEREVER YOU'VE COME FROM--YOU ARE WELCOME HERE.
AND YOU JUST MAY FIND THAT THE KINGDOM OF NOW--
--HAS MUCH TO OFFER YOU.
LORD ARIF--WHAT IS THAT OUT THERE?
THAT RIBBON OF DARKNESS--STRETCHING ACROSS SPACE?
WE CALL IT--THE BEYOND BEYOND. A PLACE...AS BEST WE CAN UNDERSTAND IT...WHERE ALL MATTER CEASES TO EXIST.
JOURNEY THERE IS FORBIDDEN TO MY PEOPLE. AND SINCE YOU THREE HAVE BECOME CITIZENS OF NOW--
--IT'S FORBIDDEN TO YOU, AS WELL.
WE'RE FED A FINE MEAL. SHOWN TO LUXURIOUS QUARTERS. LEFT ALONE...

...AND UNGUARDED.

WHAT DO YOU *THINK*, BRAND? CAN SHE WHAMMY US A WAY *OUT*?

WE'RE AS GOOD AS *HOME*.

WHEN IT COMES TO *HOCUS-POCUS*, THERE'S *NOBODY* BETTER THAN--

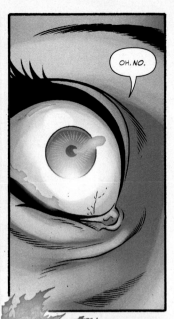

OH, *NO*.

FOOOOSHH

WHAT *HAPPENED*?

THE ENCHANTMENT... *COLLAPSED*.

SO TRY *AGAIN*.

NO, YOU DON'T *UNDER-STAND*! THE LAWS OF MAGIC DON'T *APPLY* HERE!

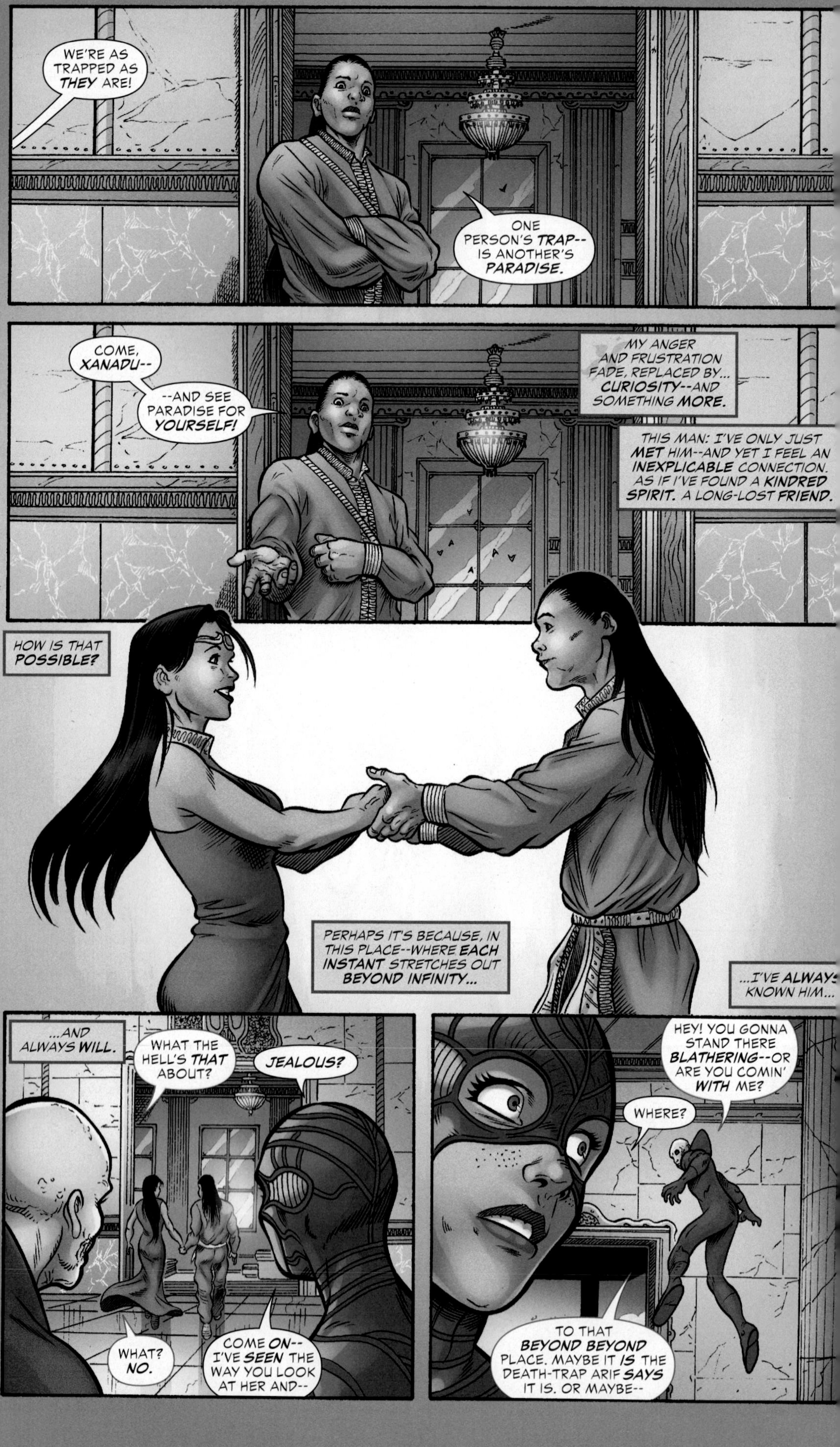
WE'RE AS TRAPPED AS THEY ARE!
ONE PERSON'S TRAP-- IS ANOTHER'S PARADISE.
COME, XANADU--
--AND SEE PARADISE FOR YOURSELF!
MY ANGER AND FRUSTRATION FADE, REPLACED BY... CURIOSITY--AND SOMETHING MORE.
THIS MAN: I'VE ONLY JUST MET HIM--AND YET I FEEL AN INEXPLICABLE CONNECTION. AS IF I'VE FOUND A KINDRED SPIRIT. A LONG-LOST FRIEND.
HOW IS THAT POSSIBLE?
PERHAPS IT'S BECAUSE, IN THIS PLACE--WHERE EACH INSTANT STRETCHES OUT BEYOND INFINITY...
...I'VE ALWAYS KNOWN HIM...
...AND ALWAYS WILL.
WHAT THE HELL'S THAT ABOUT?
JEALOUS?
WHAT? NO.
COME ON-- I'VE SEEN THE WAY YOU LOOK AT HER AND--
HEY! YOU GONNA STAND THERE BLATHERING--OR ARE YOU COMIN' WITH ME?
WHERE?
TO THAT BEYOND BEYOND PLACE. MAYBE IT IS THE DEATH-TRAP ARIF SAYS IT IS. OR MAYBE--

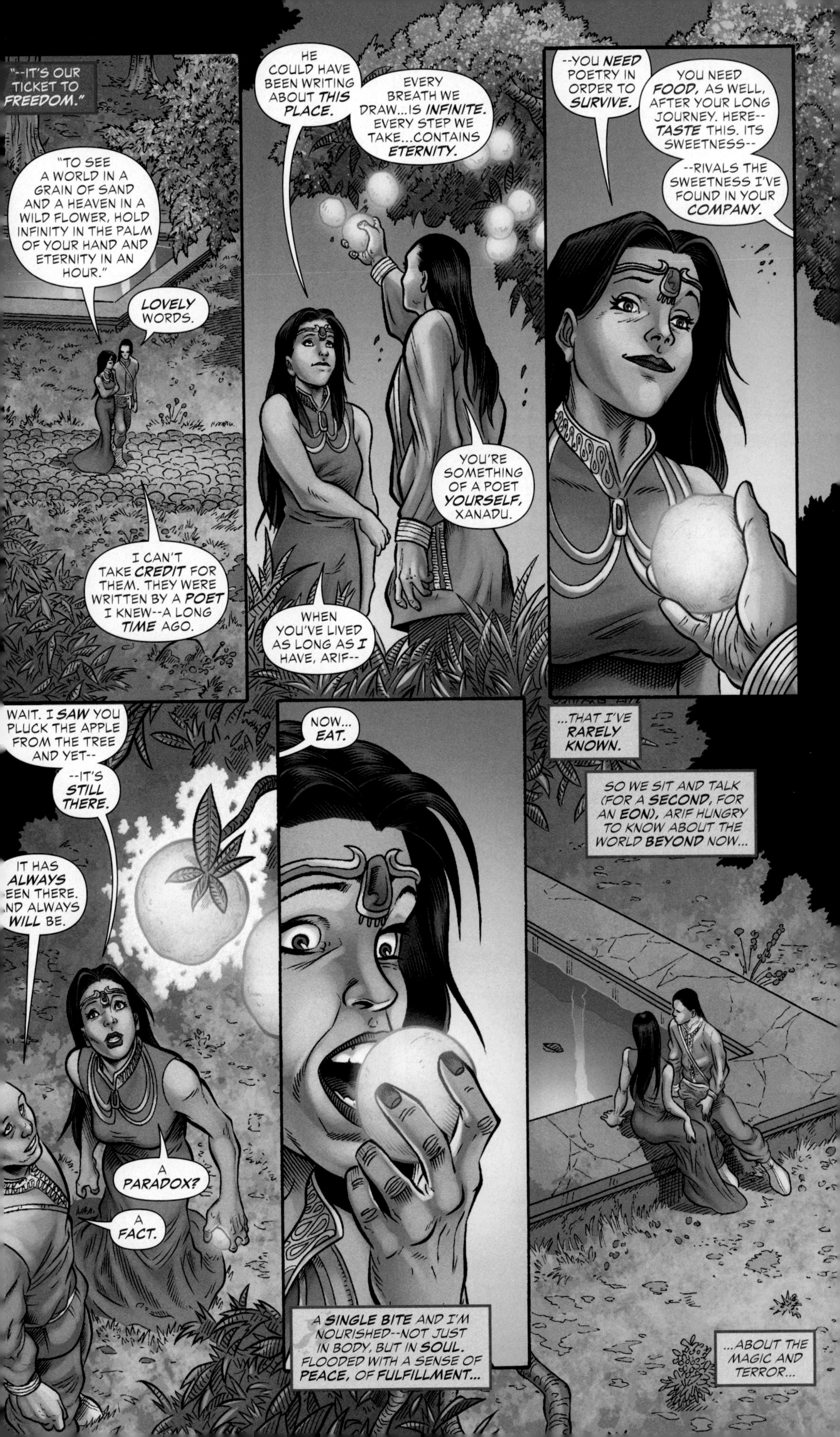

"--IT'S OUR TICKET TO FREEDOM."
"TO SEE A WORLD IN A GRAIN OF SAND AND A HEAVEN IN A WILD FLOWER, HOLD INFINITY IN THE PALM OF YOUR HAND AND ETERNITY IN AN HOUR."
LOVELY WORDS.
I CAN'T TAKE CREDIT FOR THEM. THEY WERE WRITTEN BY A POET I KNEW--A LONG TIME AGO.
HE COULD HAVE BEEN WRITING ABOUT THIS PLACE.
EVERY BREATH WE DRAW...IS INFINITE. EVERY STEP WE TAKE...CONTAINS ETERNITY.
YOU'RE SOMETHING OF A POET YOURSELF, XANADU.
WHEN YOU'VE LIVED AS LONG AS I HAVE, ARIF--
--YOU NEED POETRY IN ORDER TO SURVIVE.
YOU NEED FOOD, AS WELL, AFTER YOUR LONG JOURNEY. HERE-- TASTE THIS. ITS SWEETNESS--
--RIVALS THE SWEETNESS I'VE FOUND IN YOUR COMPANY.
WAIT. I SAW YOU PLUCK THE APPLE FROM THE TREE AND YET--
--IT'S STILL THERE.
IT HAS ALWAYS EEN THERE. ND ALWAYS WILL BE.
A PARADOX?
A FACT.
NOW... EAT.
A SINGLE BITE AND I'M NOURISHED--NOT JUST IN BODY, BUT IN SOUL. FLOODED WITH A SENSE OF PEACE, OF FULFILLMENT...
...THAT I'VE RARELY KNOWN.
SO WE SIT AND TALK (FOR A SECOND, FOR AN EON), ARIF HUNGRY TO KNOW ABOUT THE WORLD BEYOND NOW...
...ABOUT THE MAGIC AND TERROR...

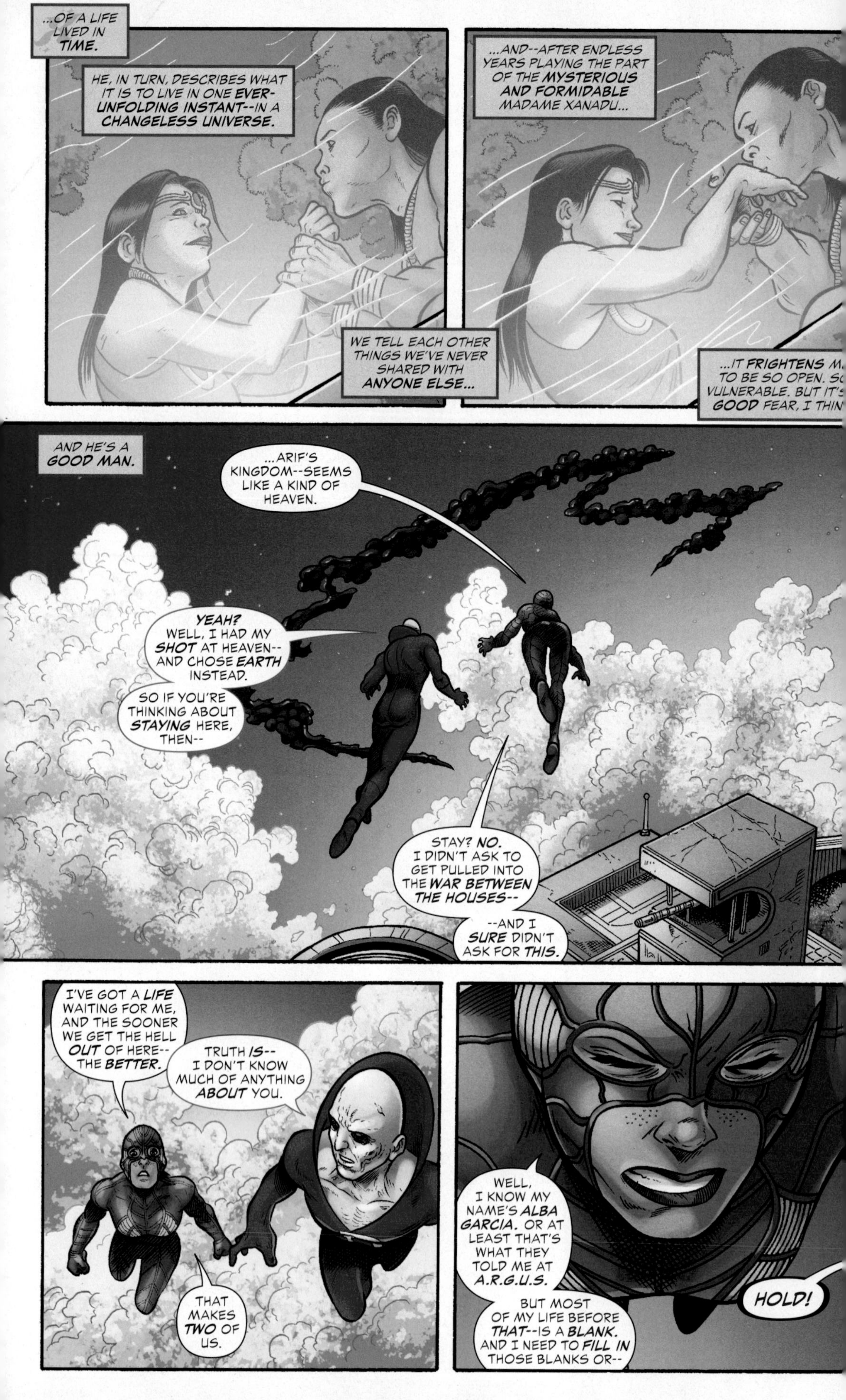
...OF A LIFE LIVED IN TIME.
HE, IN TURN, DESCRIBES WHAT IT IS TO LIVE IN ONE EVER-UNFOLDING INSTANT--IN A CHANGELESS UNIVERSE.
WE TELL EACH OTHER THINGS WE'VE NEVER SHARED WITH ANYONE ELSE...
...AND--AFTER ENDLESS YEARS PLAYING THE PART OF THE MYSTERIOUS AND FORMIDABLE MADAME XANADU...
...IT FRIGHTENS M TO BE SO OPEN. S VULNERABLE. BUT IT'S GOOD FEAR, I THIN
AND HE'S A GOOD MAN.
...ARIF'S KINGDOM--SEEMS LIKE A KIND OF HEAVEN.
YEAH? WELL, I HAD MY SHOT AT HEAVEN-- AND CHOSE EARTH INSTEAD.
SO IF YOU'RE THINKING ABOUT STAYING HERE, THEN--
STAY? NO. I DIDN'T ASK TO GET PULLED INTO THE WAR BETWEEN THE HOUSES--
--AND I SURE DIDN'T ASK FOR THIS.
I'VE GOT A LIFE WAITING FOR ME, AND THE SOONER WE GET THE HELL OUT OF HERE-- THE BETTER.
TRUTH IS-- I DON'T KNOW MUCH OF ANYTHING ABOUT YOU.
THAT MAKES TWO OF US.
WELL, I KNOW MY NAME'S ALBA GARCIA. OR AT LEAST THAT'S WHAT THEY TOLD ME AT A.R.G.U.S.
BUT MOST OF MY LIFE BEFORE THAT--IS A BLANK. AND I NEED TO FILL IN THOSE BLANKS OR--
HOLD!

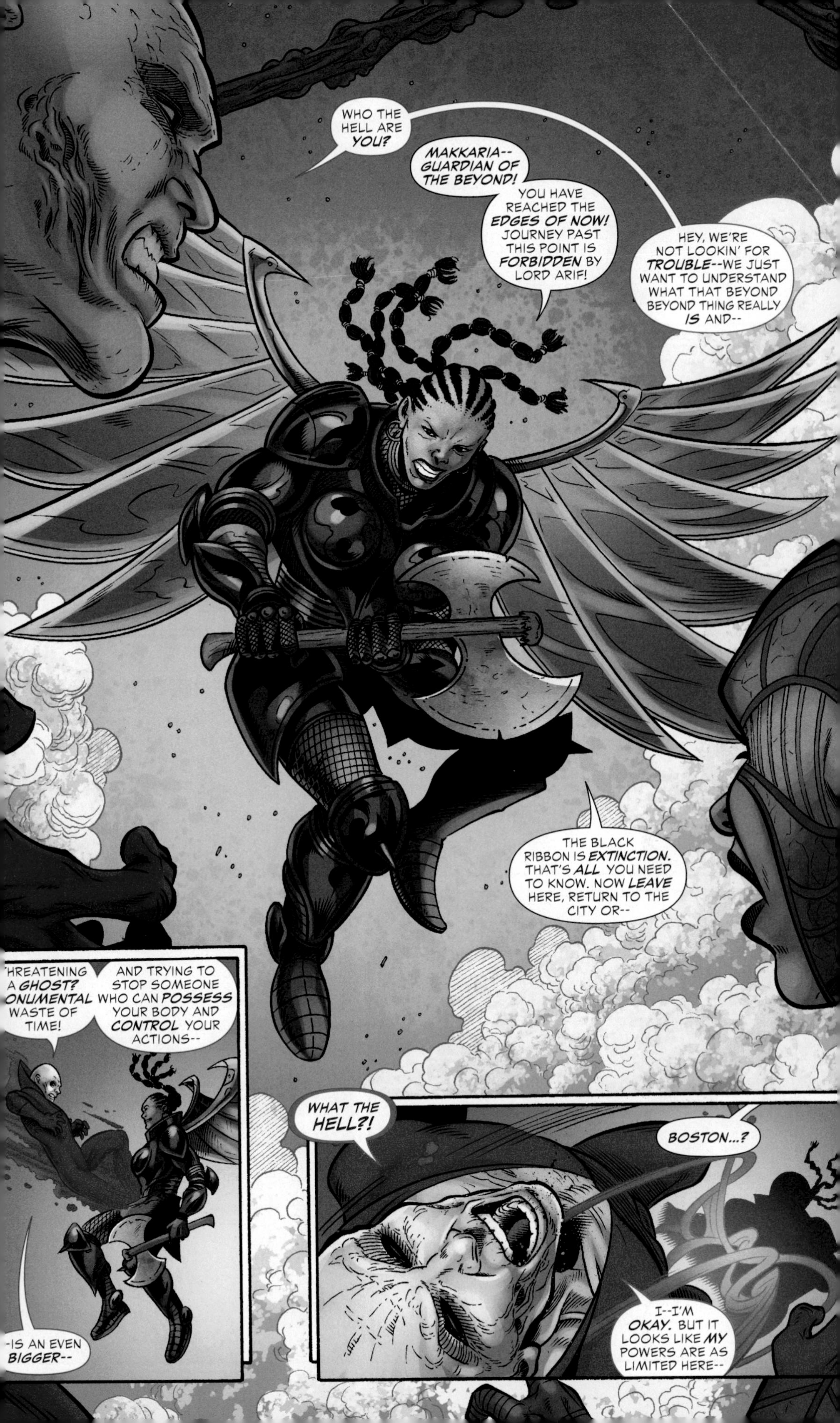

WHO THE HELL ARE YOU?
MAKKARIA-- GUARDIAN OF THE BEYOND!
YOU HAVE REACHED THE EDGES OF NOW! JOURNEY PAST THIS POINT IS FORBIDDEN BY LORD ARIF!
HEY, WE'RE NOT LOOKIN' FOR TROUBLE--WE JUST WANT TO UNDERSTAND WHAT THAT BEYOND BEYOND THING REALLY IS AND--
THE BLACK RIBBON IS EXTINCTION. THAT'S ALL YOU NEED TO KNOW. NOW LEAVE HERE, RETURN TO THE CITY OR--
HREATENING A GHOST? ONUMENTAL WASTE OF TIME!
AND TRYING TO STOP SOMEONE WHO CAN POSSESS YOUR BODY AND CONTROL YOUR ACTIONS--
-IS AN EVEN BIGGER--
WHAT THE HELL?!
BOSTON...?
I--I'M OKAY. BUT IT LOOKS LIKE MY POWERS ARE AS LIMITED HERE--

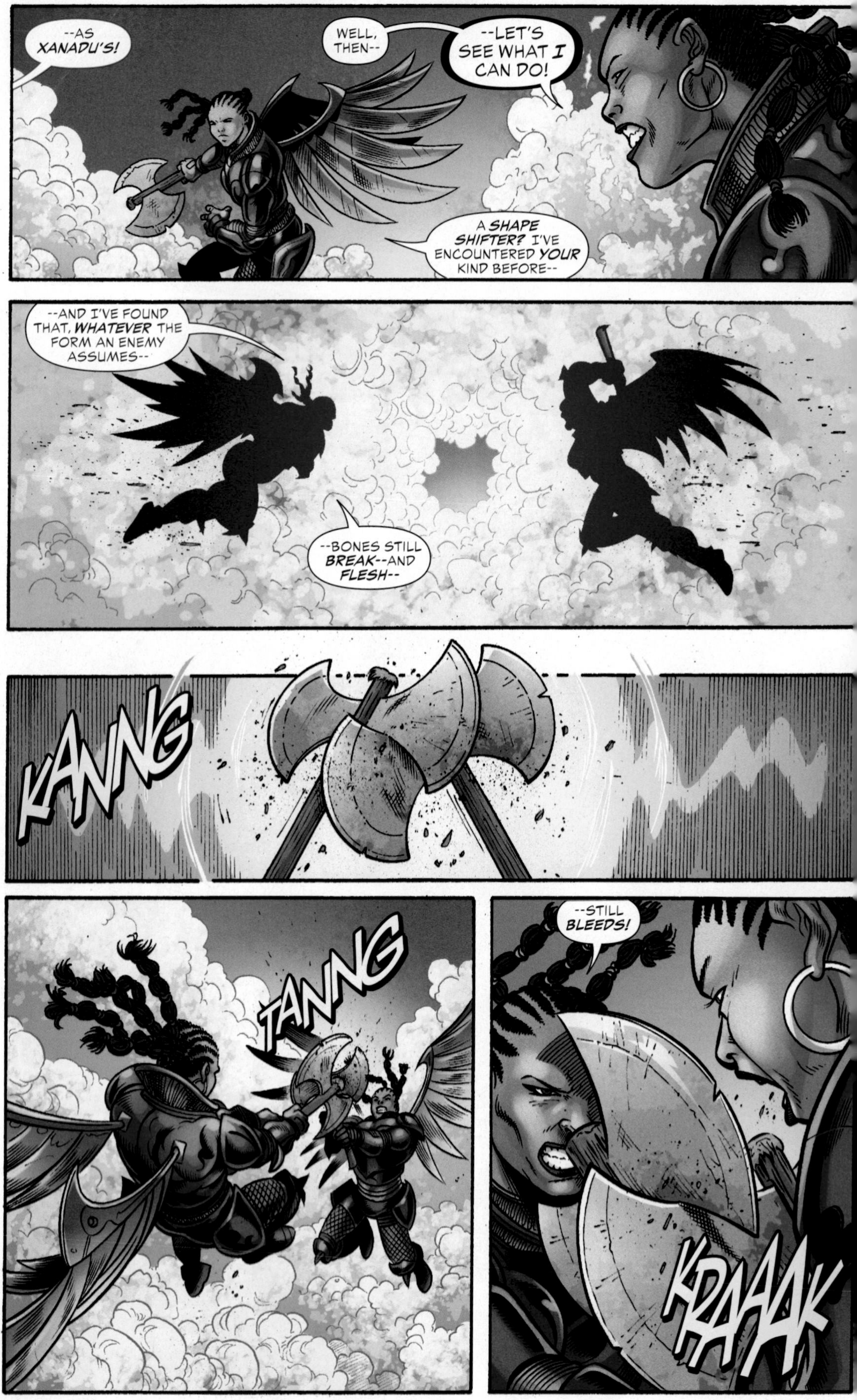
--AS XANADU'S!
WELL, THEN--
--LET'S SEE WHAT I CAN DO!
A SHAPE SHIFTER? I'VE ENCOUNTERED YOUR KIND BEFORE--
--AND I'VE FOUND THAT, WHATEVER THE FORM AN ENEMY ASSUMES--
--BONES STILL BREAK--AND FLESH--
KANNG
TANNG
--STILL BLEEDS!
KRAAAK

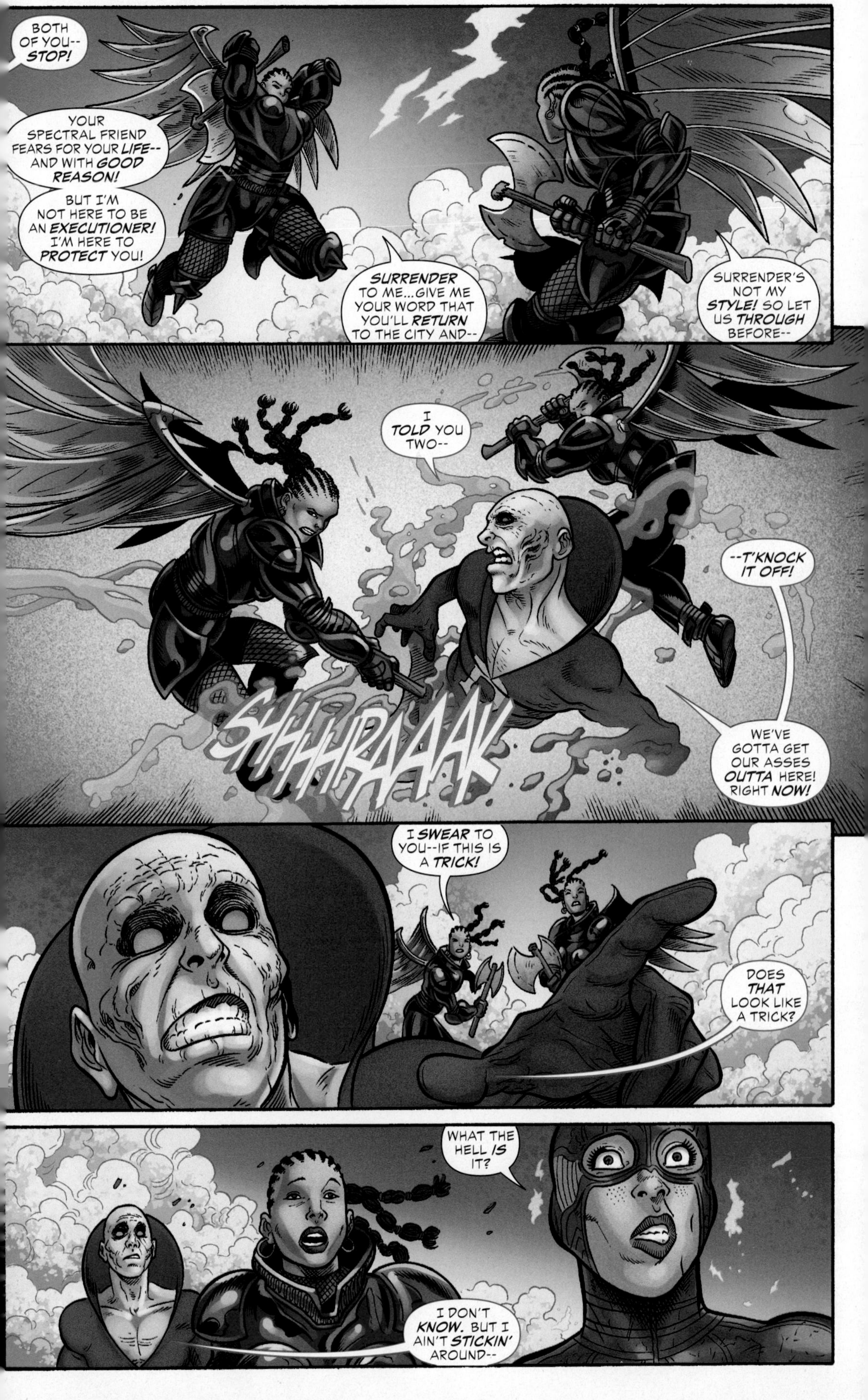
BOTH OF YOU-- STOP!
YOUR SPECTRAL FRIEND FEARS FOR YOUR LIFE-- AND WITH GOOD REASON!
BUT I'M NOT HERE TO BE AN EXECUTIONER! I'M HERE TO PROTECT YOU!
SURRENDER TO ME...GIVE ME YOUR WORD THAT YOU'LL RETURN TO THE CITY AND--
SURRENDER'S NOT MY STYLE! SO LET US THROUGH BEFORE--
I TOLD YOU TWO--
--T'KNOCK IT OFF!
SHHHRAAAK
WE'VE GOTTA GET OUR ASSES OUTTA HERE! RIGHT NOW!
I SWEAR TO YOU--IF THIS IS A TRICK!
DOES THAT LOOK LIKE A TRICK?
WHAT THE HELL IS IT?
I DON'T KNOW. BUT I AIN'T STICKIN' AROUND--

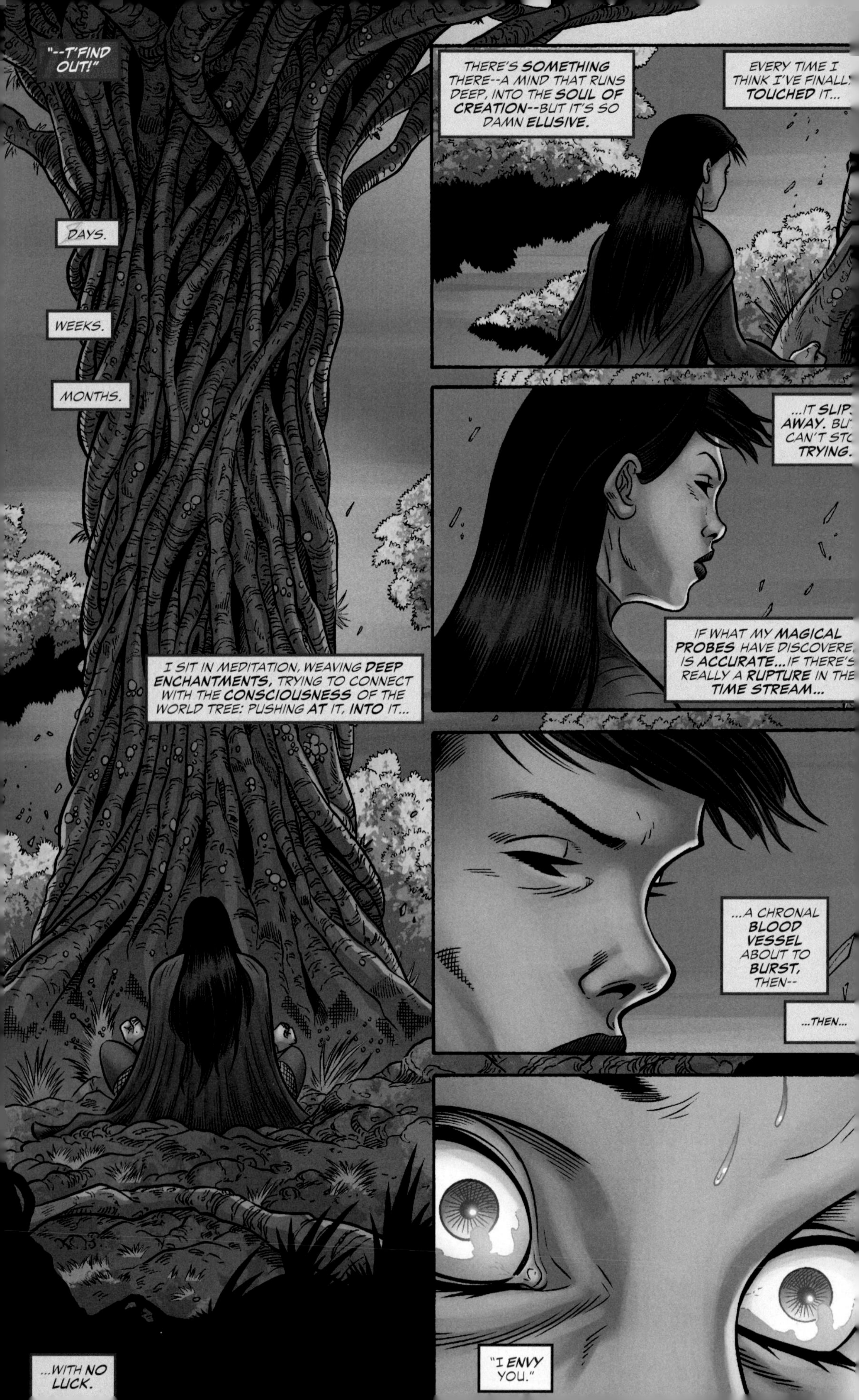
"--T'FIND OUT!"
DAYS.
WEEKS.
MONTHS.
I SIT IN MEDITATION, WEAVING DEEP ENCHANTMENTS, TRYING TO CONNECT WITH THE CONSCIOUSNESS OF THE WORLD TREE: PUSHING AT IT, INTO IT...
...WITH NO LUCK.
THERE'S SOMETHING THERE--A MIND THAT RUNS DEEP, INTO THE SOUL OF CREATION--BUT IT'S SO DAMN ELUSIVE.
EVERY TIME I THINK I'VE FINALL TOUCHED IT...
...IT SLIP AWAY. BU CAN'T STO TRYING.
IF WHAT MY MAGICAL PROBES HAVE DISCOVERE IS ACCURATE...IF THERE'S REALLY A RUPTURE IN THE TIME STREAM...
...A CHRONAL BLOOD VESSEL ABOUT TO BURST, THEN--
...THEN...
"I ENVY YOU."

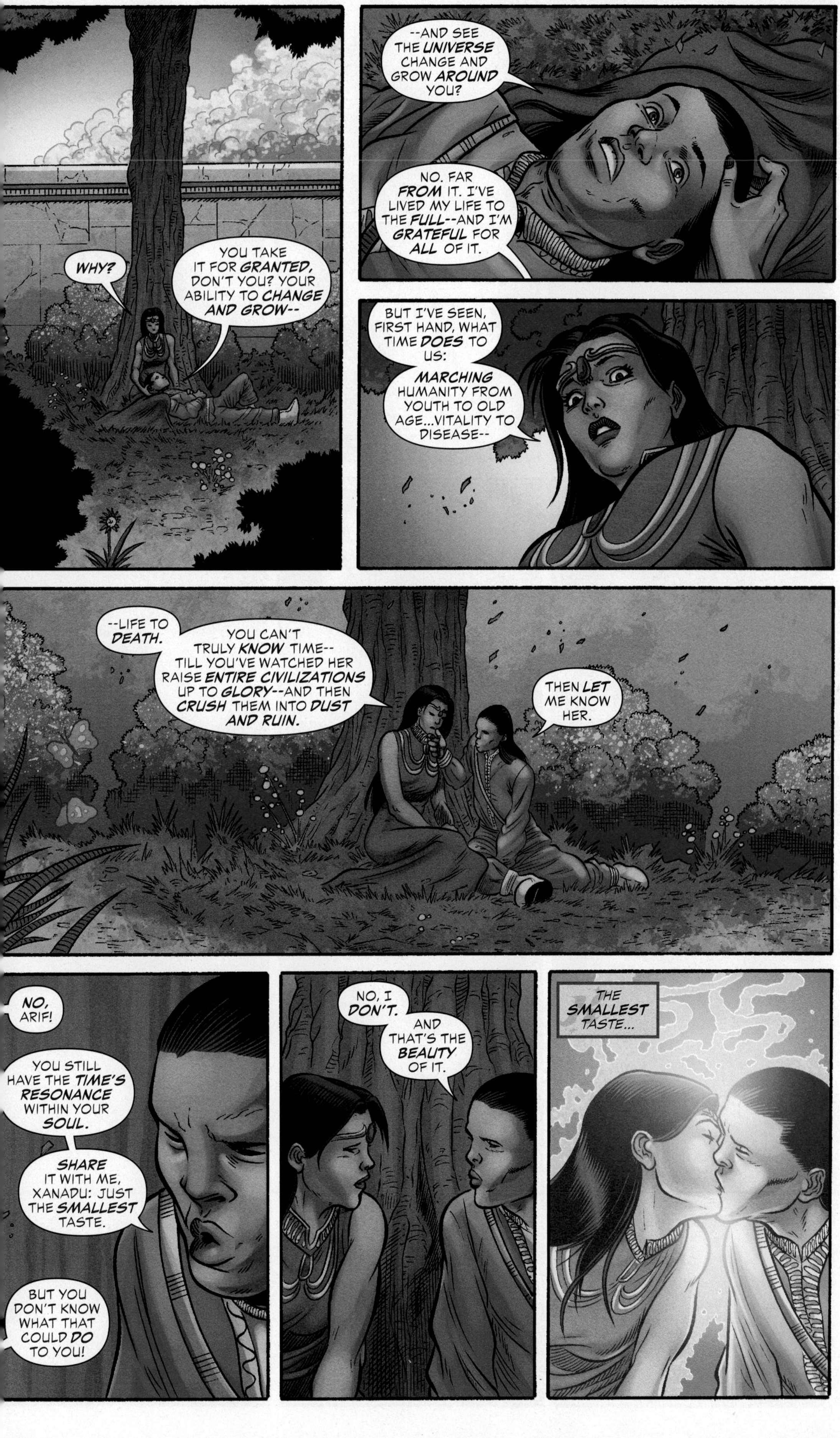
WHY?
YOU TAKE IT FOR GRANTED, DON'T YOU? YOUR ABILITY TO CHANGE AND GROW--
--AND SEE THE UNIVERSE CHANGE AND GROW AROUND YOU?
NO. FAR FROM IT. I'VE LIVED MY LIFE TO THE FULL--AND I'M GRATEFUL FOR ALL OF IT.
BUT I'VE SEEN, FIRST HAND, WHAT TIME DOES TO US:
MARCHING HUMANITY FROM YOUTH TO OLD AGE...VITALITY TO DISEASE--
--LIFE TO DEATH.
YOU CAN'T TRULY KNOW TIME--TILL YOU'VE WATCHED HER RAISE ENTIRE CIVILIZATIONS UP TO GLORY--AND THEN CRUSH THEM INTO DUST AND RUIN.
THEN LET ME KNOW HER.
NO, ARIF!
YOU STILL HAVE THE TIME'S RESONANCE WITHIN YOUR SOUL.
SHARE IT WITH ME, XANADU: JUST THE SMALLEST TASTE.
BUT YOU DON'T KNOW WHAT THAT COULD DO TO YOU!
NO, I DON'T.
AND THAT'S THE BEAUTY OF IT.
THE SMALLEST TASTE...

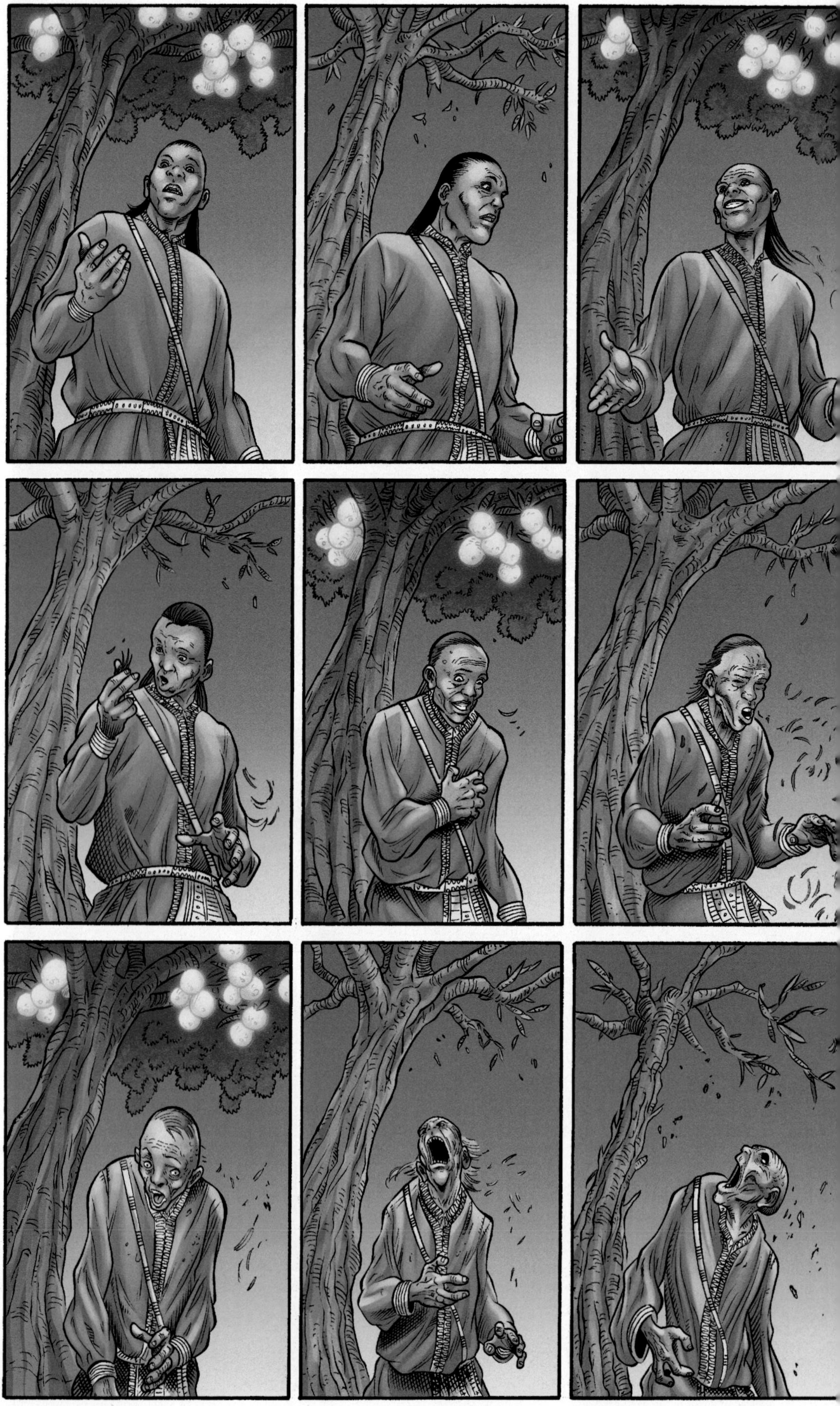

...PROVES TOO MUCH FOR HIM TO BEAR.

I CALL TIME **BACK**--HOPING TO **RENEW** ARIF, **RESTORE** HIM...

...BUT IT'S **TOO LATE**.

DON'T WEEP FOR ME, SWEET XANADU: **REJOICE**.

FOR I NOW KNOW THE **GLORY** OF THE **TRANSIENT**, THE **ECSTASY** OF THE **EPHEMERAL**. AND IN **THAT**--

--IN **YOU**--

--I'VE **FOUND**...

WHAT HAVE YOU FOUND, ARIF?

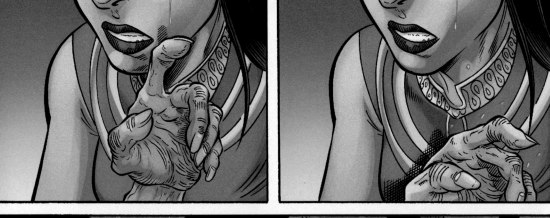

HE TOLD ME NOT TO WEEP, BUT I **DO**. AND, AS I WEEP, I WONDER:

DID I **LIBERATE** THIS MAN--OR **MURDER** HIM? AM I THE **ANGEL** AT THE GATES OF PARADISE...

...OR THE **SERPENT** IN THE GARDEN?

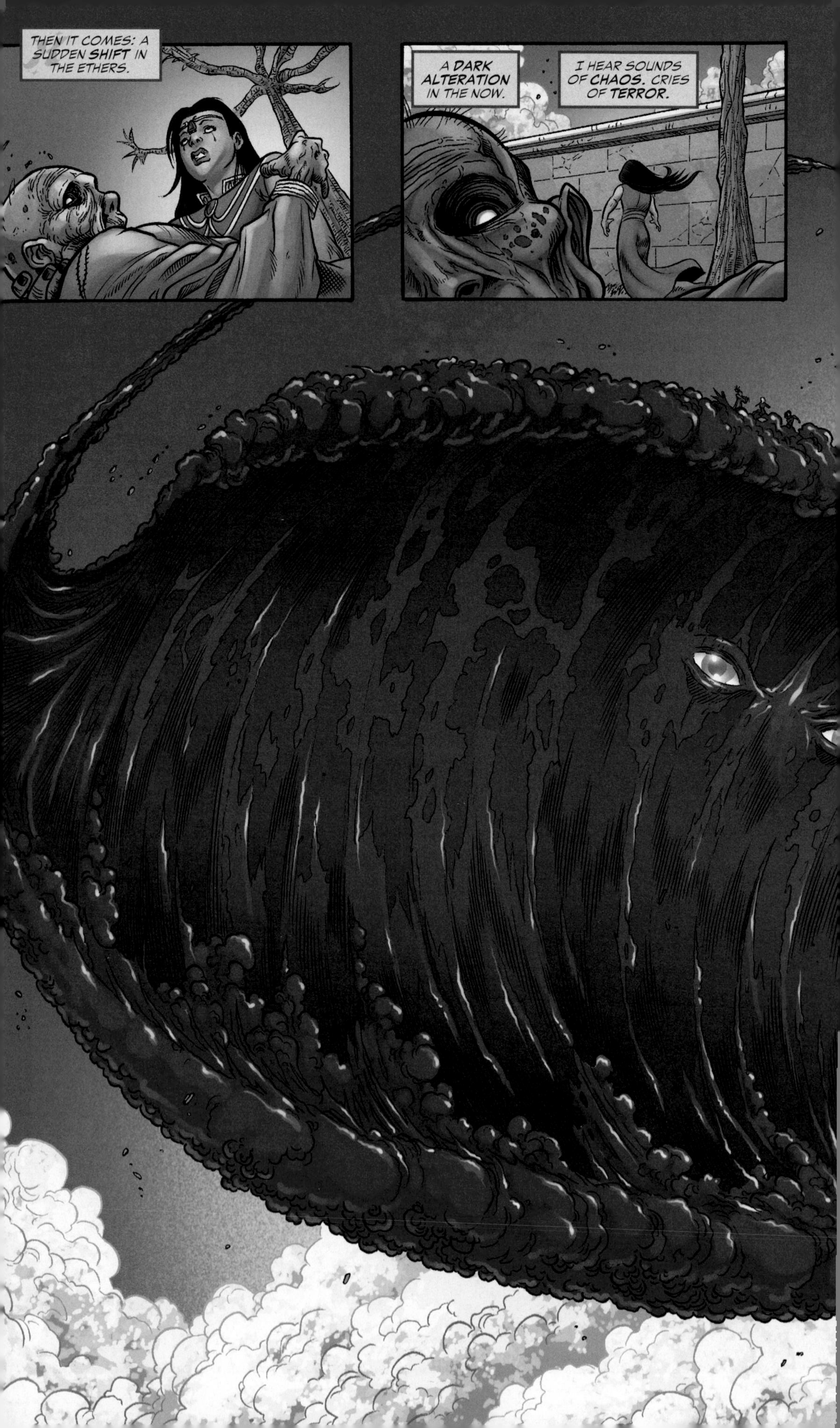
THEN IT COMES: A SUDDEN SHIFT IN THE ETHERS.
A DARK ALTERATION IN THE NOW.
I HEAR SOUNDS OF CHAOS. CRIES OF TERROR.

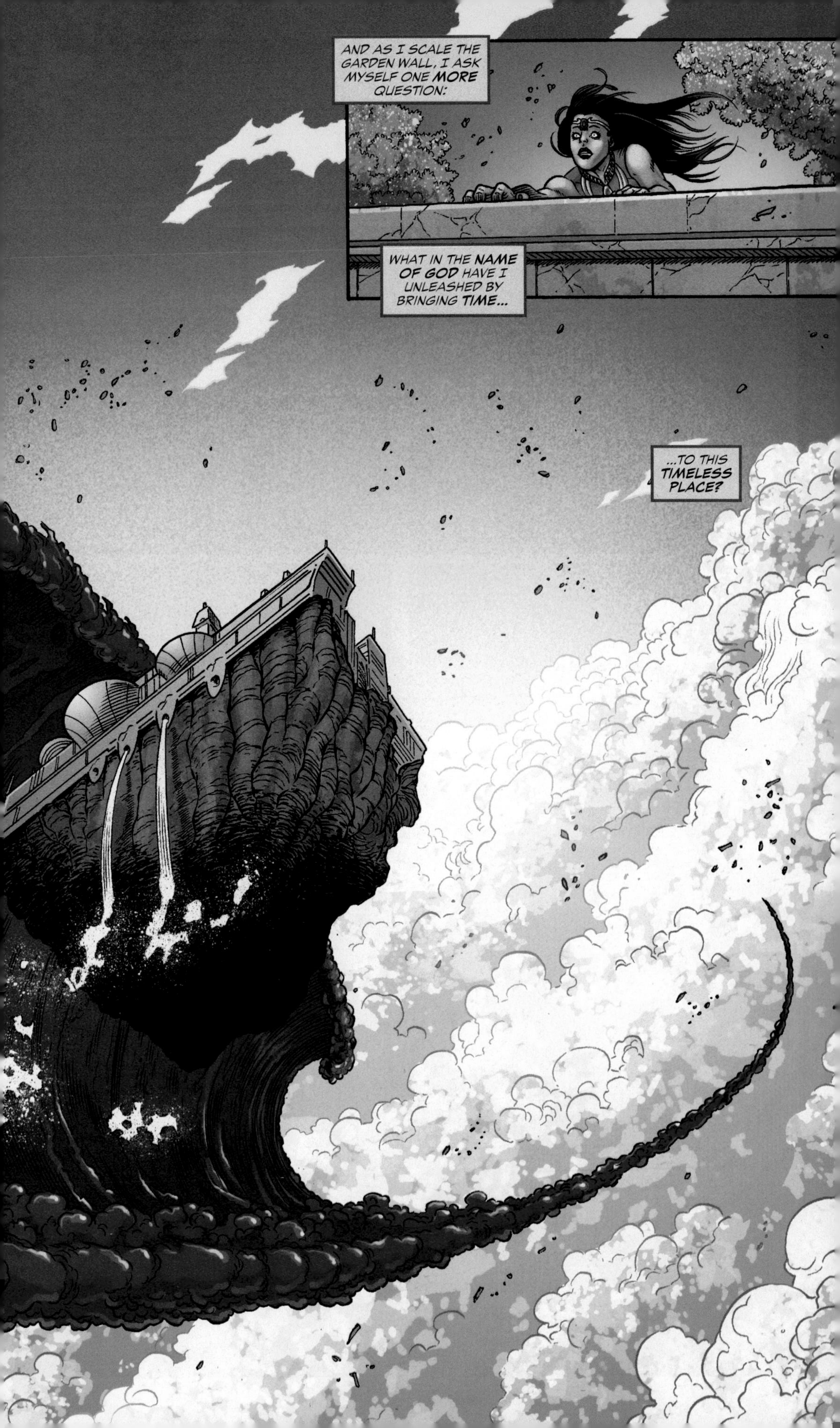
AND AS I SCALE THE GARDEN WALL, I ASK MYSELF ONE MORE QUESTION:
WHAT IN THE NAME OF GOD HAVE I UNLEASHED BY BRINGING TIME...
...TO THIS TIMELESS PLACE?

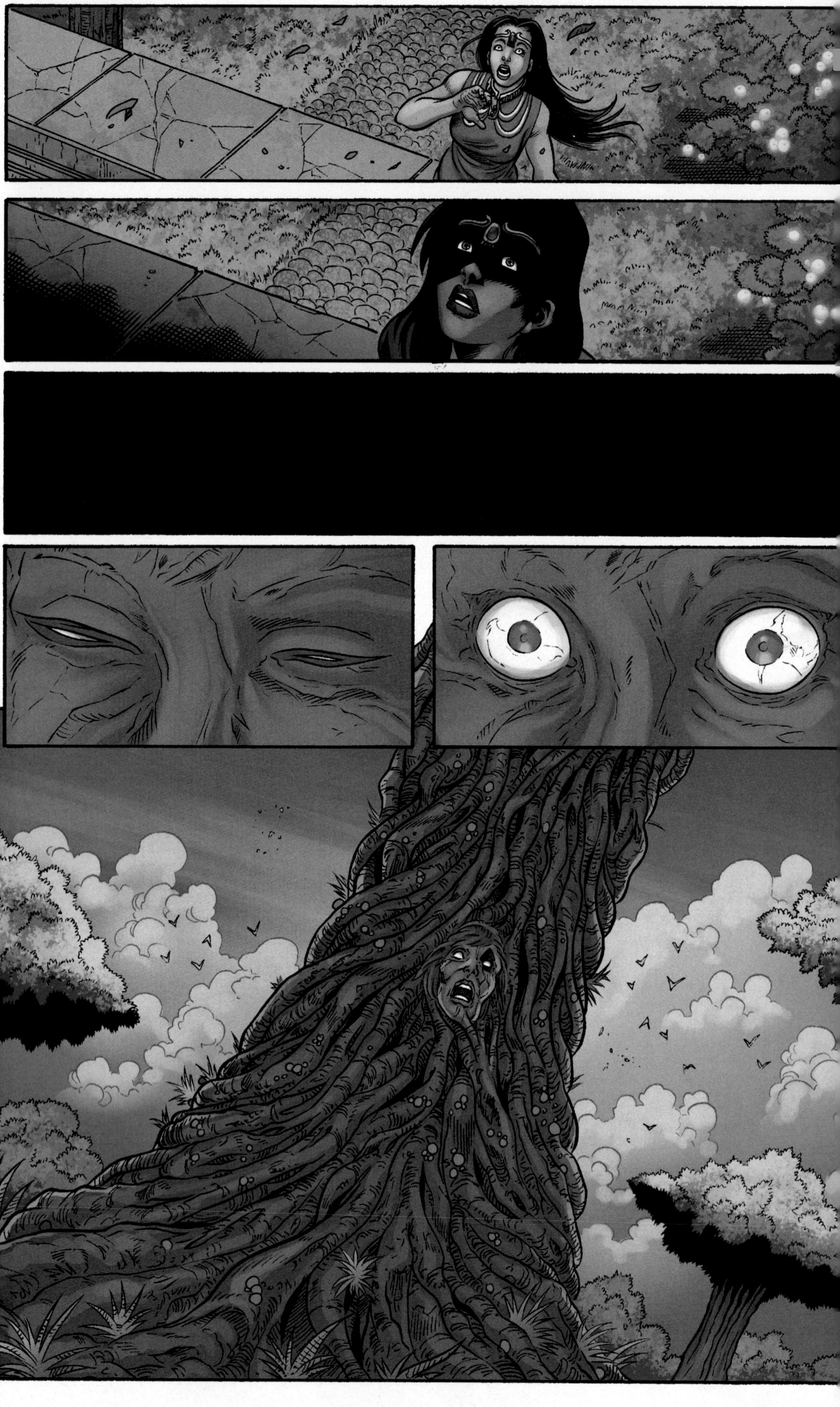

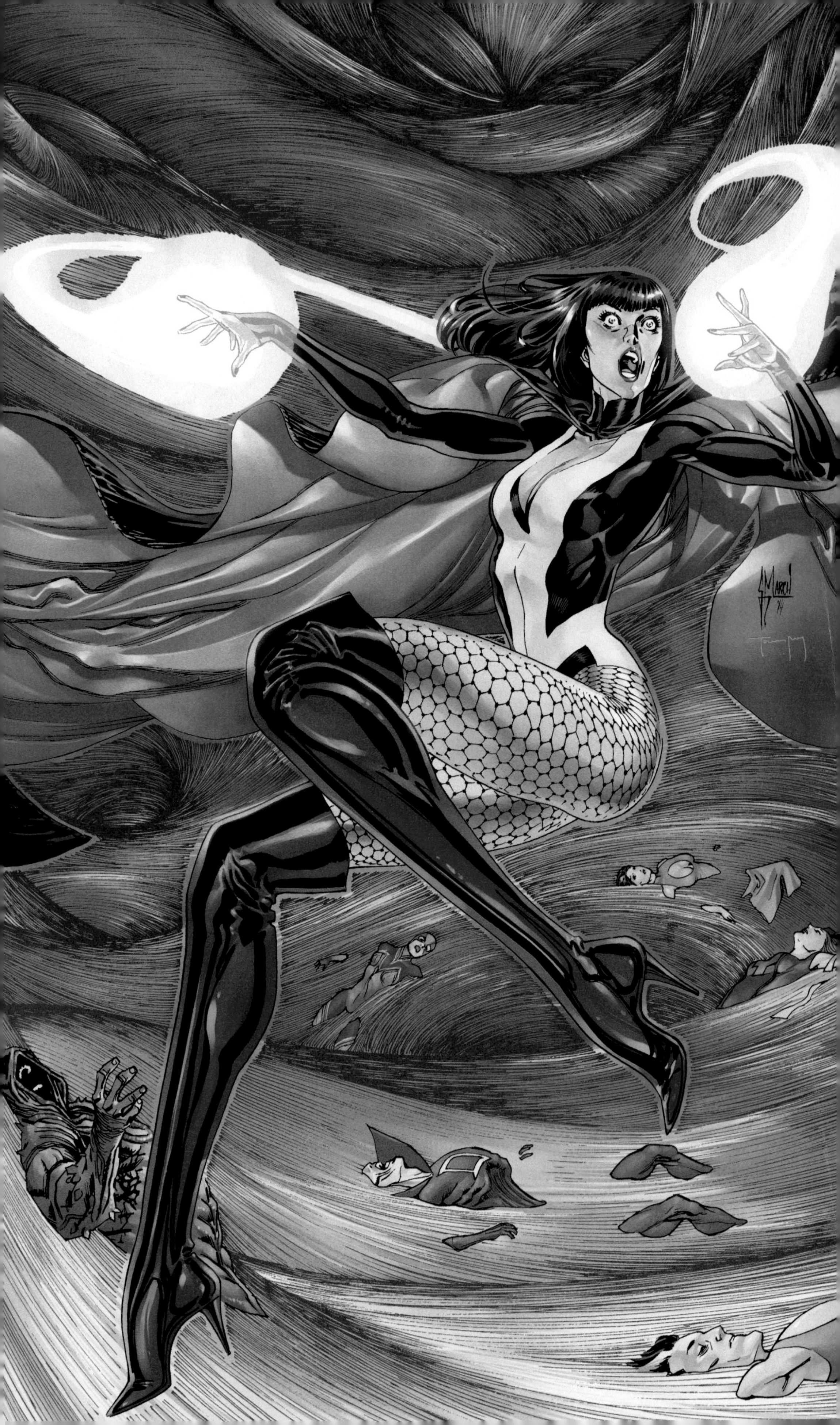

THE AMBER OF THE MOMENT PART 4: DARK REUNION

J.M. DEMATTEIS writer ANDRES GUINALDO penciller WALDEN WONG inker CHRIS SOTOMAYOR colorist TRAVIS LANHAM letterer cover by GUILLEM MARCH & TOMEU MOREY

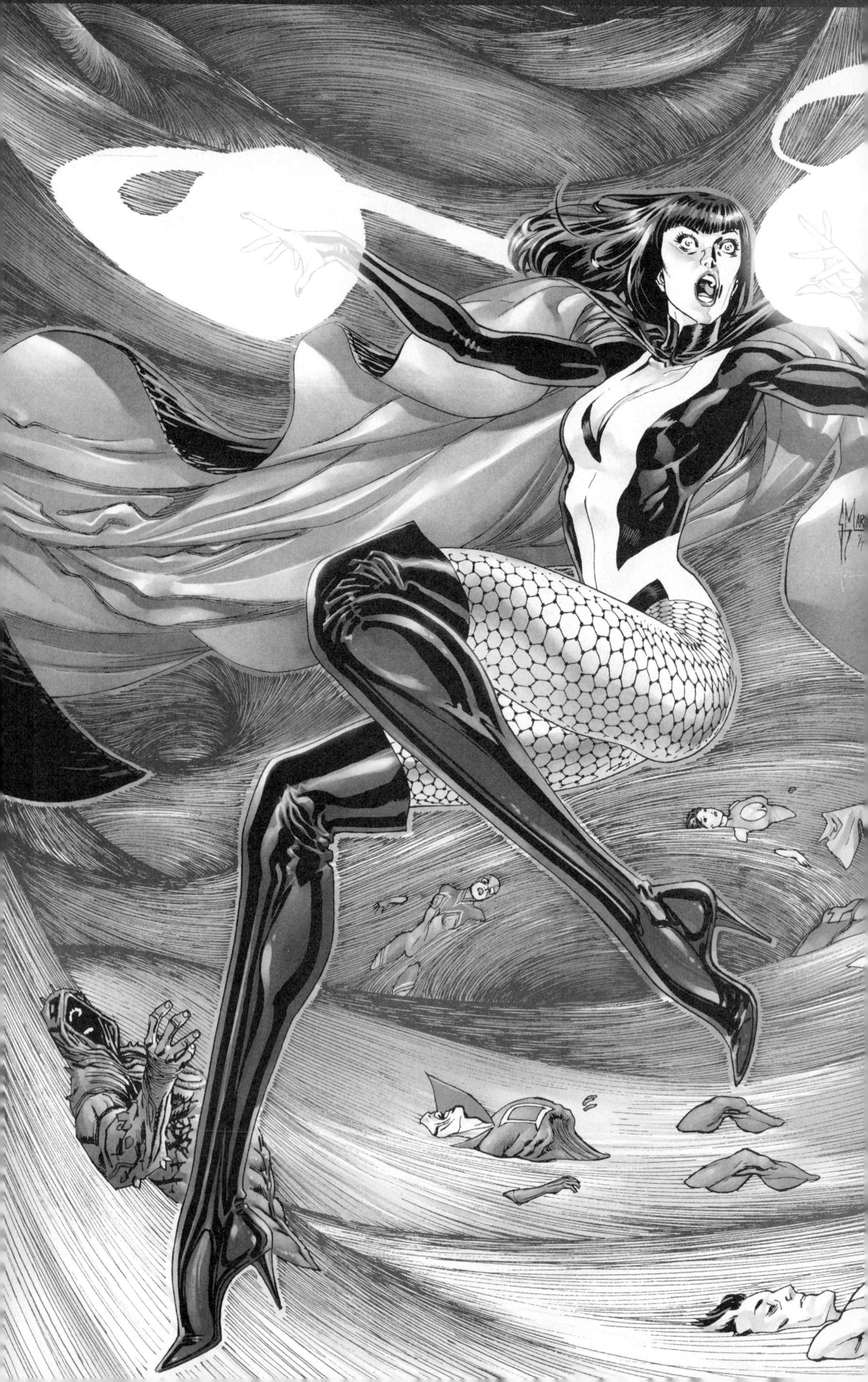

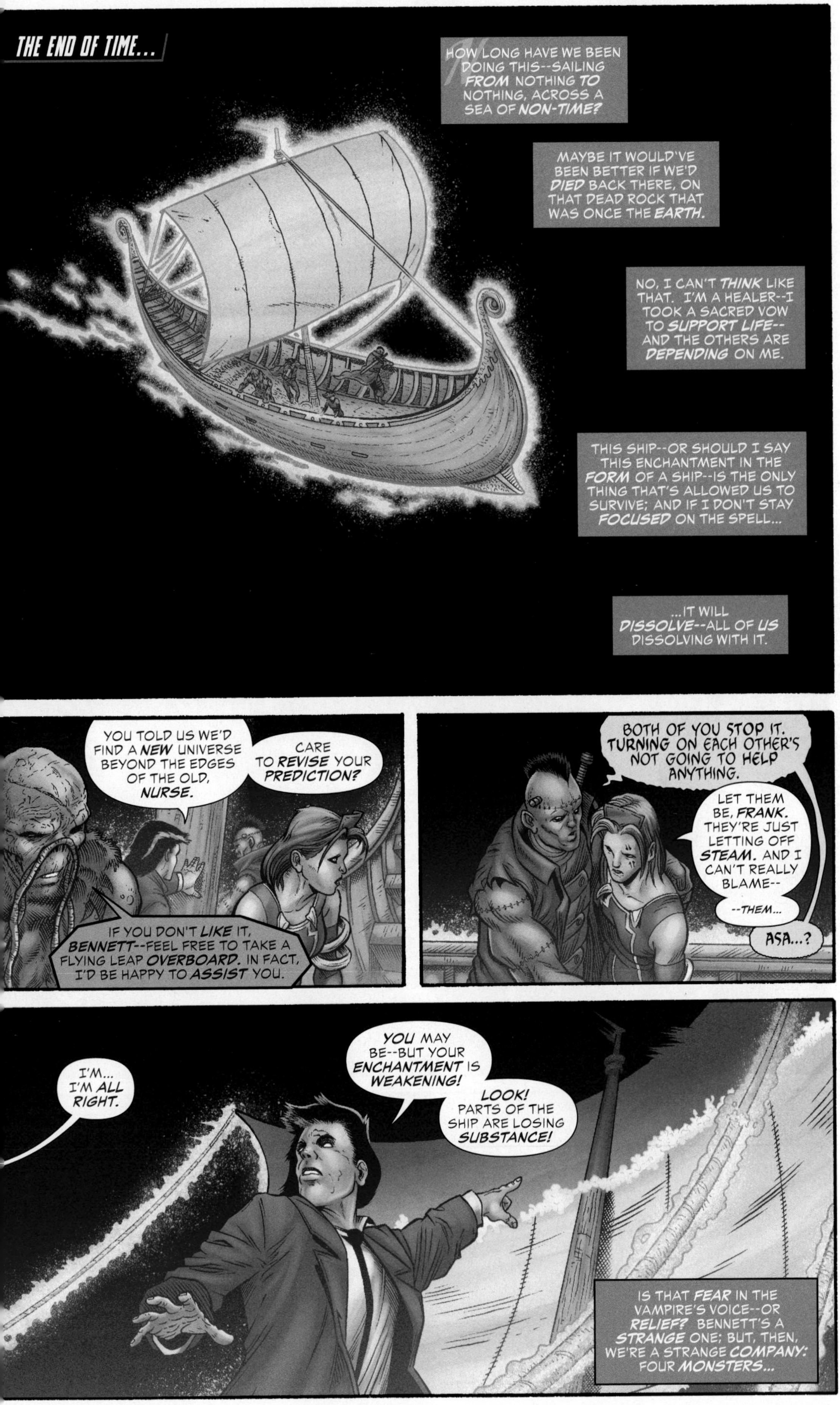

THE END OF TIME...
HOW LONG HAVE WE BEEN DOING THIS--SAILING FROM NOTHING TO NOTHING, ACROSS A SEA OF NON-TIME?
MAYBE IT WOULD'VE BEEN BETTER IF WE'D DIED BACK THERE, ON THAT DEAD ROCK THAT WAS ONCE THE EARTH.
NO, I CAN'T THINK LIKE THAT. I'M A HEALER--I TOOK A SACRED VOW TO SUPPORT LIFE--AND THE OTHERS ARE DEPENDING ON ME.
THIS SHIP--OR SHOULD I SAY THIS ENCHANTMENT IN THE FORM OF A SHIP--IS THE ONLY THING THAT'S ALLOWED US TO SURVIVE; AND IF I DON'T STAY FOCUSED ON THE SPELL...
...IT WILL DISSOLVE--ALL OF US DISSOLVING WITH IT.
YOU TOLD US WE'D FIND A NEW UNIVERSE BEYOND THE EDGES OF THE OLD, NURSE.
CARE TO REVISE YOUR PREDICTION?
IF YOU DON'T LIKE IT, BENNETT--FEEL FREE TO TAKE A FLYING LEAP OVERBOARD. IN FACT, I'D BE HAPPY TO ASSIST YOU.
BOTH OF YOU STOP IT. TURNING ON EACH OTHER'S NOT GOING TO HELP ANYTHING.
LET THEM BE, FRANK. THEY'RE JUST LETTING OFF STEAM. AND I CAN'T REALLY BLAME--
--THEM...
ASA...?
I'M... I'M ALL RIGHT.
YOU MAY BE--BUT YOUR ENCHANTMENT IS WEAKENING!
LOOK! PARTS OF THE SHIP ARE LOSING SUBSTANCE!
IS THAT FEAR IN THE VAMPIRE'S VOICE--OR RELIEF? BENNETT'S A STRANGE ONE; BUT, THEN, WE'RE A STRANGE COMPANY: FOUR MONSTERS...

...ALL OF US CLINGING TO SOME FORM OF IMAGINED *HUMANITY*.

WAIT! DO ANY OF YOU *FEEL* THAT?

FEEL, WHAT, *HOLLAND?*

IT'S LIKE... LIKE THE *FULL CONSCIOUSNESS* OF *THE GREEN*--

--BUT MULTIPLIED A THOUSAND--NO, A *MILLIONFOLD.*

I FEEL IT, *TOO.* AN...*AWARENESS*-- WASHING *OVER* ME--

--PUSHING *INTO* ME.

THERE'S SOMETHING *OUT* THERE AND IT--

IT'S *COMING.*

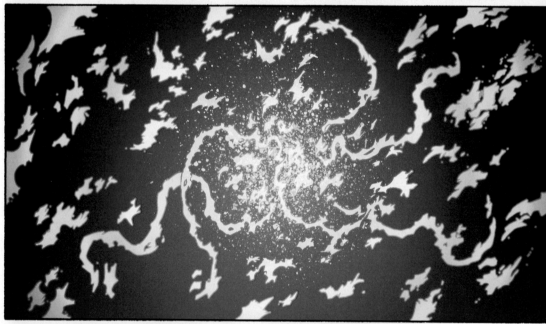

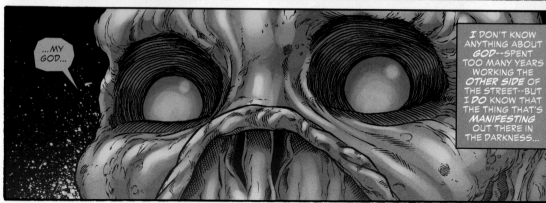

...MY GOD...

I DON'T KNOW ANYTHING ABOUT *GOD*--SPENT TOO MANY YEARS WORKING THE *OTHER SIDE* OF THE STREET--BUT I *DO* KNOW THAT THE THING THAT'S *MANIFESTING* OUT THERE IN THE DARKNESS...

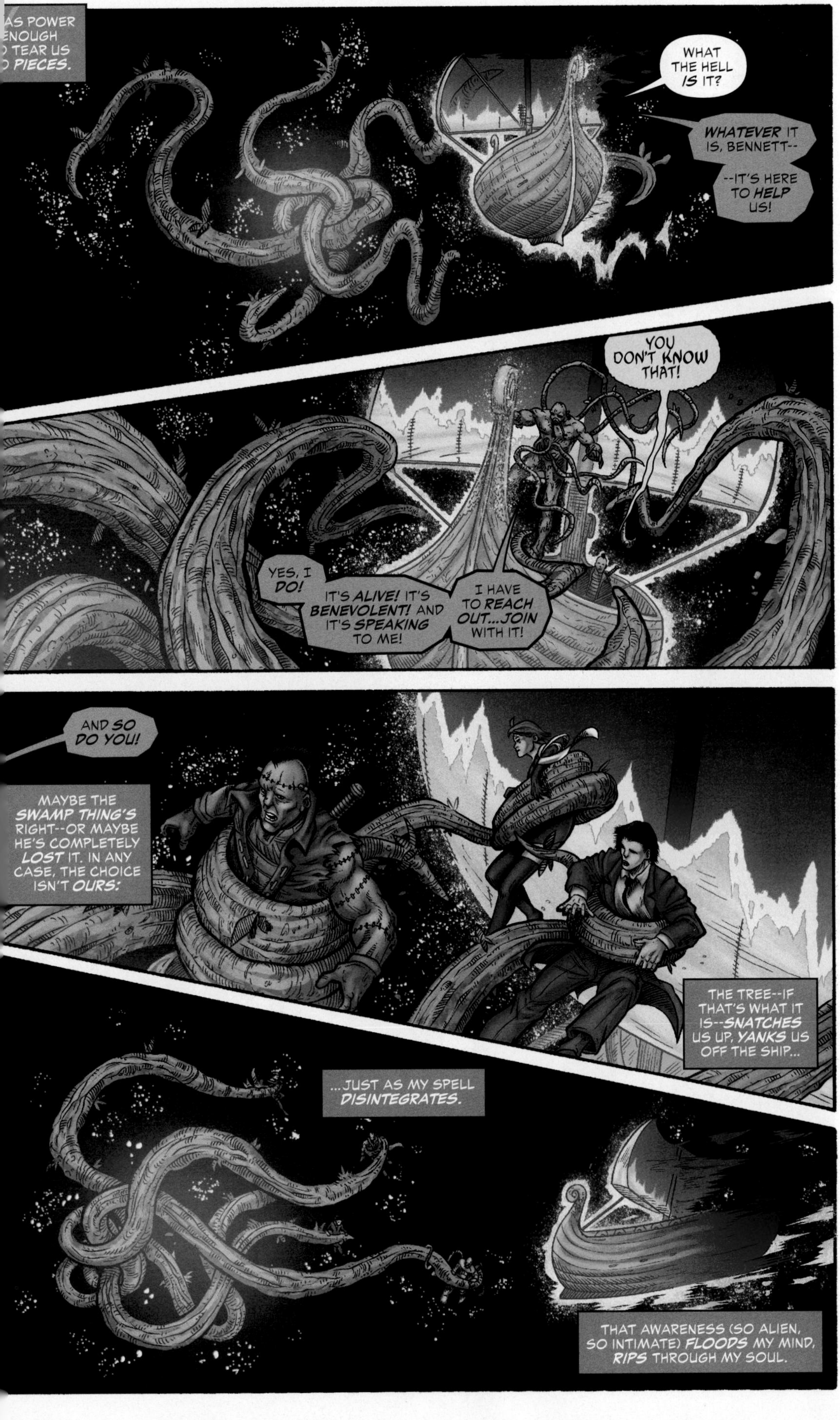

AS POWER ENOUGH O TEAR US O PIECES.
WHAT THE HELL IS IT?
WHATEVER IT IS, BENNETT--
--IT'S HERE TO HELP US!
YOU DON'T KNOW THAT!
YES, I DO!
IT'S ALIVE! IT'S BENEVOLENT! AND IT'S SPEAKING TO ME!
I HAVE TO REACH OUT...JOIN WITH IT!
AND SO DO YOU!
MAYBE THE SWAMP THING'S RIGHT--OR MAYBE HE'S COMPLETELY LOST IT. IN ANY CASE, THE CHOICE ISN'T OURS:
THE TREE--IF THAT'S WHAT IT IS--SNATCHES US UP, YANKS US OFF THE SHIP...
...JUST AS MY SPELL DISINTEGRATES.
THAT AWARENESS (SO ALIEN, SO INTIMATE) FLOODS MY MIND, RIPS THROUGH MY SOUL.

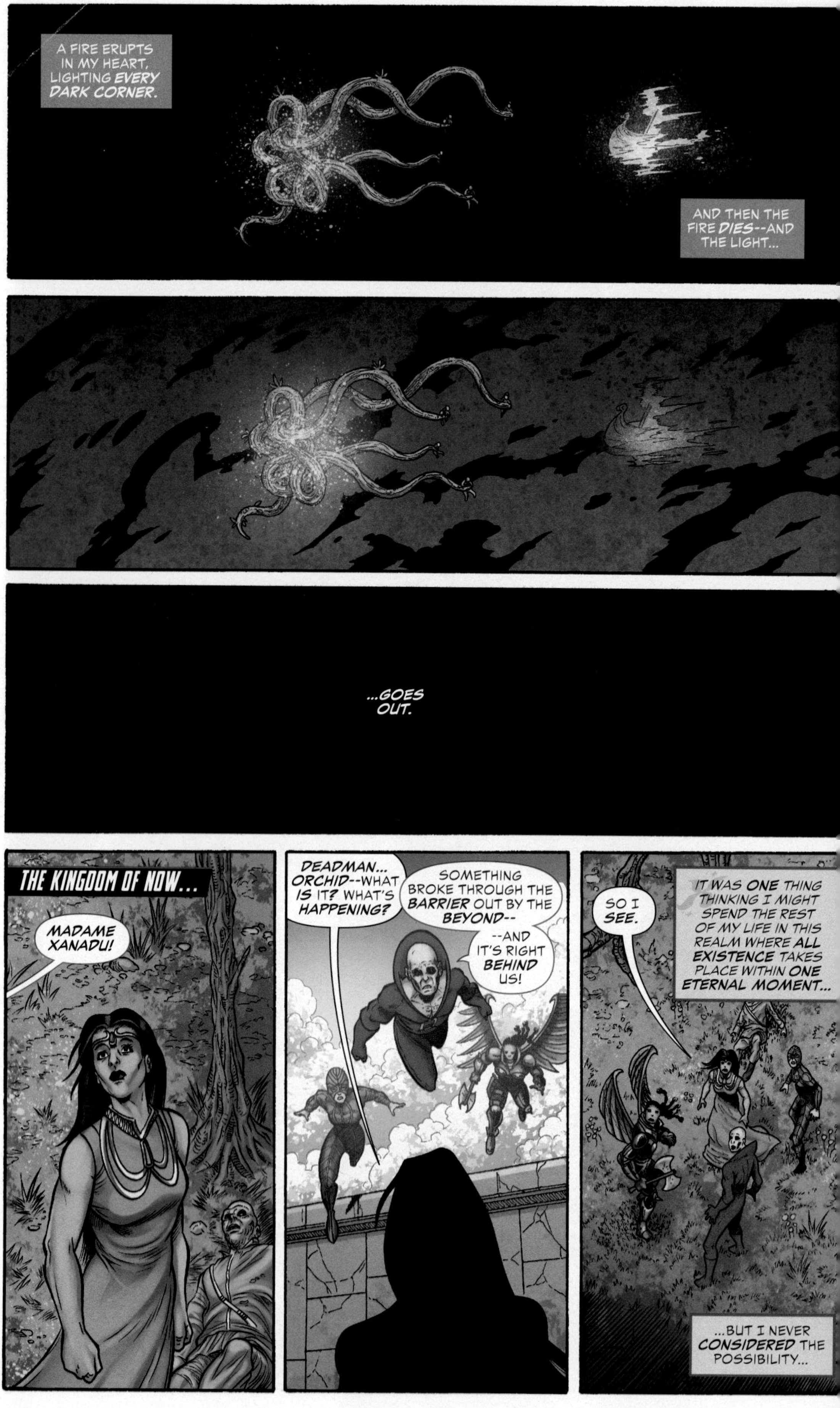
A FIRE ERUPTS IN MY HEART, LIGHTING EVERY DARK CORNER.
AND THEN THE FIRE DIES--AND THE LIGHT...
...GOES OUT.
THE KINGDOM OF NOW...
MADAME XANADU!
DEADMAN... ORCHID--WHAT IS IT? WHAT'S HAPPENING?
SOMETHING BROKE THROUGH THE BARRIER OUT BY THE BEYOND--
--AND IT'S RIGHT BEHIND US!
SO I SEE.
IT WAS ONE THING THINKING I MIGHT SPEND THE REST OF MY LIFE IN THIS REALM WHERE ALL EXISTENCE TAKES PLACE WITHIN ONE ETERNAL MOMENT...
...BUT I NEVER CONSIDERED THE POSSIBILITY...

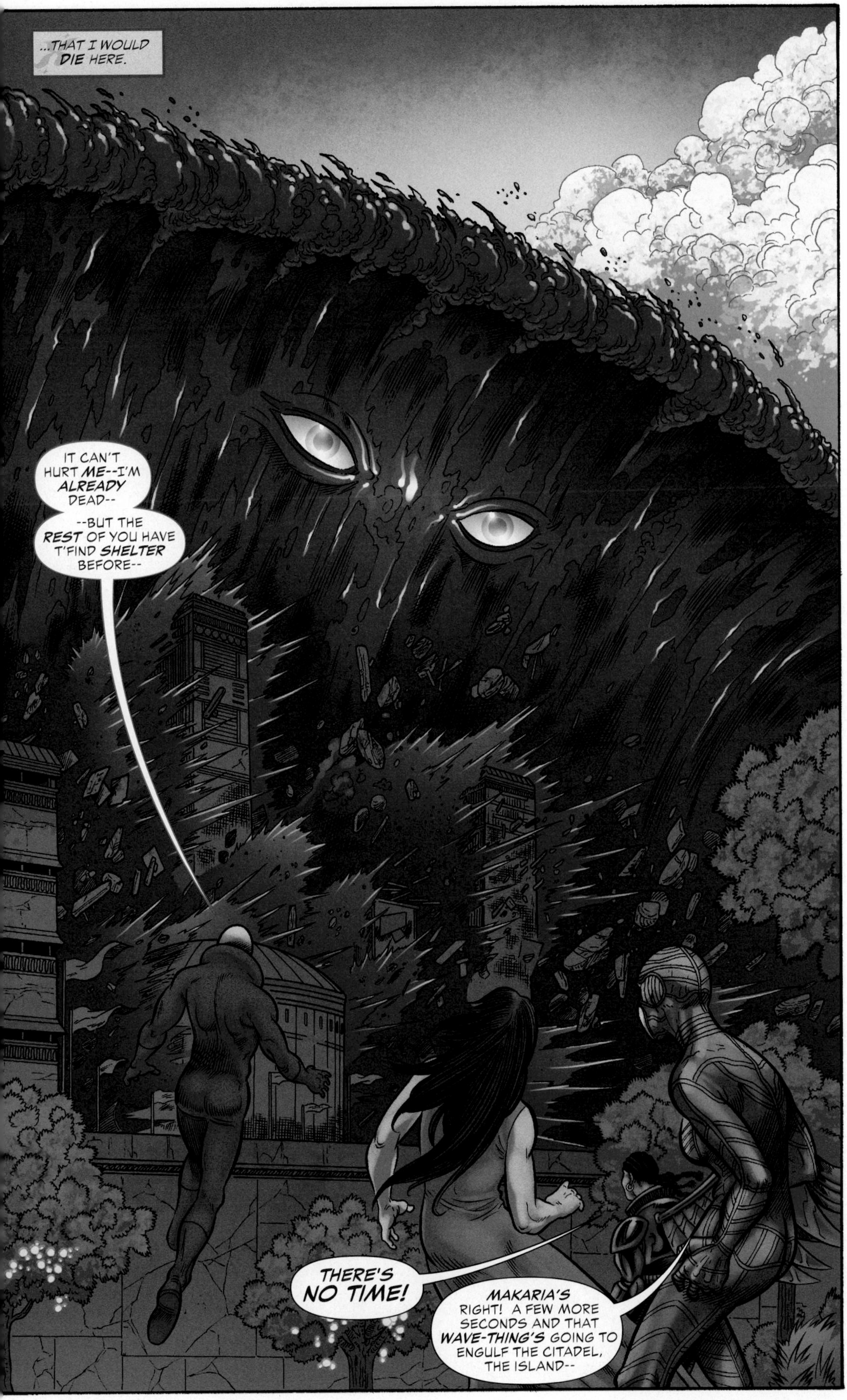
...THAT I WOULD DIE HERE.
IT CAN'T HURT ME--I'M ALREADY DEAD--
--BUT THE REST OF YOU HAVE T'FIND SHELTER BEFORE--
THERE'S NO TIME!
MAKARIA'S RIGHT! A FEW MORE SECONDS AND THAT WAVE-THING'S GOING TO ENGULF THE CITADEL, THE ISLAND--

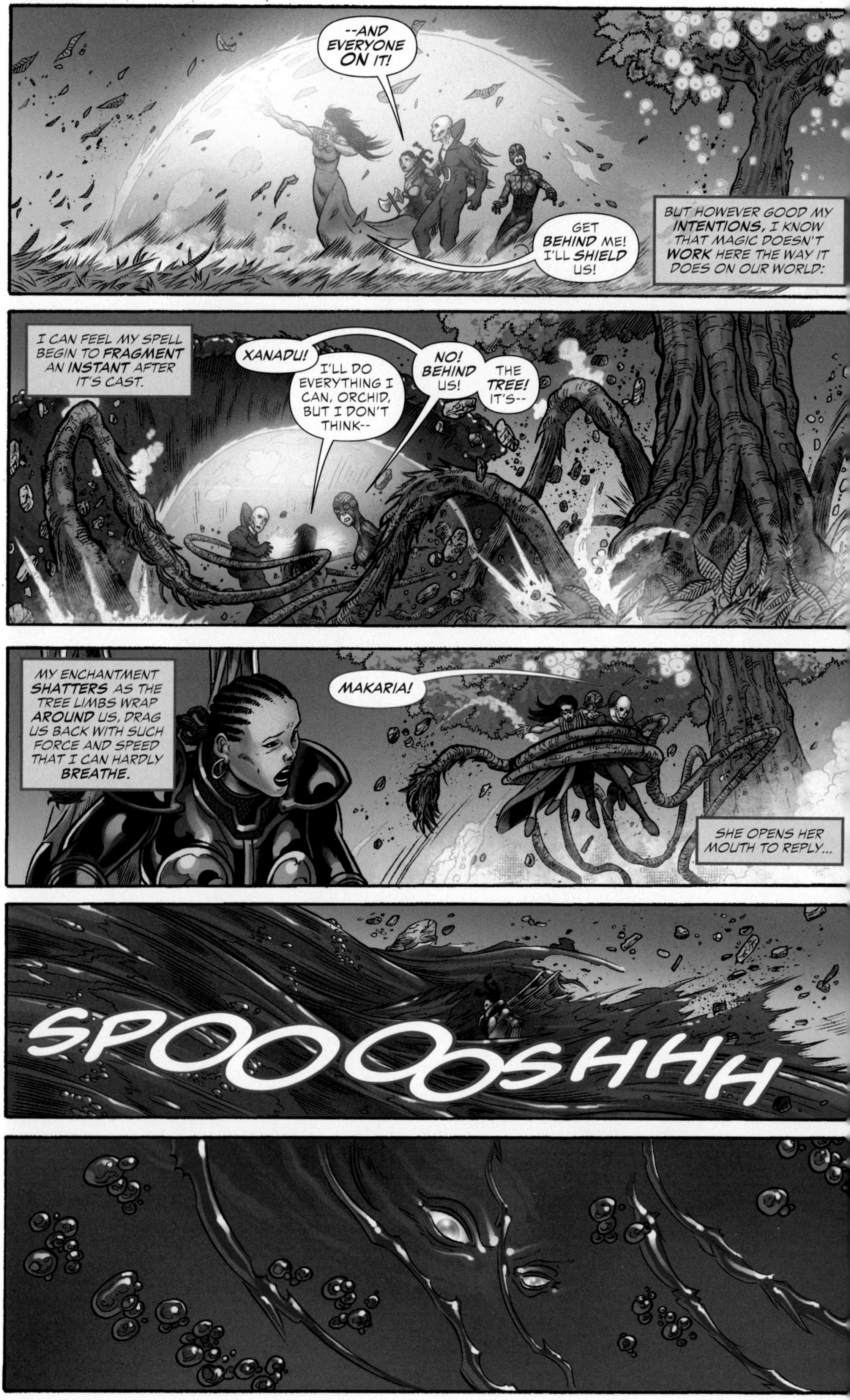
--AND EVERYONE ON IT!
GET BEHIND ME! I'LL SHIELD US!
BUT HOWEVER GOOD MY INTENTIONS, I KNOW THAT MAGIC DOESN'T WORK HERE THE WAY IT DOES ON OUR WORLD:
I CAN FEEL MY SPELL BEGIN TO FRAGMENT AN INSTANT AFTER IT'S CAST.
XANADU!
I'LL DO EVERYTHING I CAN, ORCHID, BUT I DON'T THINK--
NO! BEHIND US!
THE TREE! IT'S--
MY ENCHANTMENT SHATTERS AS THE TREE LIMBS WRAP AROUND US, DRAG US BACK WITH SUCH FORCE AND SPEED THAT I CAN HARDLY BREATHE.
MAKARIA!
SHE OPENS HER MOUTH TO REPLY...
SPOOOOSHHH

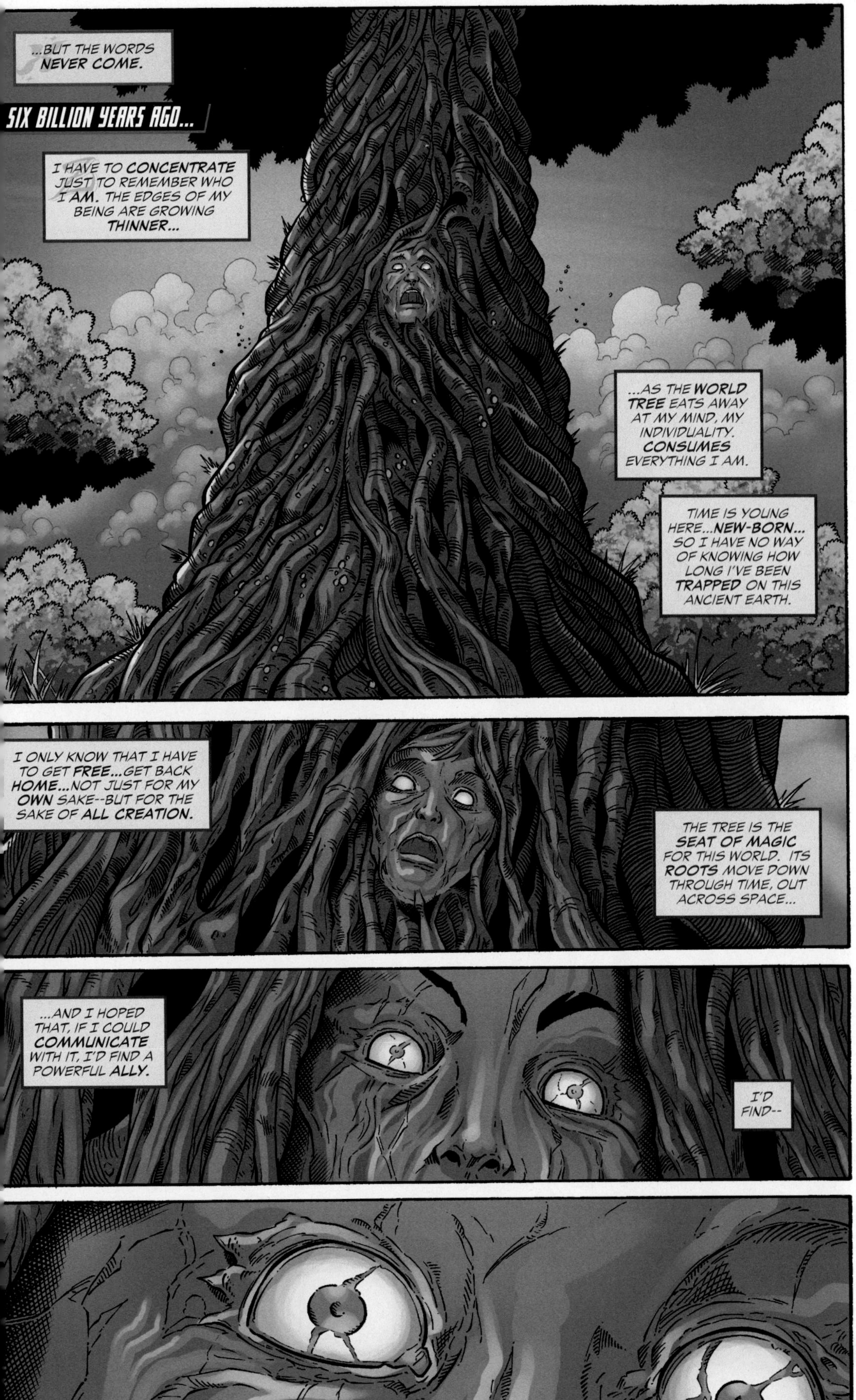
...BUT THE WORDS NEVER COME.
SIX BILLION YEARS AGO...
I HAVE TO CONCENTRATE JUST TO REMEMBER WHO I AM. THE EDGES OF MY BEING ARE GROWING THINNER...
...AS THE WORLD TREE EATS AWAY AT MY MIND, MY INDIVIDUALITY. CONSUMES EVERYTHING I AM.
TIME IS YOUNG HERE...NEW-BORN... SO I HAVE NO WAY OF KNOWING HOW LONG I'VE BEEN TRAPPED ON THIS ANCIENT EARTH.
I ONLY KNOW THAT I HAVE TO GET FREE...GET BACK HOME...NOT JUST FOR MY OWN SAKE--BUT FOR THE SAKE OF ALL CREATION.
THE TREE IS THE SEAT OF MAGIC FOR THIS WORLD. ITS ROOTS MOVE DOWN THROUGH TIME, OUT ACROSS SPACE...
...AND I HOPED THAT, IF I COULD COMMUNICATE WITH IT, I'D FIND A POWERFUL ALLY.
I'D FIND--

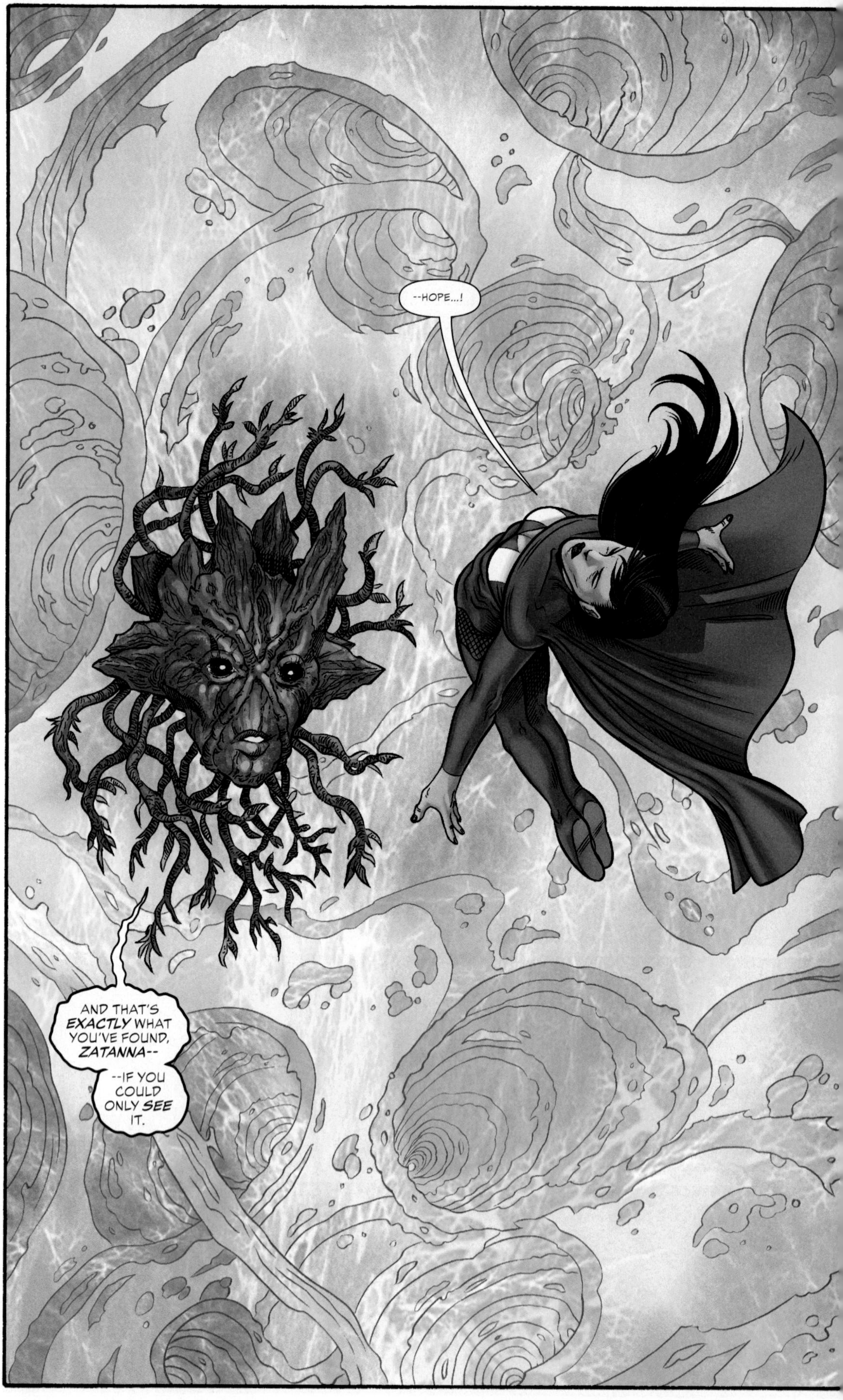
--HOPE...!
AND THAT'S EXACTLY WHAT YOU'VE FOUND, ZATANNA--
--IF YOU COULD ONLY SEE IT.

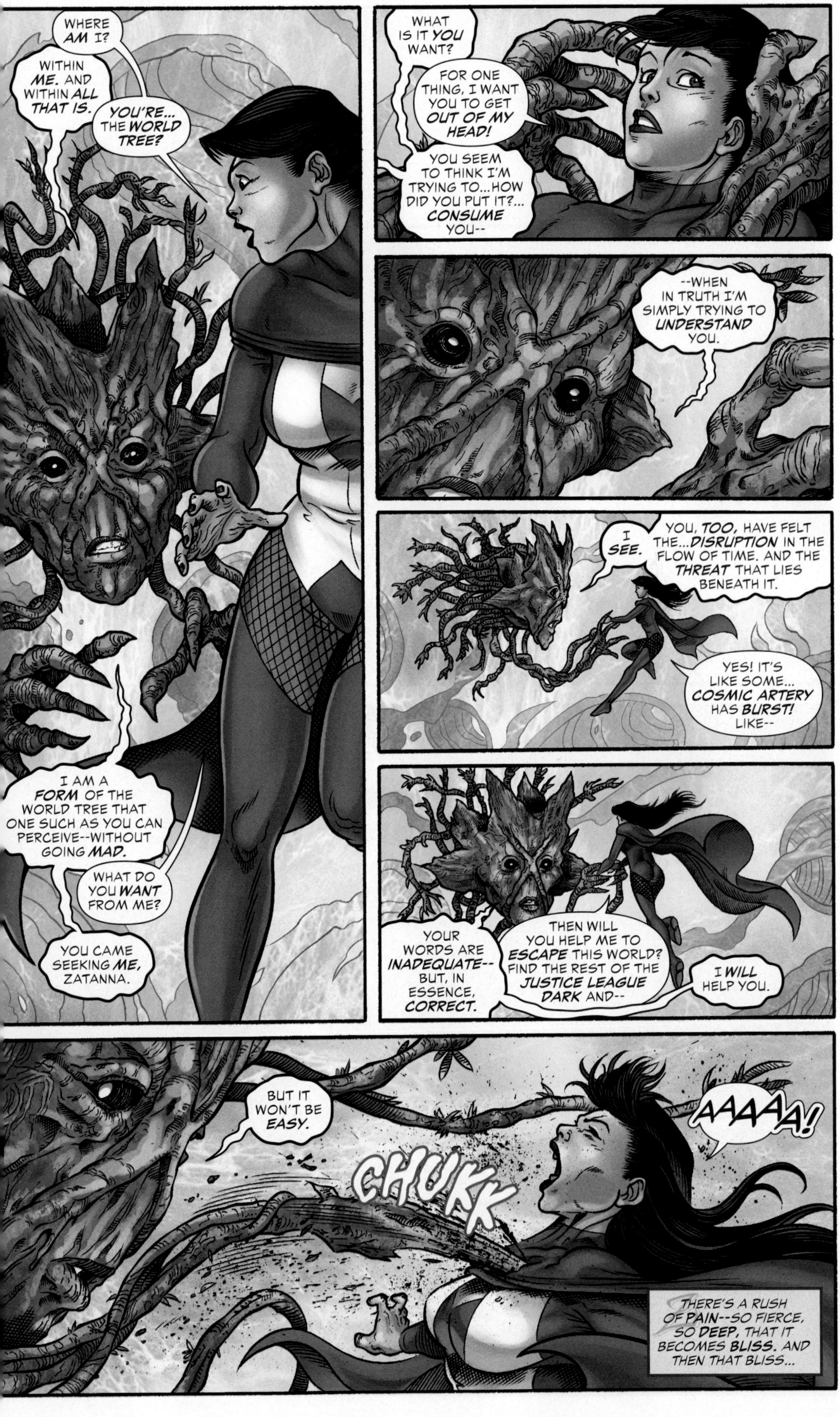
WHERE AM I?
WITHIN ME. AND WITHIN ALL THAT IS.
YOU'RE... THE WORLD TREE?
I AM A FORM OF THE WORLD TREE THAT ONE SUCH AS YOU CAN PERCEIVE--WITHOUT GOING MAD.
WHAT DO YOU WANT FROM ME?
YOU CAME SEEKING ME, ZATANNA.
WHAT IS IT YOU WANT?
FOR ONE THING, I WANT YOU TO GET OUT OF MY HEAD!
YOU SEEM TO THINK I'M TRYING TO...HOW DID YOU PUT IT?... CONSUME YOU--
--WHEN IN TRUTH I'M SIMPLY TRYING TO UNDERSTAND YOU.
I SEE.
YOU, TOO, HAVE FELT THE...DISRUPTION IN THE FLOW OF TIME. AND THE THREAT THAT LIES BENEATH IT.
YES! IT'S LIKE SOME... COSMIC ARTERY HAS BURST! LIKE--
YOUR WORDS ARE INADEQUATE--BUT, IN ESSENCE, CORRECT.
THEN WILL YOU HELP ME TO ESCAPE THIS WORLD? FIND THE REST OF THE JUSTICE LEAGUE DARK AND--
I WILL HELP YOU.
BUT IT WON'T BE EASY.
AAAAA!
CHUKK
THERE'S A RUSH OF PAIN--SO FIERCE, SO DEEP, THAT IT BECOMES BLISS. AND THEN THAT BLISS...

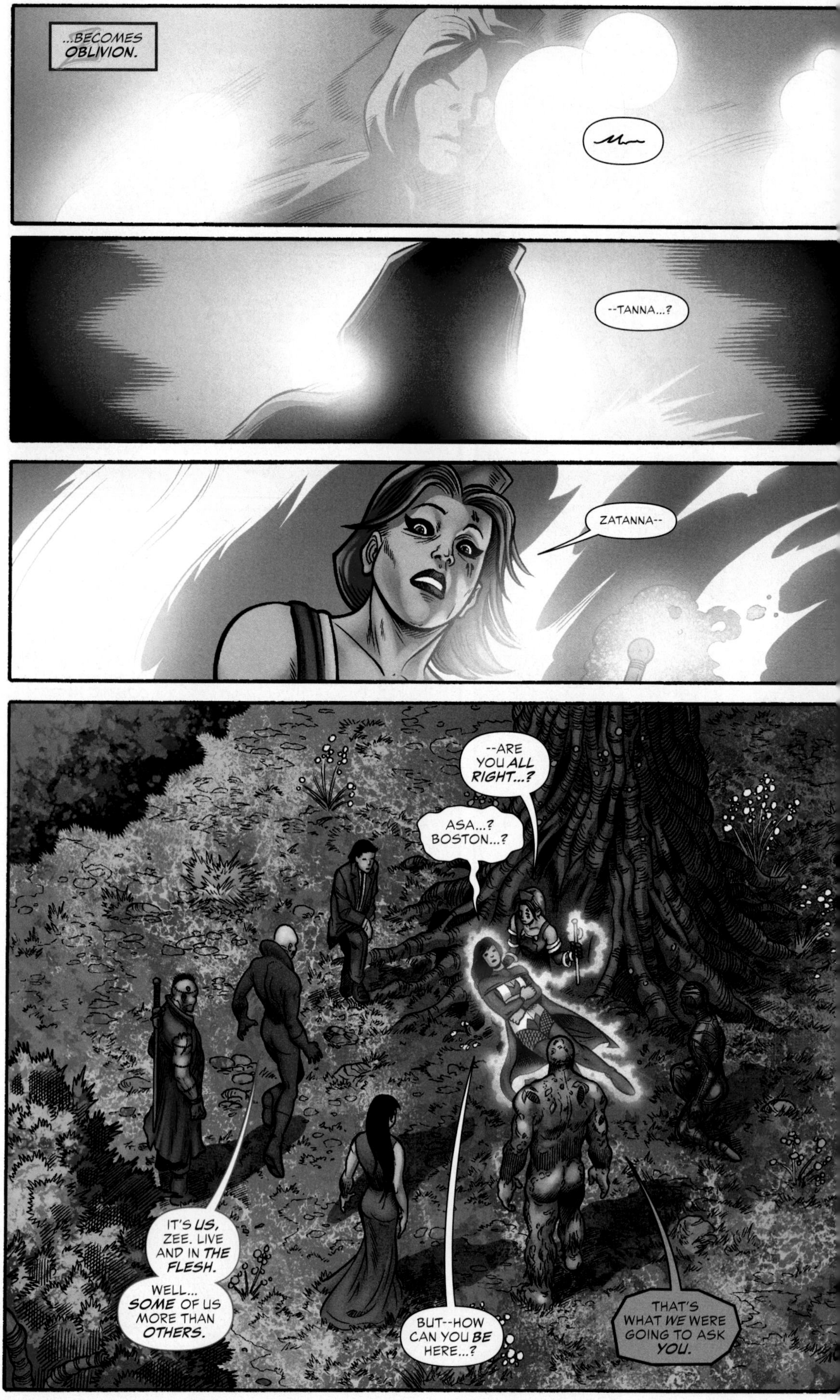
...BECOMES OBLIVION.
--TANNA...?
ZATANNA--
--ARE YOU ALL RIGHT...?
ASA...? BOSTON...?
IT'S US, ZEE. LIVE AND IN THE FLESH.
WELL... SOME OF US MORE THAN OTHERS.
BUT--HOW CAN YOU BE HERE...?
THAT'S WHAT WE WERE GOING TO ASK YOU.

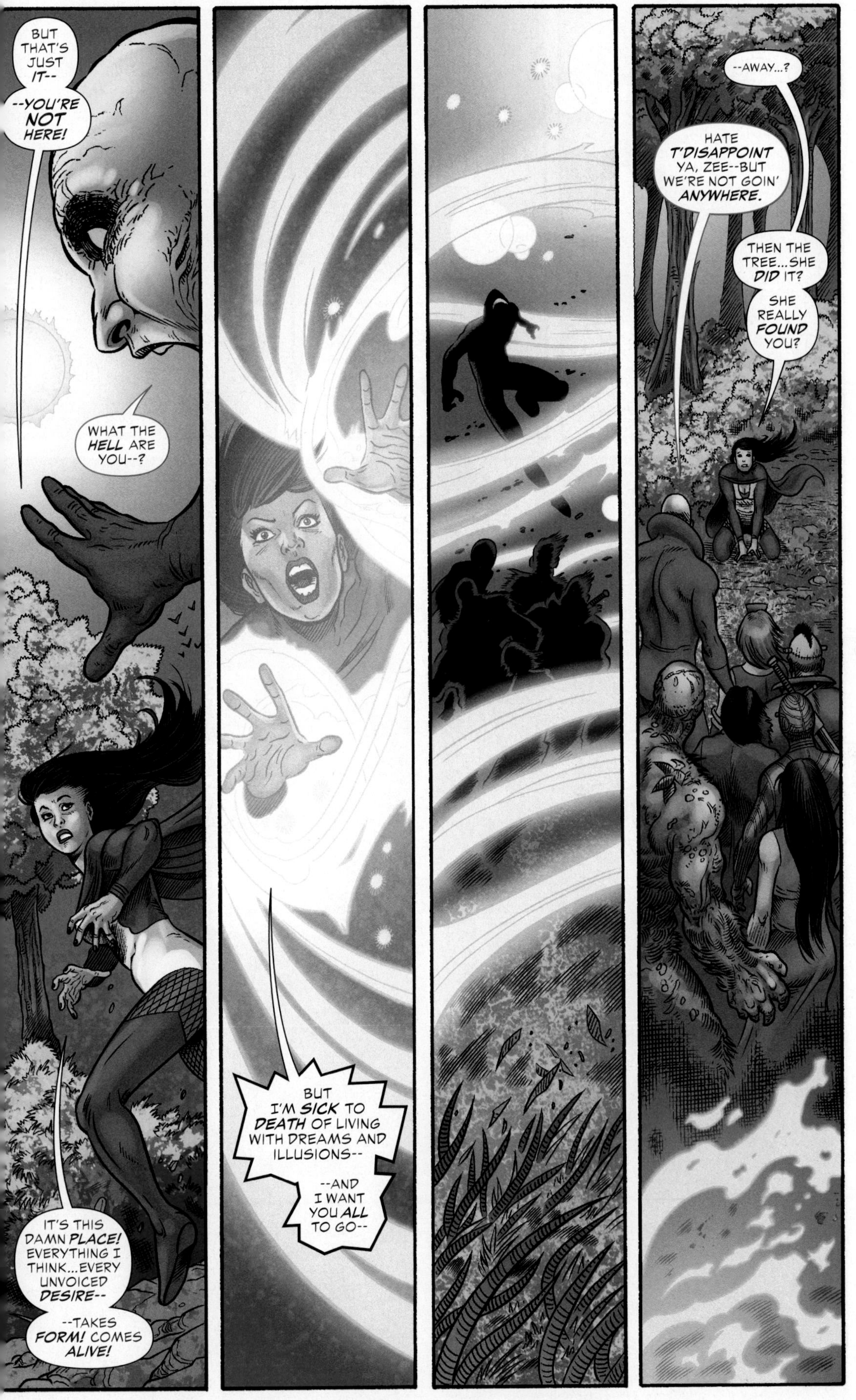

BUT THAT'S JUST *IT*--
--*YOU'RE NOT HERE!*
WHAT THE *HELL* ARE YOU--?
IT'S THIS DAMN *PLACE!* EVERYTHING I THINK...EVERY UNVOICED *DESIRE*--
--TAKES *FORM!* COMES *ALIVE!*
BUT I'M *SICK* TO *DEATH* OF LIVING WITH DREAMS AND ILLUSIONS--
--AND I WANT YOU *ALL* TO GO--
--AWAY...?
HATE *T'DISAPPOINT* YA, ZEE--BUT WE'RE NOT GOIN' *ANYWHERE.*
THEN THE TREE...SHE *DID* IT?
SHE REALLY *FOUND* YOU?

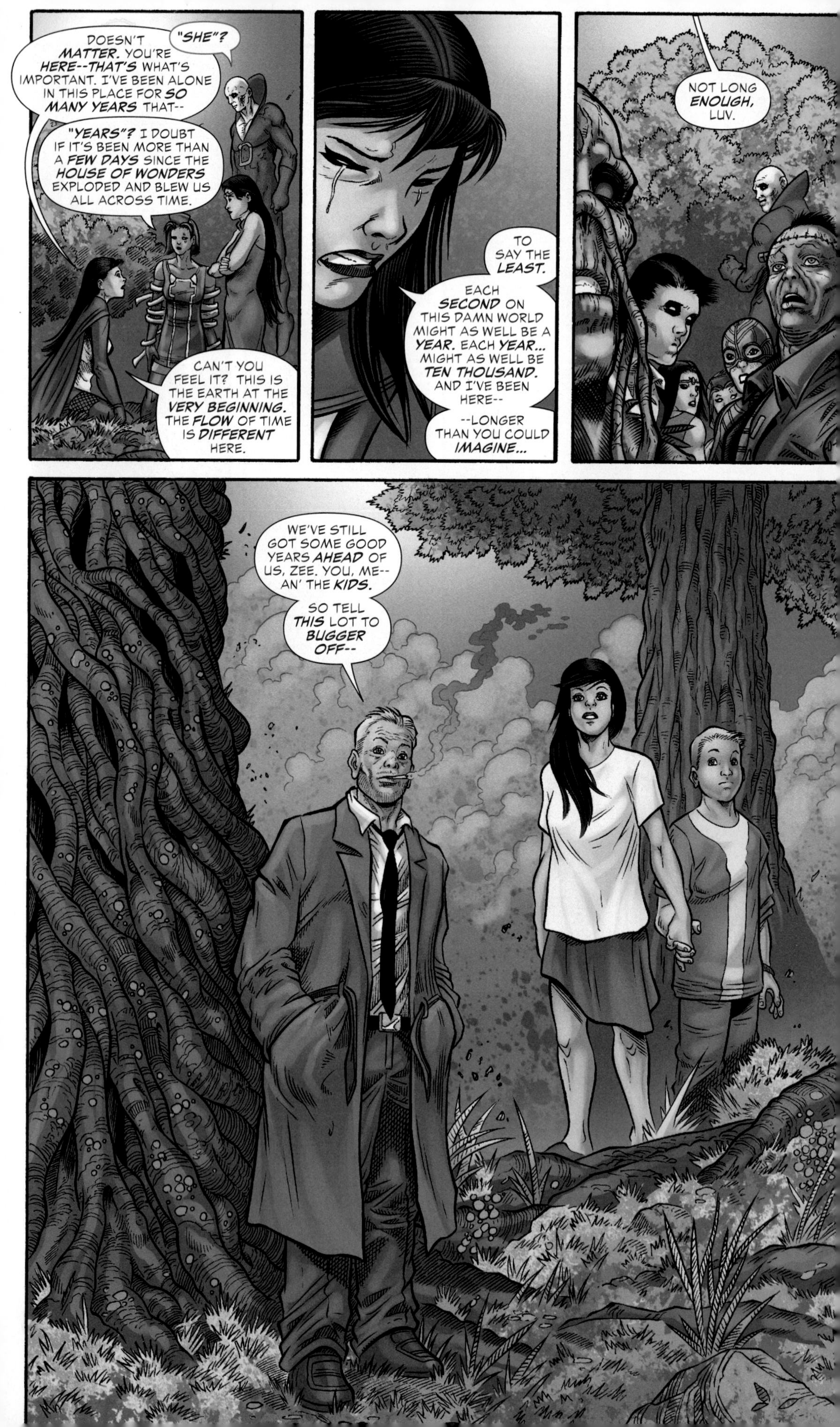
DOESN'T MATTER. YOU'RE HERE--THAT'S WHAT'S IMPORTANT. I'VE BEEN ALONE IN THIS PLACE FOR SO MANY YEARS THAT--
"SHE"?
"YEARS"? I DOUBT IF IT'S BEEN MORE THAN A FEW DAYS SINCE THE HOUSE OF WONDERS EXPLODED AND BLEW US ALL ACROSS TIME.
CAN'T YOU FEEL IT? THIS IS THE EARTH AT THE VERY BEGINNING. THE FLOW OF TIME IS DIFFERENT HERE.
TO SAY THE LEAST.
EACH SECOND ON THIS DAMN WORLD MIGHT AS WELL BE A YEAR. EACH YEAR... MIGHT AS WELL BE TEN THOUSAND. AND I'VE BEEN HERE--
--LONGER THAN YOU COULD IMAGINE...
NOT LONG ENOUGH, LUV.
WE'VE STILL GOT SOME GOOD YEARS AHEAD OF US, ZEE. YOU, ME-- AN' THE KIDS.
SO TELL THIS LOT TO BUGGER OFF--

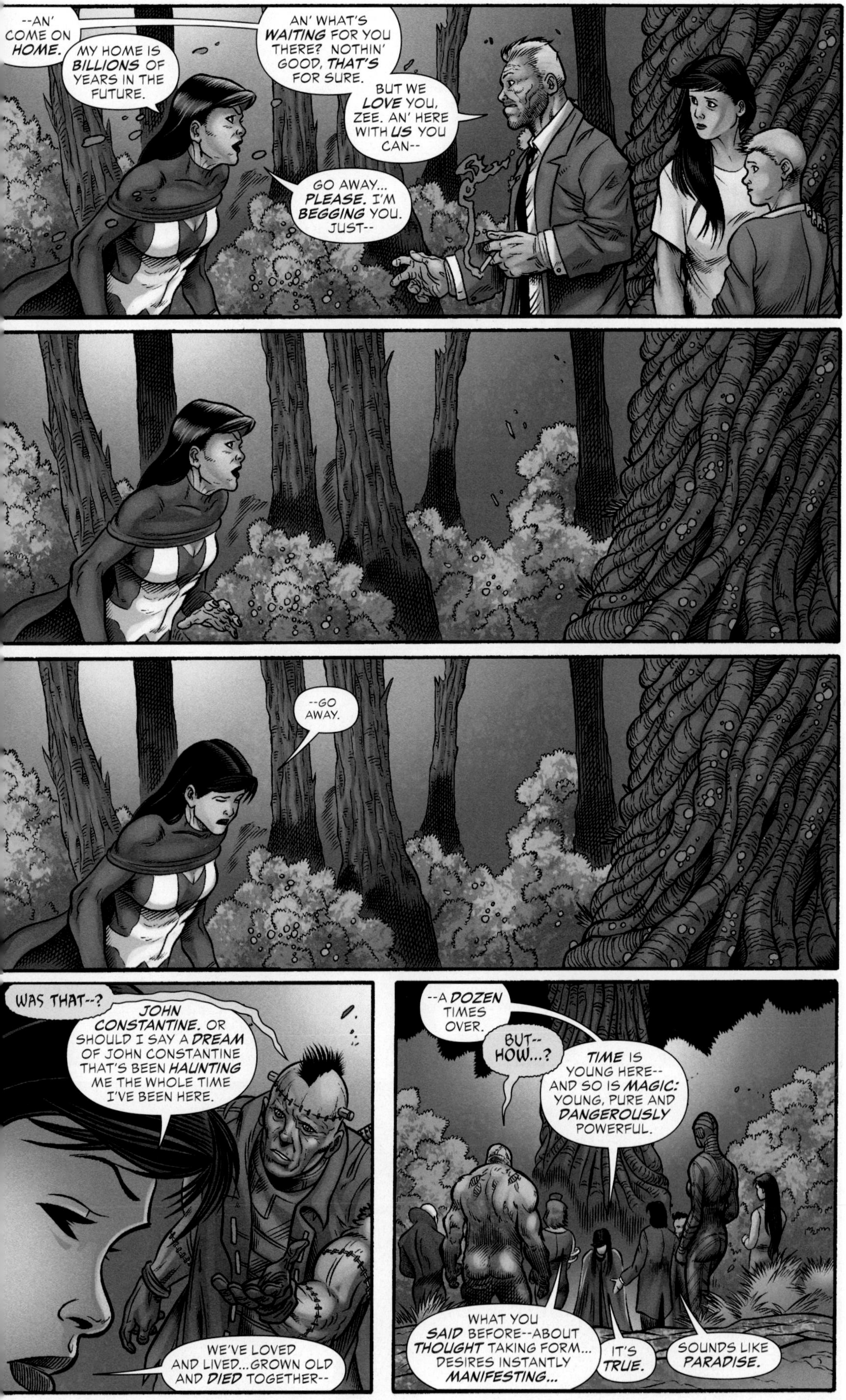

--AN' COME ON HOME.
MY HOME IS BILLIONS OF YEARS IN THE FUTURE.
AN' WHAT'S WAITING FOR YOU THERE? NOTHIN' GOOD, THAT'S FOR SURE.
BUT WE LOVE YOU, ZEE. AN' HERE WITH US YOU CAN--
GO AWAY... PLEASE. I'M BEGGING YOU. JUST--
--GO AWAY.
WAS THAT--?
JOHN CONSTANTINE. OR SHOULD I SAY A DREAM OF JOHN CONSTANTINE THAT'S BEEN HAUNTING ME THE WHOLE TIME I'VE BEEN HERE.
WE'VE LOVED AND LIVED...GROWN OLD AND DIED TOGETHER--
--A DOZEN TIMES OVER.
BUT-- HOW...?
TIME IS YOUNG HERE-- AND SO IS MAGIC: YOUNG, PURE AND DANGEROUSLY POWERFUL.
WHAT YOU SAID BEFORE--ABOUT THOUGHT TAKING FORM... DESIRES INSTANTLY MANIFESTING...
IT'S TRUE.
SOUNDS LIKE PARADISE.

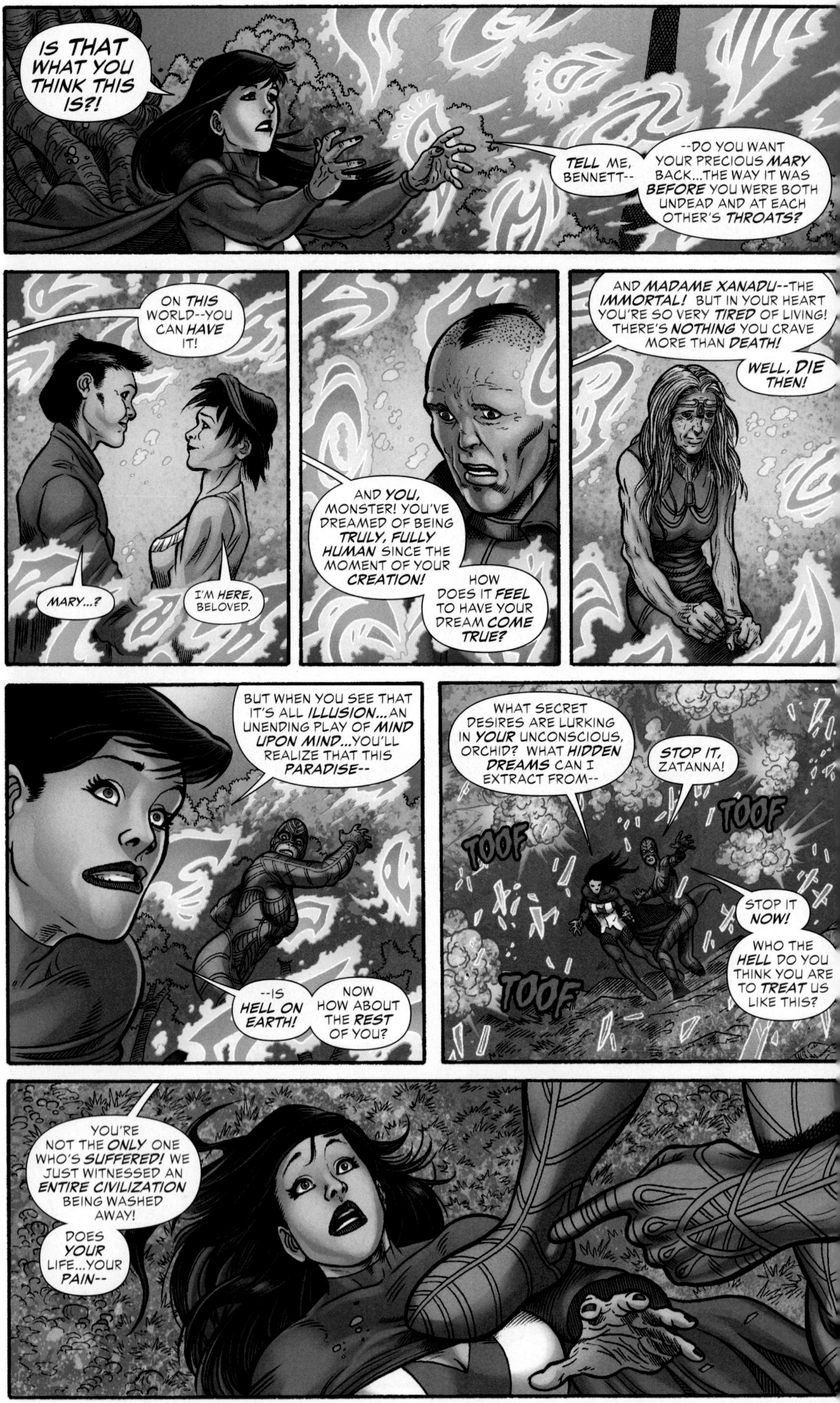

IS THAT WHAT YOU THINK THIS IS?!
TELL ME, BENNETT--
--DO YOU WANT YOUR PRECIOUS MARY BACK...THE WAY IT WAS BEFORE YOU WERE BOTH UNDEAD AND AT EACH OTHER'S THROATS?
ON THIS WORLD--YOU CAN HAVE IT!
MARY...?
I'M HERE, BELOVED.
AND YOU, MONSTER! YOU'VE DREAMED OF BEING TRULY, FULLY HUMAN SINCE THE MOMENT OF YOUR CREATION!
HOW DOES IT FEEL TO HAVE YOUR DREAM COME TRUE?
AND MADAME XANADU--THE IMMORTAL! BUT IN YOUR HEART YOU'RE SO VERY TIRED OF LIVING! THERE'S NOTHING YOU CRAVE MORE THAN DEATH!
WELL, DIE THEN!
BUT WHEN YOU SEE THAT IT'S ALL ILLUSION...AN UNENDING PLAY OF MIND UPON MIND...YOU'LL REALIZE THAT THIS PARADISE--
--IS HELL ON EARTH!
NOW HOW ABOUT THE REST OF YOU?
WHAT SECRET DESIRES ARE LURKING IN YOUR UNCONSCIOUS, ORCHID? WHAT HIDDEN DREAMS CAN I EXTRACT FROM--
STOP IT, ZATANNA!
TOOF
TOOF
TOOF
STOP IT NOW!
WHO THE HELL DO YOU THINK YOU ARE TO TREAT US LIKE THIS?
YOU'RE NOT THE ONLY ONE WHO'S SUFFERED! WE JUST WITNESSED AN ENTIRE CIVILIZATION BEING WASHED AWAY!
DOES YOUR LIFE...YOUR PAIN--

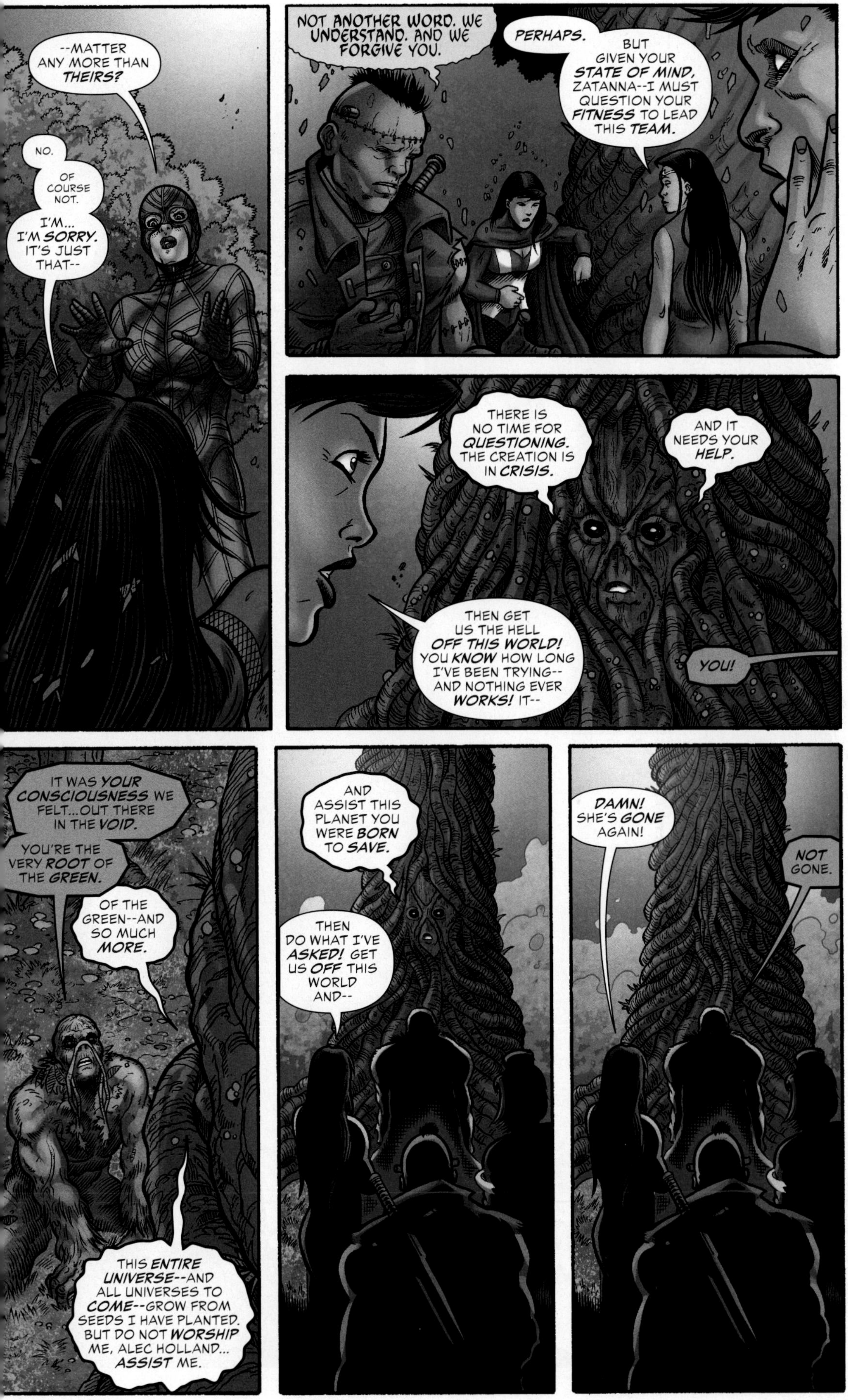
--MATTER ANY MORE THAN THEIRS?
NO.
OF COURSE NOT.
I'M... I'M SORRY. IT'S JUST THAT--
NOT ANOTHER WORD. WE UNDERSTAND. AND WE FORGIVE YOU.
PERHAPS.
BUT GIVEN YOUR STATE OF MIND, ZATANNA--I MUST QUESTION YOUR FITNESS TO LEAD THIS TEAM.
THERE IS NO TIME FOR QUESTIONING. THE CREATION IS IN CRISIS.
AND IT NEEDS YOUR HELP.
THEN GET US THE HELL OFF THIS WORLD! YOU KNOW HOW LONG I'VE BEEN TRYING--AND NOTHING EVER WORKS! IT--
YOU!
IT WAS YOUR CONSCIOUSNESS WE FELT...OUT THERE IN THE VOID.
YOU'RE THE VERY ROOT OF THE GREEN.
OF THE GREEN--AND SO MUCH MORE.
THIS ENTIRE UNIVERSE--AND ALL UNIVERSES TO COME--GROW FROM SEEDS I HAVE PLANTED. BUT DO NOT WORSHIP ME, ALEC HOLLAND... ASSIST ME.
AND ASSIST THIS PLANET YOU WERE BORN TO SAVE.
THEN DO WHAT I'VE ASKED! GET US OFF THIS WORLD AND--
DAMN! SHE'S GONE AGAIN!
NOT GONE.

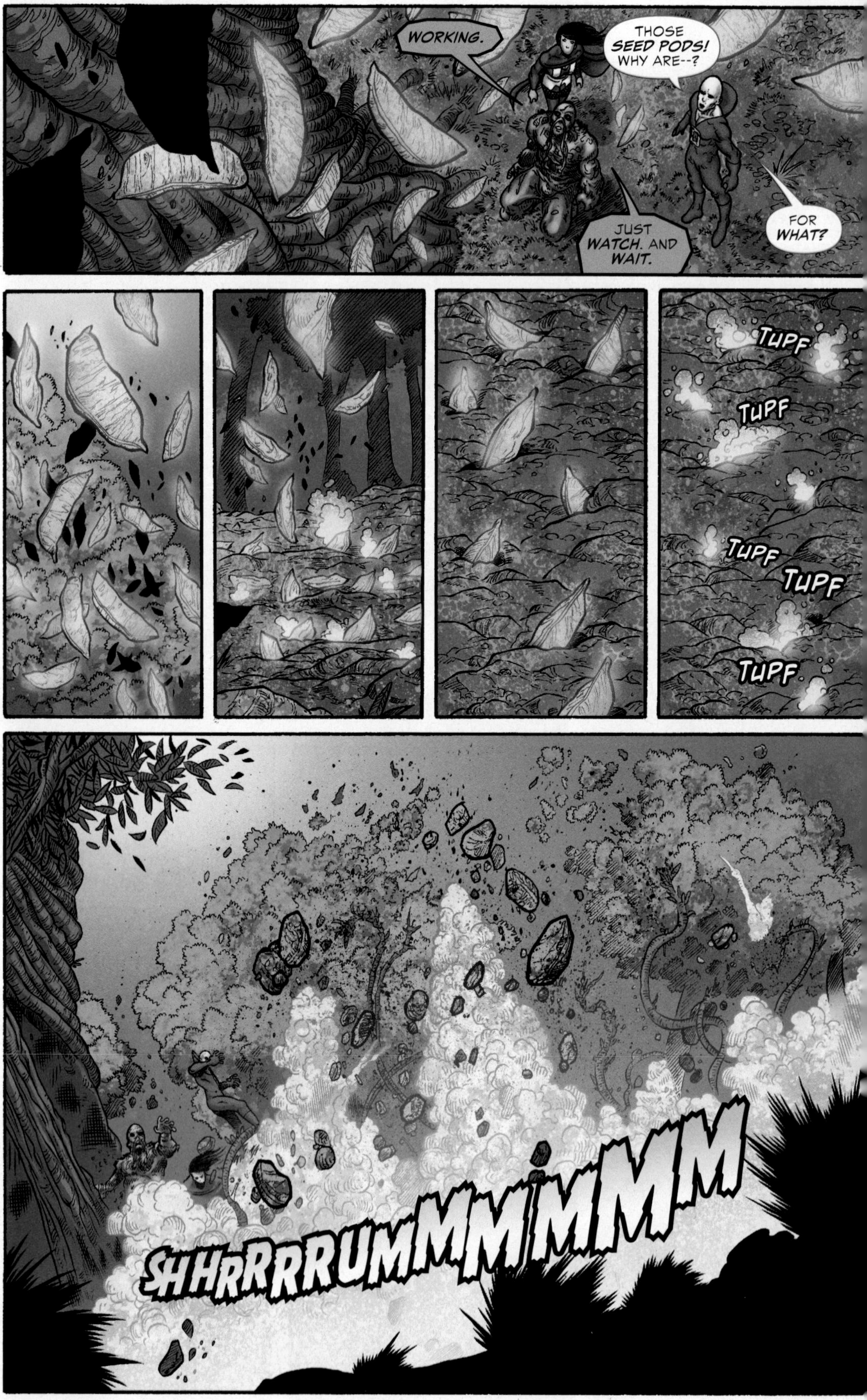
WORKING.
THOSE SEED PODS! WHY ARE--?
JUST WATCH. AND WAIT.
FOR WHAT?
TUPF
TUPF
TUPF
TUPF
TUPF
SHHRRRRUMMMMMMMMM

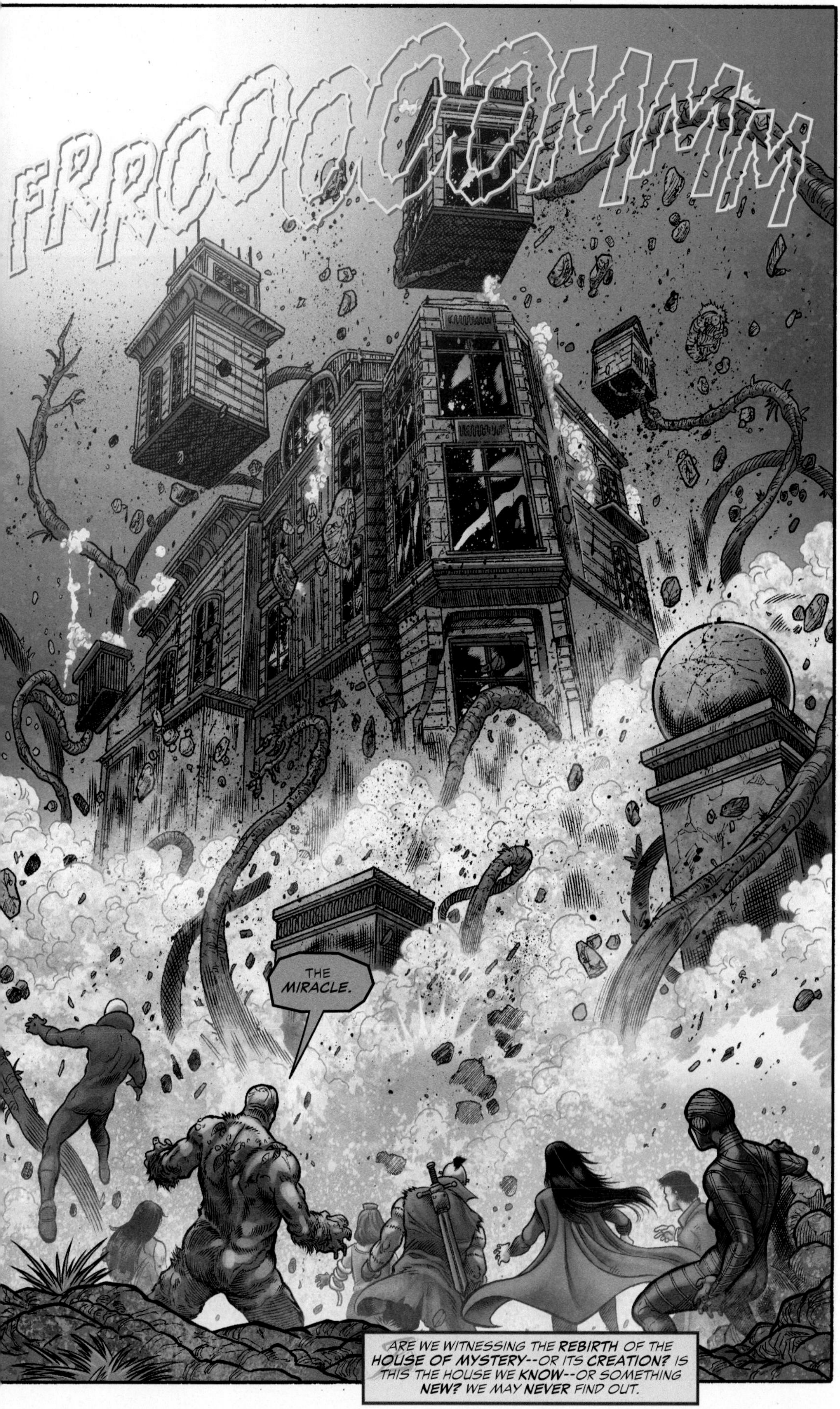
FRROOOOOMMM
THE MIRACLE.
ARE WE WITNESSING THE REBIRTH OF THE HOUSE OF MYSTERY--OR ITS CREATION? IS THIS THE HOUSE WE KNOW--OR SOMETHING NEW? WE MAY NEVER FIND OUT.

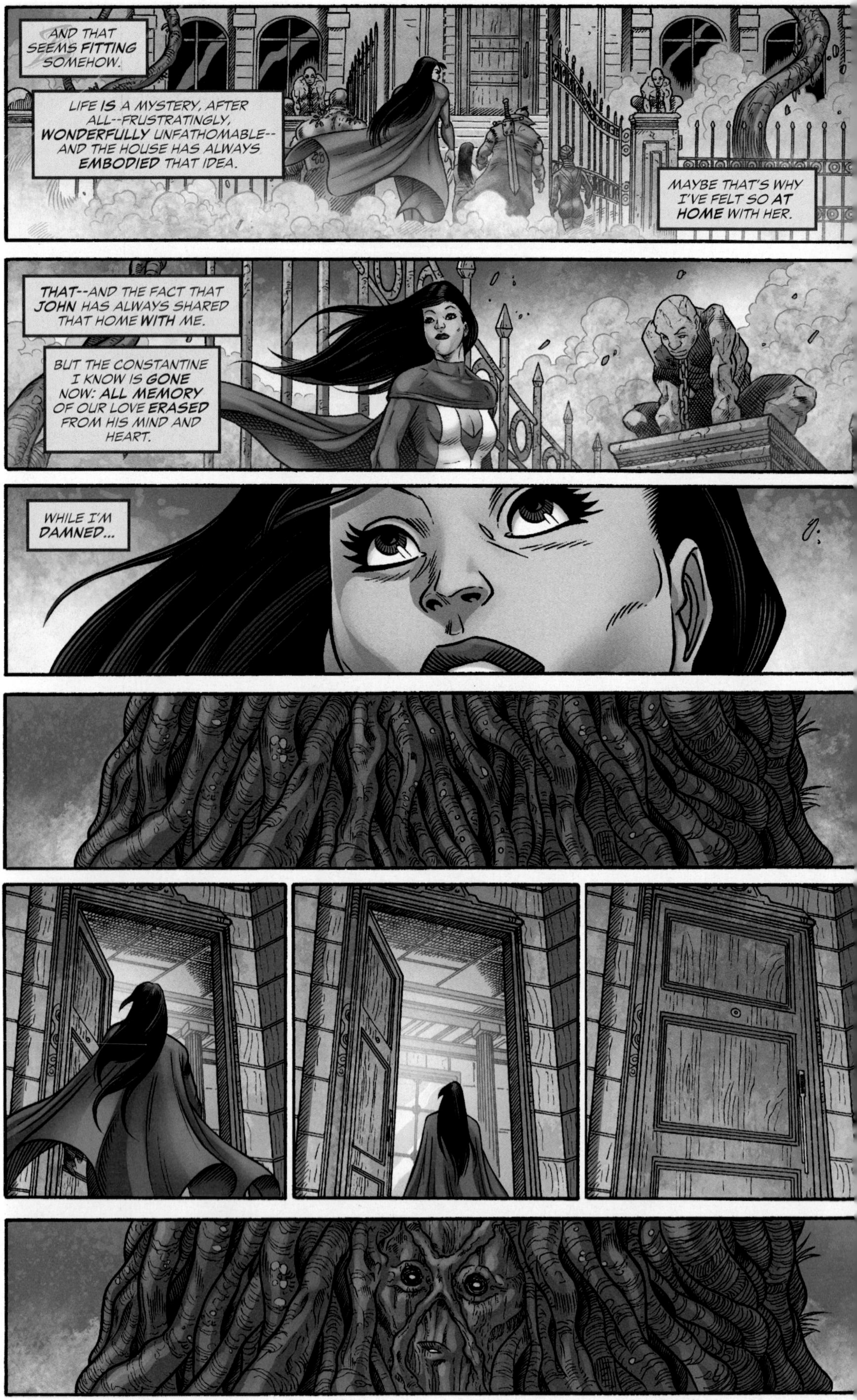
AND THAT SEEMS FITTING SOMEHOW.
LIFE IS A MYSTERY, AFTER ALL--FRUSTRATINGLY, WONDERFULLY UNFATHOMABLE-- AND THE HOUSE HAS ALWAYS EMBODIED THAT IDEA.
MAYBE THAT'S WHY I'VE FELT SO AT HOME WITH HER.
THAT--AND THE FACT THAT JOHN HAS ALWAYS SHARED THAT HOME WITH ME.
BUT THE CONSTANTINE I KNOW IS GONE NOW: ALL MEMORY OF OUR LOVE ERASED FROM HIS MIND AND HEART.
WHILE I'M DAMNED...

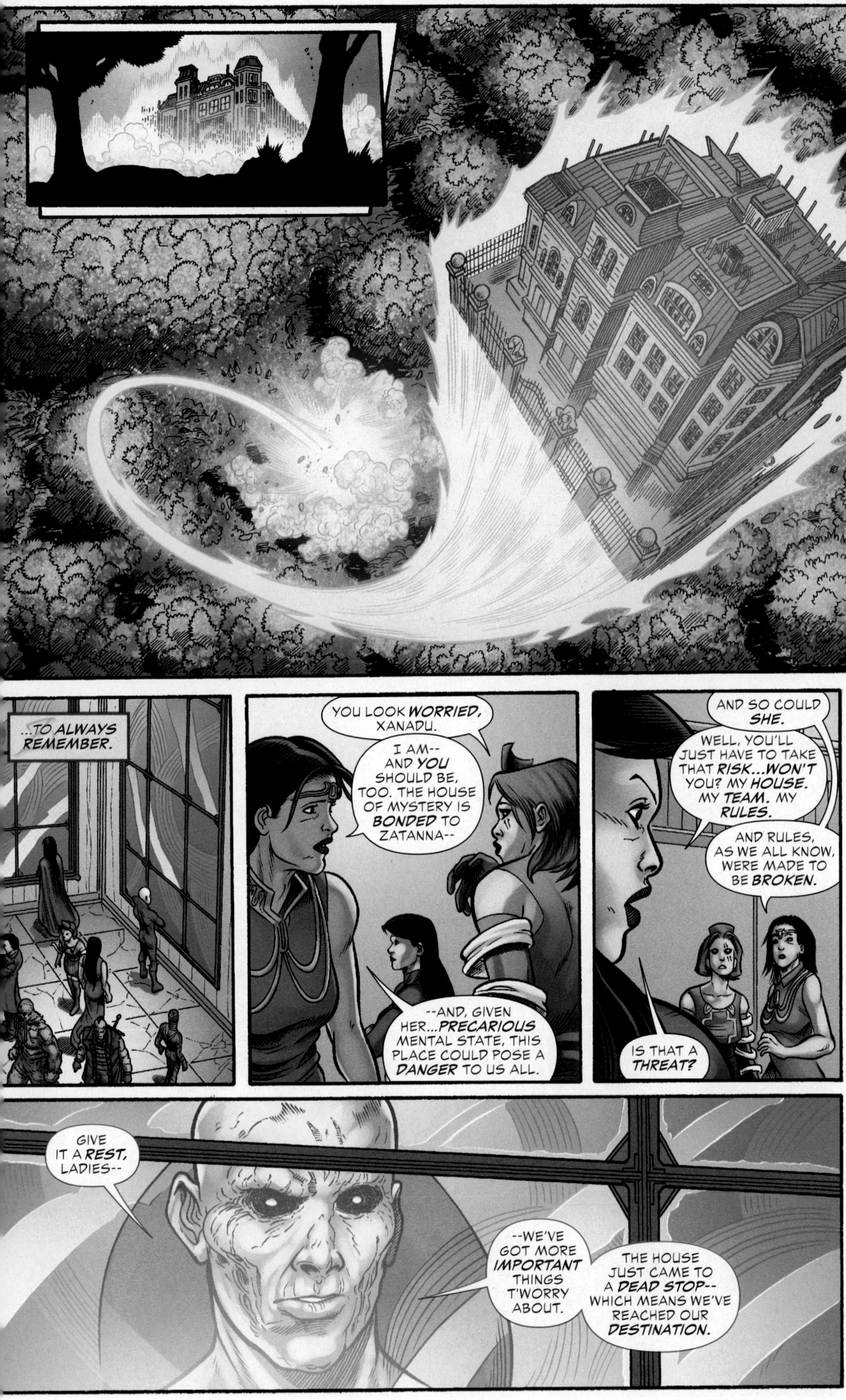
...TO ALWAYS REMEMBER.
YOU LOOK WORRIED, XANADU.
I AM-- AND YOU SHOULD BE, TOO. THE HOUSE OF MYSTERY IS BONDED TO ZATANNA--
--AND, GIVEN HER...PRECARIOUS MENTAL STATE, THIS PLACE COULD POSE A DANGER TO US ALL.
IS THAT A THREAT?
AND SO COULD SHE.
WELL, YOU'LL JUST HAVE TO TAKE THAT RISK...WON'T YOU? MY HOUSE. MY TEAM. MY RULES.
AND RULES, AS WE ALL KNOW, WERE MADE TO BE BROKEN.
GIVE IT A REST, LADIES--
--WE'VE GOT MORE IMPORTANT THINGS T'WORRY ABOUT.
THE HOUSE JUST CAME TO A DEAD STOP-- WHICH MEANS WE'VE REACHED OUR DESTINATION.

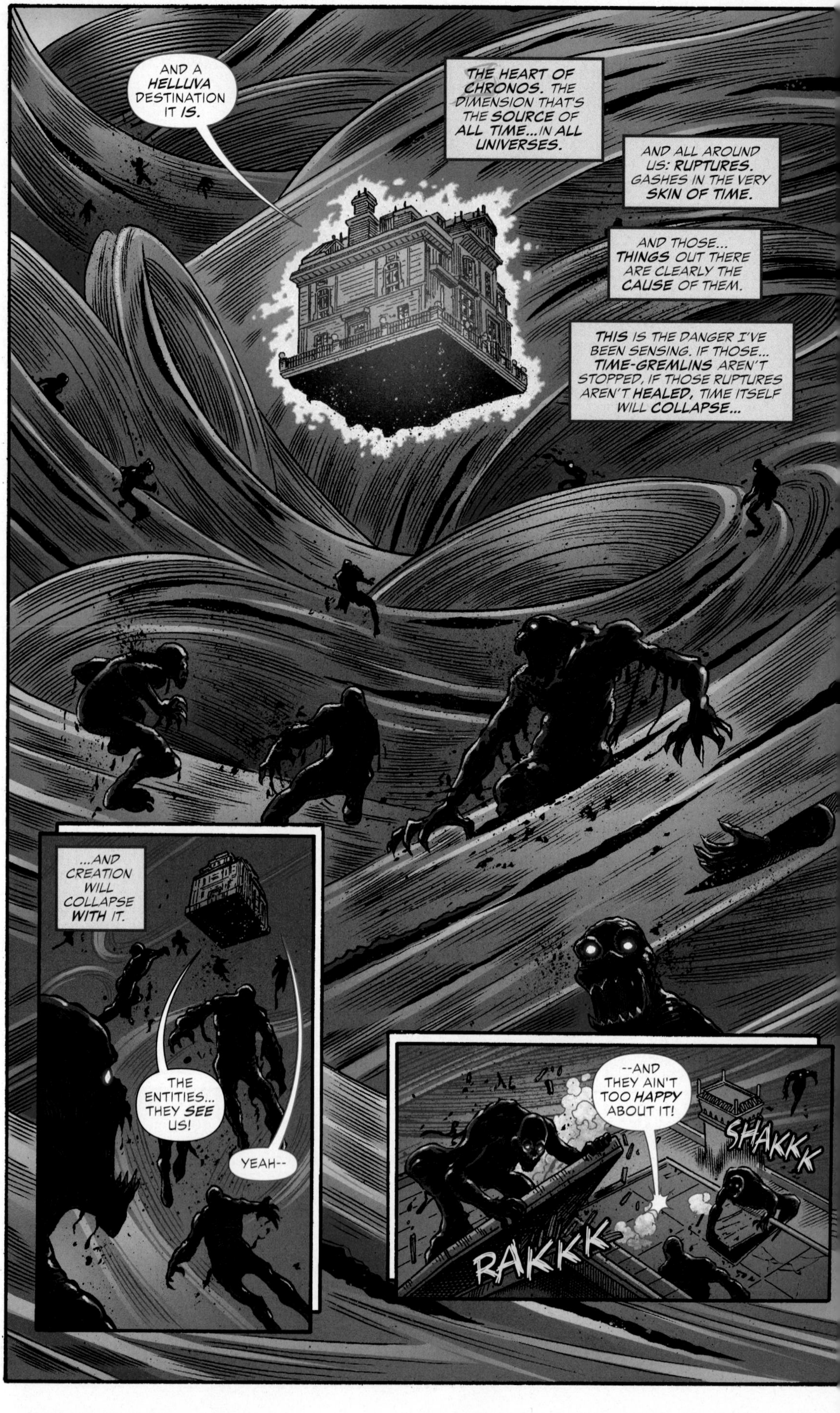
THE HEART OF CHRONOS. THE DIMENSION THAT'S THE SOURCE OF ALL TIME...IN ALL UNIVERSES.
AND A HELLUVA DESTINATION IT IS.
AND ALL AROUND US: RUPTURES. GASHES IN THE VERY SKIN OF TIME.
AND THOSE... THINGS OUT THERE ARE CLEARLY THE CAUSE OF THEM.
THIS IS THE DANGER I'VE BEEN SENSING. IF THOSE... TIME-GREMLINS AREN'T STOPPED, IF THOSE RUPTURES AREN'T HEALED, TIME ITSELF WILL COLLAPSE...
...AND CREATION WILL COLLAPSE WITH IT.
THE ENTITIES... THEY SEE US!
YEAH--
--AND THEY AIN'T TOO HAPPY ABOUT IT!
SHAKKK
RAKKK

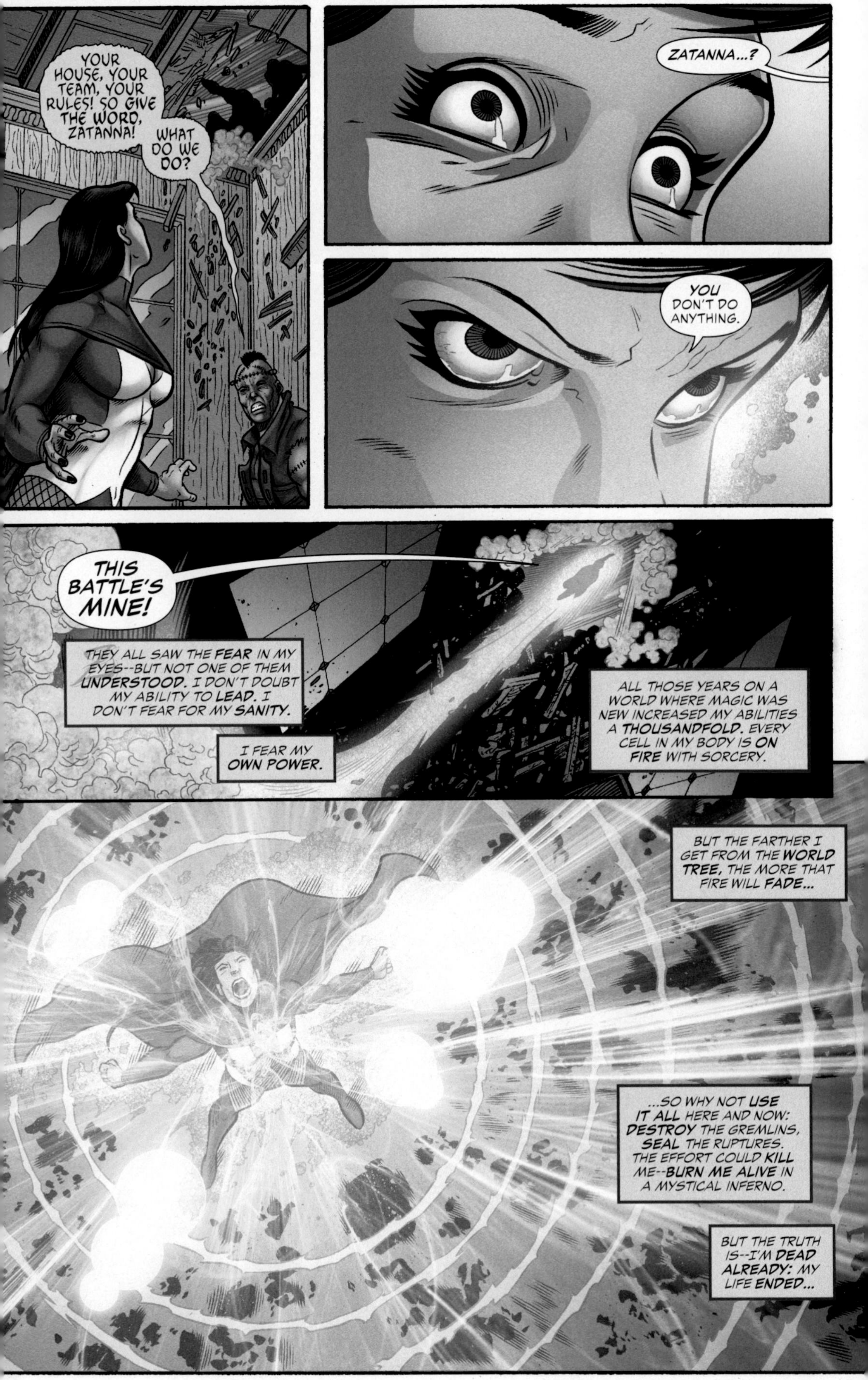
YOUR HOUSE, YOUR TEAM, YOUR RULES! SO GIVE THE WORD, ZATANNA!
WHAT DO WE DO?
ZATANNA...?
YOU DON'T DO ANYTHING.
THIS BATTLE'S MINE!
THEY ALL SAW THE FEAR IN MY EYES--BUT NOT ONE OF THEM UNDERSTOOD. I DON'T DOUBT MY ABILITY TO LEAD. I DON'T FEAR FOR MY SANITY.
I FEAR MY OWN POWER.
ALL THOSE YEARS ON A WORLD WHERE MAGIC WAS NEW INCREASED MY ABILITIES A THOUSANDFOLD. EVERY CELL IN MY BODY IS ON FIRE WITH SORCERY.
BUT THE FARTHER I GET FROM THE WORLD TREE, THE MORE THAT FIRE WILL FADE...
...SO WHY NOT USE IT ALL HERE AND NOW: DESTROY THE GREMLINS, SEAL THE RUPTURES. THE EFFORT COULD KILL ME--BURN ME ALIVE IN A MYSTICAL INFERNO.
BUT THE TRUTH IS--I'M DEAD ALREADY: MY LIFE ENDED...

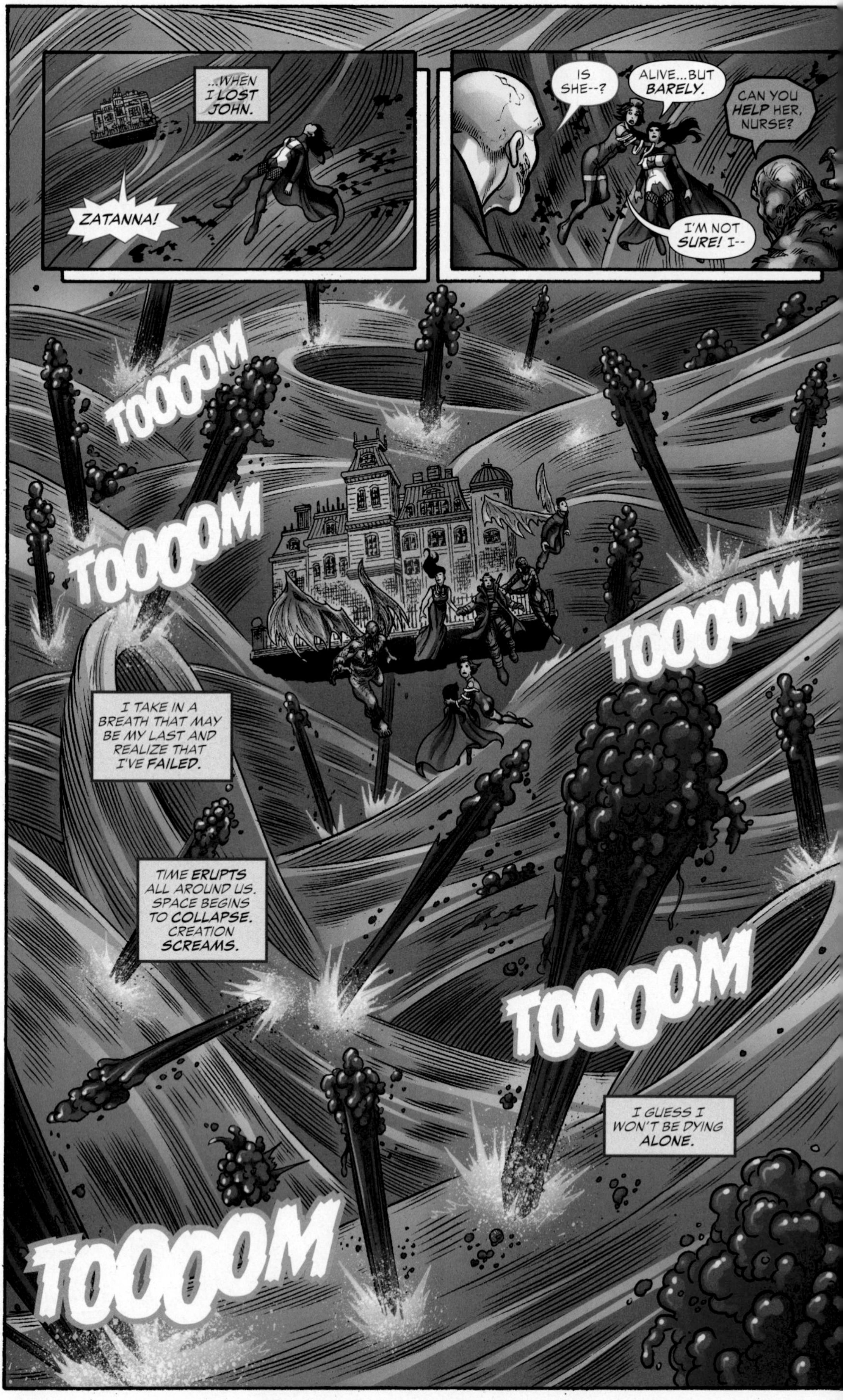
...WHEN I LOST JOHN.
ZATANNA!
IS SHE--?
ALIVE...BUT BARELY.
CAN YOU HELP HER, NURSE?
I'M NOT SURE! I--
TOOOOM
TOOOOM
TOOOOM
I TAKE IN A BREATH THAT MAY BE MY LAST AND REALIZE THAT I'VE FAILED.
TIME ERUPTS ALL AROUND US. SPACE BEGINS TO COLLAPSE. CREATION SCREAMS.
TOOOOM
I GUESS I WON'T BE DYING ALONE.
TOOOOM

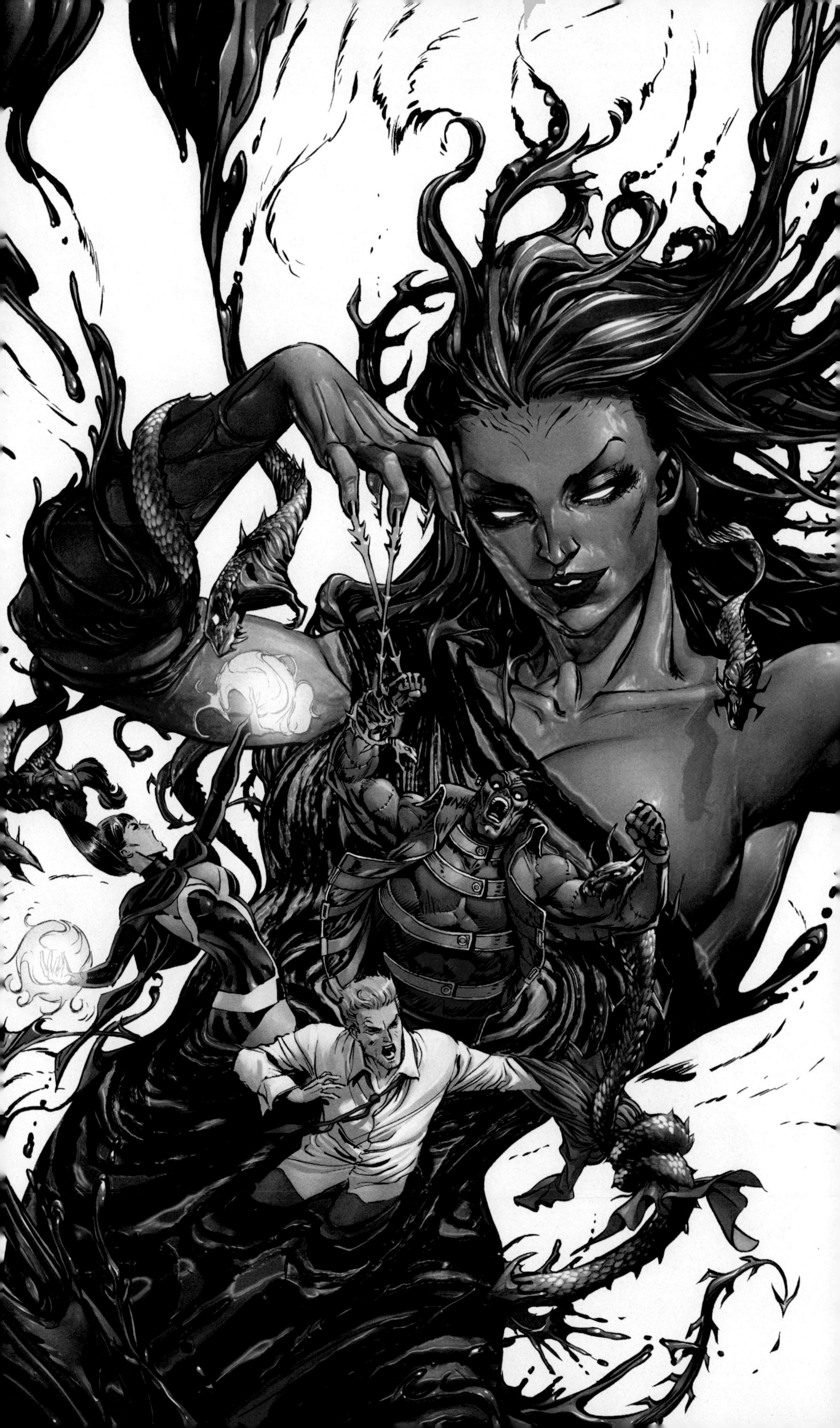

THE AMBER OF THE MOMENT PART 5: PRALAYA

J.M. DEMATTEIS writer ANDRES GUINALDO penciller WALDEN WONG inker CHRIS SOTOMAYOR colorist
TRAVIS LANHAM letterer cover by GUILLEM MARCH & TOMEU MOREY

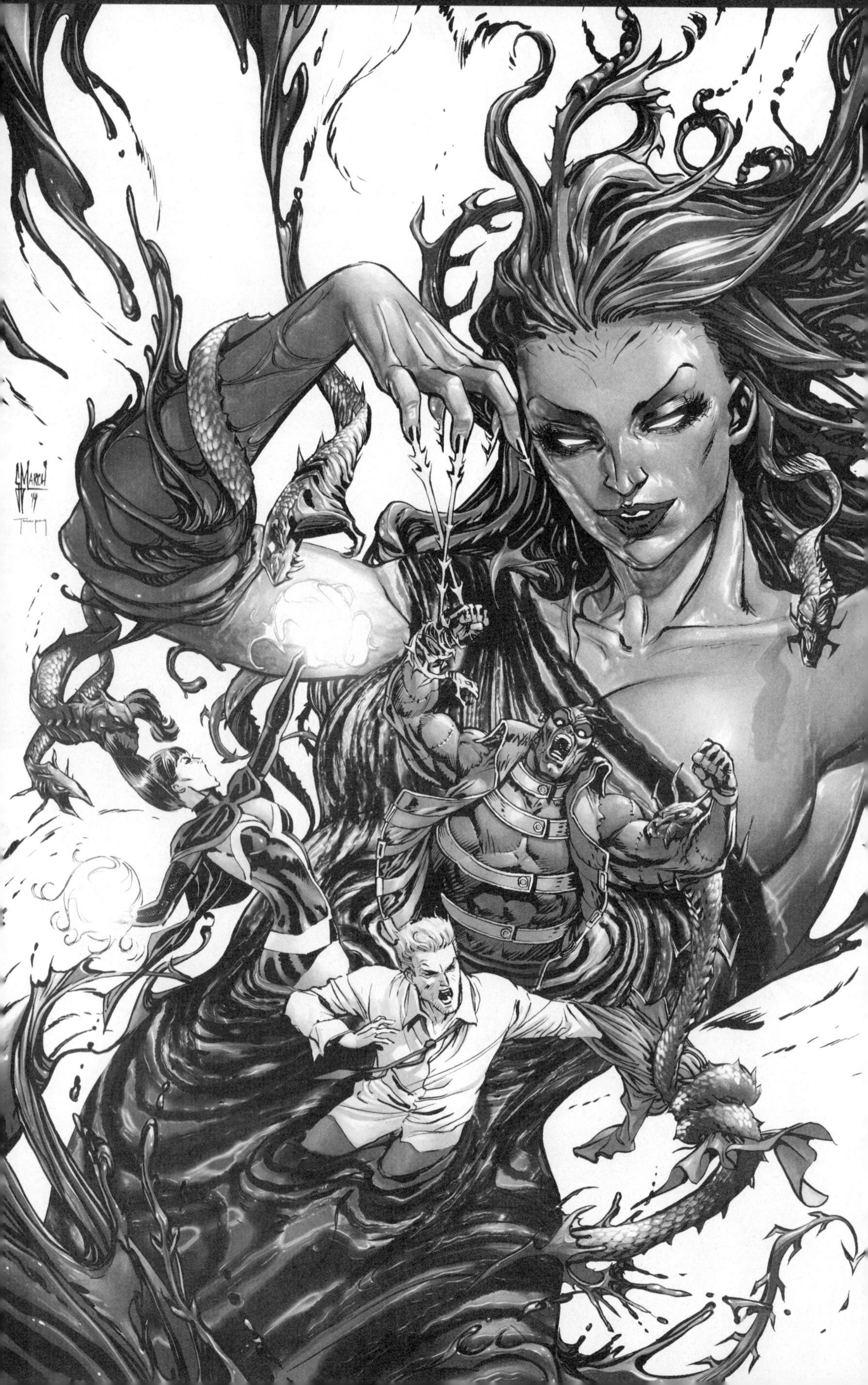

G.MARCH '14

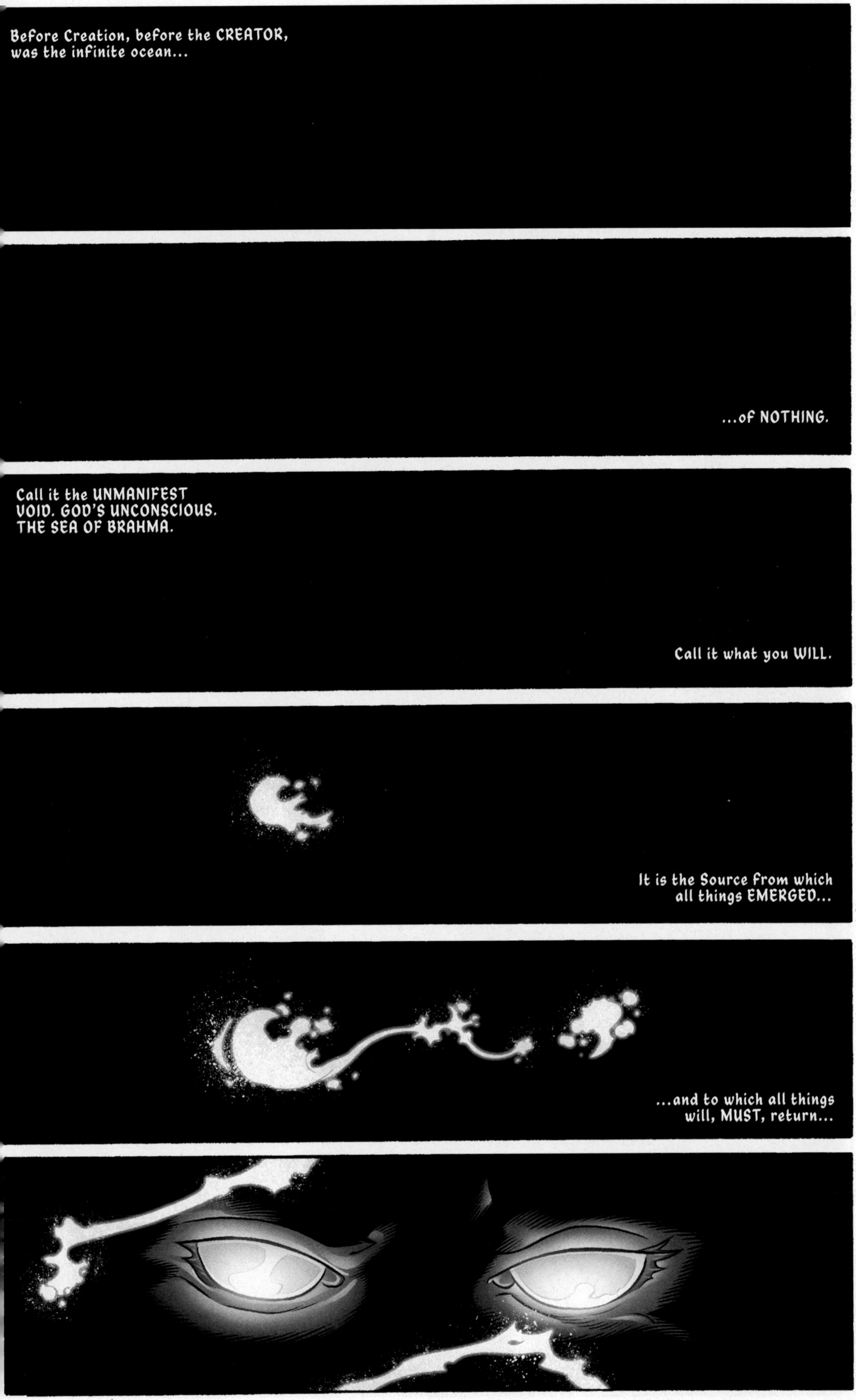
Before Creation, before the CREATOR, was the infinite ocean...
...of NOTHING.
Call it the UNMANIFEST VOID. GOD'S UNCONSCIOUS. THE SEA OF BRAHMA.
Call it what you WILL.
It is the Source from which all things EMERGED...
...and to which all things will, MUST, return...

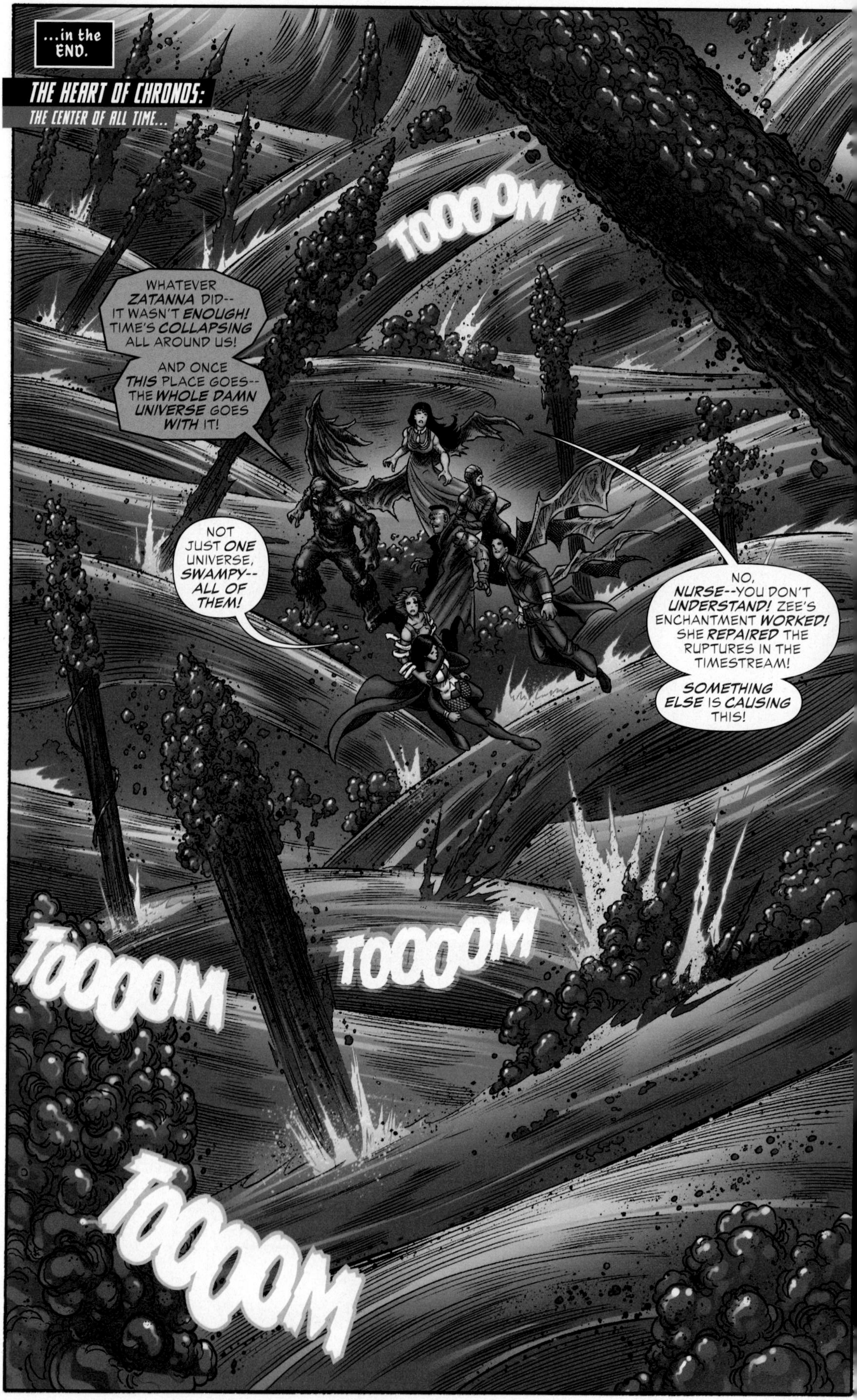

...in the END.
THE HEART OF CHRONOS: THE CENTER OF ALL TIME...
TOOOOM
WHATEVER ZATANNA DID-- IT WASN'T ENOUGH! TIME'S COLLAPSING ALL AROUND US!
AND ONCE THIS PLACE GOES-- THE WHOLE DAMN UNIVERSE GOES WITH IT!
NOT JUST ONE UNIVERSE, SWAMPY-- ALL OF THEM!
NO, NURSE--YOU DON'T UNDERSTAND! ZEE'S ENCHANTMENT WORKED! SHE REPAIRED THE RUPTURES IN THE TIMESTREAM!
SOMETHING ELSE IS CAUSING THIS!
TOOOOM
TOOOOM
TOOOOM

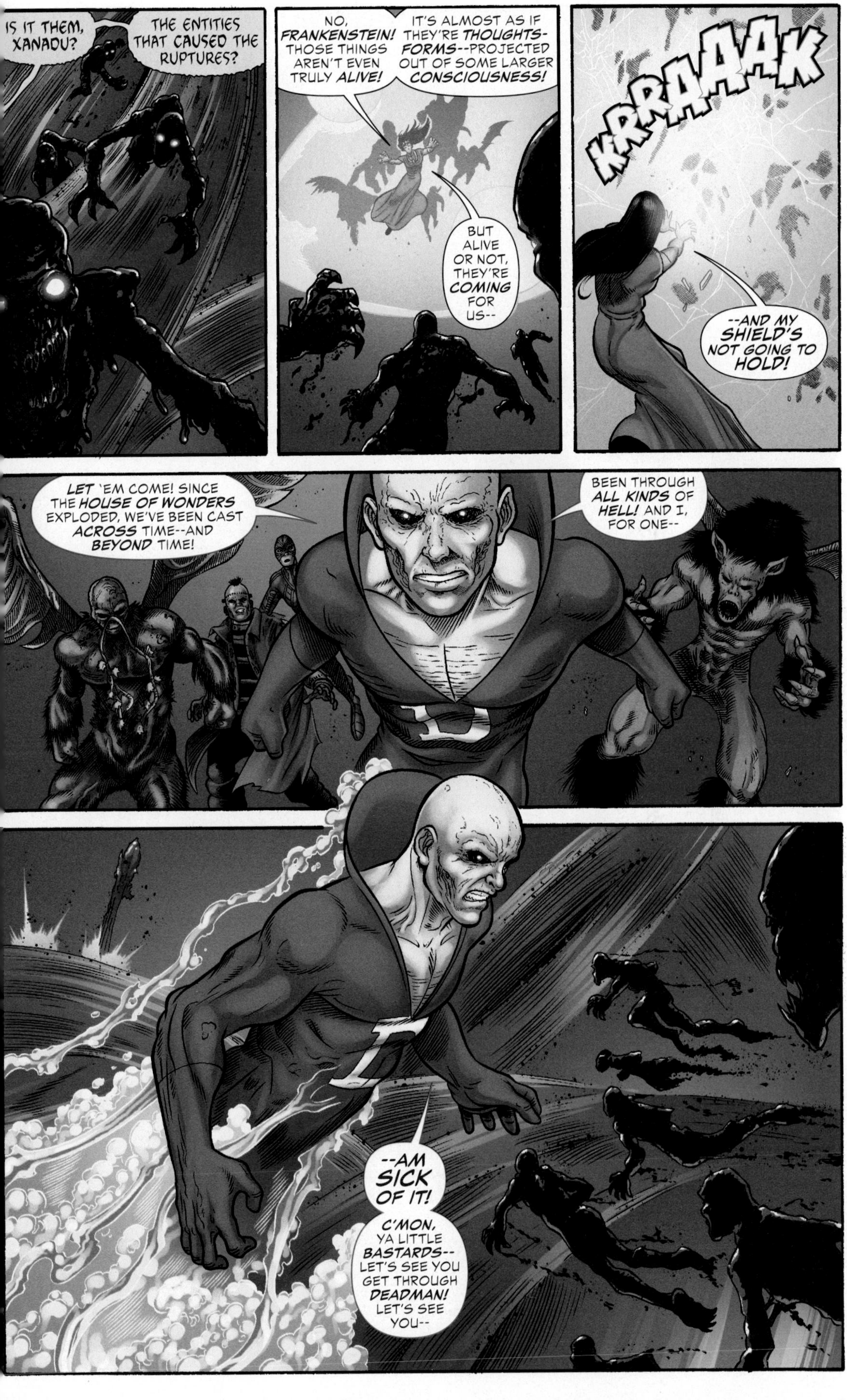
IS IT THEM, XANADU?
THE ENTITIES THAT CAUSED THE RUPTURES?
NO, FRANKENSTEIN! THOSE THINGS AREN'T EVEN TRULY ALIVE!
IT'S ALMOST AS IF THEY'RE THOUGHTS-FORMS--PROJECTED OUT OF SOME LARGER CONSCIOUSNESS!
BUT ALIVE OR NOT, THEY'RE COMING FOR US--
KRRAAAK
--AND MY SHIELD'S NOT GOING TO HOLD!
LET 'EM COME! SINCE THE HOUSE OF WONDERS EXPLODED, WE'VE BEEN CAST ACROSS TIME--AND BEYOND TIME!
BEEN THROUGH ALL KINDS OF HELL! AND I, FOR ONE--
--AM SICK OF IT!
C'MON, YA LITTLE BASTARDS--LET'S SEE YOU GET THROUGH DEADMAN! LET'S SEE YOU--

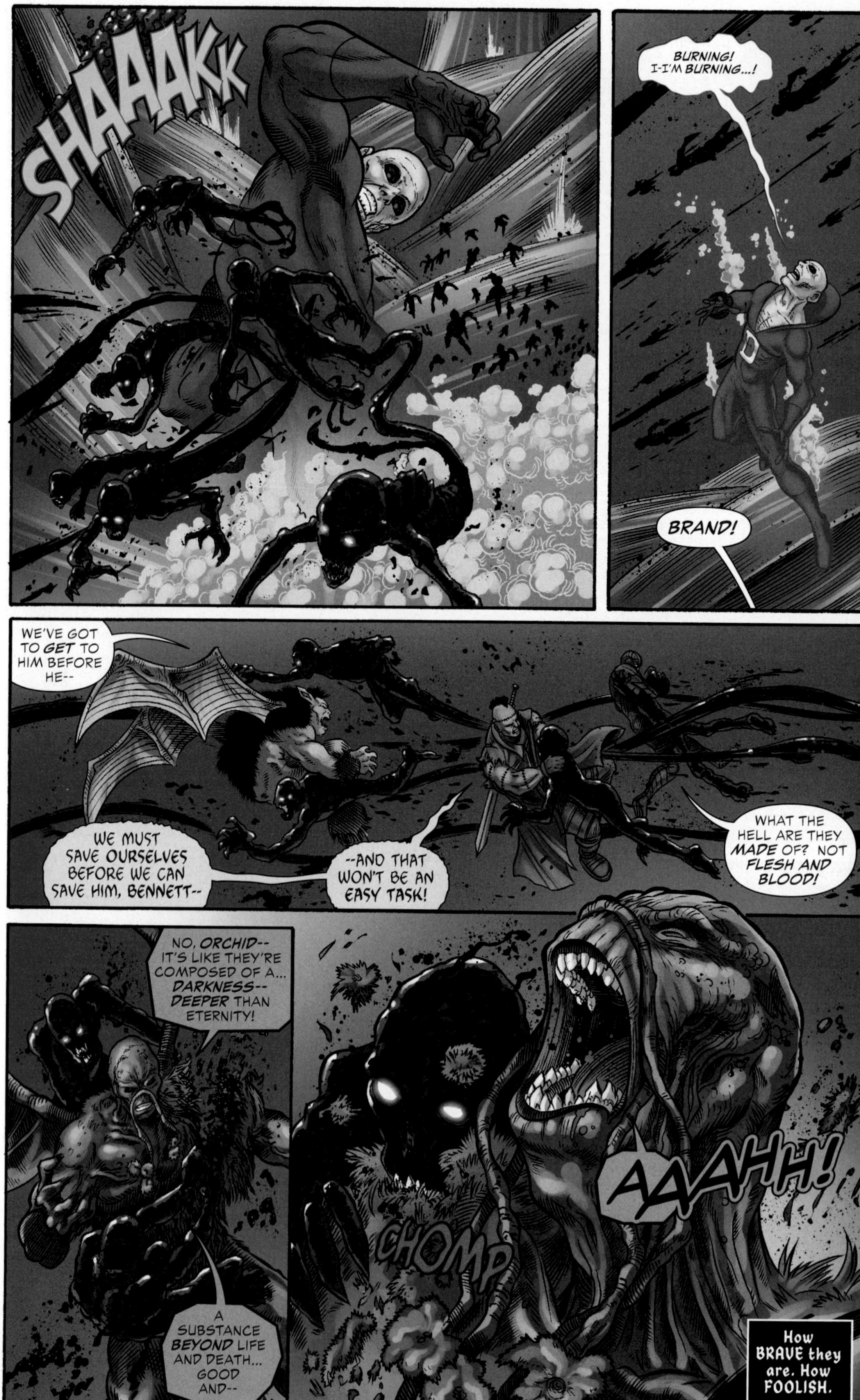
SHAAAKK
BURNING! I-I'M BURNING...!
BRAND!
WE'VE GOT TO GET TO HIM BEFORE HE--
WE MUST SAVE OURSELVES BEFORE WE CAN SAVE HIM, BENNETT--
--AND THAT WON'T BE AN EASY TASK!
WHAT THE HELL ARE THEY MADE OF? NOT FLESH AND BLOOD!
NO, ORCHID-- IT'S LIKE THEY'RE COMPOSED OF A... DARKNESS-- DEEPER THAN ETERNITY!
A SUBSTANCE BEYOND LIFE AND DEATH... GOOD AND--
CHOMP
AAAHH!
How BRAVE they are. How FOOLISH.

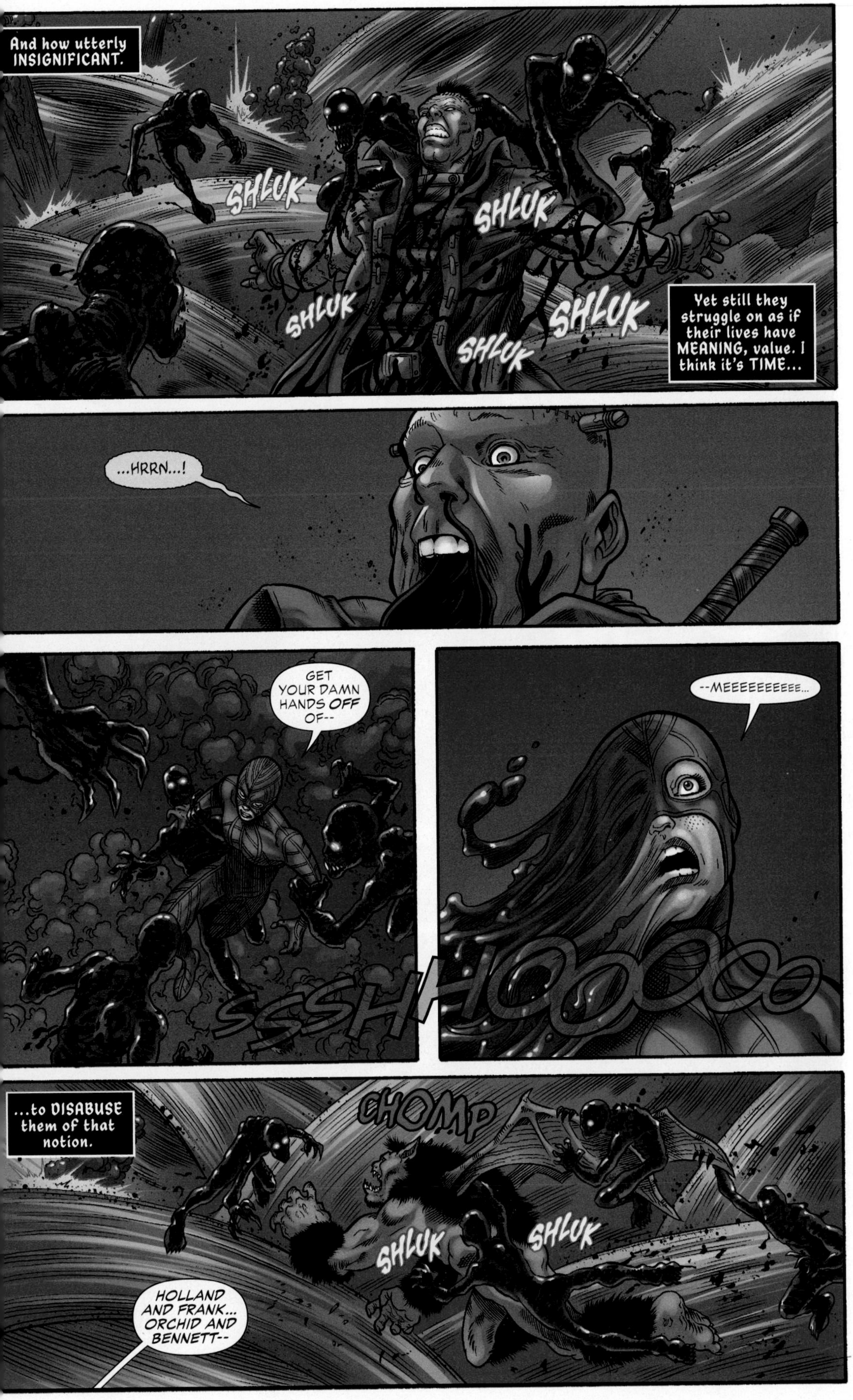
And how utterly INSIGNIFICANT.
SHLUK
SHLUK
SHLUK
SHLUK
SHLUK
Yet still they struggle on as if their lives have MEANING, value. I think it's TIME...
...HRRN...!
GET YOUR DAMN HANDS OFF OF--
--MEEEEEEEEEE...
SSSHHOOOOOO
...to DISABUSE them of that notion.
CHOMP
SHLUK
SHLUK
HOLLAND AND FRANK... ORCHID AND BENNETT--

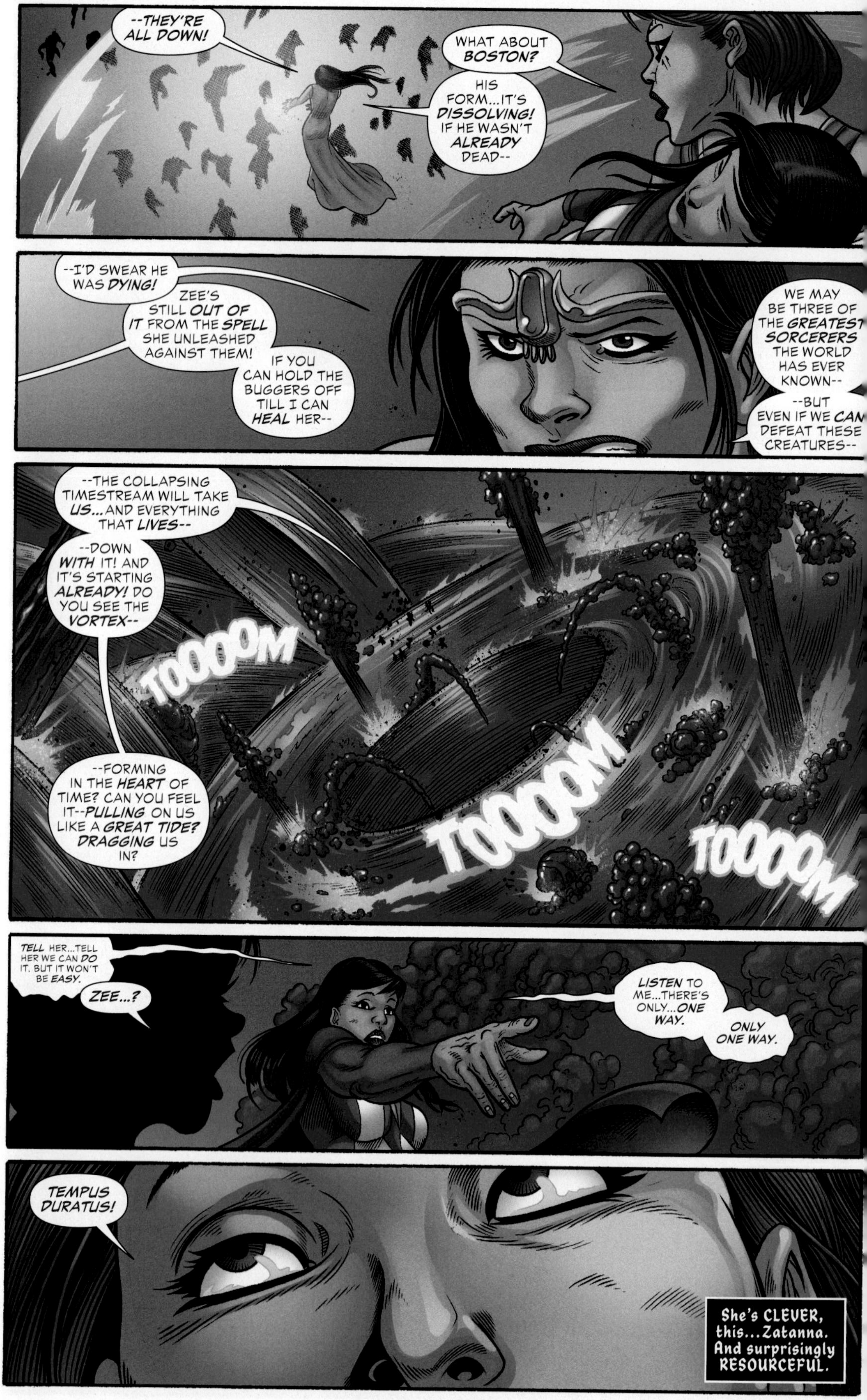
--THEY'RE ALL DOWN!
WHAT ABOUT BOSTON?
HIS FORM...IT'S DISSOLVING! IF HE WASN'T ALREADY DEAD--
--I'D SWEAR HE WAS DYING!
ZEE'S STILL OUT OF IT FROM THE SPELL SHE UNLEASHED AGAINST THEM!
IF YOU CAN HOLD THE BUGGERS OFF TILL I CAN HEAL HER--
WE MAY BE THREE OF THE GREATEST SORCERERS THE WORLD HAS EVER KNOWN--
--BUT EVEN IF WE CAN DEFEAT THESE CREATURES--
--THE COLLAPSING TIMESTREAM WILL TAKE US...AND EVERYTHING THAT LIVES--
--DOWN WITH IT! AND IT'S STARTING ALREADY! DO YOU SEE THE VORTEX--
TOOOOM
--FORMING IN THE HEART OF TIME? CAN YOU FEEL IT--PULLING ON US LIKE A GREAT TIDE? DRAGGING US IN?
TOOOOOM
TOOOOM
TELL HER...TELL HER WE CAN DO IT. BUT IT WON'T BE EASY.
ZEE...?
LISTEN TO ME...THERE'S ONLY...ONE WAY.
ONLY ONE WAY.
TEMPUS DURATUS!
She's CLEVER, this...Zatanna. And surprisingly RESOURCEFUL.

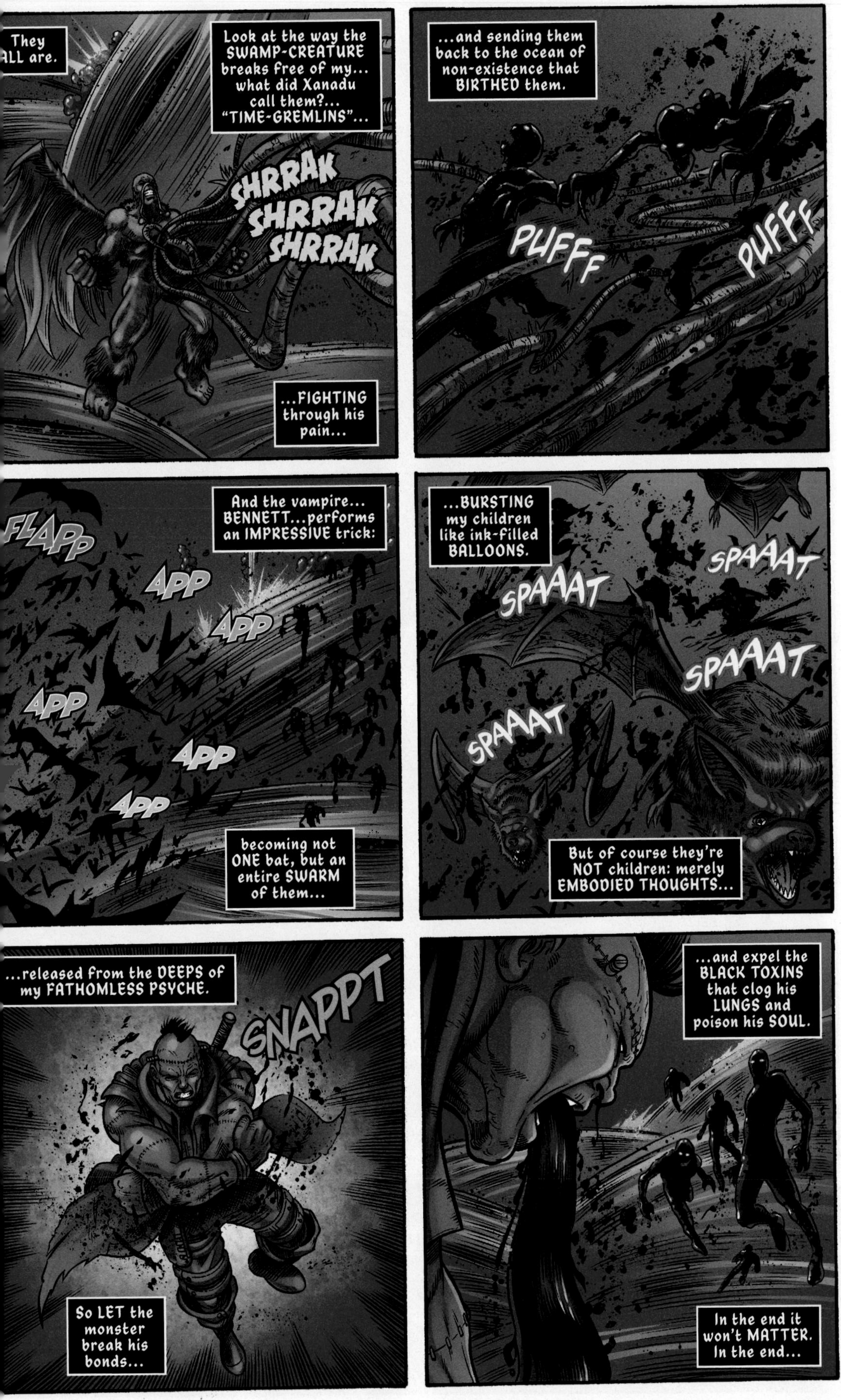

They ALL are.
Look at the way the SWAMP-CREATURE breaks free of my... what did Xanadu call them?... "TIME-GREMLINS"...
SHRRAK SHRRAK SHRRAK
...FIGHTING through his pain...
...and sending them back to the ocean of non-existence that BIRTHED them.
PUFFF
PUFFF
And the vampire... BENNETT...performs an IMPRESSIVE trick:
FLAPP
APP
APP
APP
APP
APP
becoming not ONE bat, but an entire SWARM of them...
...BURSTING my children like ink-filled BALLOONS.
SPAAAT
SPAAAT
SPAAAT
SPAAAT
But of course they're NOT children: merely EMBODIED THOUGHTS...
...released from the DEEPS of my FATHOMLESS PSYCHE.
SNAPPT
So LET the monster break his bonds...
...and expel the BLACK TOXINS that clog his LUNGS and poison his SOUL.
In the end it won't MATTER. In the end...

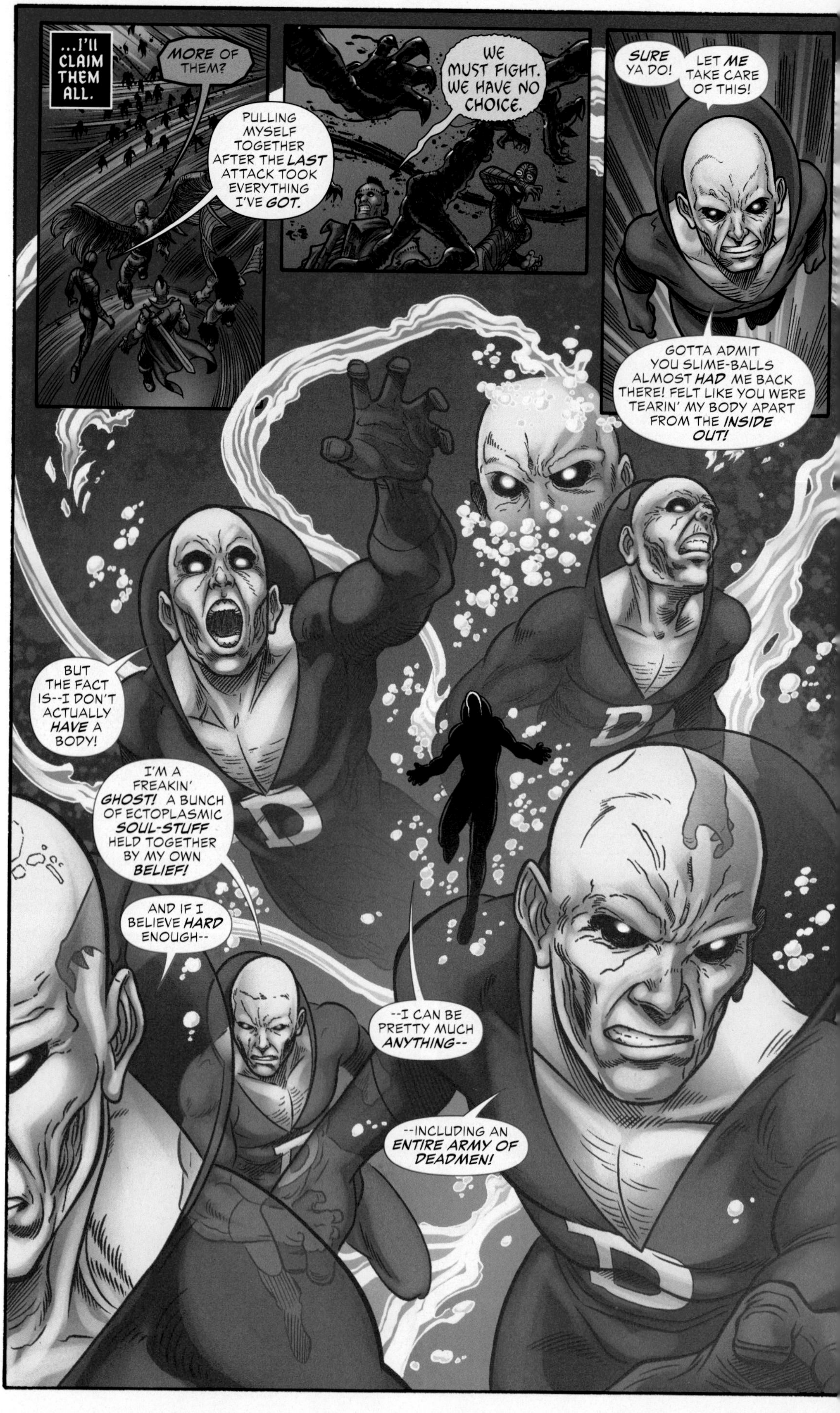
...I'll CLAIM THEM ALL.
MORE OF THEM?
PULLING MYSELF TOGETHER AFTER THE LAST ATTACK TOOK EVERYTHING I'VE GOT.
WE MUST FIGHT. WE HAVE NO CHOICE.
SURE YA DO!
LET ME TAKE CARE OF THIS!
GOTTA ADMIT YOU SLIME-BALLS ALMOST HAD ME BACK THERE! FELT LIKE YOU WERE TEARIN' MY BODY APART FROM THE INSIDE OUT!
BUT THE FACT IS--I DON'T ACTUALLY HAVE A BODY!
I'M A FREAKIN' GHOST! A BUNCH OF ECTOPLASMIC SOUL-STUFF HELD TOGETHER BY MY OWN BELIEF!
AND IF I BELIEVE HARD ENOUGH--
--I CAN BE PRETTY MUCH ANYTHING--
--INCLUDING AN ENTIRE ARMY OF DEADMEN!

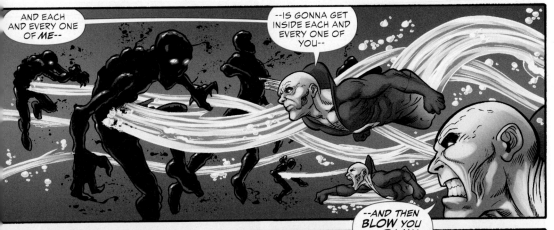

AND EACH AND EVERY ONE OF *ME*--

--IS GONNA GET INSIDE EACH AND EVERY ONE OF YOU--

--AND THEN *BLOW* YOU TO *DAMN PIECES!*

TOOOF

TOOOF

TOOOOF

TOOOF

A *NOBLE* EFFORT, BOSTON-- BUT A *FUTILE* ONE.

FOR EVERY ONE OF THESE ENTITIES WE DESTROY-- A HUNDRED MORE RISE UP TO TAKE THEIR PLACE.

A HUNDRED? TAKE A *GOOD LOOK*, FRANK. IT'S MORE LIKE A *THOUSAND!*

WHERE THE HELL ARE THEY *COMING* FROM?

From *ME*, Orchid. And since my *MIND* is INFINITE...

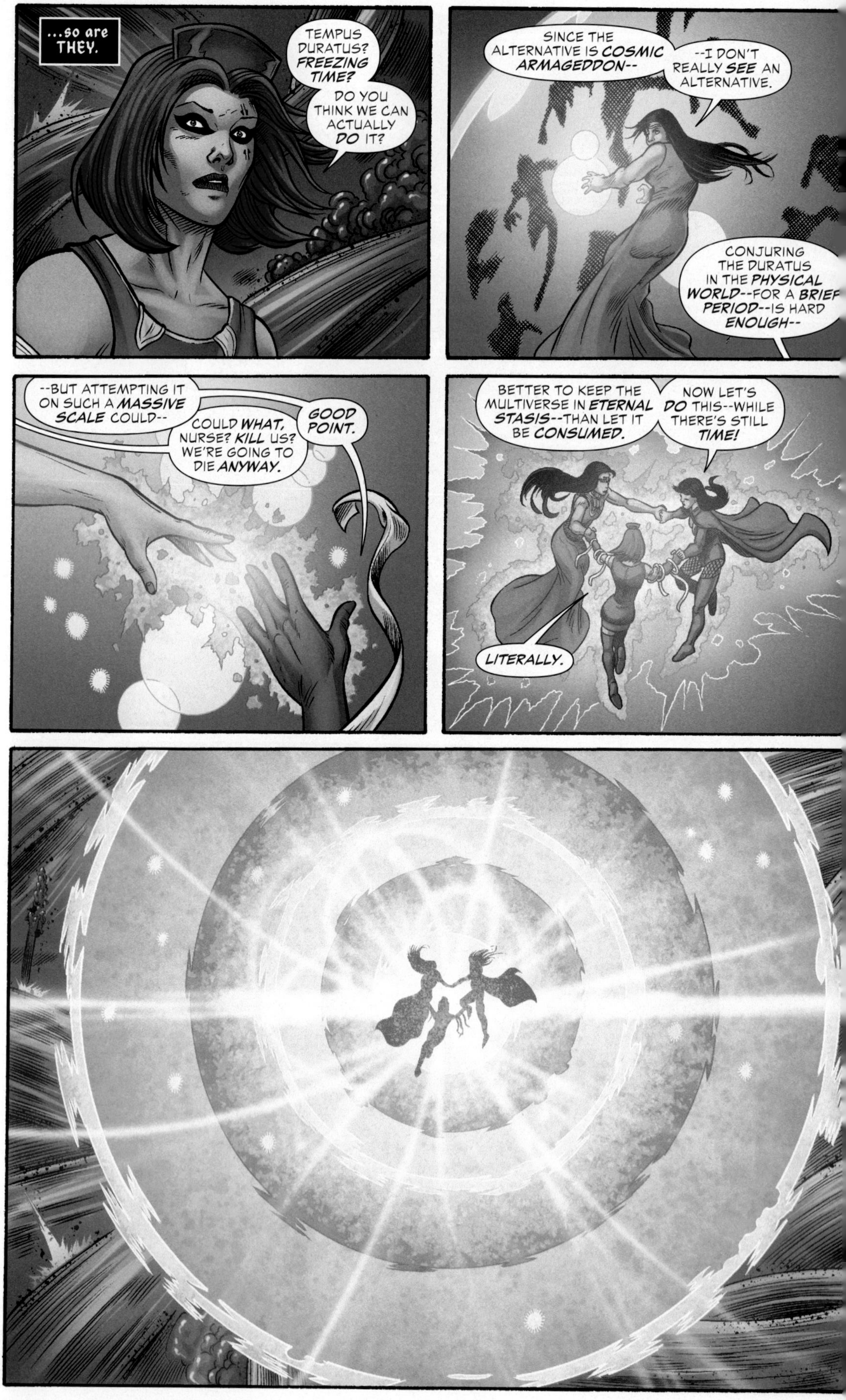
...so are THEY.
TEMPUS DURATUS? FREEZING TIME?
DO YOU THINK WE CAN ACTUALLY DO IT?
SINCE THE ALTERNATIVE IS COSMIC ARMAGEDDON--
--I DON'T REALLY SEE AN ALTERNATIVE.
CONJURING THE DURATUS IN THE PHYSICAL WORLD--FOR A BRIEF PERIOD--IS HARD ENOUGH--
--BUT ATTEMPTING IT ON SUCH A MASSIVE SCALE COULD--
COULD WHAT, NURSE? KILL US? WE'RE GOING TO DIE ANYWAY.
GOOD POINT.
BETTER TO KEEP THE MULTIVERSE IN ETERNAL STASIS--THAN LET IT BE CONSUMED.
NOW LET'S DO THIS--WHILE THERE'S STILL TIME!
LITERALLY.

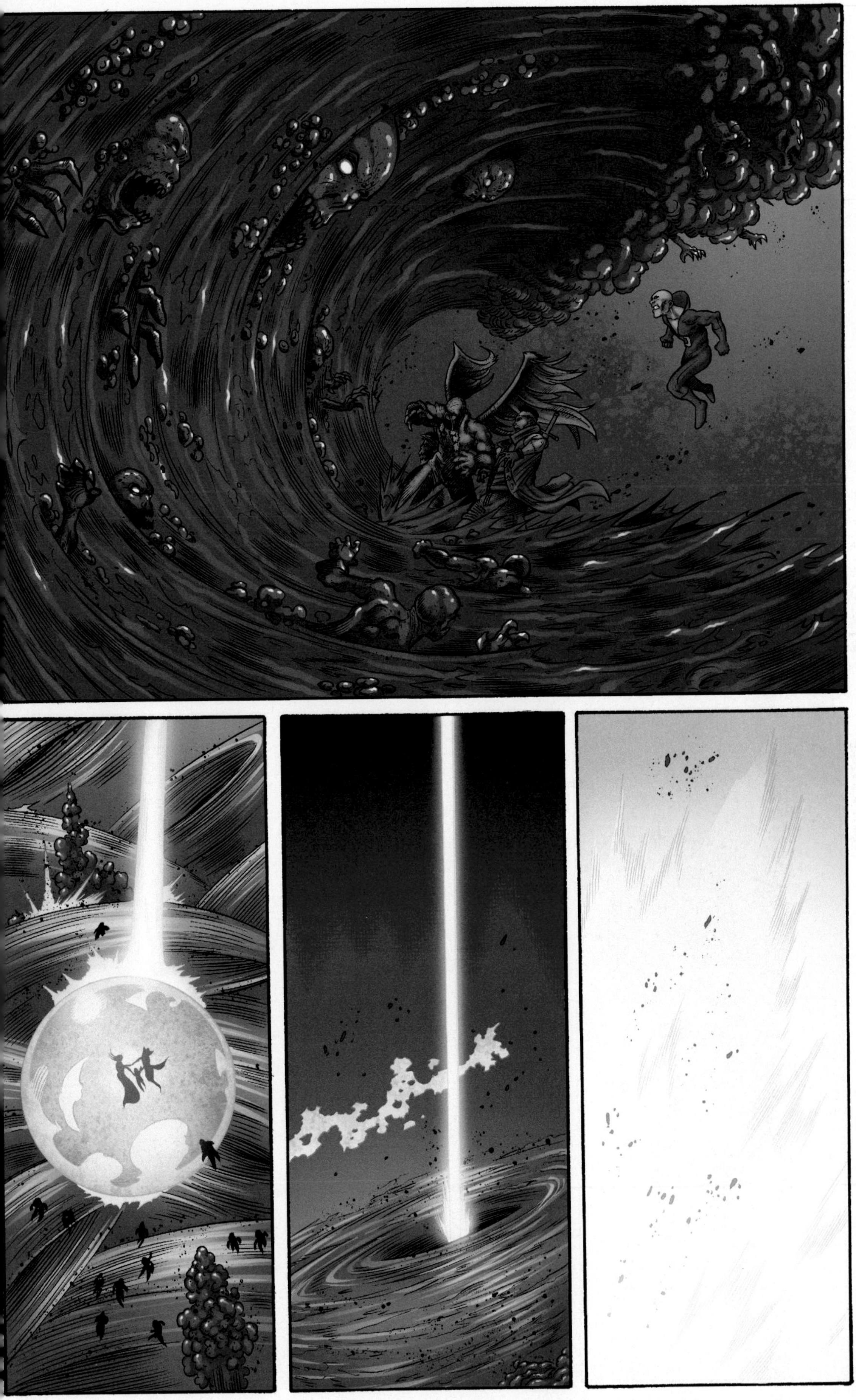

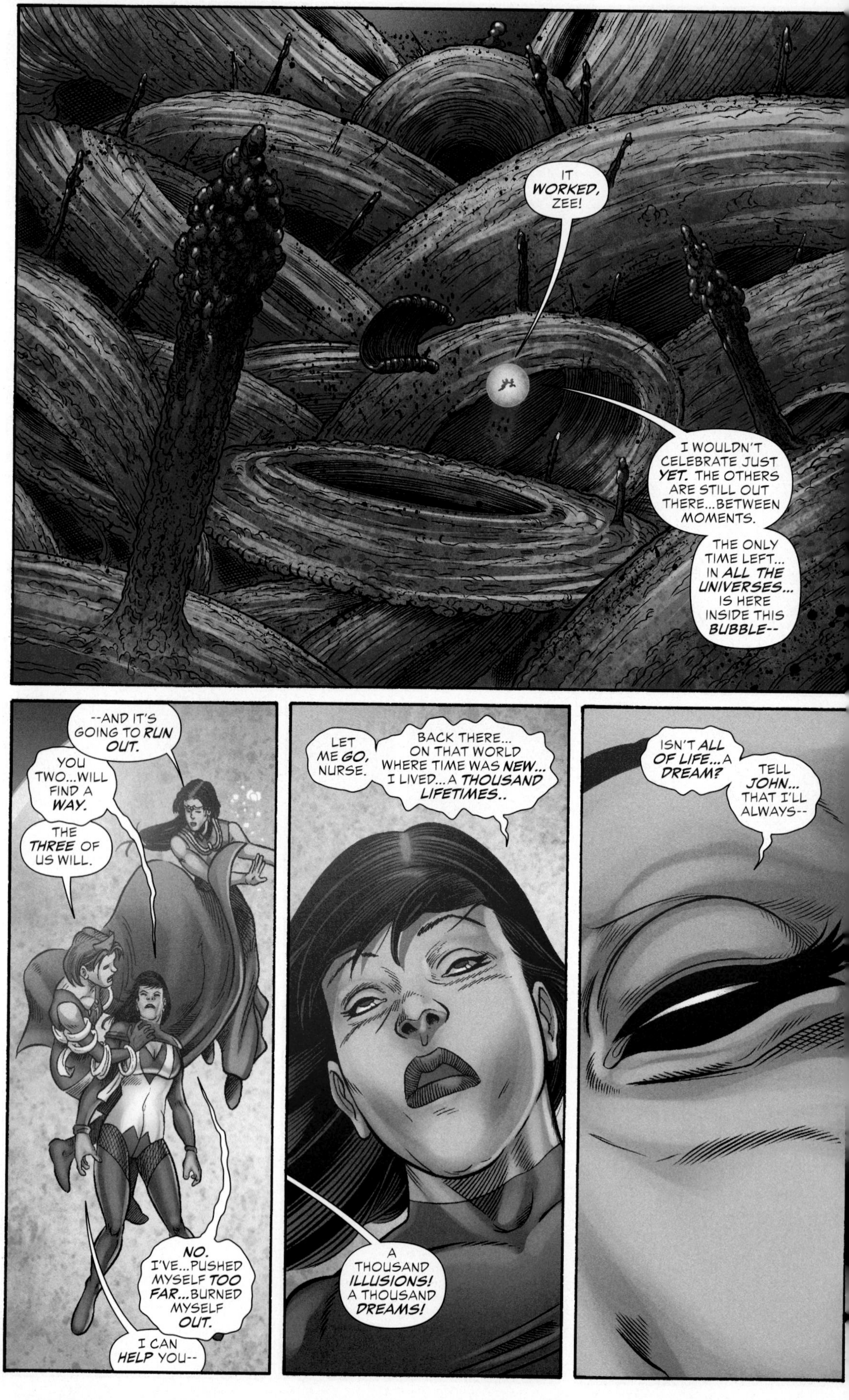

IT WORKED, ZEE!
I WOULDN'T CELEBRATE JUST YET. THE OTHERS ARE STILL OUT THERE...BETWEEN MOMENTS.
THE ONLY TIME LEFT... IN ALL THE UNIVERSES... IS HERE INSIDE THIS BUBBLE--
--AND IT'S GOING TO RUN OUT.
YOU TWO...WILL FIND A WAY.
THE THREE OF US WILL.
NO. I'VE...PUSHED MYSELF TOO FAR...BURNED MYSELF OUT.
I CAN HELP YOU--
LET ME GO, NURSE.
BACK THERE... ON THAT WORLD WHERE TIME WAS NEW... I LIVED...A THOUSAND LIFETIMES..
A THOUSAND ILLUSIONS! A THOUSAND DREAMS!
ISN'T ALL OF LIFE...A DREAM?
TELL JOHN... THAT I'LL ALWAYS--

TELL HIM *YOURSELF!*

I'M A *HEALER,* DAMMIT--I SWORE AN OATH TO *APOLLO* AND *PANACEA*--AND I'M NOT LETTING YOU *GIVE UP!*

I'M NOT LETTING YOU *DIE!*

XANADU! I'VE WOVEN A *DOZEN* ENCHANTMENTS TOGETHER--BUT I CAN'T DO THIS *ALONE!*

I NEED YOU TO CHANNEL YOUR MAGIC THROUGH THE *ROD OF ASCLEPIUS!*

DONE!

COME ON, ZATANNA! WE CAN'T SET THINGS RIGHT *WITHOUT* YOU!

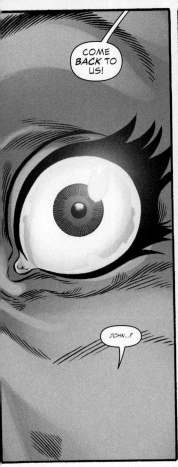

COME *BACK TO* US!

JOHN...?

DAMN WE'RE GOOD.

HOW'RE YOU *FEELING,* ZEE?

MY *HEAD'S* POUNDING...MY BODY'S *SHAKING...* AND I'M SICK TO MY *STOMACH.*

OTHER THAN THAT-- *PERFECT.*

GOOD. NOW LET'S SEE WHAT WE CAN DO TO GET THE MULTIVERSE BACK ON *TRACK.*

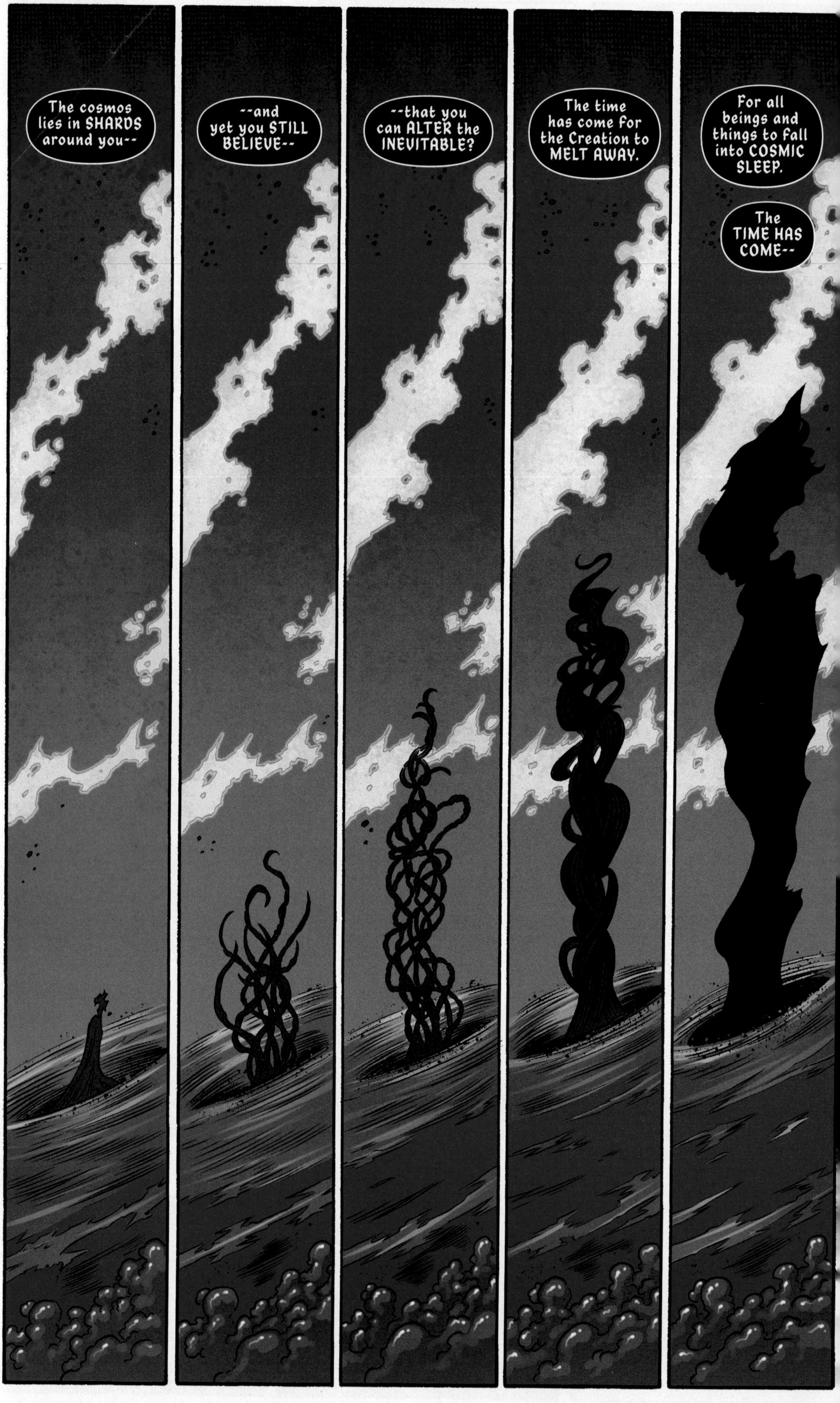
The cosmos lies in SHARDS around you--
--and yet you STILL BELIEVE--
--that you can ALTER the INEVITABLE?
The time has come for the Creation to MELT AWAY.
For all beings and things to fall into COSMIC SLEEP.
The TIME HAS COME--

--FOR PRALAYA.
THE GODDESS OF THE VOID?
To call me a goddess is an INSULT--for I am BEYOND such things.
What you see before you is as much a PROJECTION as my TIME GREMLINS were.
If you looked upon me in my TRUE FORM--your minds would COLLAPSE.
THEN YOU'RE THE ONE WHO RUPTURED THE TIMESTREAM?
I simply accelerated a process--
--that YOU BEGAN.
US?

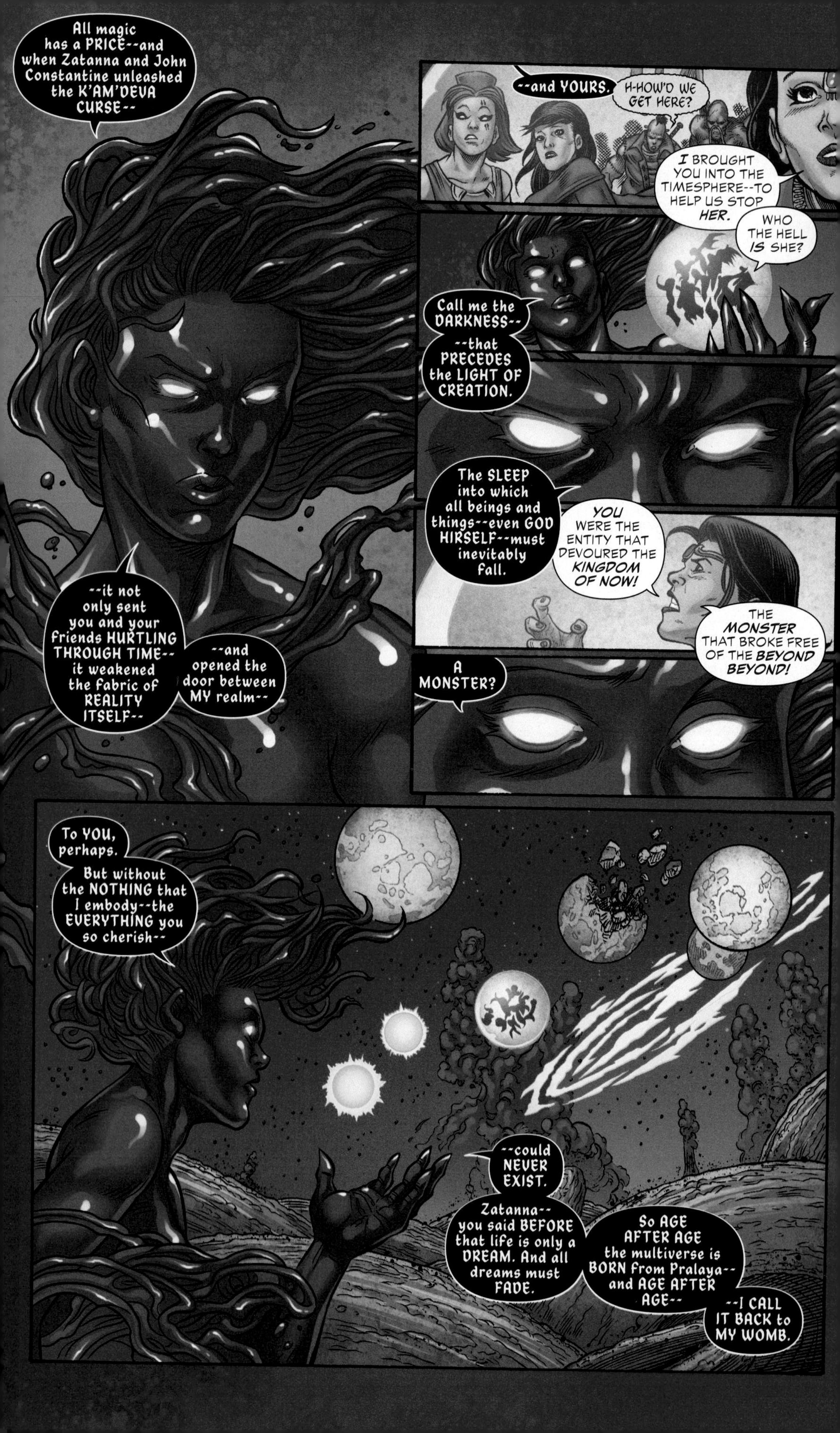
All magic has a PRICE--and when Zatanna and John Constantine unleashed the K'AM'DEVA CURSE--
--and YOURS.
H-HOW'D WE GET HERE?
I BROUGHT YOU INTO THE TIMESPHERE--TO HELP US STOP HER.
WHO THE HELL IS SHE?
Call me the DARKNESS--
--that PRECEDES the LIGHT OF CREATION.
The SLEEP into which all beings and things--even GOD HIRSELF--must inevitably fall.
YOU WERE THE ENTITY THAT DEVOURED THE KINGDOM OF NOW!
THE MONSTER THAT BROKE FREE OF THE BEYOND BEYOND!
--it not only sent you and your friends HURTLING THROUGH TIME--it weakened the fabric of REALITY ITSELF--
--and opened the door between MY realm--
A MONSTER?
To YOU, perhaps.
But without the NOTHING that I embody--the EVERYTHING you so cherish--
--could NEVER EXIST.
Zatanna--you said BEFORE that life is only a DREAM. And all dreams must FADE.
So AGE AFTER AGE the multiverse is BORN from Pralaya--and AGE AFTER AGE--
--I CALL IT BACK to MY WOMB.

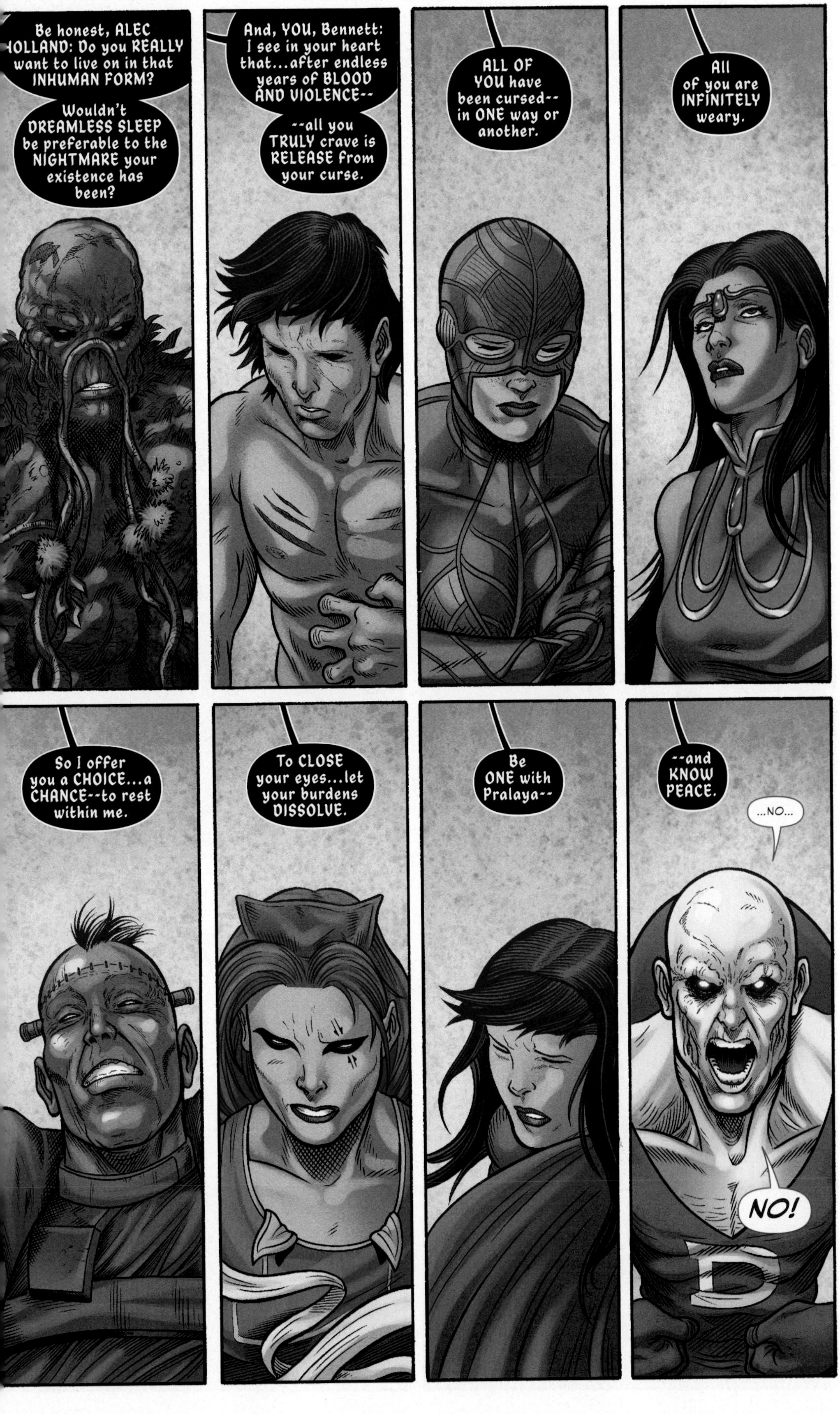
Be honest, ALEC HOLLAND: Do you REALLY want to live on in that INHUMAN FORM?
Wouldn't DREAMLESS SLEEP be preferable to the NIGHTMARE your existence has been?
And, YOU, Bennett: I see in your heart that...after endless years of BLOOD AND VIOLENCE--
--all you TRULY crave is RELEASE from your curse.
ALL OF YOU have been cursed--in ONE way or another.
All of you are INFINITELY weary.
So I offer you a CHOICE...a CHANCE--to rest within me.
To CLOSE your eyes...let your burdens DISSOLVE.
Be ONE with Pralaya--
--and KNOW PEACE.
...NO...
NO!

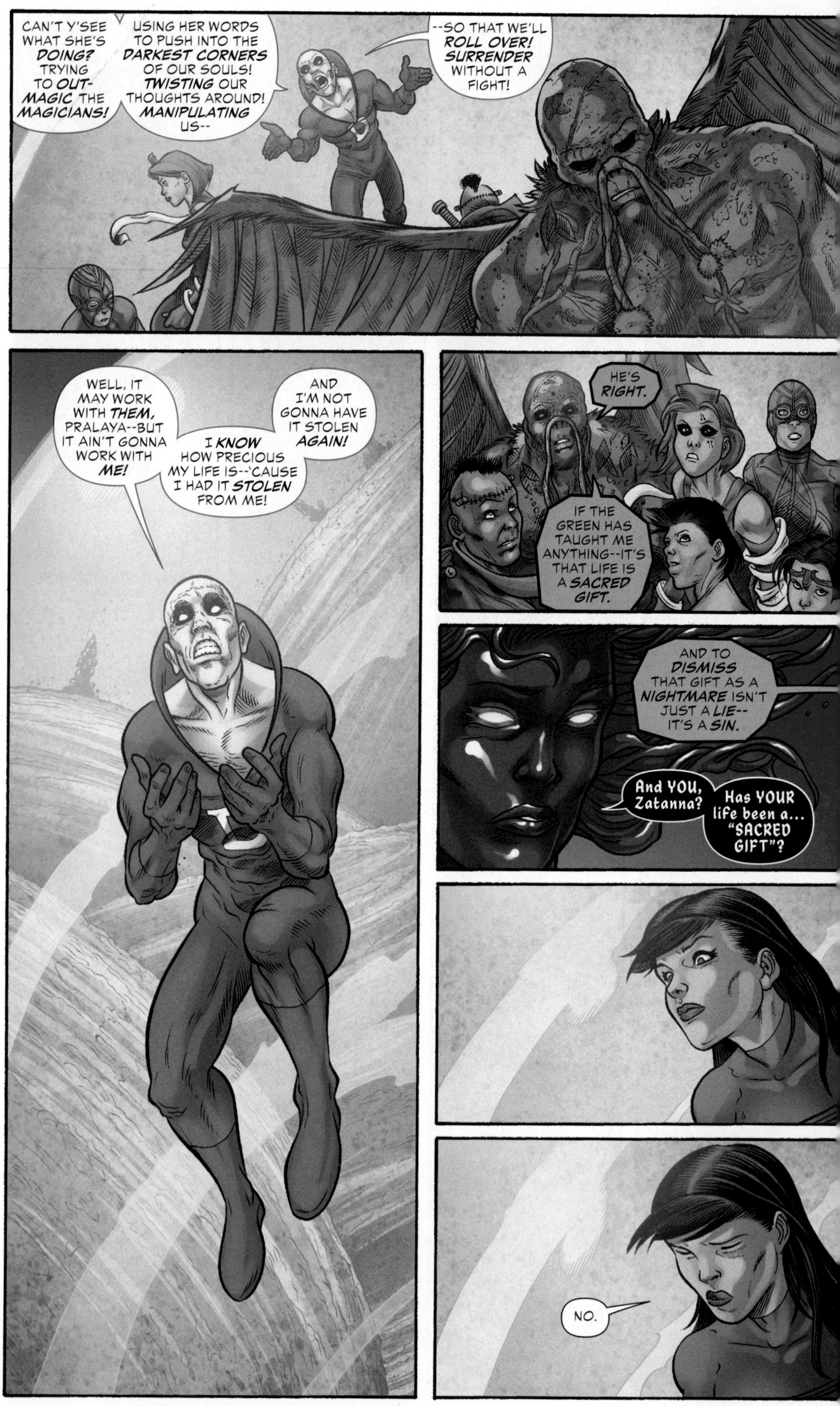
CAN'T Y'SEE WHAT SHE'S DOING? TRYING TO OUT-MAGIC THE MAGICIANS!
USING HER WORDS TO PUSH INTO THE DARKEST CORNERS OF OUR SOULS! TWISTING OUR THOUGHTS AROUND! MANIPULATING US--
--SO THAT WE'LL ROLL OVER! SURRENDER WITHOUT A FIGHT!
WELL, IT MAY WORK WITH THEM, PRALAYA--BUT IT AIN'T GONNA WORK WITH ME!
I KNOW HOW PRECIOUS MY LIFE IS--'CAUSE I HAD IT STOLEN FROM ME!
AND I'M NOT GONNA HAVE IT STOLEN AGAIN!
HE'S RIGHT.
IF THE GREEN HAS TAUGHT ME ANYTHING--IT'S THAT LIFE IS A SACRED GIFT.
AND TO DISMISS THAT GIFT AS A NIGHTMARE ISN'T JUST A LIE-- IT'S A SIN.
And YOU, Zatanna?
Has YOUR life been a... "SACRED GIFT"?
NO.

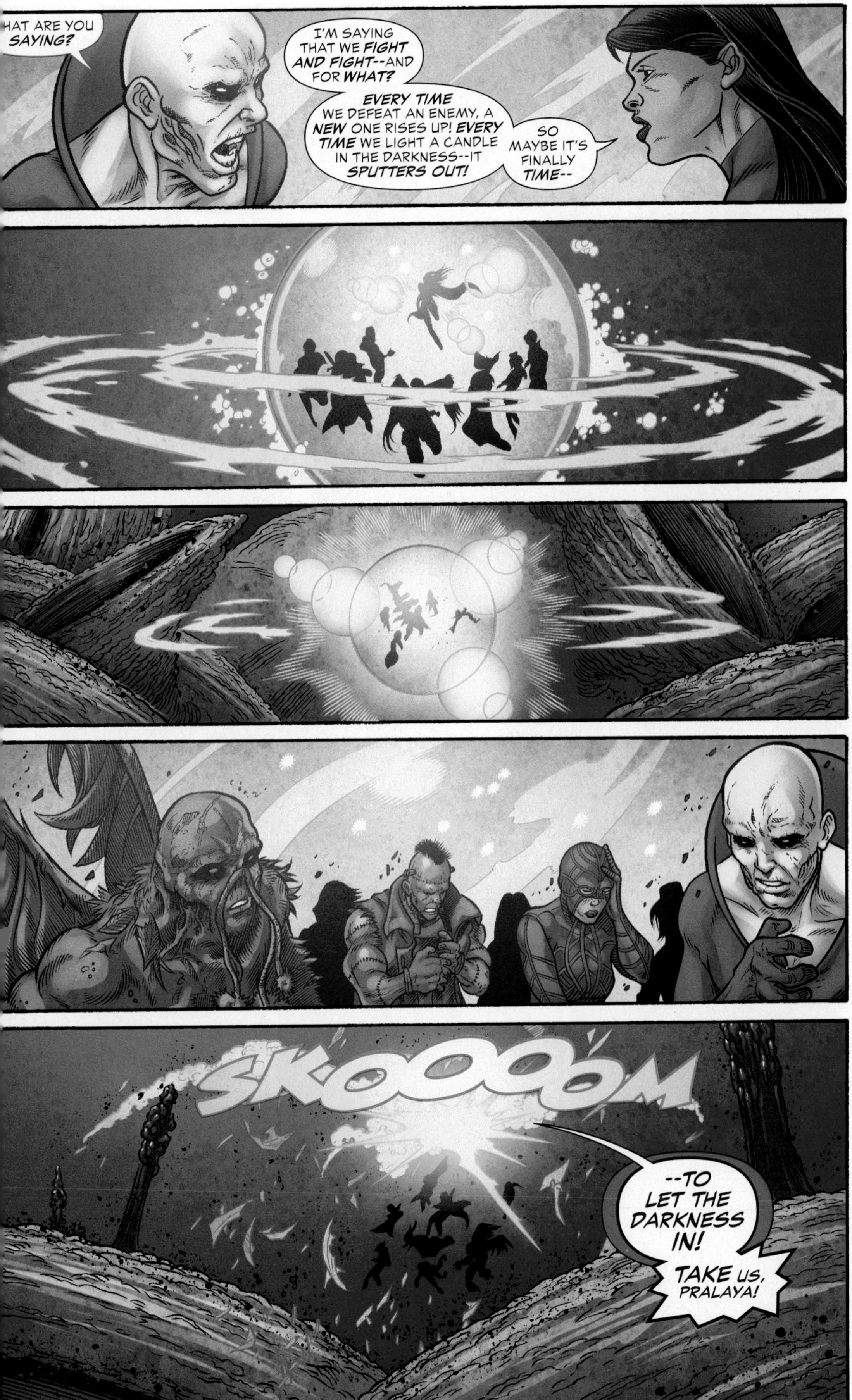
HAT ARE YOU SAYING?
I'M SAYING THAT WE FIGHT AND FIGHT--AND FOR WHAT?
EVERY TIME WE DEFEAT AN ENEMY, A NEW ONE RISES UP! EVERY TIME WE LIGHT A CANDLE IN THE DARKNESS--IT SPUTTERS OUT!
SO MAYBE IT'S FINALLY TIME--
SKOOOOOM
--TO LET THE DARKNESS IN!
TAKE US, PRALAYA!

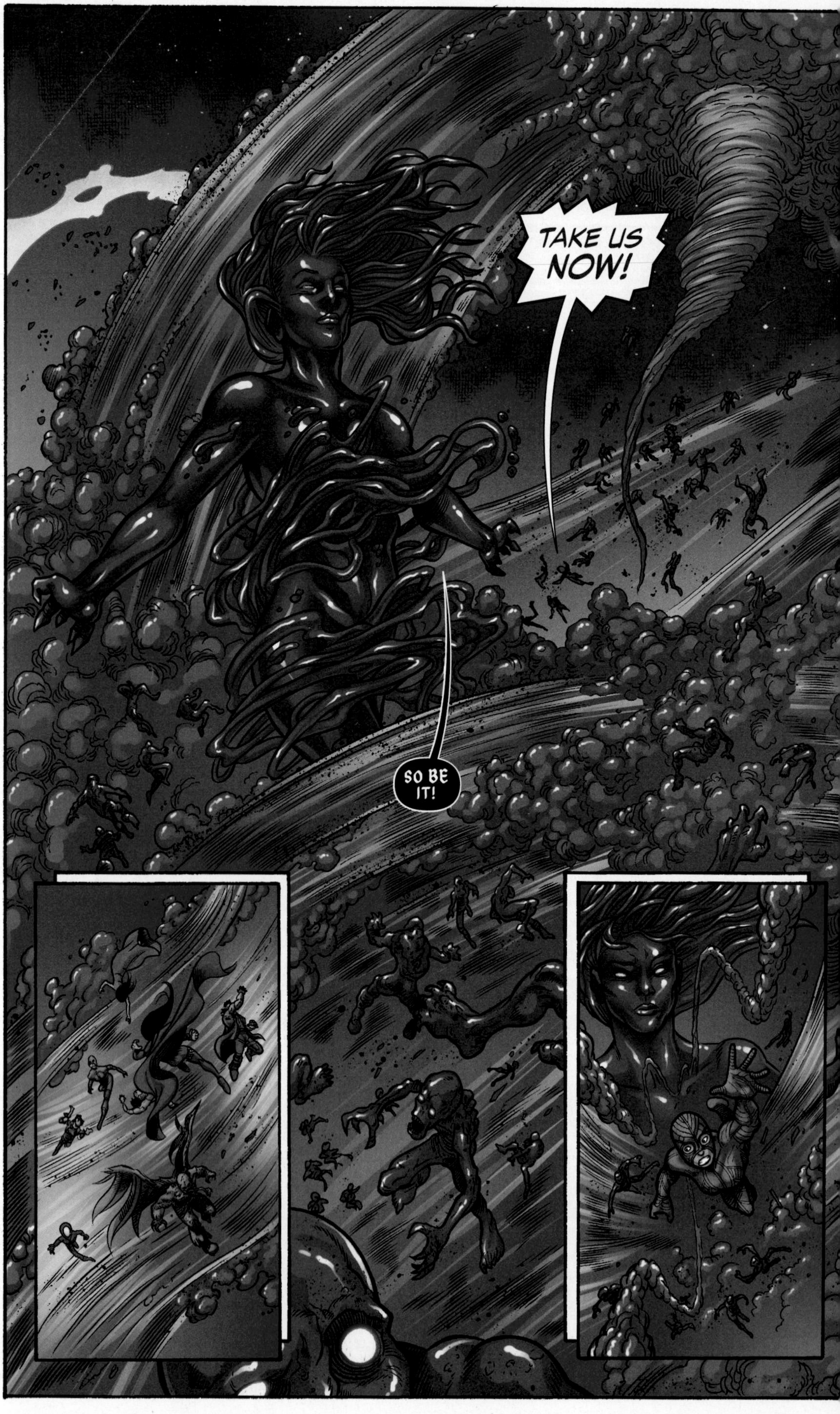
TAKE US NOW!
SO BE IT!

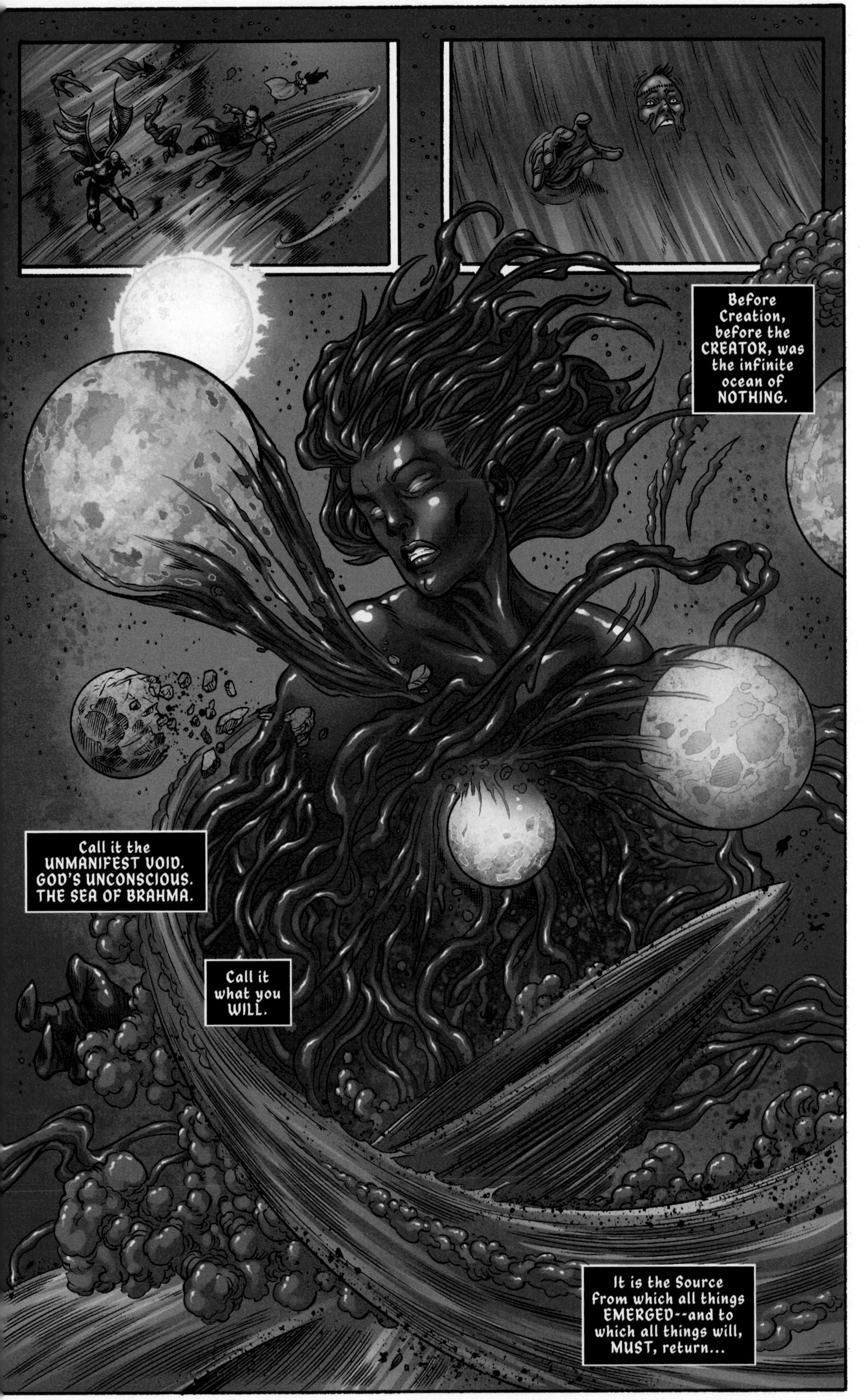

Before Creation, before the CREATOR, was the infinite ocean of NOTHING.
Call it the UNMANIFEST VOID. GOD'S UNCONSCIOUS. THE SEA OF BRAHMA.
Call it what you WILL.
It is the Source from which all things EMERGED--and to which all things will, MUST, return...

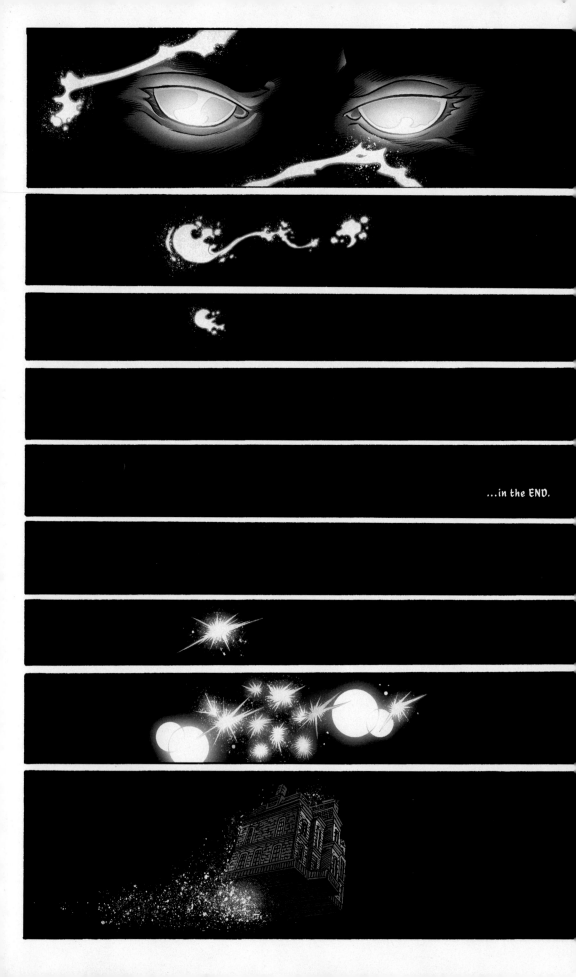

...in the END.

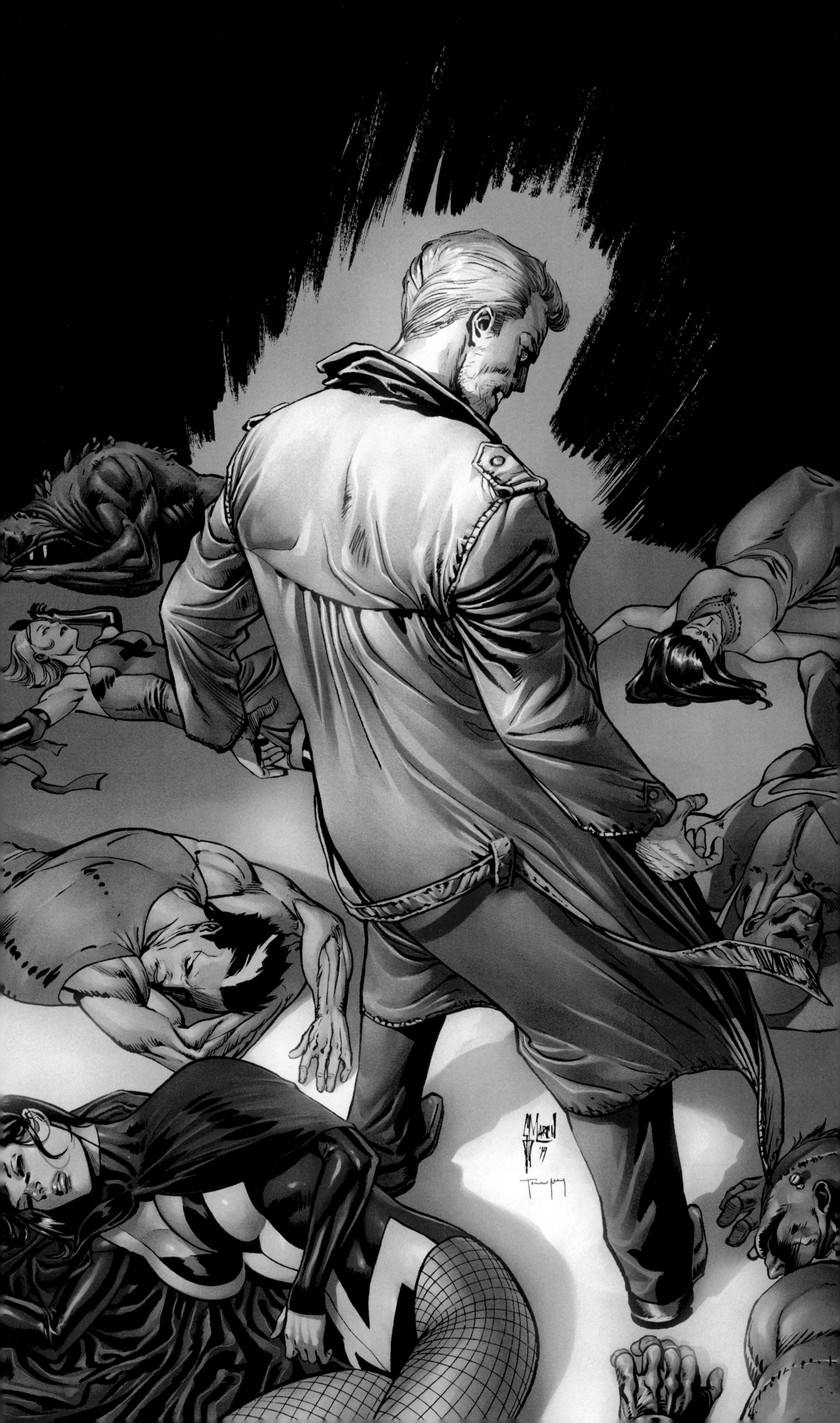

THE AMBER OF THE MOMENT PART 6: OUROBOROS

J.M. DeMATTEIS writer ANDRES GUINALDO penciller WALDEN WONG inker CHRIS SOTOMAYOR colorist
TRAVIS LANHAM letterer cover by GUILLEM MARCH & TOMEU MOREY

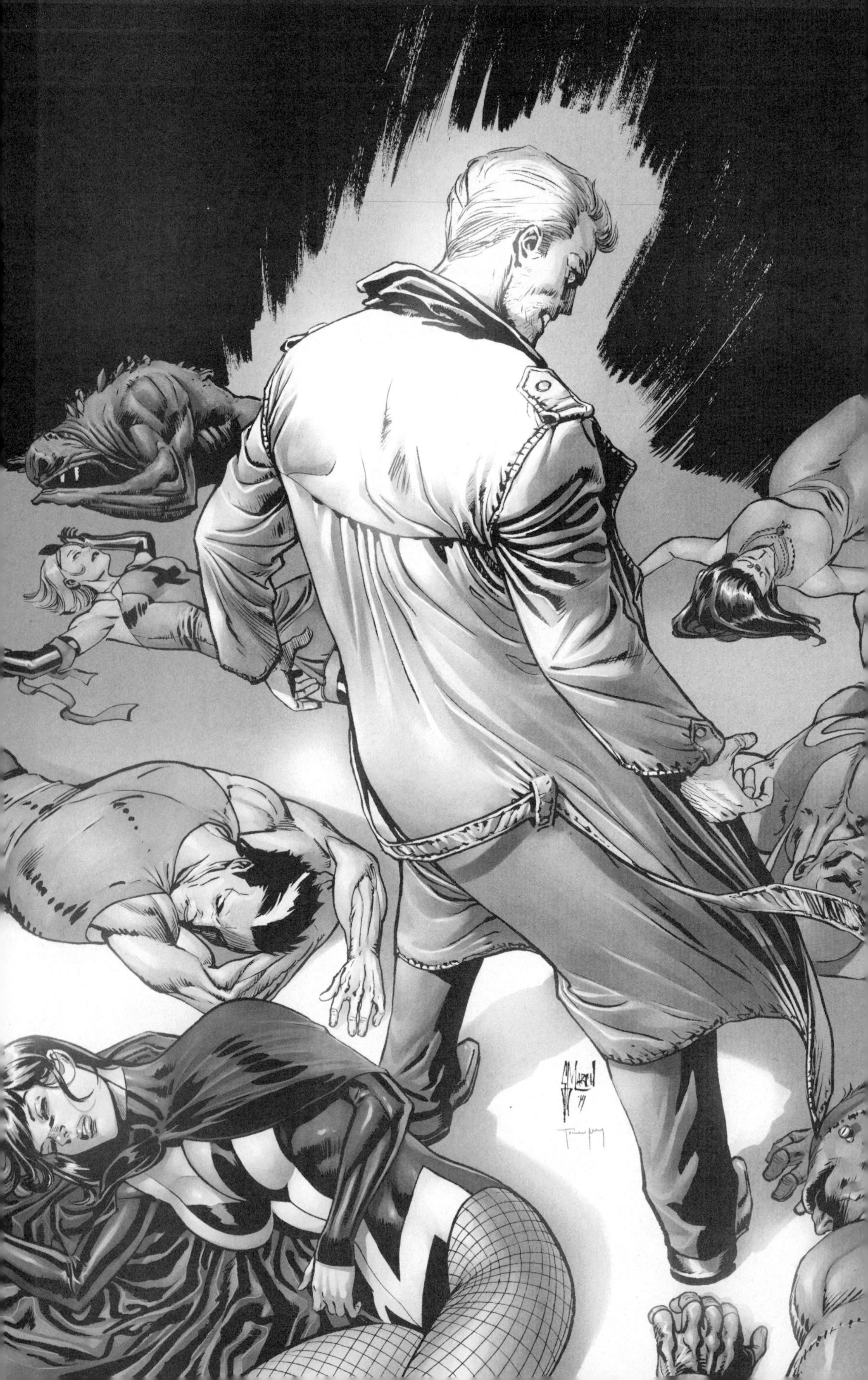

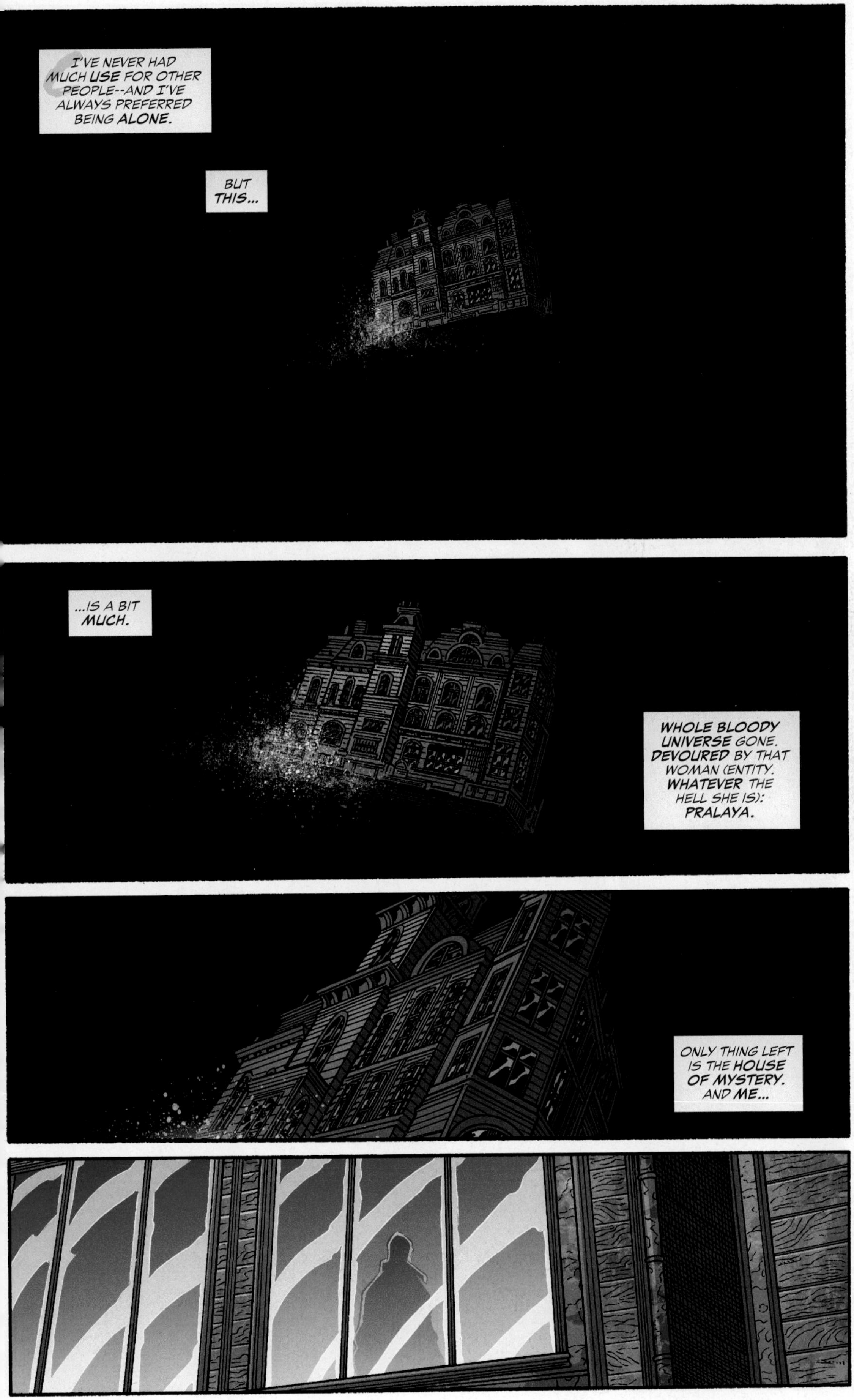

I'VE NEVER HAD MUCH USE FOR OTHER PEOPLE--AND I'VE ALWAYS PREFERRED BEING ALONE.
BUT THIS...
...IS A BIT MUCH.
WHOLE BLOODY UNIVERSE GONE. DEVOURED BY THAT WOMAN (ENTITY. WHATEVER THE HELL SHE IS): PRALAYA.
ONLY THING LEFT IS THE HOUSE OF MYSTERY. AND ME...

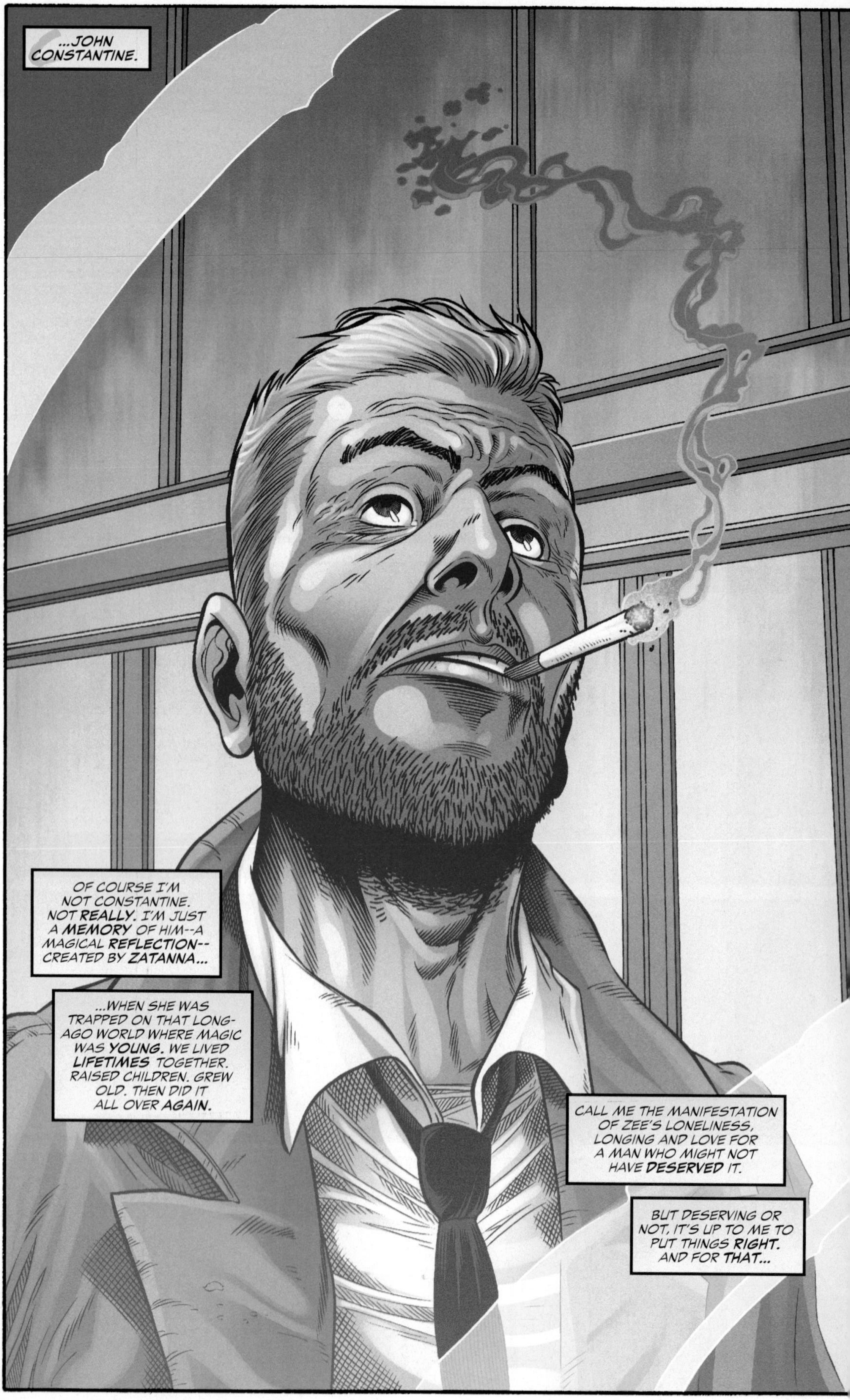
...JOHN CONSTANTINE.
OF COURSE I'M NOT CONSTANTINE. NOT REALLY. I'M JUST A MEMORY OF HIM--A MAGICAL REFLECTION-- CREATED BY ZATANNA...
...WHEN SHE WAS TRAPPED ON THAT LONG-AGO WORLD WHERE MAGIC WAS YOUNG. WE LIVED LIFETIMES TOGETHER. RAISED CHILDREN. GREW OLD. THEN DID IT ALL OVER AGAIN.
CALL ME THE MANIFESTATION OF ZEE'S LONELINESS, LONGING AND LOVE FOR A MAN WHO MIGHT NOT HAVE DESERVED IT.
BUT DESERVING OR NOT, IT'S UP TO ME TO PUT THINGS RIGHT. AND FOR THAT...

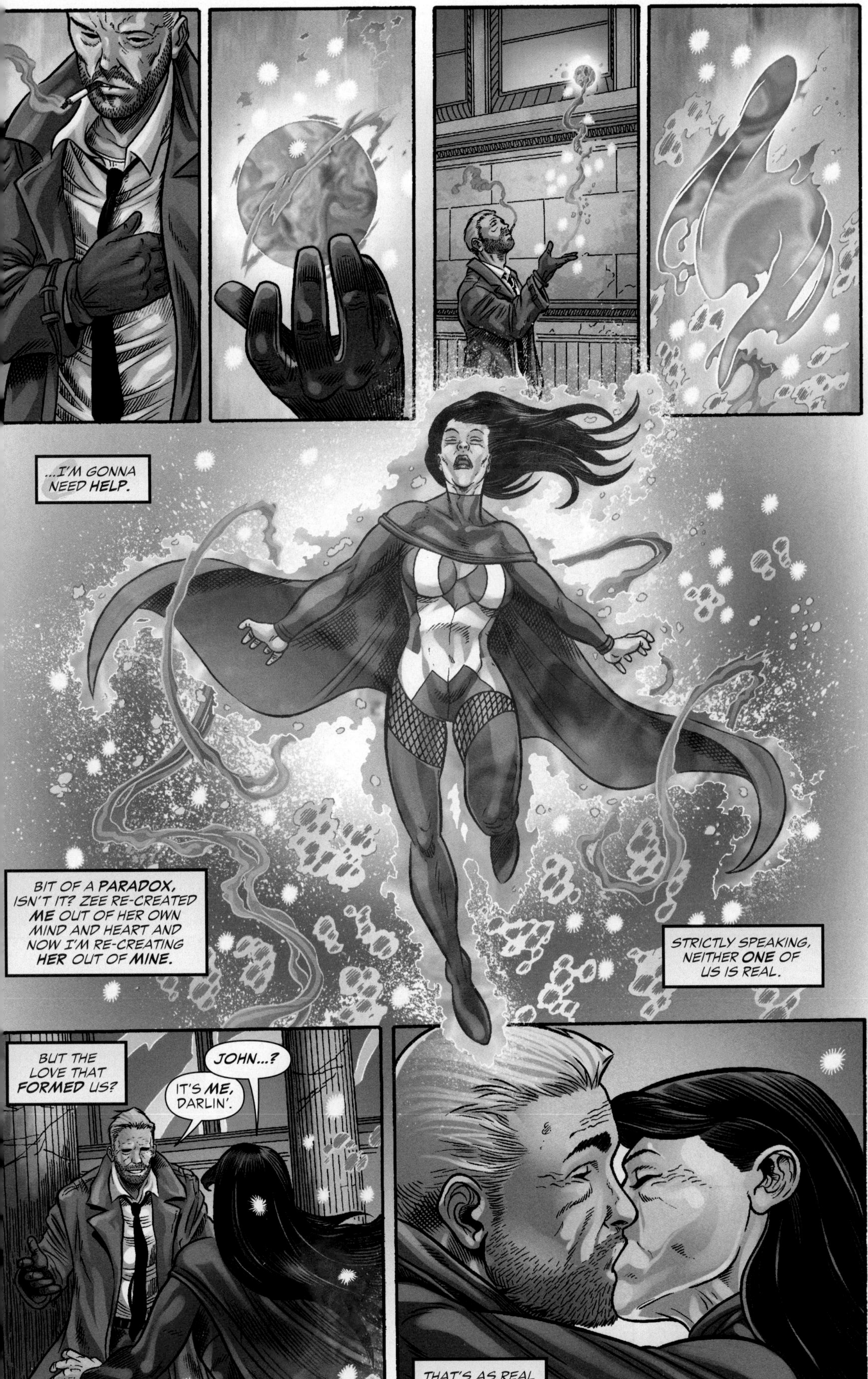

...I'M GONNA NEED HELP.
BIT OF A PARADOX, ISN'T IT? ZEE RE-CREATED ME OUT OF HER OWN MIND AND HEART AND NOW I'M RE-CREATING HER OUT OF MINE.
STRICTLY SPEAKING, NEITHER ONE OF US IS REAL.
BUT THE LOVE THAT FORMED US?
JOHN...?
IT'S ME, DARLIN'.
THAT'S AS REAL AS ANYTHING.

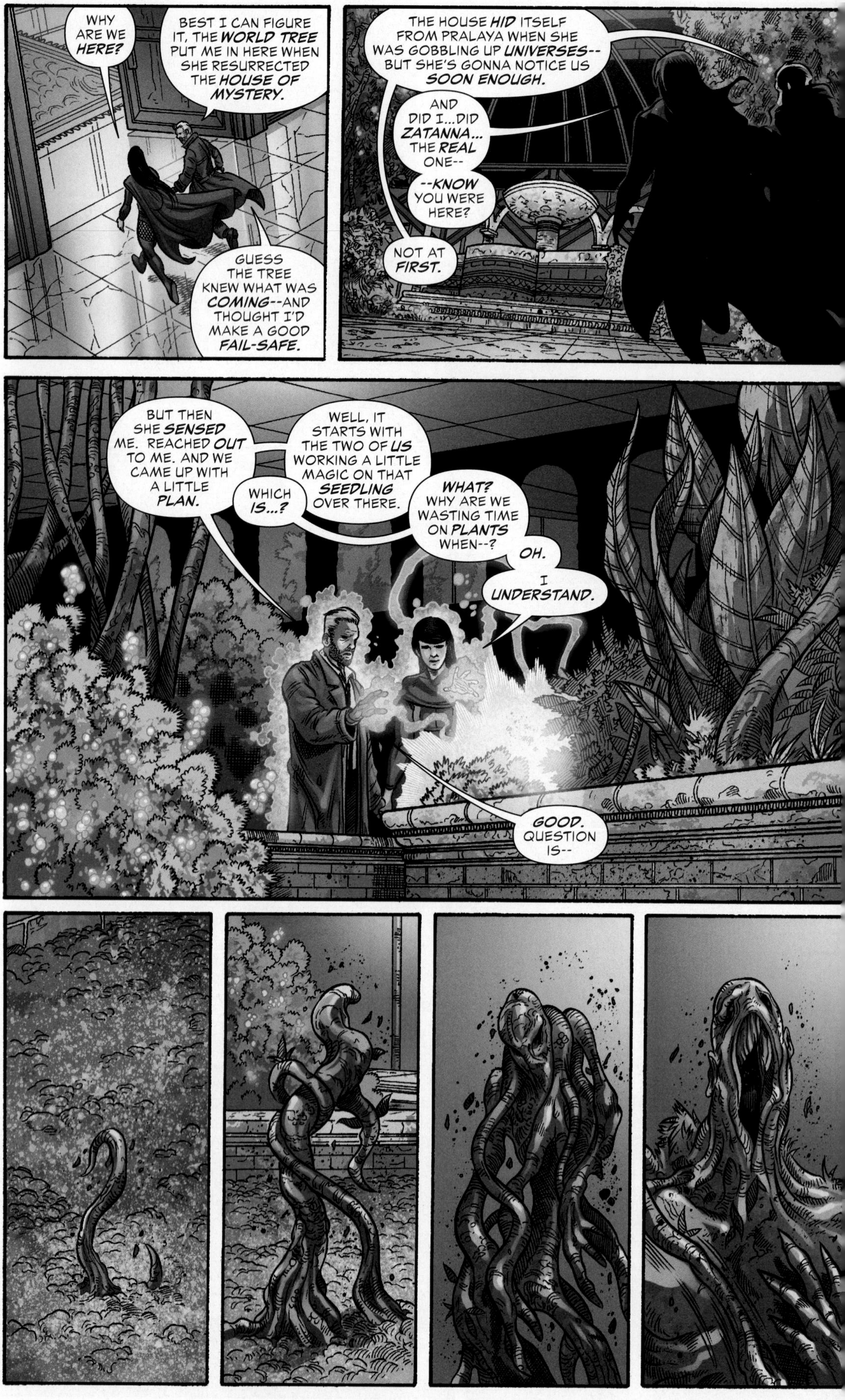
WHY ARE WE HERE?
BEST I CAN FIGURE IT, THE WORLD TREE PUT ME IN HERE WHEN SHE RESURRECTED THE HOUSE OF MYSTERY.
GUESS THE TREE KNEW WHAT WAS COMING--AND THOUGHT I'D MAKE A GOOD FAIL-SAFE.
THE HOUSE HID ITSELF FROM PRALAYA WHEN SHE WAS GOBBLING UP UNIVERSES--BUT SHE'S GONNA NOTICE US SOON ENOUGH.
AND DID I...DID ZATANNA... THE REAL ONE--
--KNOW YOU WERE HERE?
NOT AT FIRST.
BUT THEN SHE SENSED ME. REACHED OUT TO ME. AND WE CAME UP WITH A LITTLE PLAN.
WHICH IS...?
WELL, IT STARTS WITH THE TWO OF US WORKING A LITTLE MAGIC ON THAT SEEDLING OVER THERE.
WHAT? WHY ARE WE WASTING TIME ON PLANTS WHEN--?
OH.
I UNDERSTAND.
GOOD. QUESTION IS--

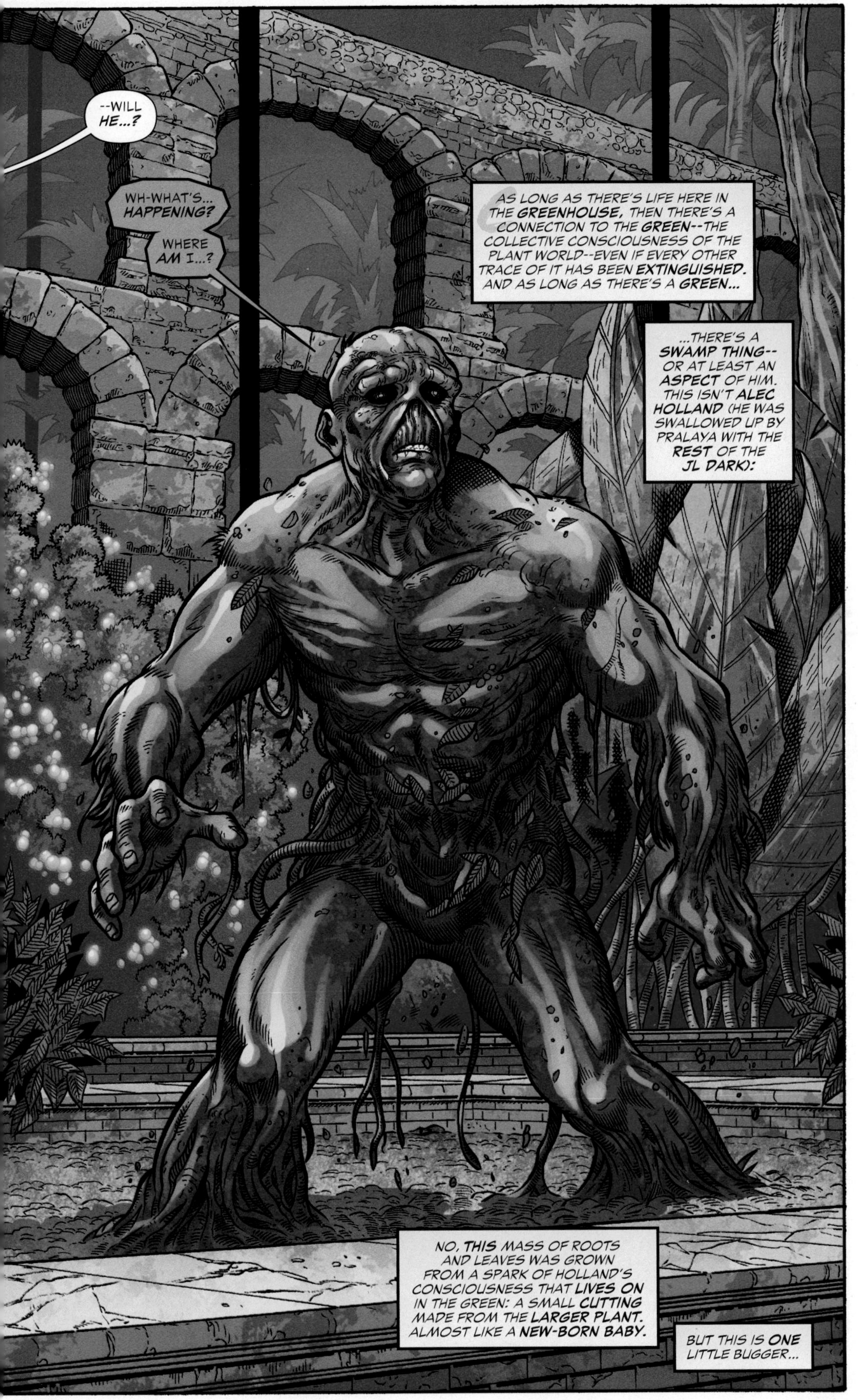

--WILL HE...?
WH-WHAT'S... HAPPENING?
WHERE AM I...?
AS LONG AS THERE'S LIFE HERE IN THE GREENHOUSE, THEN THERE'S A CONNECTION TO THE GREEN--THE COLLECTIVE CONSCIOUSNESS OF THE PLANT WORLD--EVEN IF EVERY OTHER TRACE OF IT HAS BEEN EXTINGUISHED. AND AS LONG AS THERE'S A GREEN...
...THERE'S A SWAMP THING--OR AT LEAST AN ASPECT OF HIM. THIS ISN'T ALEC HOLLAND (HE WAS SWALLOWED UP BY PRALAYA WITH THE REST OF THE JL DARK):
NO, THIS MASS OF ROOTS AND LEAVES WAS GROWN FROM A SPARK OF HOLLAND'S CONSCIOUSNESS THAT LIVES ON IN THE GREEN: A SMALL CUTTING MADE FROM THE LARGER PLANT. ALMOST LIKE A NEW-BORN BABY.
BUT THIS IS ONE LITTLE BUGGER...

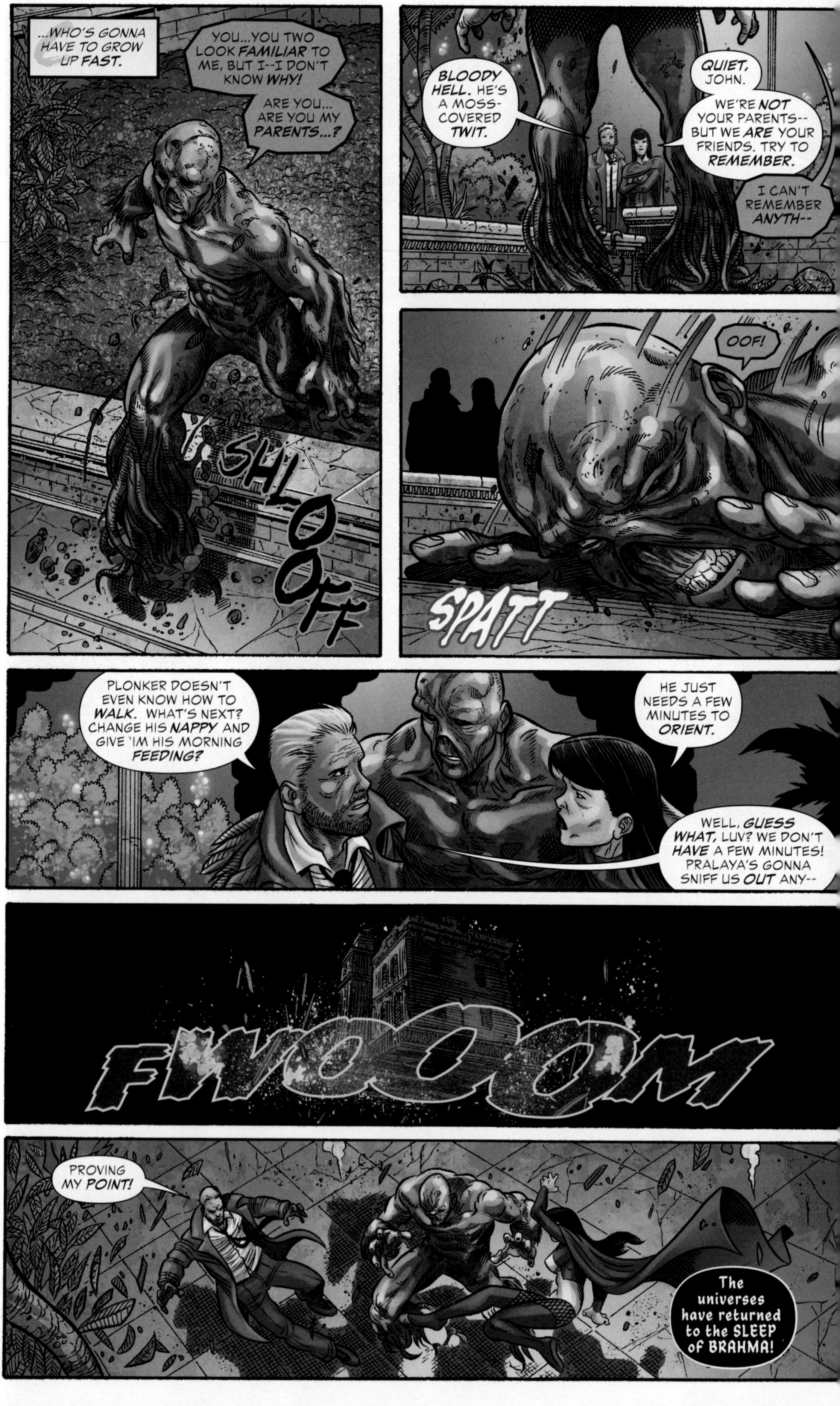
...WHO'S GONNA HAVE TO GROW UP FAST.
YOU...YOU TWO LOOK FAMILIAR TO ME, BUT I--I DON'T KNOW WHY!
ARE YOU... ARE YOU MY PARENTS...?
SHLOOFF
BLOODY HELL. HE'S A MOSS-COVERED TWIT.
QUIET, JOHN.
WE'RE NOT YOUR PARENTS-- BUT WE ARE YOUR FRIENDS. TRY TO REMEMBER.
I CAN'T REMEMBER ANYTH--
OOF!
SPATT
PLONKER DOESN'T EVEN KNOW HOW TO WALK. WHAT'S NEXT? CHANGE HIS NAPPY AND GIVE 'IM HIS MORNING FEEDING?
HE JUST NEEDS A FEW MINUTES TO ORIENT.
WELL, GUESS WHAT, LUV? WE DON'T HAVE A FEW MINUTES! PRALAYA'S GONNA SNIFF US OUT ANY--
FWOOOM
PROVING MY POINT!
The universes have returned to the SLEEP of BRAHMA!

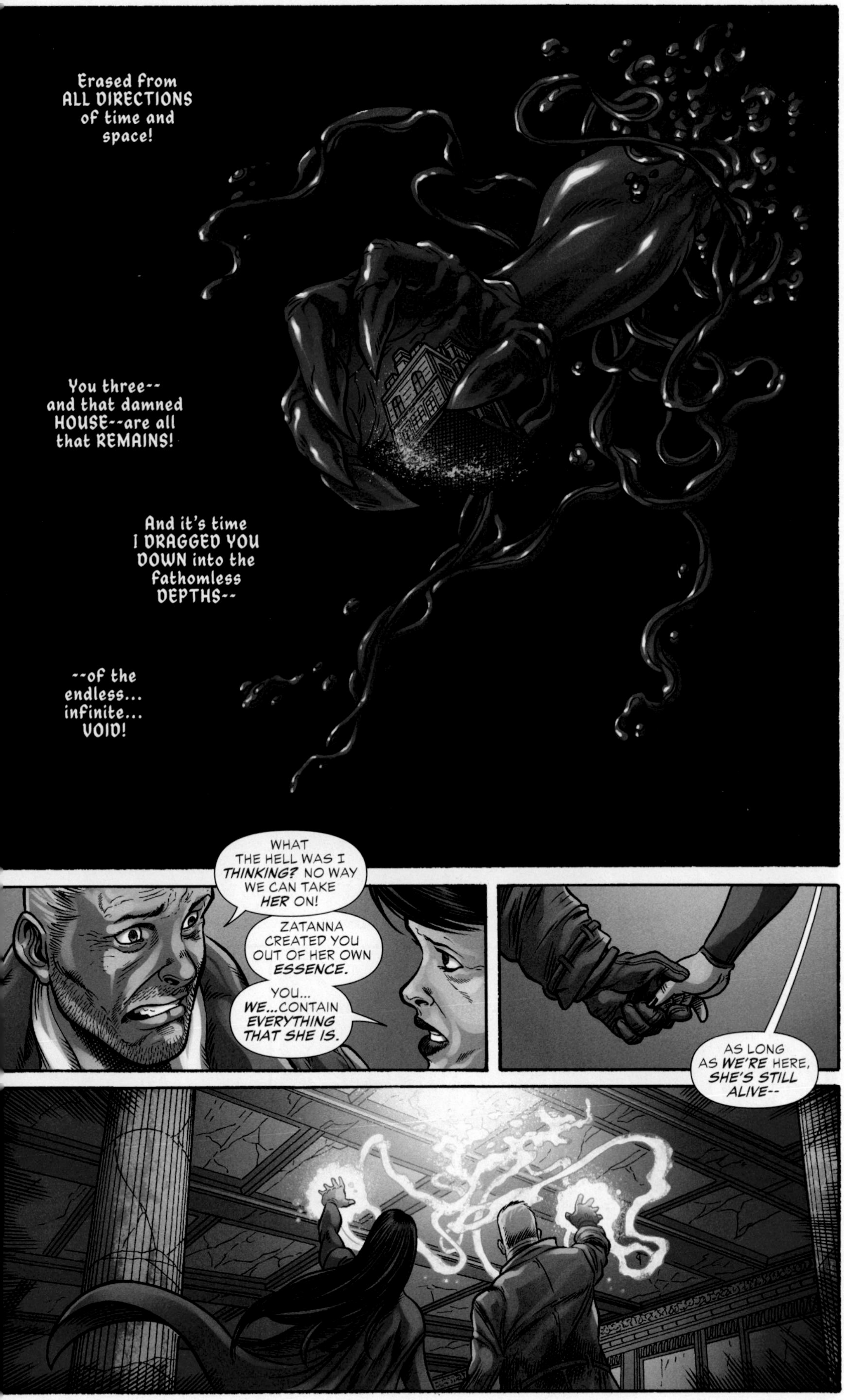
Erased from ALL DIRECTIONS of time and space!
You three--and that damned HOUSE--are all that REMAINS!
And it's time I DRAGGED YOU DOWN into the fathomless DEPTHS--
--of the endless... infinite... VOID!
WHAT THE HELL WAS I THINKING? NO WAY WE CAN TAKE HER ON!
ZATANNA CREATED YOU OUT OF HER OWN ESSENCE.
YOU... WE...CONTAIN EVERYTHING THAT SHE IS.
AS LONG AS WE'RE HERE, SHE'S STILL ALIVE--

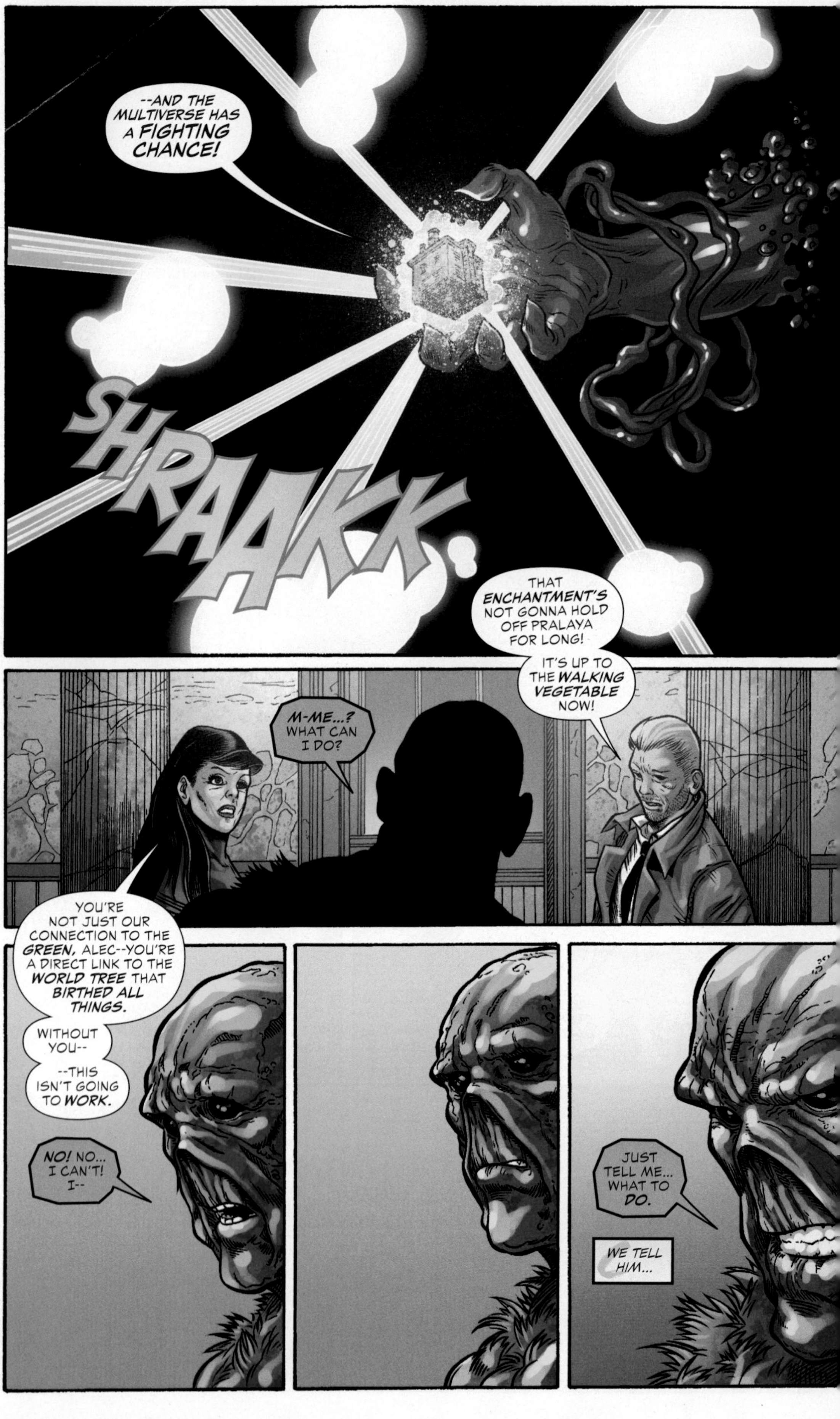
--AND THE MULTIVERSE HAS A FIGHTING CHANCE!
SHRAAKK
THAT ENCHANTMENT'S NOT GONNA HOLD OFF PRALAYA FOR LONG!
IT'S UP TO THE WALKING VEGETABLE NOW!
M-ME...? WHAT CAN I DO?
YOU'RE NOT JUST OUR CONNECTION TO THE GREEN, ALEC--YOU'RE A DIRECT LINK TO THE WORLD TREE THAT BIRTHED ALL THINGS.
WITHOUT YOU--
--THIS ISN'T GOING TO WORK.
NO! NO... I CAN'T! I--
JUST TELL ME... WHAT TO DO.
WE TELL HIM...

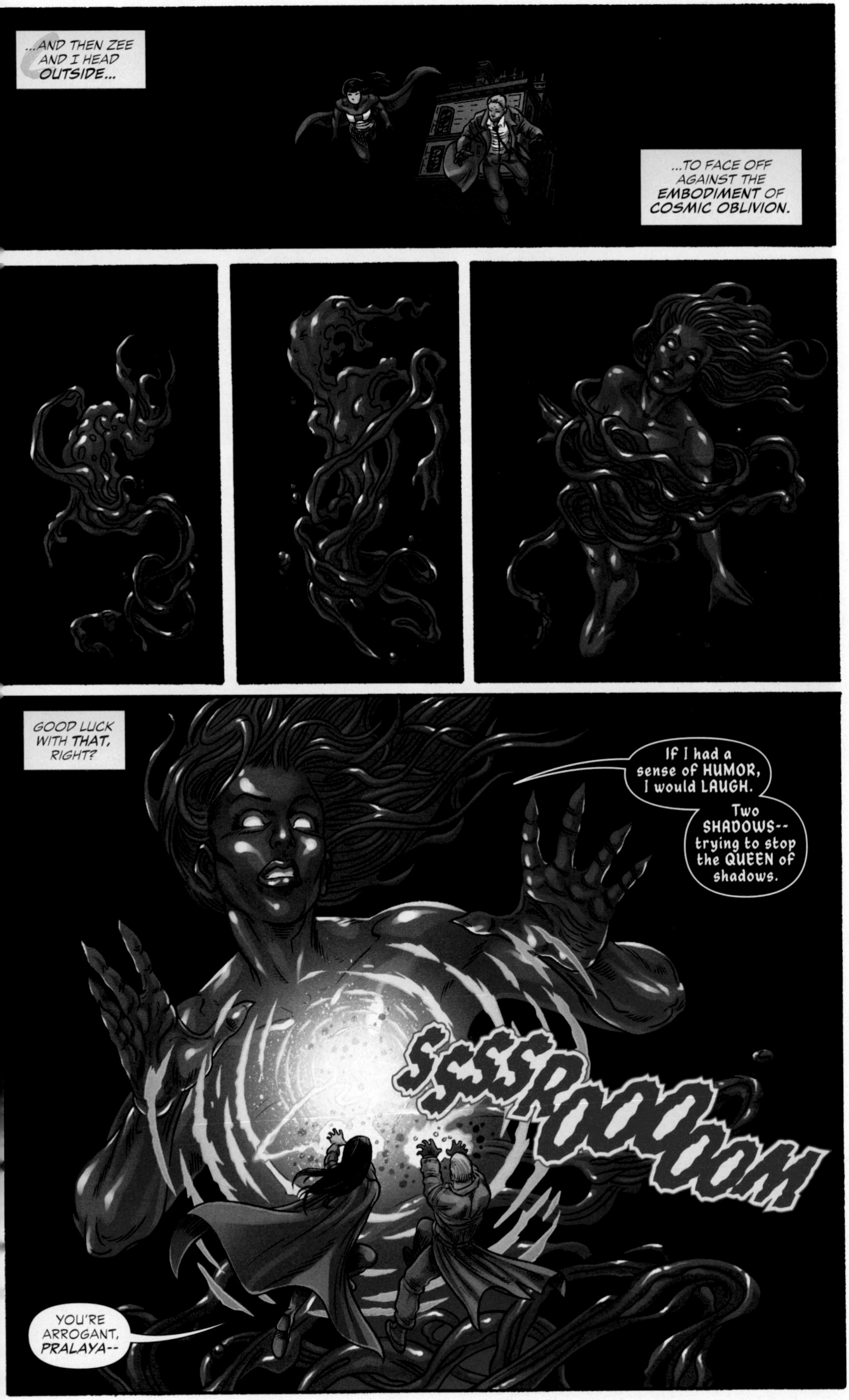
...AND THEN ZEE AND I HEAD OUTSIDE...
...TO FACE OFF AGAINST THE EMBODIMENT OF COSMIC OBLIVION.
GOOD LUCK WITH THAT, RIGHT?
If I had a sense of HUMOR, I would LAUGH.
Two SHADOWS-- trying to stop the QUEEN of shadows.
SSSSROOOOOM
YOU'RE ARROGANT, PRALAYA--

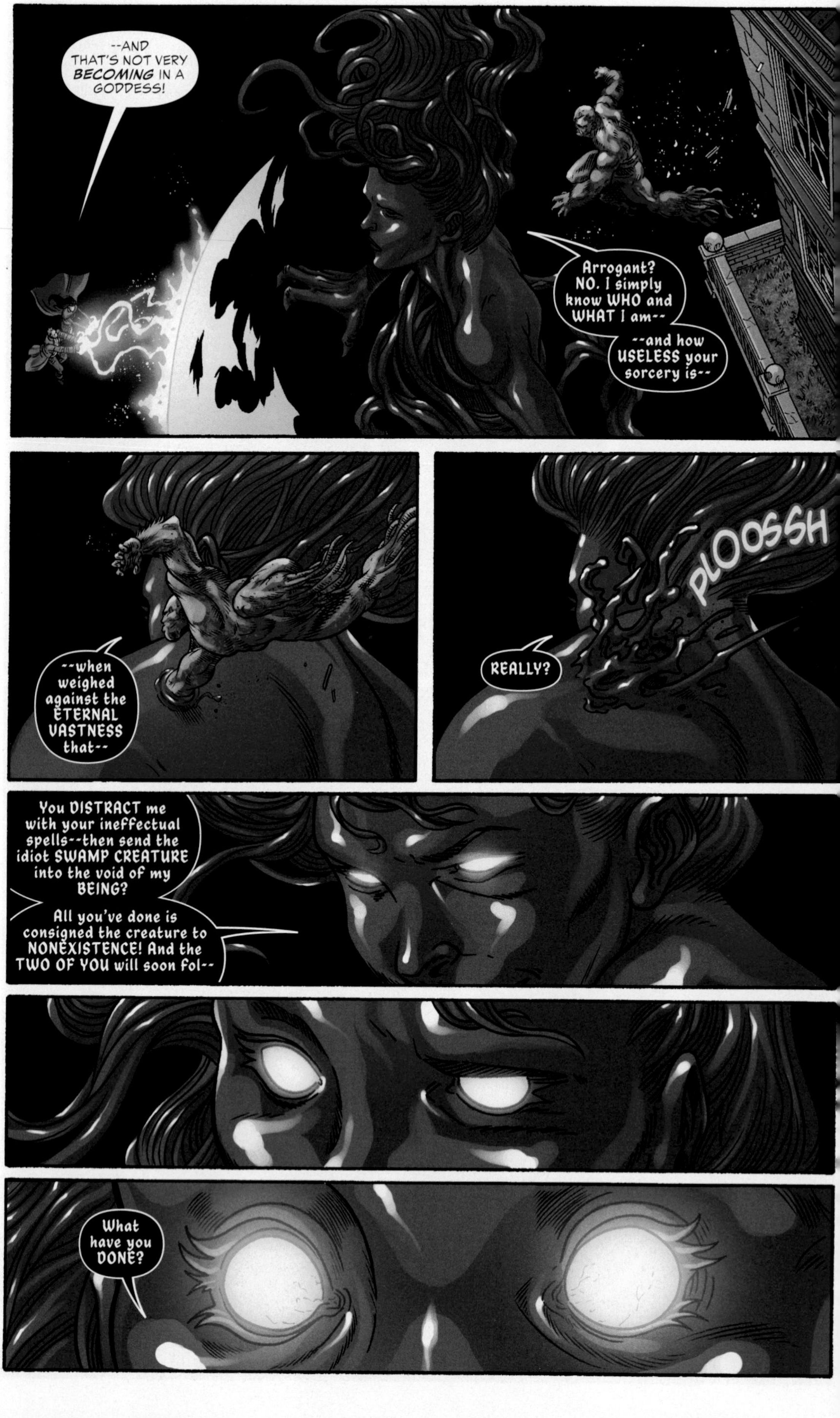
--AND THAT'S NOT VERY *BECOMING* IN A GODDESS!
Arrogant? NO. I simply know WHO and WHAT I am--
--and how USELESS your sorcery is--
--when weighed against the ETERNAL VASTNESS that--
REALLY?
PLOOSSH
You DISTRACT me with your ineffectual spells--then send the idiot SWAMP CREATURE into the void of my BEING?
All you've done is consigned the creature to NONEXISTENCE! And the TWO OF YOU will soon fol--
What have you DONE?

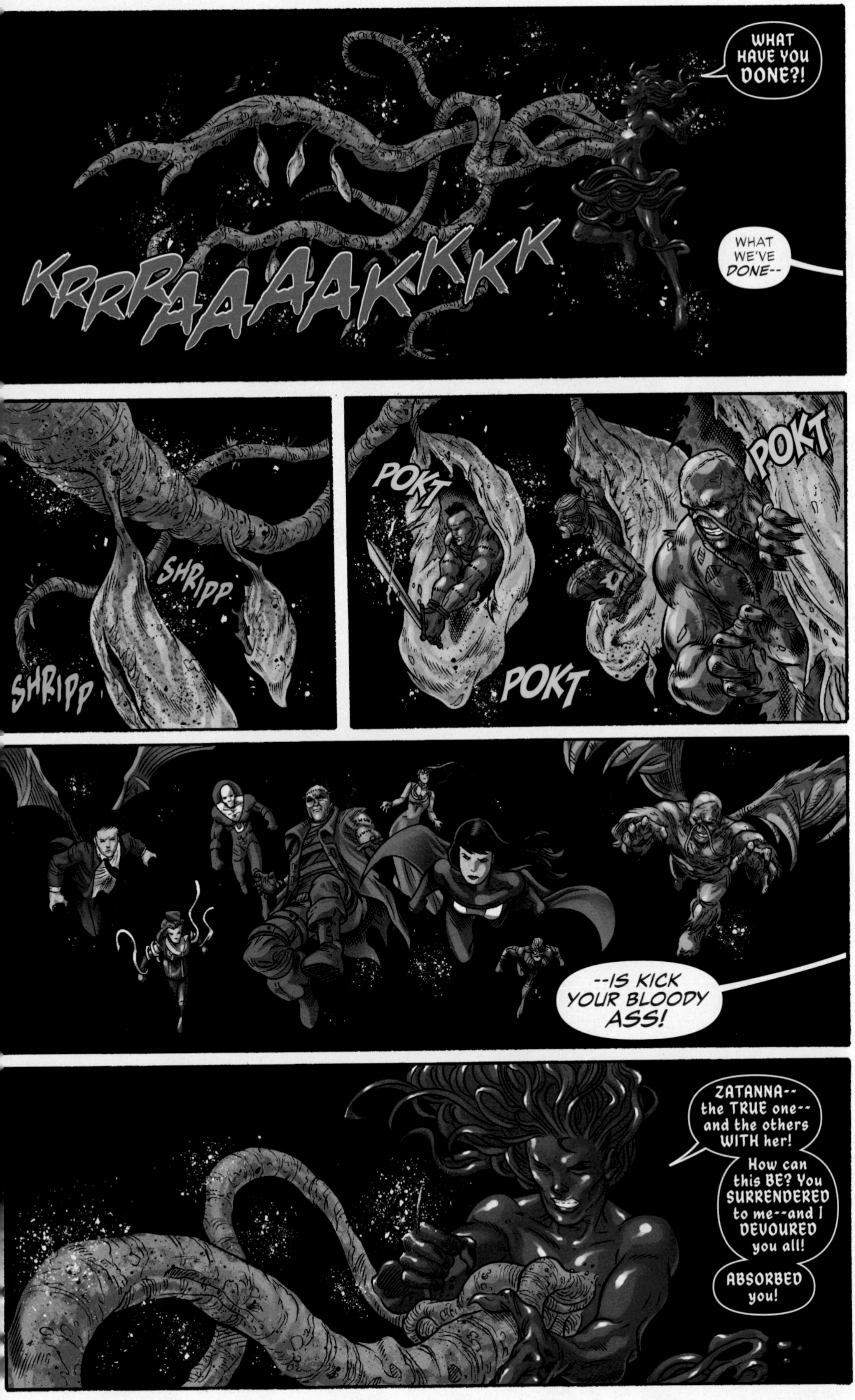
WHAT HAVE YOU DONE?!
KRRRAAAAKKKK
WHAT WE'VE DONE--
SHRIPP
SHRIPP
POKT
POKT
POKT
--IS KICK YOUR BLOODY ASS!
ZATANNA-- the TRUE one-- and the others WITH her!
How can this BE? You SURRENDERED to me--and I DEVOURED you all!
ABSORBED you!

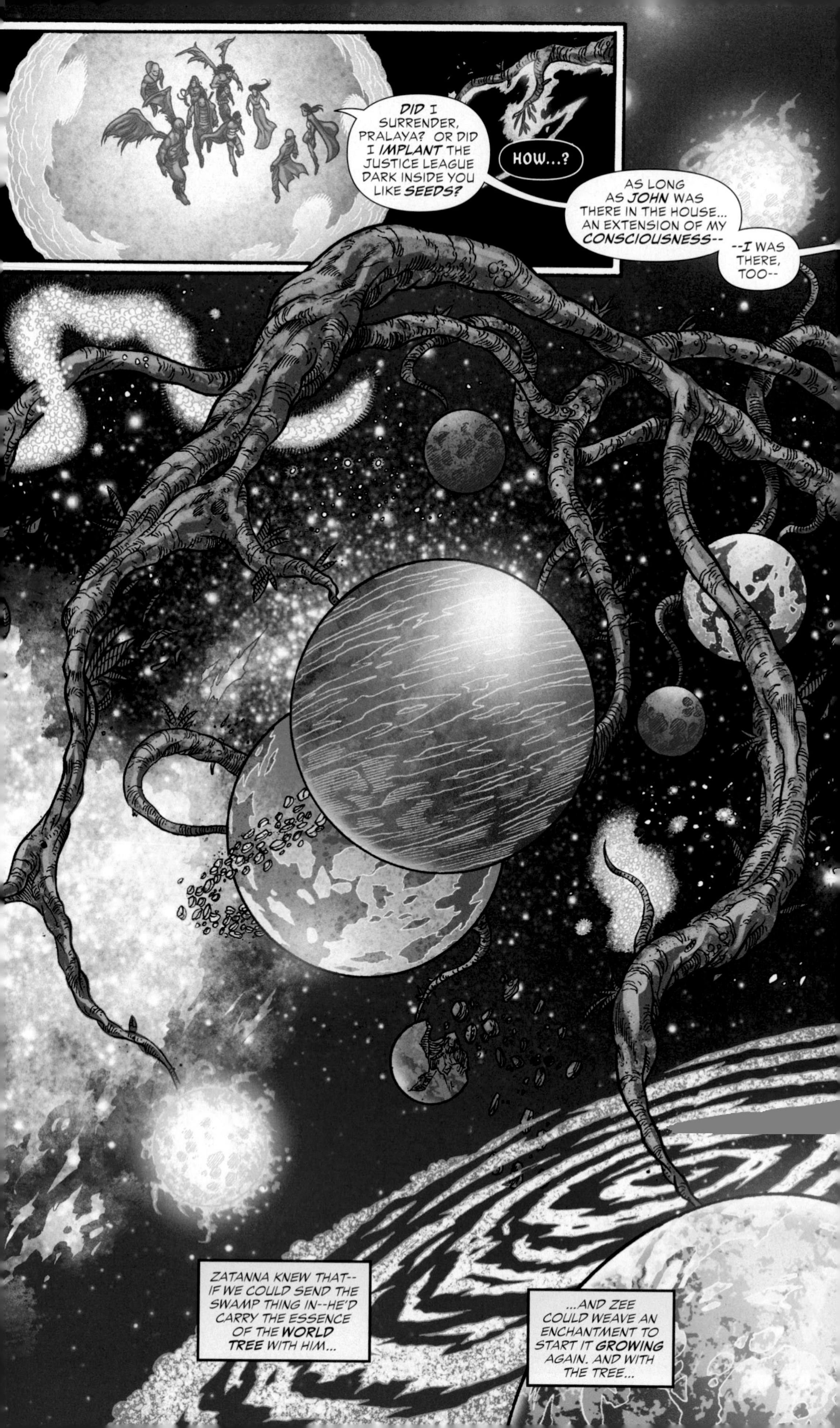
DID I SURRENDER, PRALAYA? OR DID I IMPLANT THE JUSTICE LEAGUE DARK INSIDE YOU LIKE SEEDS?
HOW...?
AS LONG AS JOHN WAS THERE IN THE HOUSE... AN EXTENSION OF MY CONSCIOUSNESS--
--I WAS THERE, TOO--
ZATANNA KNEW THAT-- IF WE COULD SEND THE SWAMP THING IN--HE'D CARRY THE ESSENCE OF THE WORLD TREE WITH HIM...
...AND ZEE COULD WEAVE AN ENCHANTMENT TO START IT GROWING AGAIN. AND WITH THE TREE...

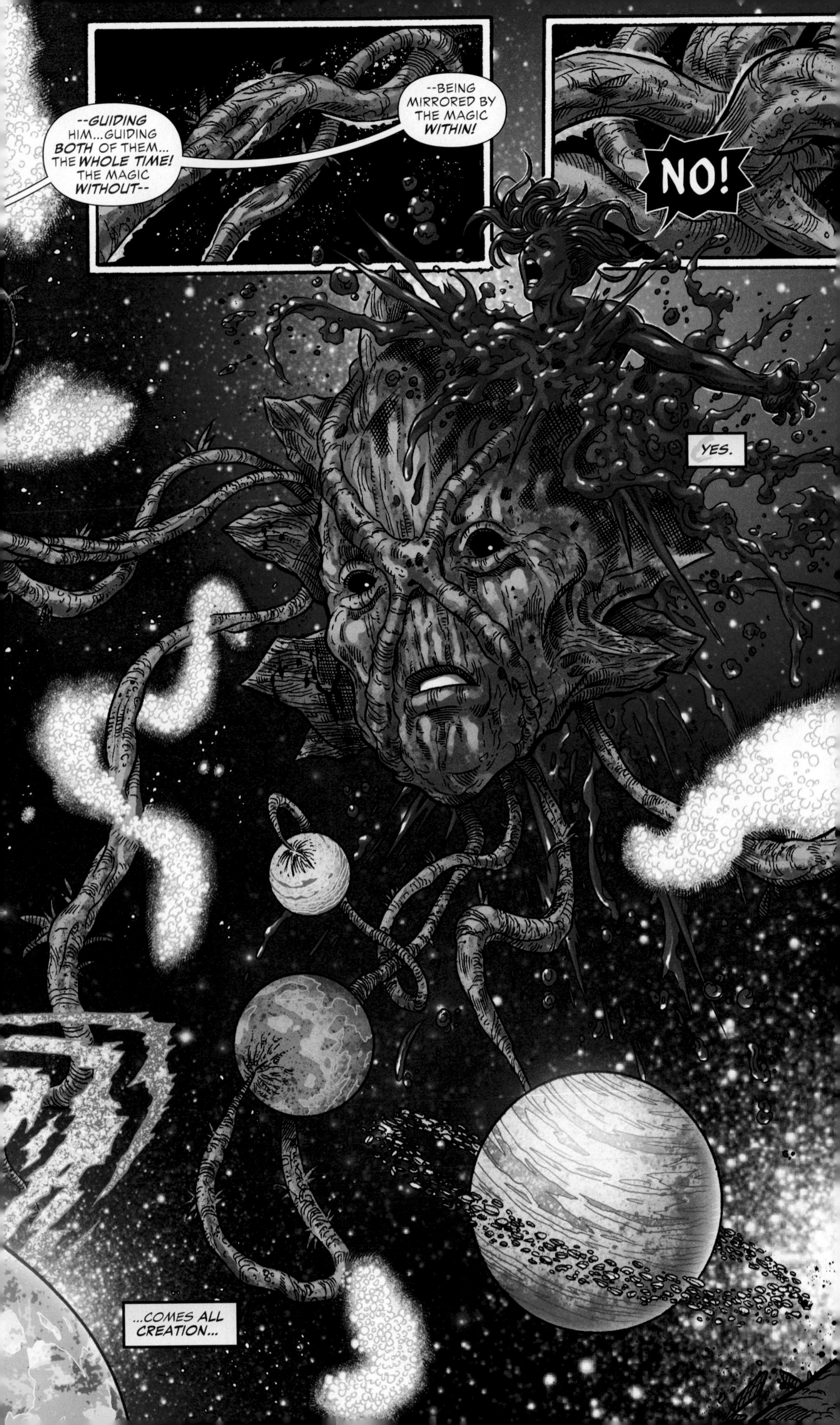

--GUIDING HIM...GUIDING BOTH OF THEM... THE WHOLE TIME! THE MAGIC WITHOUT--
--BEING MIRRORED BY THE MAGIC WITHIN!
NO!
YES.
...COMES ALL CREATION...

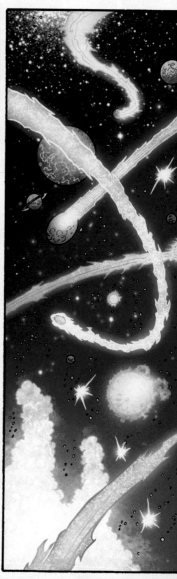

...REBORN.

NO, NOT REBORN:
RESTORED.

AWAKENED FROM
COSMIC SLEEP--AND
RETURNED TO THE EXACT
MOMENT BEFORE PRALAYA
CONSUMED IT. AND WE'RE
THE ONLY ONES...

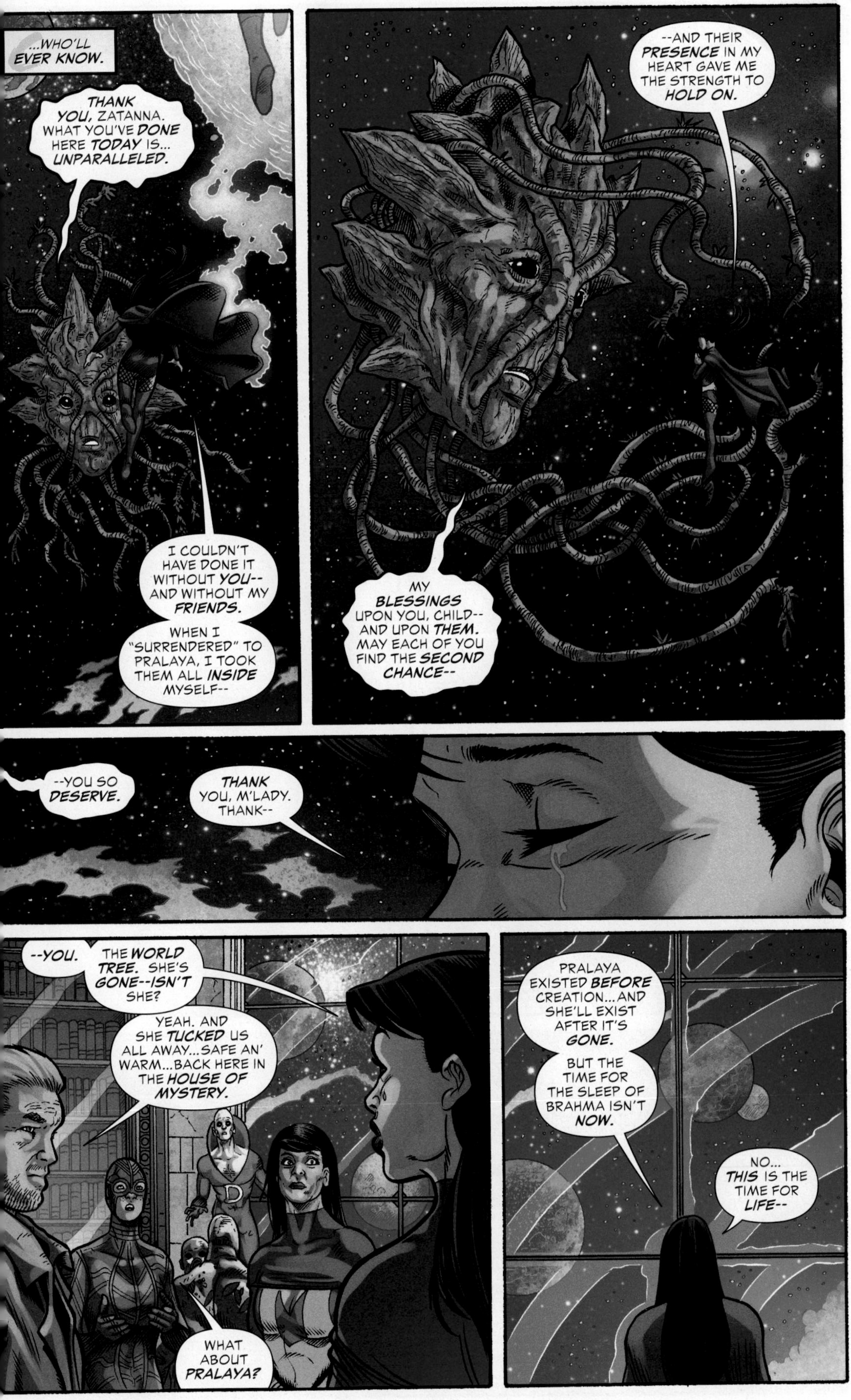
...WHO'LL EVER KNOW.
THANK YOU, ZATANNA. WHAT YOU'VE DONE HERE TODAY IS... UNPARALLELED.
I COULDN'T HAVE DONE IT WITHOUT YOU-- AND WITHOUT MY FRIENDS.
WHEN I "SURRENDERED" TO PRALAYA, I TOOK THEM ALL INSIDE MYSELF--
--AND THEIR PRESENCE IN MY HEART GAVE ME THE STRENGTH TO HOLD ON.
MY BLESSINGS UPON YOU, CHILD-- AND UPON THEM. MAY EACH OF YOU FIND THE SECOND CHANCE--
--YOU SO DESERVE.
THANK YOU, M'LADY. THANK--
--YOU.
THE WORLD TREE. SHE'S GONE--ISN'T SHE?
YEAH. AND SHE TUCKED US ALL AWAY...SAFE AN' WARM...BACK HERE IN THE HOUSE OF MYSTERY.
WHAT ABOUT PRALAYA?
PRALAYA EXISTED BEFORE CREATION...AND SHE'LL EXIST AFTER IT'S GONE.
BUT THE TIME FOR THE SLEEP OF BRAHMA ISN'T NOW.
NO... THIS IS THE TIME FOR LIFE--

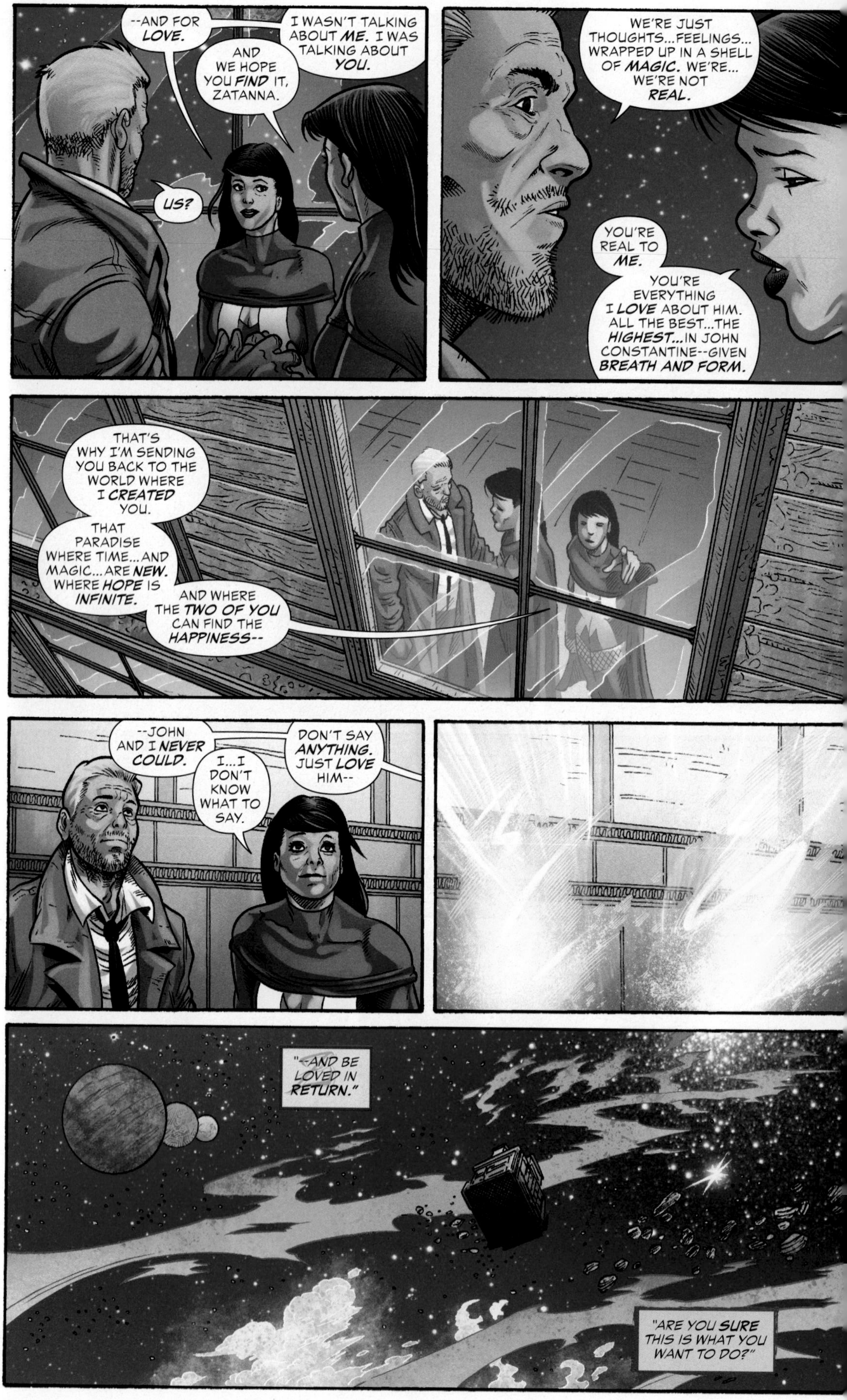
--AND FOR LOVE.
I WASN'T TALKING ABOUT ME. I WAS TALKING ABOUT YOU.
AND WE HOPE YOU FIND IT, ZATANNA.
US?
WE'RE JUST THOUGHTS...FEELINGS... WRAPPED UP IN A SHELL OF MAGIC. WE'RE... WE'RE NOT REAL.
YOU'RE REAL TO ME.
YOU'RE EVERYTHING I LOVE ABOUT HIM. ALL THE BEST...THE HIGHEST...IN JOHN CONSTANTINE--GIVEN BREATH AND FORM.
THAT'S WHY I'M SENDING YOU BACK TO THE WORLD WHERE I CREATED YOU.
THAT PARADISE WHERE TIME...AND MAGIC...ARE NEW. WHERE HOPE IS INFINITE.
AND WHERE THE TWO OF YOU CAN FIND THE HAPPINESS--
--JOHN AND I NEVER COULD.
I...I DON'T KNOW WHAT TO SAY.
DON'T SAY ANYTHING. JUST LOVE HIM--
"--AND BE LOVED IN RETURN."
"ARE YOU SURE THIS IS WHAT YOU WANT TO DO?"

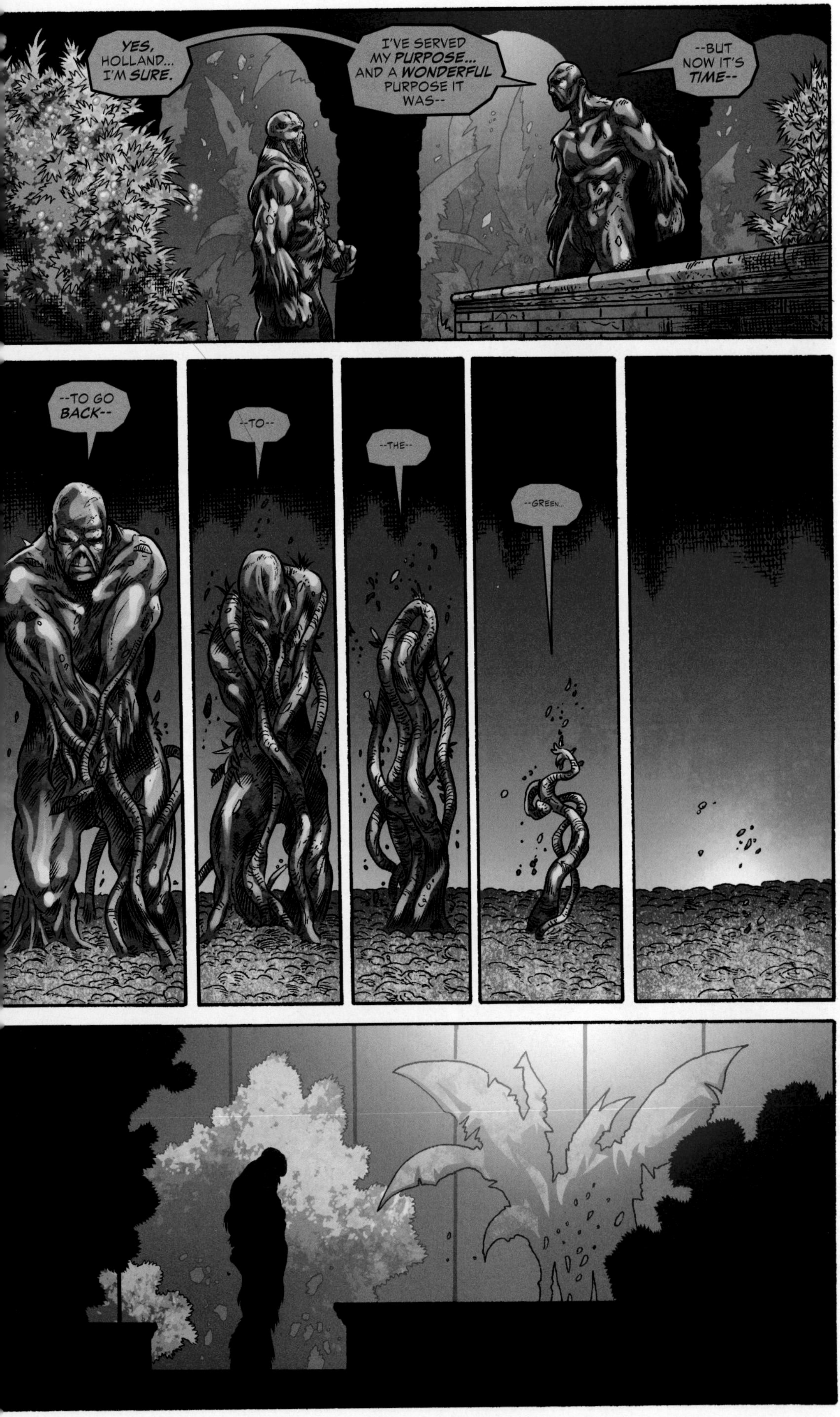
YES, HOLLAND... I'M SURE.
I'VE SERVED MY PURPOSE... AND A WONDERFUL PURPOSE IT WAS--
--BUT NOW IT'S TIME--
--TO GO BACK--
--TO--
--THE--
--GREEN...

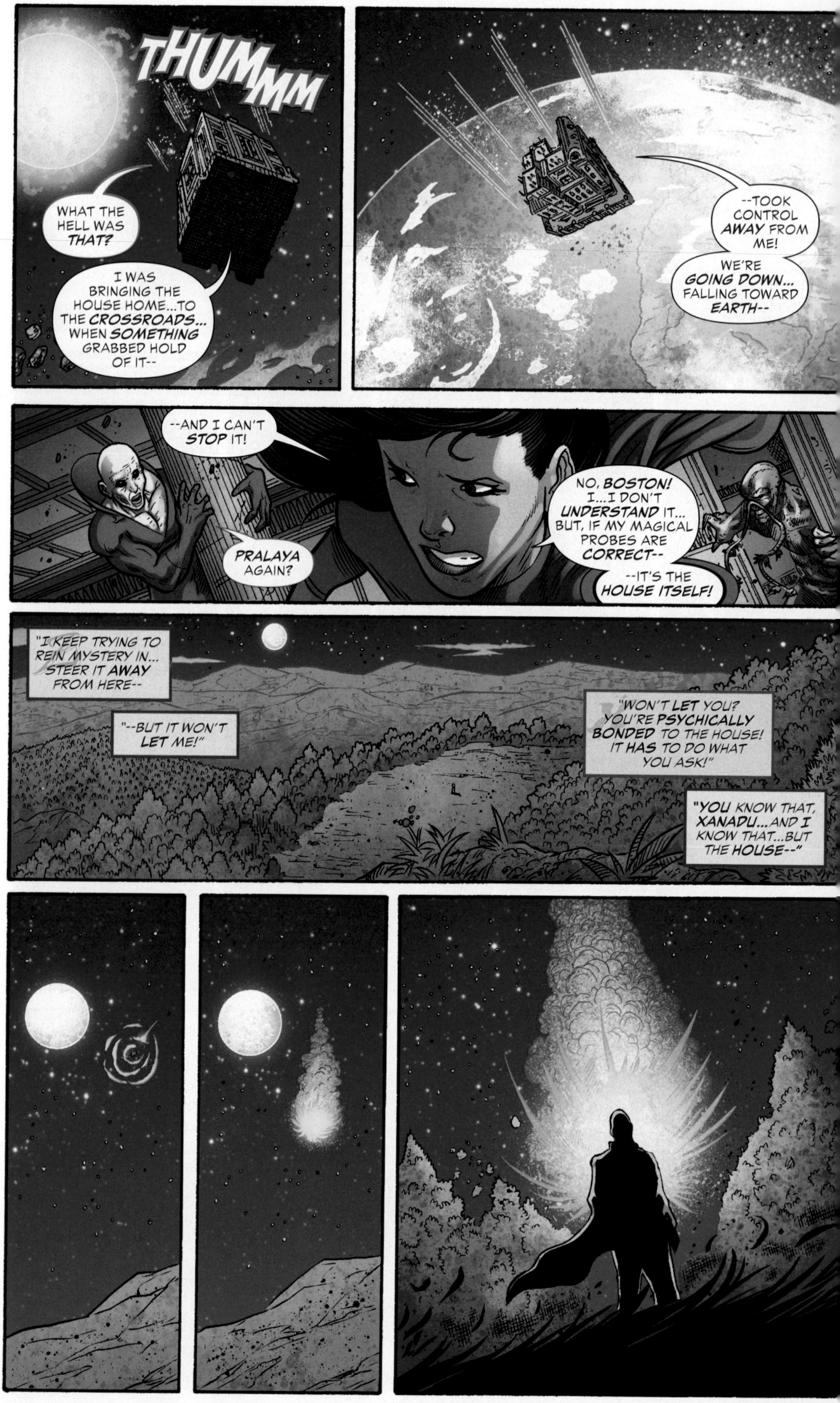
THUMMM
WHAT THE HELL WAS THAT?
I WAS BRINGING THE HOUSE HOME...TO THE CROSSROADS... WHEN SOMETHING GRABBED HOLD OF IT--
--TOOK CONTROL AWAY FROM ME!
WE'RE GOING DOWN... FALLING TOWARD EARTH--
--AND I CAN'T STOP IT!
PRALAYA AGAIN?
NO, BOSTON! I...I DON'T UNDERSTAND IT... BUT, IF MY MAGICAL PROBES ARE CORRECT--
--IT'S THE HOUSE ITSELF!
"I KEEP TRYING TO REIN MYSTERY IN... STEER IT AWAY FROM HERE--
"--BUT IT WON'T LET ME!"
"WON'T LET YOU? YOU'RE PSYCHICALLY BONDED TO THE HOUSE! IT HAS TO DO WHAT YOU ASK!"
"YOU KNOW THAT, XANADU...AND I KNOW THAT...BUT THE HOUSE--"

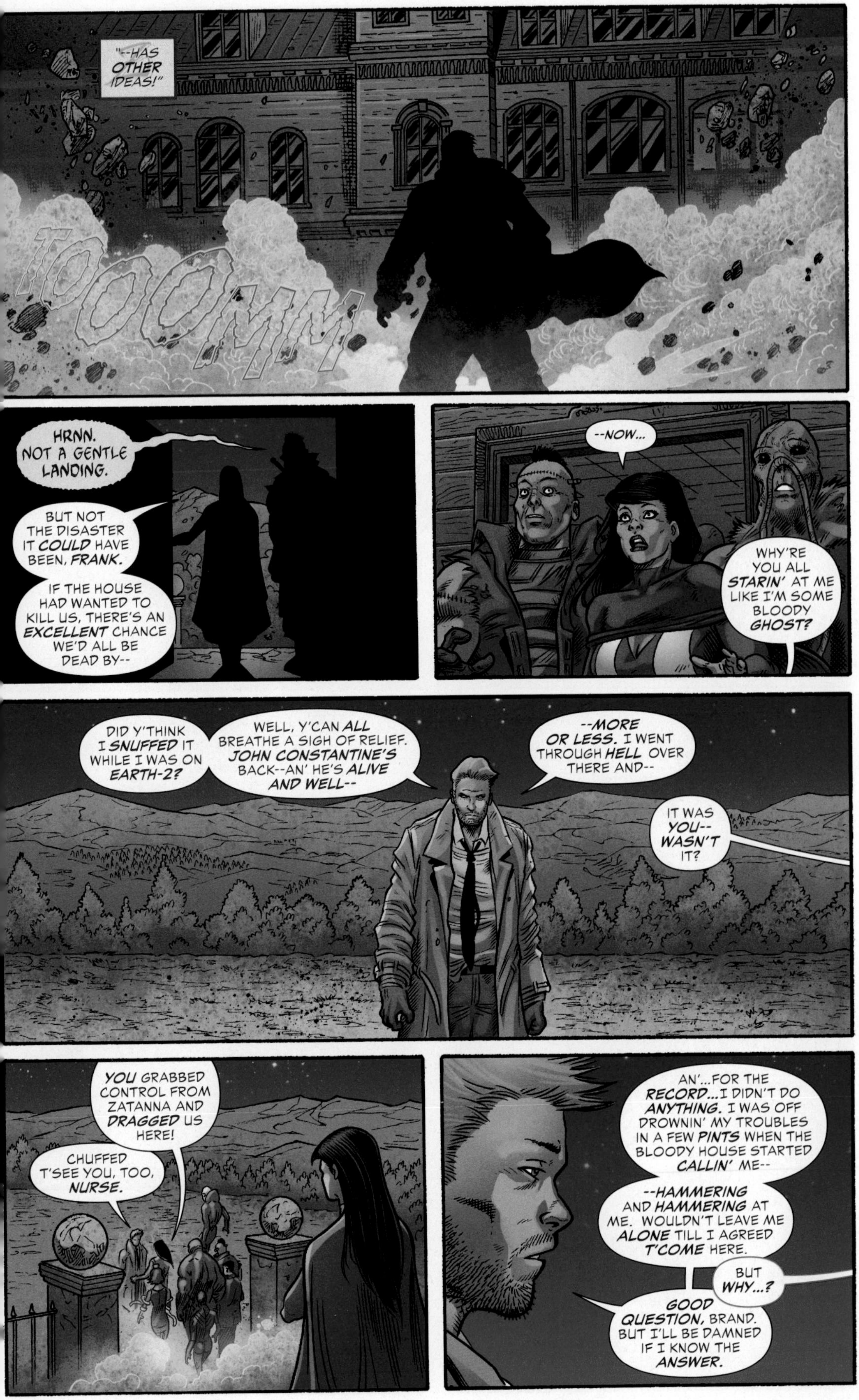
"--HAS OTHER IDEAS!"
TOOOMM
HRNN. NOT A GENTLE LANDING.
BUT NOT THE DISASTER IT COULD HAVE BEEN, FRANK.
IF THE HOUSE HAD WANTED TO KILL US, THERE'S AN EXCELLENT CHANCE WE'D ALL BE DEAD BY--
--NOW...
WHY'RE YOU ALL STARIN' AT ME LIKE I'M SOME BLOODY GHOST?
DID Y'THINK I SNUFFED IT WHILE I WAS ON EARTH-2?
WELL, Y'CAN ALL BREATHE A SIGH OF RELIEF. JOHN CONSTANTINE'S BACK--AN' HE'S ALIVE AND WELL--
--MORE OR LESS. I WENT THROUGH HELL OVER THERE AND--
IT WAS YOU-- WASN'T IT?
YOU GRABBED CONTROL FROM ZATANNA AND DRAGGED US HERE!
CHUFFED T'SEE YOU, TOO, NURSE.
AN'...FOR THE RECORD...I DIDN'T DO ANYTHING. I WAS OFF DROWNIN' MY TROUBLES IN A FEW PINTS WHEN THE BLOODY HOUSE STARTED CALLIN' ME--
--HAMMERING AND HAMMERING AT ME. WOULDN'T LEAVE ME ALONE TILL I AGREED T'COME HERE.
BUT WHY...?
GOOD QUESTION, BRAND. BUT I'LL BE DAMNED IF I KNOW THE ANSWER.

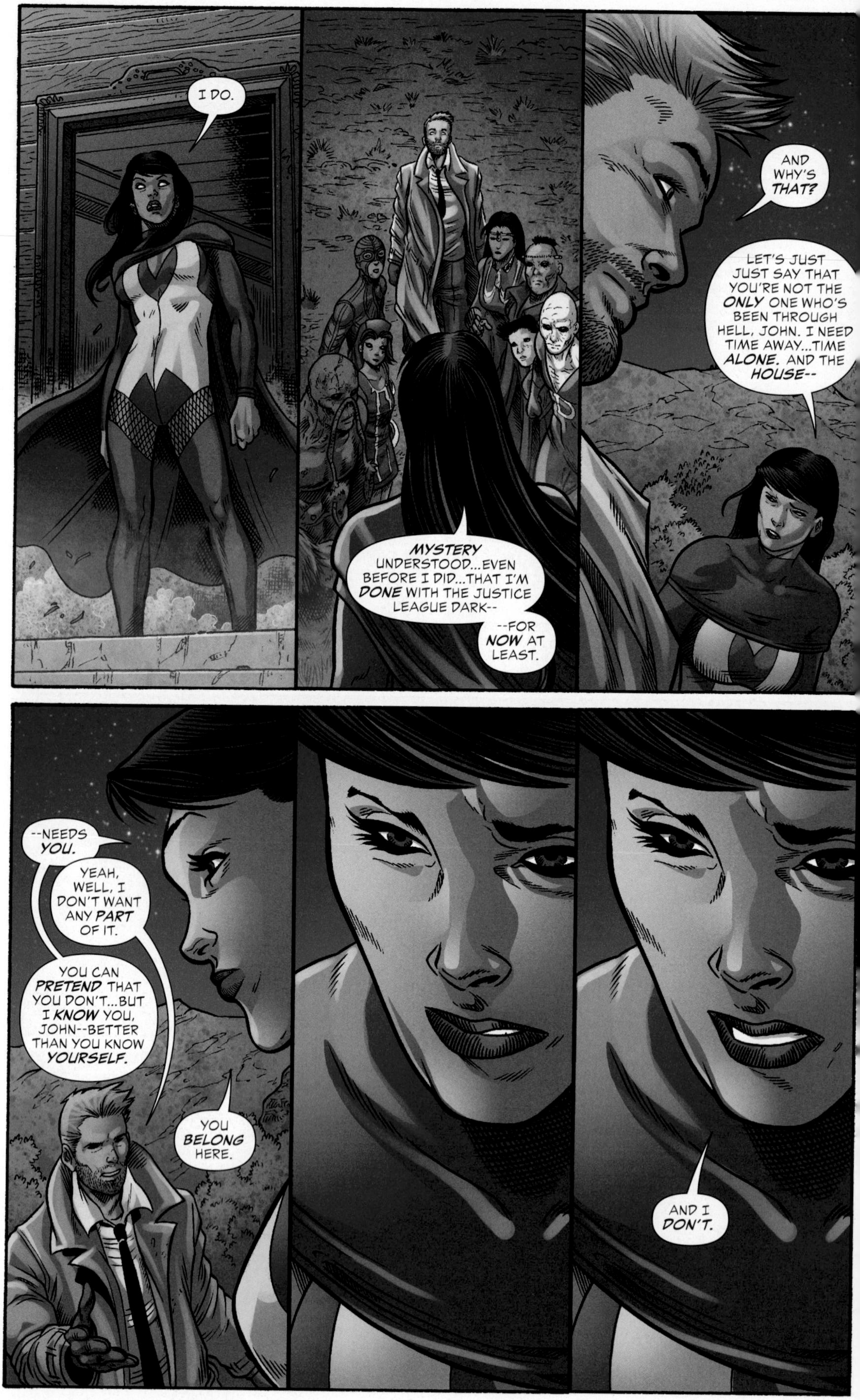
I DO.
MYSTERY UNDERSTOOD...EVEN BEFORE I DID...THAT I'M DONE WITH THE JUSTICE LEAGUE DARK--
--FOR NOW AT LEAST.
AND WHY'S THAT?
LET'S JUST JUST SAY THAT YOU'RE NOT THE ONLY ONE WHO'S BEEN THROUGH HELL, JOHN. I NEED TIME AWAY...TIME ALONE. AND THE HOUSE--
--NEEDS YOU.
YEAH, WELL, I DON'T WANT ANY PART OF IT.
YOU CAN PRETEND THAT YOU DON'T...BUT I KNOW YOU, JOHN--BETTER THAN YOU KNOW YOURSELF.
YOU BELONG HERE.
AND I DON'T.

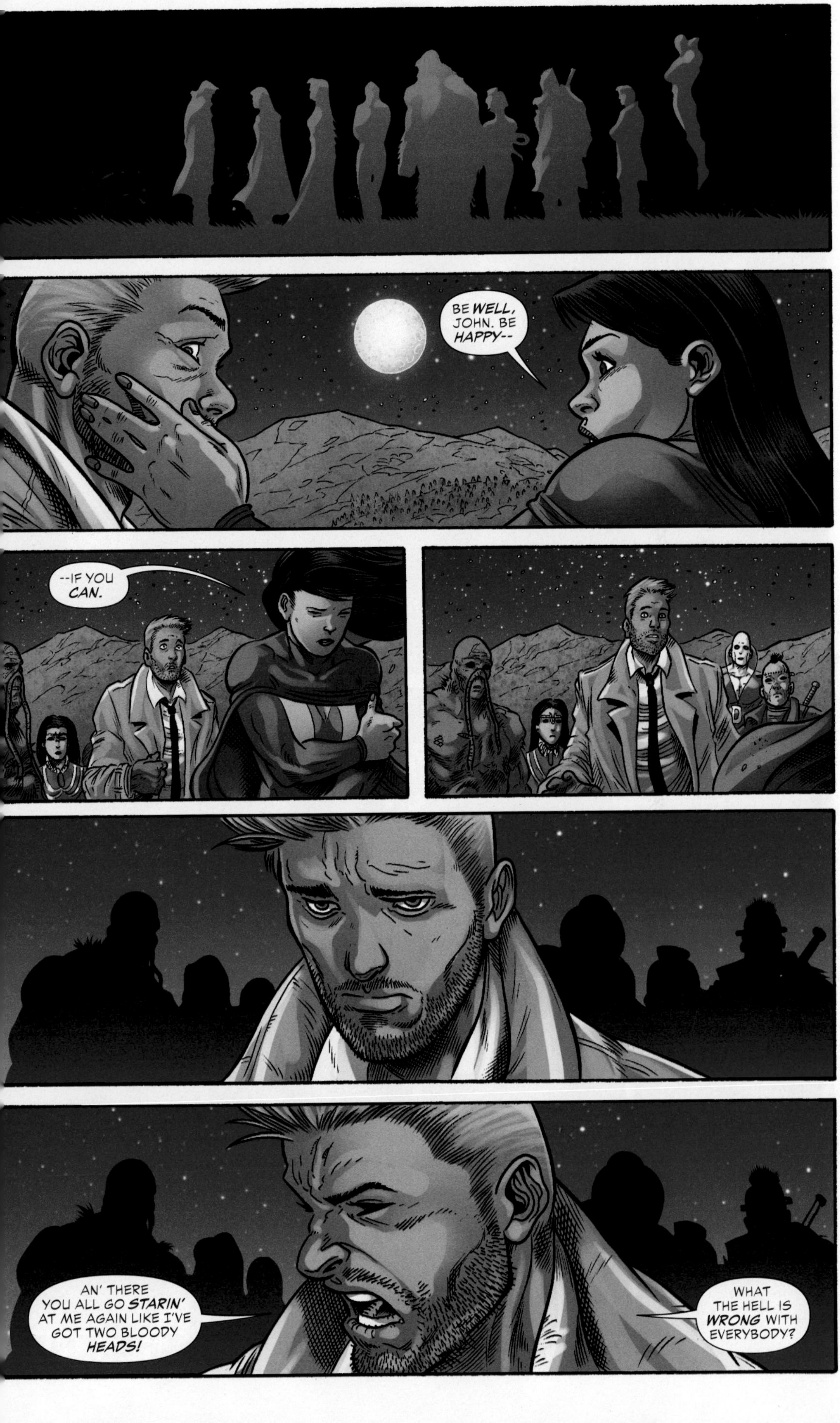
BE WELL, JOHN. BE HAPPY--
--IF YOU CAN.
AN' THERE YOU ALL GO STARIN' AT ME AGAIN LIKE I'VE GOT TWO BLOODY HEADS!
WHAT THE HELL IS WRONG WITH EVERYBODY?

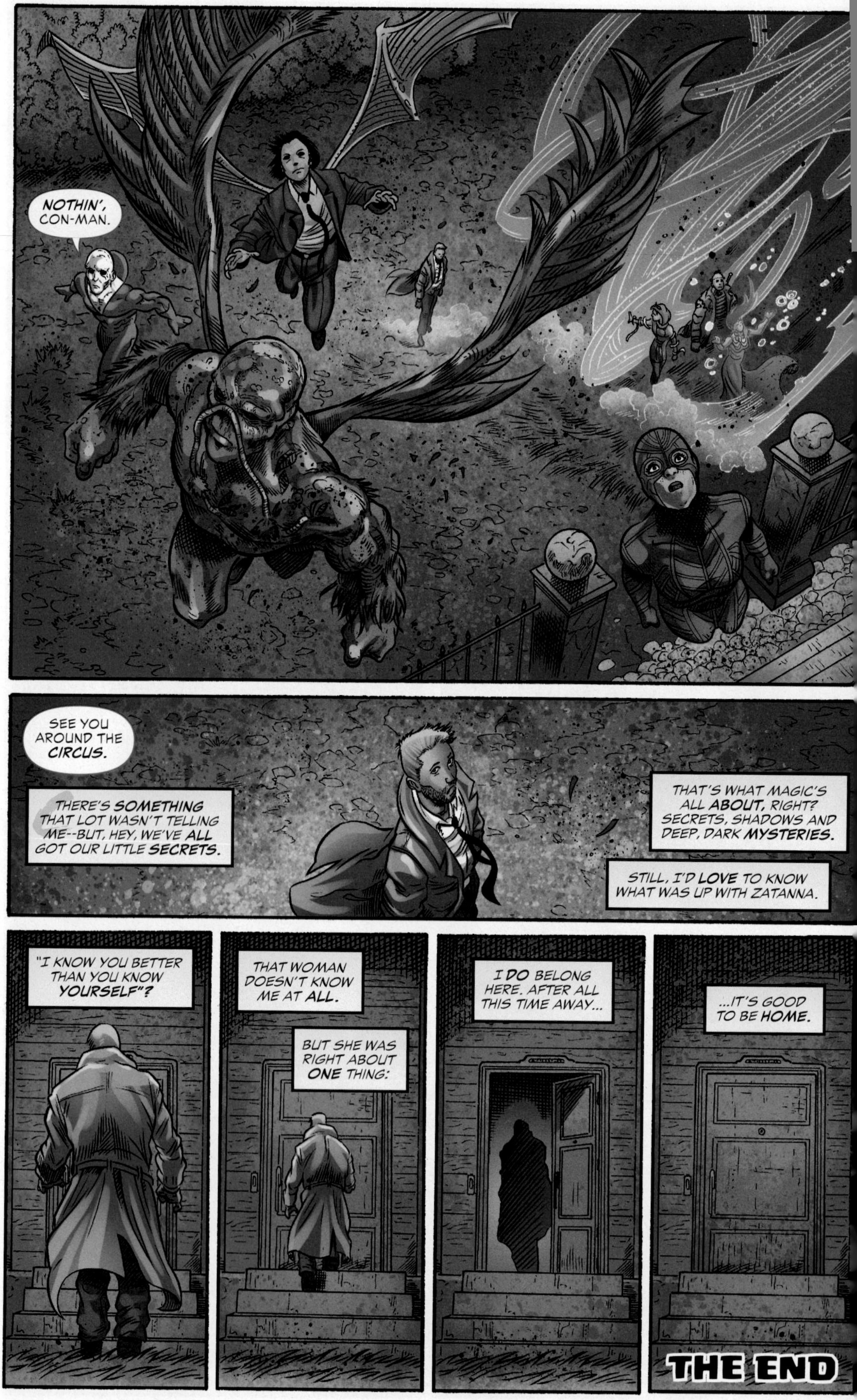
NOTHIN', CON-MAN.
SEE YOU AROUND THE CIRCUS.
THERE'S SOMETHING THAT LOT WASN'T TELLING ME--BUT, HEY, WE'VE ALL GOT OUR LITTLE SECRETS.
THAT'S WHAT MAGIC'S ALL ABOUT, RIGHT? SECRETS, SHADOWS AND DEEP, DARK MYSTERIES.
STILL, I'D LOVE TO KNOW WHAT WAS UP WITH ZATANNA.
"I KNOW YOU BETTER THAN YOU KNOW YOURSELF"?
THAT WOMAN DOESN'T KNOW ME AT ALL.
BUT SHE WAS RIGHT ABOUT ONE THING:
I DO BELONG HERE. AFTER ALL THIS TIME AWAY...
...IT'S GOOD TO BE HOME.
THE END

VARIANT COVER GALLERY

JUSTICE LEAGUE DARK #35
Monster of the Month variant cover by Eric Gist

JUSTICE LEAGUE DARK #36
LEGO Month variant cover art

JUSTICE LEAGUE DARK #37
variant cover by Darwyn Cooke

JUSTICE LEAGUE DARK #38
Flash 75th Anniversary variant cover by Kelley Jones

JUSTICE LEAGUE DARK #39
Harley Quinn variant cover by Joe Quinones

JUSTICE LEAGUE DARK #40
Movie Poster variant cover by Joe Quinones

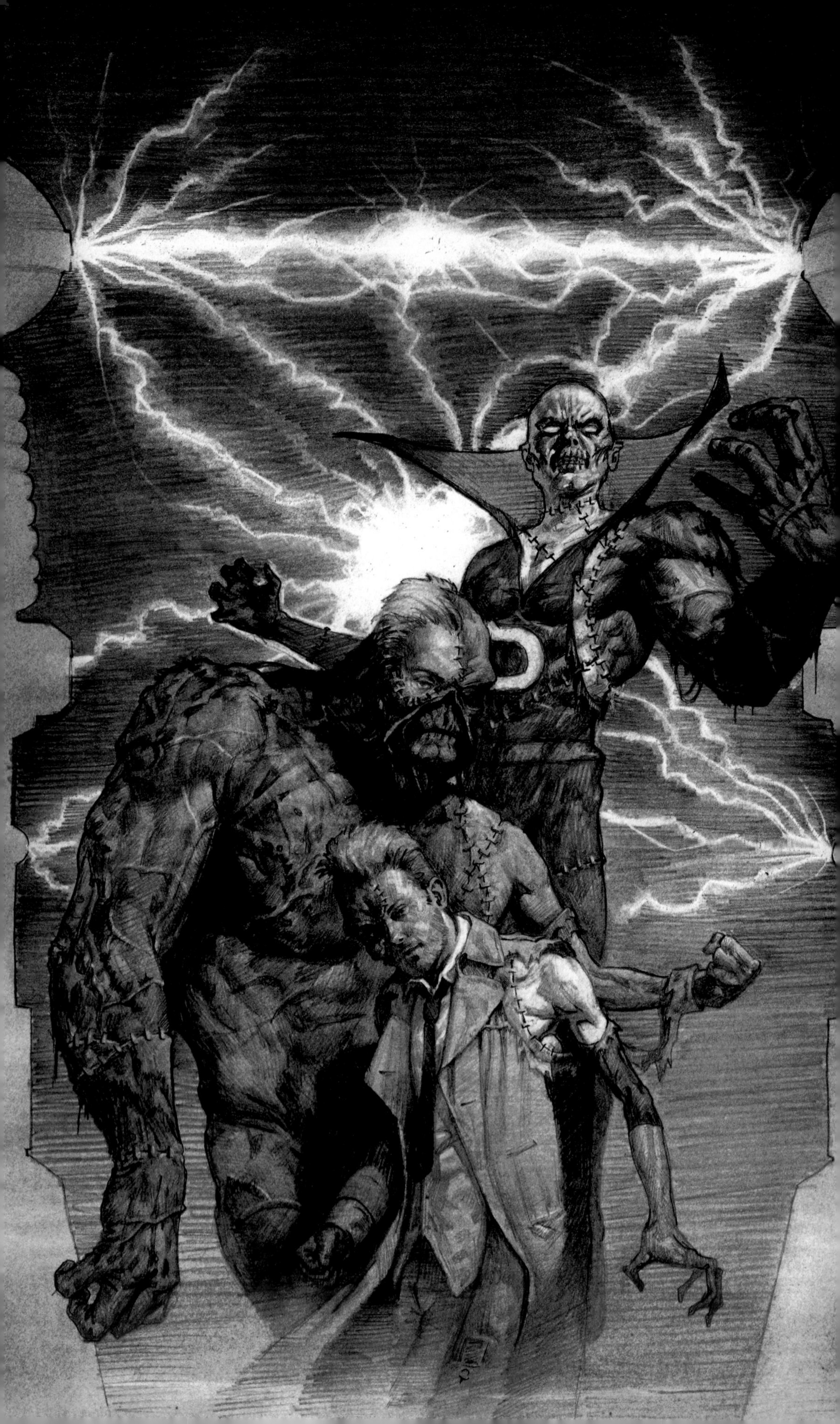

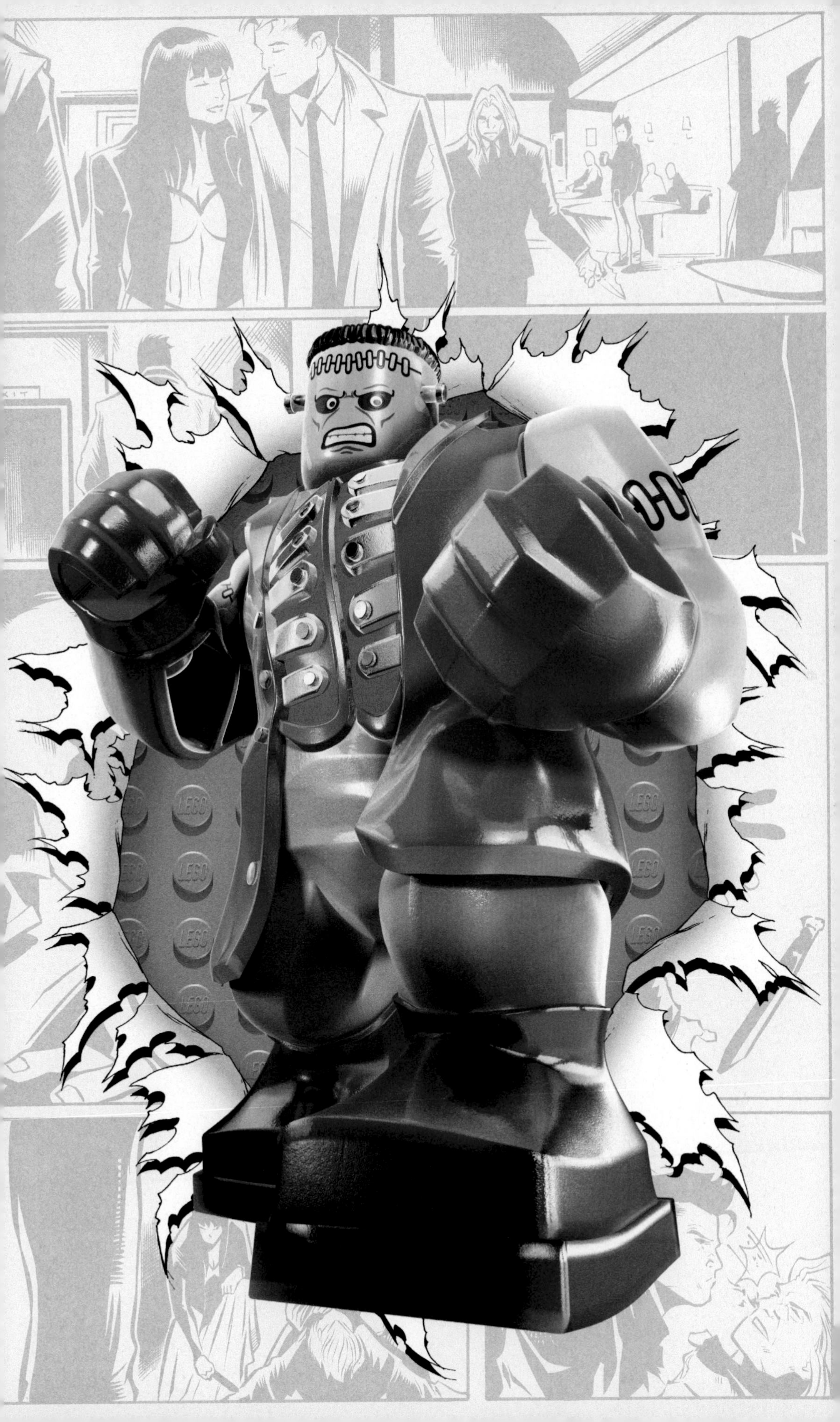

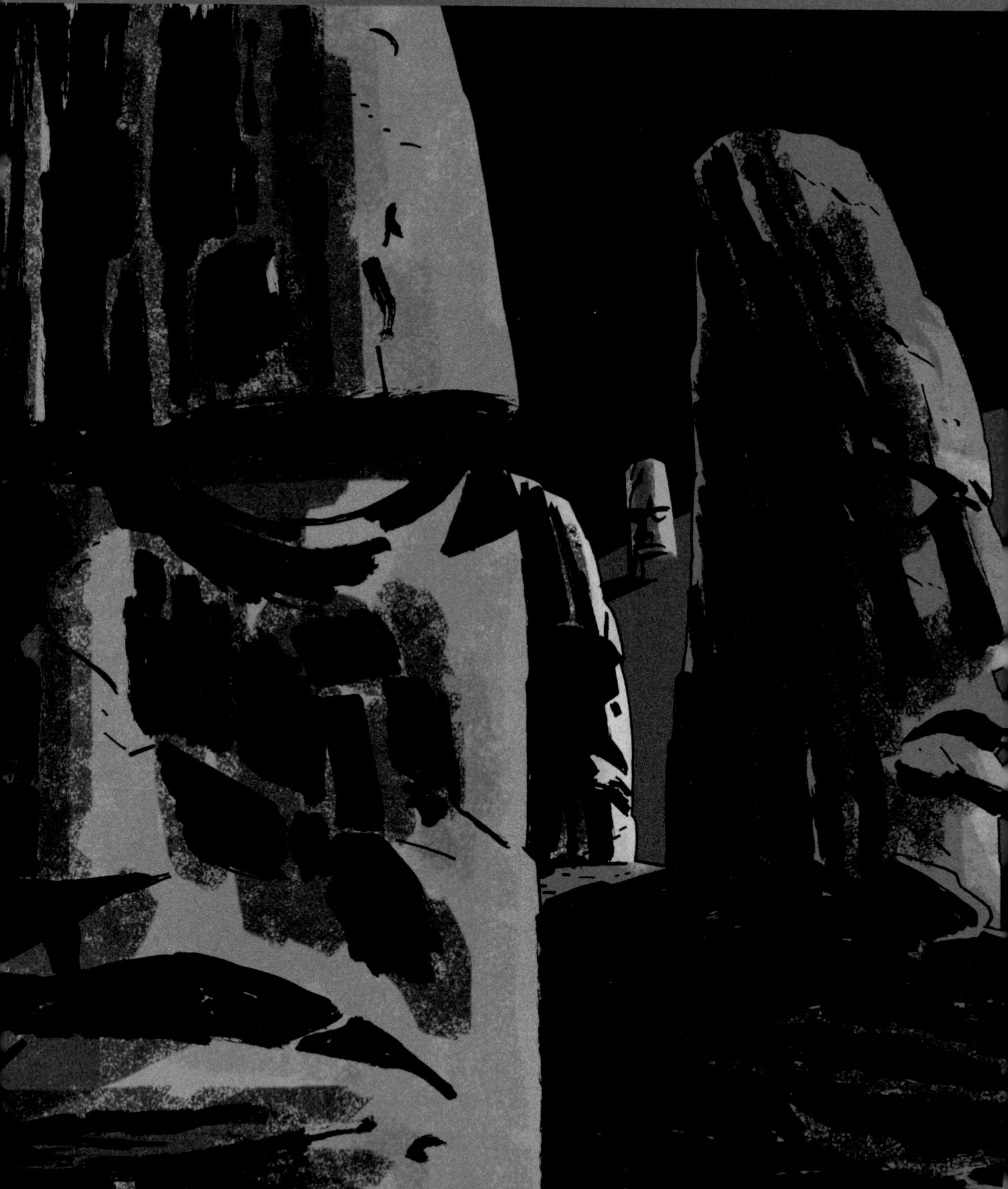

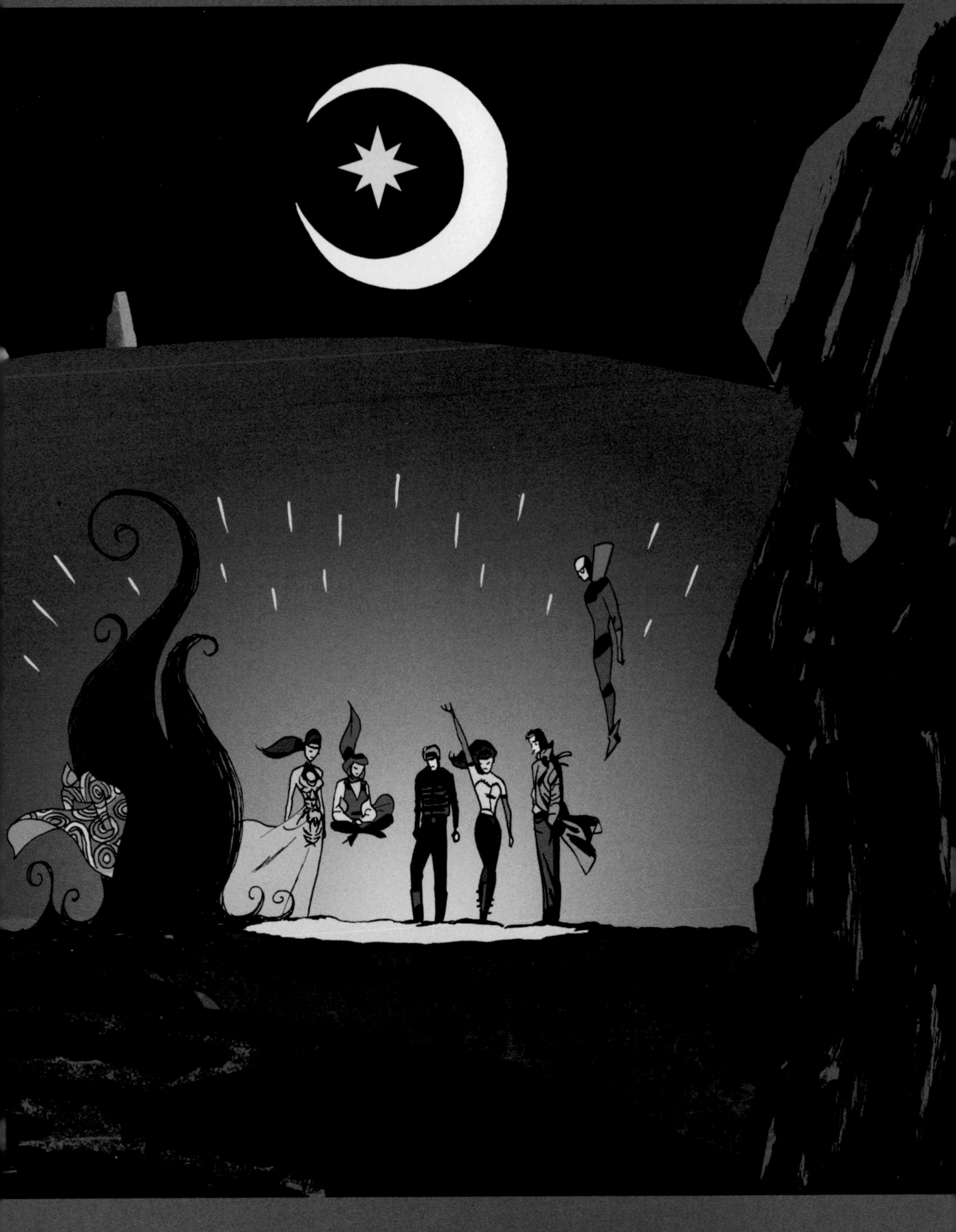

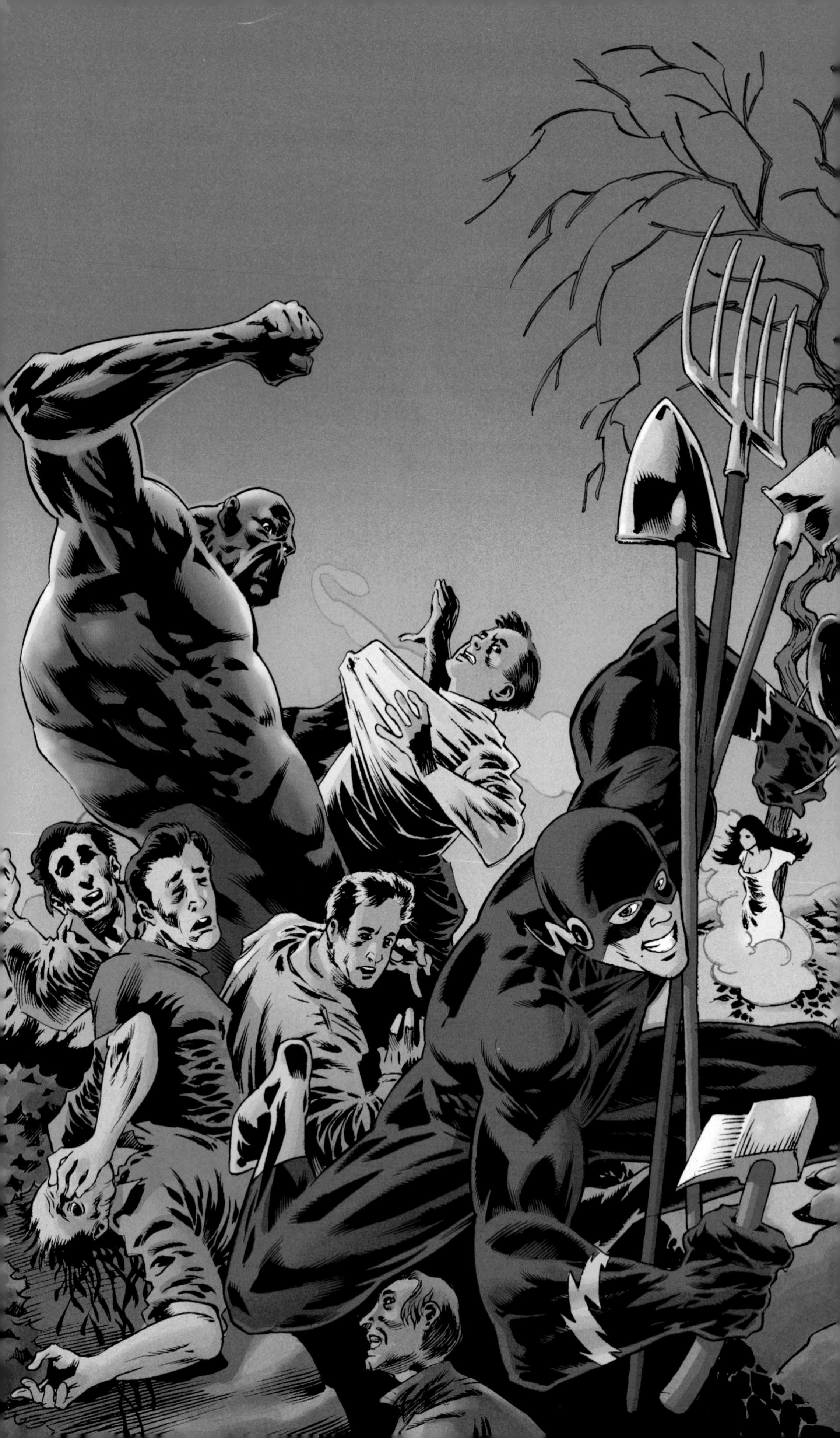

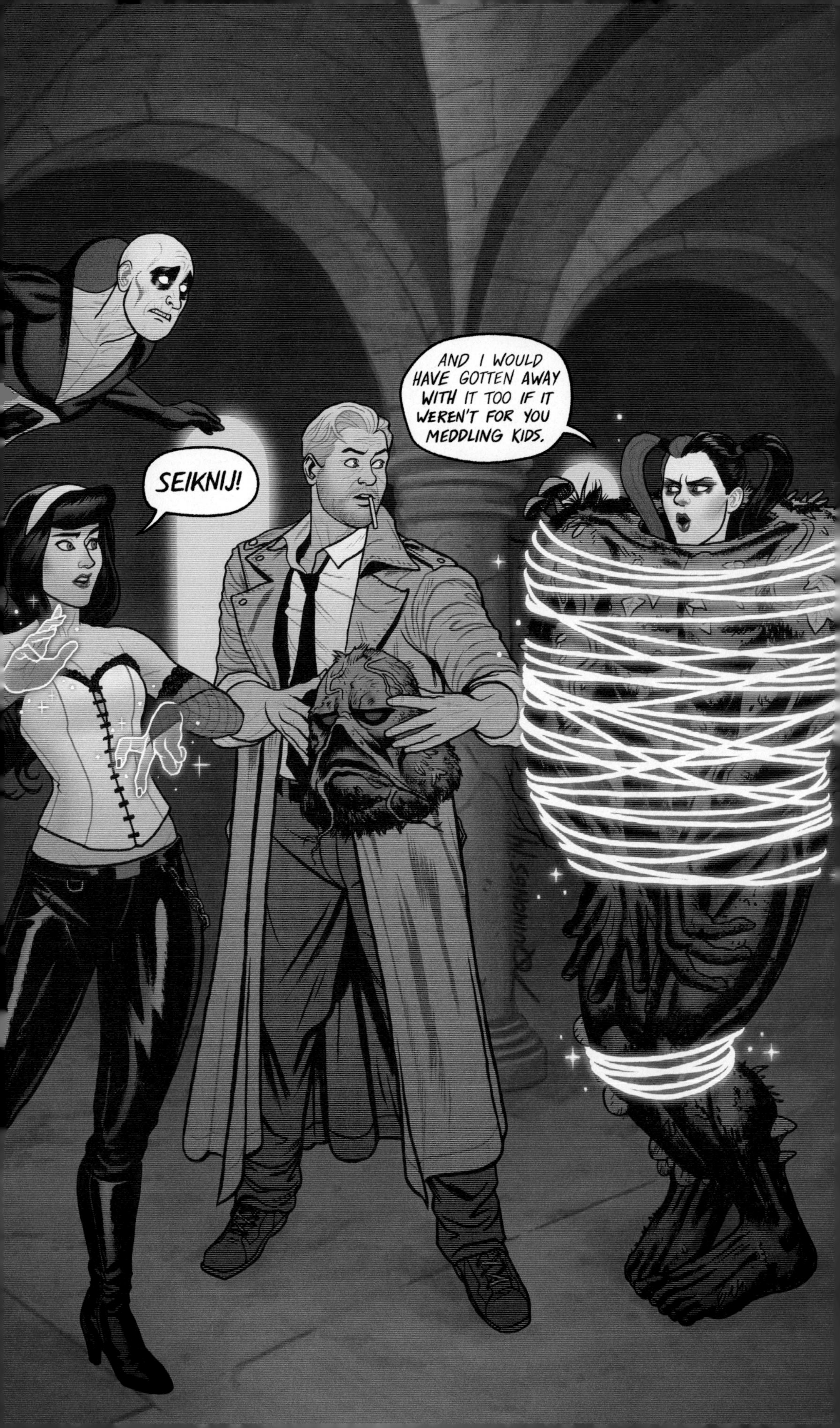
AND I WOULD HAVE GOTTEN AWAY WITH IT TOO IF IT WEREN'T FOR YOU MEDDLING KIDS.
SEIKNIJ!

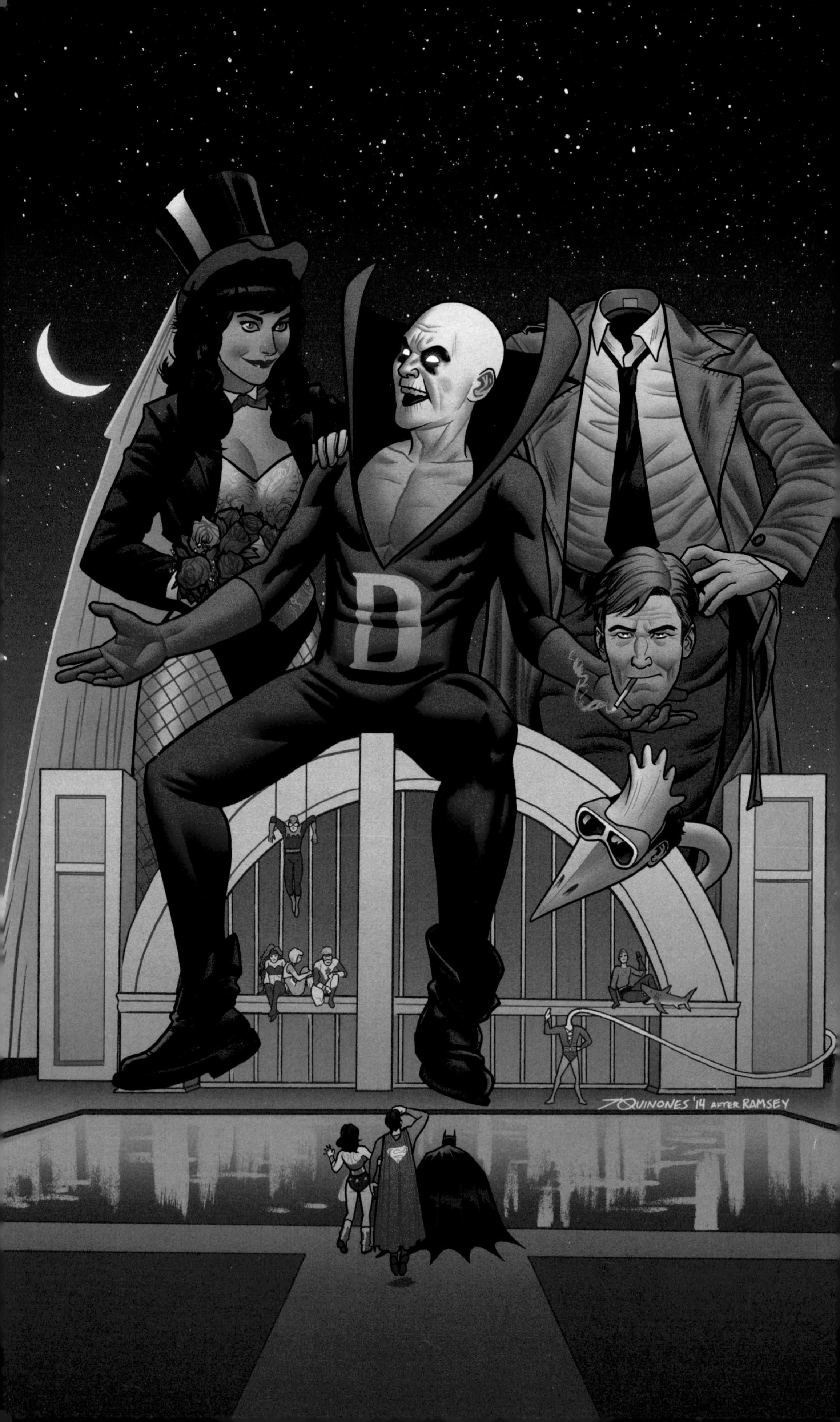

D
JQUINONES '14 AFTER RAMSEY

"Worthy of the adjective, but in a good way."
—THE NEW YORK TIMES

"There are some threats that are too much for
even Superman, Batman and Wonder Woman
to handle. That's when you call the people
who make magic their method."—CRAVE ONLINE

START AT THE BEGINNING!

JUSTICE LEAGUE DARK
VOLUME 1: IN THE DARK

JUSTICE LEAGUE
DARK VOL. 2: THE
BOOKS OF MAGIC

with JEFF LEMIRE

JUSTICE LEAGUE
DARK VOL. 3:
THE DEATH OF MAGIC

with JEFF LEMIRE
CONSTANTINE
VOL. 1: THE SPARKLE
AND THE FLAME

"THIS WILL BE A BOOK TO WATCH."
— THE ONION/AV CLUB

THE NEW 52!

DC COMICS™

JUSTICE LEAGUE DARK

VOLUME 1
IN THE DARK

PETER **MILLIGAN**   MIKEL **JANIN**

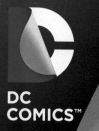

DC
COMICS™

"A pretty irresistible hook. What if the good guys assembl
a bunch of bad guys to work as a Dirty Dozen-like supertea
and do the dirty work traditional heroes would never tou
(or want to know about)?"—THE ONION/AV CL

START AT THE BEGINNING!

SUICIDE SQUAD
VOLUME 1: KICKED IN THE TEETH

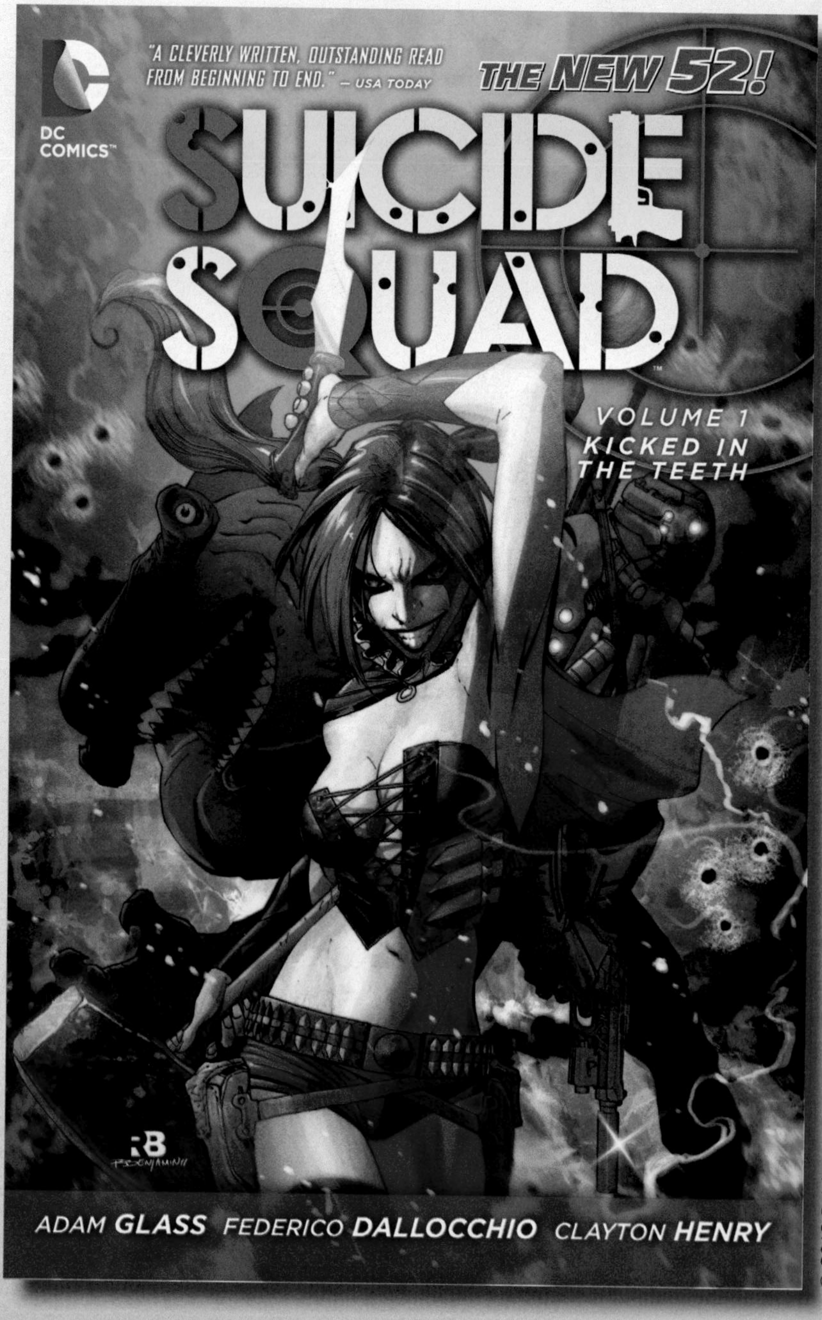
"A CLEVERLY WRITTEN, OUTSTANDING READ FROM BEGINNING TO END." – USA TODAY
DC COMICS
THE NEW 52!
SUICIDE SQUAD
VOLUME 1 KICKED IN THE TEETH
ADAM GLASS FEDERICO DALLOCCHIO CLAYTON HENRY

SUICIDE SQUAD VOL. 2: BASILISK RISING

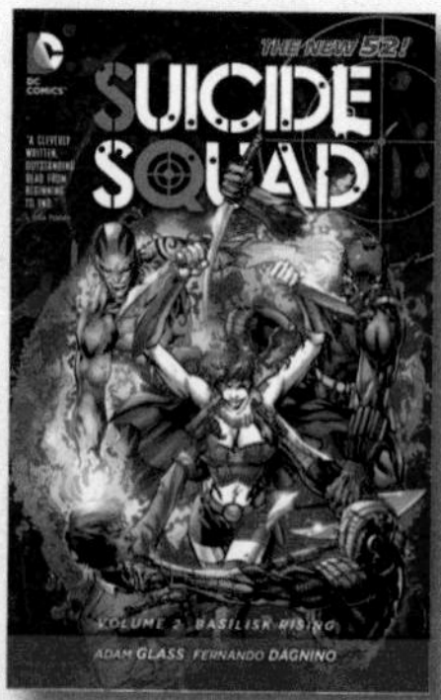
THE NEW 52!
SUICIDE SQUAD
VOLUME 2 BASILISK RISING
ADAM GLASS FERNANDO DAGNINO

SUICIDE SQUAD VOL. 3: DEATH IS FOR SUCKERS

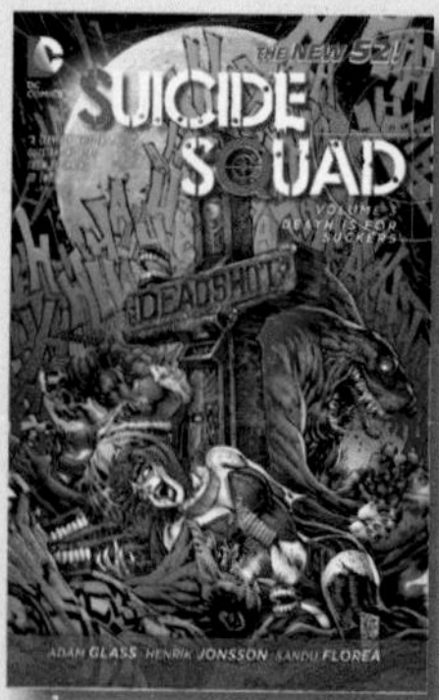
THE NEW 52!
SUICIDE SQUAD
DEADSHOT
ADAM GLASS HENRIK JONSSON SANDU FLOREA

DEATHSTROKE VOL. 1: LEGACY

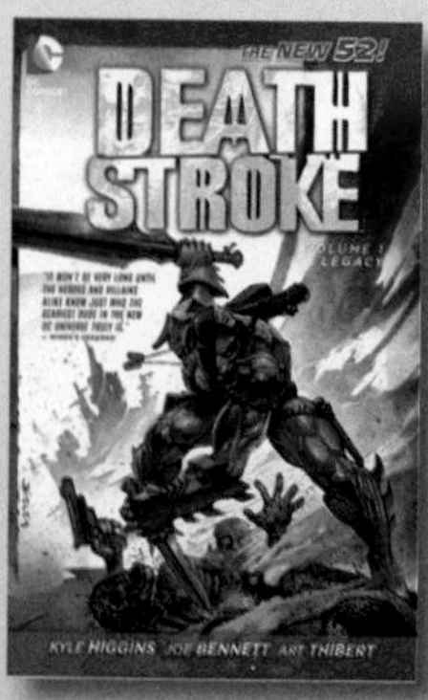
THE NEW 52!
DEATHSTROKE
KYLE HIGGINS JOE BENNETT ART THIBERT

START AT THE BEGINNING!

SWAMP THING VOLUME 1: RAISE THEM BONES

START AT THE BEGINNING!

ANIMAL MAN
VOLUME 1: THE HUNT

**JUSTICE LEAGUE DARK
VOLUME 1:
IN THE DARK**

**RESURRECTION MAN
VOLUME 1:
DEAD AGAIN**

**FRANKENSTEIN
AGENT OF S.H.A.D.E.
VOLUME 1: WAR OF
THE MONSTERS**

VOLUME 1
THE HUNT

*"TRAVEL FOREMAN'S ART
IS INNOVATIVE AND
EXCELLENTLY CREEPY...
AS LEMIRE'S EVERYMAN
HERO MAKES HIS MARK IN
THE NEW DC UNIVERSE."*

— USA TODAY